D0082706

WEAK COURTS, STRONG RIGHTS

WEAK COURTS, STRONG RIGHTS

JUDICIAL REVIEW AND SOCIAL WELFARE RIGHTS
IN COMPARATIVE CONSTITUTIONAL LAW

Mark Tushnet

PRINCETON UNIVERSITY PRESS

PRINCETON AND OXFORD

Copyright © 2008 by Princeton University Press

Published by Princeton University Press, 41 William Street, Princeton, New Jersey 08540

In the United Kingdom: Princeton University Press, 3 Market Place, Woodstock, Oxfordshire OX20 1SY

All Rights Reserved

Library of Congress Cataloging-in-Publication Data

Tushnet, Mark V., 1945–
     Weak courts, strong rights : judicial review and social welfare rights in comparative
constitutional law / Mark Tushnet.
          p. cm.
     Includes bibliographical references and index.
     ISBN-13: 978-0-691-13092-7 (hardcover : alk. paper)
     1. Judicial review—United States. 2. Social rights—United States. 3. Judicial review.
4. Social rights. I. Title.
     KF4575.T873 2008
     347.73'12—dc22

                                                                                    2007003095

British Library Cataloging-in-Publication Data is available

This book has been composed in Goudy

Printed on acid-free paper. ∞

press.princeton.edu

Printed in the United States of America

10 9 8 7 6 5 4 3 2 1

KF4575
.T875
2008

0 80460670

TO MY COLLEAGUES

At the Georgetown University Law Center

Contents

Preface

THIS BOOK BRINGS together two of the important intellectual or theoretical issues of concern to students of comparative constitutional law as it has developed in the United States over the past decade. First, what is the proper role of courts in constitutional systems that generally comply with rule-of-law requirements? Second, what substantive rights do, should, or can constitutions guarantee? Should they protect second-generation social and economic rights and third-generation cultural and environmental rights, and if so, how, and in what venues? I argue that the comparative study of constitutions brings out underappreciated connections between the answers to these two questions.

The reason is that the "new Commonwealth model" of judicial review offers an important alternative to the form of judicial review familiar in the United States.* In that new model, courts assess legislation against constitutional norms, but do not have the final word on whether statutes comply with those norms. In some versions the courts are directed to interpret legislation to make it consistent with constitutional norms if doing so is fairly possible according to (previously) accepted standards of statutory interpretation. In other versions the courts gain the additional power to declare statutes inconsistent with constitutional norms, but not to enforce such judgments coercively against a losing party. In still others, the courts can enforce the judgment coercively, but the legislature may respond by reinstating the original legislation by some means other than a cumbersome amendment process.

I call the new model of judicial review *weak-form* judicial review, in contrast with the strong form of judicial review in the United States. Strong-form review itself has numerous variants. At its heart is the power of courts to declare statutes enacted by a nation's highest legislature unconstitutional, and to make that declaration practically effective by using the standard weapons at a court's hands—injunctions against further enforcement of the statute by executive officials, dismissals of prosecutions under the statute, awards of damages on behalf of people injured by the statute's operation backed up by the potential to seize the defendant's property. (None of these weapons are powerful enough to defeat a recalcitrant legislature and executive backed by strong public opinion. The U.S. experience has never pushed strong-form review to the point where its exercise has provoked a real constitutional crisis when nonjudicial officials fight hard against a court's orders.)

---

* The terminology originated in Stephen Gardbaum, "The New Commonwealth Model of Constitutionalism," 49 Am. J. Comp. L. 707 (2001).

Some variants of strong-form review involve differences in the degree to which courts defer to constitutional interpretations offered by the other branches—interpretations sometimes described as being made by the legislature when it enacted the very legislation under constitutional challenge. Another variant confines strong-form review to areas directly implicating the courts themselves. This variant, sometimes called *departmentalism*, allows a court to strike down a statute unconstitutionally expanding or limiting its jurisdiction, the issue in the U.S. classic *Marbury v. Madison* (1803), or depriving plaintiffs of jury trials to which they are constitutionally entitled, and the like. Seemingly narrower than other variants of strong-form review, departmentalist review can actually be quite expansive, because any government seeking to operate reasonably effectively is likely to call upon the courts for assistance, at which point departmentalist strong-form review comes into play. A statute making flag burning as a means of political protest illegal, for example, does not in itself ask the courts to do anything, and so might seem immune from departmentalist strong-form review. Yet, as soon as prosecutors bring a criminal case against a flag burner, departmentalism kicks in, allowing the courts to dismiss the case if they see the executive branch prosecutors asking the courts' help in enforcing what the judges find to be an unconstitutional statute. Yet another variant of strong-form judicial review is judicial supremacy, in which the courts' judgments of constitutionality are taken to be conclusive on *all* constitutional issues that can be presented to the courts.

Every variant of strong-form judicial review raises basic questions about democratic self-governance, because every variant allows the courts to displace the present-day judgments of contemporary majorities in the service of judgments the courts attribute to the constitution's adopters. Of course, constitutionalism is all about limiting contemporary majorities. The problem with strong-form judicial review is that the courts' determinations of what the constitution means are frequently simultaneously reasonable ones and ones with which other reasonable people could disagree. This is especially true when the courts interpret the relatively abstract statements of principle contained in bills of rights.

Take the issue of affirmative action as an example. A conscientious legislature could think about what the constitution's ban on discrimination means and decide that broad race-based affirmative action programs are consistent with the nation's commitment to equality because such programs are appropriate ways of rectifying the legacy of a history of racism. The courts might conclude, in contrast, that the national commitment to equality means that legislation can take race into account only under much more restricted circumstances, and not merely to rectify historical injustices. The conclusions drawn by the legislature would hardly be unreasonable even if disputable. Yet, in a system of strong-form judicial review the courts' different conclusion, itself reasonable, prevails over the legislature's. This is a substantial restriction on the power of the people to govern themselves. When—as if often the case—reasonable people can disagree about what the constitution actually means in connection with challenges to particular statutes, the restriction on self-government is difficult to defend simply by invoking the basic idea of constitutionalism.

Proponents of the new model of weak-form judicial review describe it as an attractive way to reconcile democratic self-governance with constitutionalism. As Jeffrey Goldsworthy puts it, the new model "offers the possibility of a compromise that combines the best features of both the traditional models, by conferring on courts constitutional responsibility to review the consistency of legislation with protected rights, while preserving the authority of legislatures to have the last word."[†]

This characteristic of weak-form judicial review is the bridge between it and the second question I mentioned earlier, that of the propriety of incorporating social and economic rights in constitutions. Two arguments against doing so are widely accepted: courts, it is said, lack the capacity to give appropriate content to general social welfare rights in the context of particular controversies, and, it is said as well, judicial enforcement of social welfare rights is particularly intrusive on legislative—and therefore democratic—choice because enforcing social and economic rights typically has substantially larger implications for a government's budgets than enforcing first-generation rights does. The creation of weak-form review undermines these arguments by providing an institutional mechanism for the *provisional* identification and enforcement of social and economic rights. Weak-form systems allow legislatures to respond to judicial decisions by saying that the courts misspecified the content of constitutional social or economic rights, or insisted on excessively expensive modes of realizing such rights.

I begin in chapter 1 by arguing for the value of comparative constitutional study, not to determine the proper interpretation of specific constitutional provisions but rather to assist thinking about issues of domestic constitutional law. This methodological point pervades the book. Chapters 2 and 3 then introduce and examine in some detail the different forms of judicial review, with particular attention to the less familiar weak forms. Chapter 3 draws on the experience in weak-form systems over the past few decades to ask whether weak-form systems are stable, in the sense that they remain weak-form and do not have a tendency to become strong-form systems—and, if they are not stable in that sense, how such a transformation might be explained and perhaps justified.

Part 2 turns to a question implicit in the argument that, in Goldsworthy's terms, weak-form systems are attractive in part because they preserve legislative authority: weak-form systems assume that legislatures given responsibility

[†] Jeffrey Goldsworthy, "Homogenizing Constitutions," 23 Ox. J. Leg. Stud. 484, 484 (2003).

for participating in the development of constitutional meaning, in dialogue with the courts, will do so reasonably well. Many people, including many of this book's readers, will be skeptical about the claim that legislatures, staffed by politicians interested more in reelection than in advancing the constitution's commitments, will actually do a decent job of it. After identifying the precise questions we ought to ask about legislative performance and indicating some difficulties in investigating actual legislative performance, chapter 4 develops criteria for evaluating the quality of legislative performance in the constitutional arena. These criteria are complex and, perhaps surprisingly, much more generous to legislatures than one might have thought beforehand. Chapter 5 provides some case studies in actual legislative performance, with those criteria in mind. The case studies also bring out some aspects of constitutional design in both strong-form and weak-form systems that affect legislative performance.

Part 3 then takes up social and economic rights themselves, connecting the institution of weak-form judicial review to those rights. It addresses two arguments prominent in skeptical discussions of judicial enforcement of social and economic rights, particularly in connection with the U.S. Constitution. The first is that doing so is *novel*, that the U.S. Constitution is a constitution of negative rights, in contrast to the positive social and economic rights contained in more recently adopted constitutions. The second is that doing so is beyond judicial *capacity*, especially because coercive judicial enforcement of social and economic rights interferes with legislative prerogatives more substantially than judicial enforcement of classical liberal rights. Part 3 argues that each of these arguments is mistaken. Chapter 6 looks at the so-called state action doctrine in U.S. constitutional law and the related doctrines of horizontal effect in other constitutional systems and demonstrates that, under the guise of enforcing that doctrine (or of considering whether to give constitutional provisions horizontal effect), constitutional courts *already* enforce such rights, thereby weakening the "novelty" objection. Drawing on experience in the United States and Canada, I show that liberal constitutions cannot avoid the question of social welfare rights because they must do *something* about the constitutional implications of what I call the background rights of property, contract, and tort law. I then argue that substantive constitutional law is entirely adequate to deal with whatever troubling implications the constitutionalization of social welfare rights is something thought to have.

Chapters 7 and 8, drawing on South Africa's developing jurisprudence of social welfare rights, show that the "capacity" objection to judicial enforcement of social and economic rights rests on the assumption that such enforcement must take a strong form, and argues that this assumption is weakened by the creation of weak-form judicial review, which might be an attractive method for enforcing social and economic rights. Weak-form judicial review can recognize social welfare rights in a way that has no larger implications for government budgets than do judicial decisions enforcing such first-generation rights as the right to free speech.

The argument in part 3 does not establish that enforcing social and economic rights is necessarily a good thing; it simply attempts to clear away some rather thick underbrush that has developed around the issue so that other arguments about enforcing those rights—for example, that doing so will have good or bad effects on a nation's economy—can take their proper, prominent place in our consideration of the question. Nor, of course, does the argument attempt to explain why the United States has a strong-form system of judicial review or to examine the political reasons (as distinct from the institutional reasons associated specifically with judicial review) that might explain why substantive arguments for social and economic rights have so little purchase in U.S. political discourse.

⁓᯽⁓

One point of terminology (or typography): Throughout this book, I use phrases like *the constitution* with a small *c* when I am referring to the constitution of a generic democratic nation. I capitalize *Constitution* when I am referring to a specific constitution, which I identify either immediately (as in "U.S. Constitution") or in the sentences preceding the reference.

Acknowledgments

MATERIAL IN THE book previously appeared, in a different form, in the following publications and is reprinted with permission of the publishers:

"Alternative Forms of Judicial Review," Reprinted from the Michigan Law Review, August 2003, vol. 101, No. 8. Copyright 2003 by The Michigan Law Review Association.

"Book Review," 2 International Journal of Constitutional Law 734 (2004).

"Evaluating Congressional Constitutional Interpretation: Some Criteria and Two Informal Case Studies," 50 Duke Law Journal 1395 (2001).

"Forms of Judicial Review as Expressions of Constitutional Patriotism," 22 Law and Philosophy 353 (2003). Copyright © 2003 Kluwer Academic Publishers. No part of the material protected by this copyright notice may be reproduced or utilized in any form or by any means, electronic or mechanical, including photocopying, recording or by any information storage and retrieval system, without written permission from the copyright owner. Reprinted with kind permission of Springer Science and Business Media.

"Institutions for Implementing Constitutional Law," originally published in Rethinking Political Institutions: The Art of the State (Ian Shapiro, Stephen Skowronek, and Daniel Galvin, eds., New York University Press, 2006).

"Interpretation in Legislatures and Courts: Incentives and Institutional Design," in The Least Examined Branch: The Role of Legislatures in the Constitutional State (Richard W. Bauman and Tsvi Kahana eds. 2006). Reprinted with permission of the publisher, Cambridge University Press © 2006.

"Interpreting Constitutions Comparatively: Some Cautionary Notes, with Reference to Affirmative Action," 36 Connecticut Law Review 649 (2004).

"Judicial Activism or Restraint in a Section 33 World," 52 University of Toronto Law Journal 89 (2002). © University of Toronto Press Incorporated 2003. All rights reserved.

"New Forms of Judicial Review and the Persistence of Rights- and Democracy-Based Worries," 38 Wake Forest Law Review 813 (2003).

"Social Welfare Rights and the Forms of Judicial Review," 82 Texas Law Review 1895 (2004). Reprinted with permission of the publisher, Texas Law Review © 2004.

"State Action and a New Birth of Freedom," 92 Georgetown Law Journal 779 (2004) (with Gary Peller). Reprinted with permission of the publisher, Georgetown Law Journal © 2004.

"State Action, Social Welfare Rights, and the Judicial Role: Some Comparative Observations," 3 University of Chicago Journal of International Law 435 (2002). Reprinted with permission of the publisher, Chicago Journal of International Law © 2002.

"The Issue of State Action/Horizontal Effect in Comparative Constitutional Law," 1 International Journal of Constitutional Law 79 (2003).

"Weak-Form Judicial Review: Its Implications for Legislatures," (2004) S.C.L.R. (2d) 213, and in Constitutionalism in the Charter Era (Grant Huscroft and Ian Brodie eds., 2005).

PART I

Strong-Form and Weak-Form Judicial Review

CHAPTER 1

Why Comparative Constitutional Law?

RECENT SUPREME COURT opinions mentioning constitutional decisions by courts outside the United States have generated a strong—and grossly overstated—critique by conservative commentators.[1] The thrust of the critique is that these opinions portend inroads on the sovereign ability of the American people to govern ourselves, and the embedding in the U.S. Constitution—through judicial interpretation—of the values of a cosmopolitan elite that could not persuade the American people to adopt those values through purely domestic legal processes.

Only a brief comment on these "arguments" is appropriate here.[2] First, Supreme Court mention of decisions by courts outside the United States is no recent development, but at most a revival of an earlier tradition that had been submerged for perhaps a decade or two.[3] Second, *mention* is the right word. Only one recent opinion relies on the substance of a decision by a non-U.S. court to support a proposition that played some role in the Court's reasoning.[4] Other references to such decisions have been in the form of factual observations about what other courts have done. Third, the idea that references to non-U.S. decisions might somehow produce decisions that would not be reached by using other materials for interpreting the Constitution is quite implausible. It seems to require that some justice who would not otherwise be

---

[1] The most prominent are Robert Bork and Richard Posner. *See* Robert H. Bork, Coercing Virtue: The Worldwide Rule of Judges (2003); Richard A. Posner, "Foreword: A Political Court," 119 Harv. L. Rev. 31, 85–88 (2005). Probably the most extended analysis is Roger P. Alford, "In Search of a Theory for Constitutional Comparativism," 52 UCLA L. Rev. 639 (2005).

[2] For my more extended observations, see Mark Tushnet, "Transnational/Domestic Constitutional Law," 37 Loyola L.A. L. Rev. 239 (2003); Mark Tushnet, "When Is Knowing Less Better than Knowing More? Unpacking the Controversy Over Supreme Court Reference to Non-U.S. Law," 90 Minn. L. Rev. 1275 (2006); Mark Tushnet, "Referring to Foreign Law in Constitutional Interpretation: An Episode in the Culture Wars," 35 Balt. L. Rev. 299 (2006).

[3] For a compilation of materials showing how long the tradition is (with some effort to massage the characterization of the tradition to establish the novelty of recent references to non-U.S. law), see Steven G. Calabresi & Stephanie Dotson Zimdahl, "The Supreme Court and Foreign Sources of Law: Two Hundred Years of Practice and the Juvenile Death Penalty Decision," 47 Wm. & Mary L. Rev. 743 (2005).

[4] Lawrence v. Texas, 539 U.S. 558 (2003), referred to a 1981 decision by the European Court of Human Rights to show the inaccuracy of an assertion made in 1985 by then chief justice Warren Burger that "condemnation of [homosexual] practices is firmly rooted in Judeo-Christian moral and ethical standards." Bowers v. Hardwick, 478 U.S. 186, 196 (Burger, C. J., concurring).

persuaded by those other materials would nonetheless change his or her mind when confronted with the non-U.S. materials. That might happen, someday, for one justice perhaps, but surely not on a large enough scale for anyone to care about. Fourth, the concern about sovereignty seems equally misplaced. The U.S. Supreme Court is, after all, a domestic lawmaker no less than is, for example, the U.S. Senate, which ratifies treaties limiting what the U.S. government as a whole can do. That is, a domestic institution would impose any restrictions on U.S. lawmaking by references to non-U.S. court decisions. There is no impairment of sovereignty in that. And, finally, the concerns about self-government expressed by critics of these Supreme Court decisions are valid ones—when made about judicial review itself. There is nothing, though, that distinguishes non-U.S. decisions from anything else the Court might rely on to limit self-government through judicial review.

This recent tempest in a teapot has placed the question of the value of comparative constitutional study on the table. Why study comparative constitutional law? For a scholar, of course, the value seems obvious: more knowledge is generally better than less. Others have a more instrumental interest. They might want to know whether studying comparative constitutional law might improve our ability to make domestic constitutional law. Responding to that inquiry requires some examination of how we can actually *do* comparative constitutional law.[5]

I confine my attention to questions implicated in doing comparative constitutional law *as law*. There is, of course, a large field of comparative studies of governmental organization, conducted by political scientists as well as lawyers, and some of that field overlaps with the field of comparative constitutional law. There is, though, one large difference between the fields. Comparative constitutional law involves doing law. And, as I have learned, it is quite difficult to be comfortable in doing law in more than one legal system. Even when language barriers do not intervene, legal cultures do. For example, I have been persuaded—despite my initial skepticism—that Australian constitutional culture is far more formalist than U.S. constitutional culture. It is less open to what seem to me the inevitable intellectual challenges from those influenced by American legal realism and its legacy. As a result, constitutional doctrines in Australia, such as those dealing with the allocation of authority between the national and the state governments, are more stable than similar doctrines in the United States, even doctrines framed in language that seems

---

[5] There is a large literature on the methods of comparative law generally. The more general field, though, has included discussions of matters that I personally find not terribly interesting, such as the classification of legal systems into families and the phenomenon of borrowing by one legal system or tradition from another. For examples of writing in comparative constitutional law on the latter topic, see Constitutionalism and Rights: The Influence of the United States Constitution Abroad (Louis Henkin & Albert Rosenthal eds., 1990); Symposium on Constitutional Borrowing, 1 Int'l J. Con. L. 181–324 (2003).

parallel to that used in the Australian cases. These and other differences in constitutional cultures complicate the task of doing comparative constitutional law, perhaps to the point where the payoff in any terms other than the increase of knowledge is small.

An Overview of Methods in Comparative Constitutional Law

I think it useful to identify two ways of doing comparative constitutional law, as a preliminary to criticizing and deepening them to suggest a third method. Without insisting that they are sharply different, I call the first two methods *normative universalism* and *functionalism*.[6] These two methods involve efforts to see how constitutional ideas developed in one system might be related to those in another, either because the ideas attempt to capture the same normative value or because they attempt to organize a government to carry out the same tasks. I call the third method *contextualism*. This method comes in two variants, which I call *simple* contextualism and *expressivism*. Simple contextualism insists that constitutional ideas can be understood only in the full institutional and doctrinal context within which they are placed. Expressivism takes constitutional ideas to be expressions of a particular nation's self-understanding. Both methods raise questions about the coherence of the idea that constitutional ideas can migrate (without substantial modification) from one system to another.[7]

Universalism and Functionalism

Normative universalism emerges primarily from the dialogue between those who study comparative constitutional law and those who study international human rights. The idea is simple: constitutionalism itself entails— everywhere—some fundamental principles. Some of those principles involve human rights: the protection of some universal human rights, such as rights to political participation, to equal treatment under the law, to freedom of

---

[6] There is a sense in which normative universalism and functionalism are variants of a more general universalism, as will become clear later. I have been unable to devise labels that preserve a parallelism in formulations, though.

[7] It may be worth noting that legal scholars attracted to normative universalism are likely to be influenced by normative jurisprudence and political theory, that those attracted to functionalism are likely to be influenced by political scientists, and that those attracted to contextualism are likely to be influenced by anthropologists. And here yet another complexity intrudes. Not only will the scholar of comparative constitutional law have to be comfortable in more than one constitutional system, but he or she may think it helpful to be comfortable with the discipline other than law that seems likely to illuminate comparative constitutional questions in the way the legal scholar finds useful.

conscience and expression, and, for many human rights advocates, much more. Others involve structures of government. Here the list is typically shorter: independent courts for sure, perhaps some version of the separation between law enactment and law execution (another aspect of the separation of powers), and probably little more.

Universalists study comparative constitutional law to identify how particular constitutions instantiate those universal principles. By comparing different versions, we can better understand the principles themselves. Then we might be able to improve a domestic system's version of one or another principle by using that enhanced understanding to modify it.

Three examples from free speech law, two controversial, the other not, illustrate the universalist method in comparative constitutional law. The uncontroversial one is the law of sedition, a criminal offense consisting of criticism of existing government policies. Over the past century, the United States Supreme Court has grappled with the problem of reconciling the law of sedition with the First Amendment's protection of free expression. Its sustained attention to the problem has yielded two conclusions. The first is widely accepted. Government efforts to suppress speech critical of its policies must be treated with extreme skepticism, captured variously in formulations like "clear and present danger" or "intended to and likely to cause imminent lawless conduct."[8] The latter formulation indicates the second conclusion we can draw from the U.S. sedition cases. The problem of seditious speech, analysis has shown, is only one aspect of a broader problem—how can governments regulate speech that, they fear, will cause people to break the law?

Governments around the world have confronted the problem of seditious speech, and all governments must deal with the problem of speech that increases the risk that laws will be broken. Comparative constitutional study allows us to examine the different ways in which they deal with the problem. And, most scholars and many constitutional courts believe, something like the U.S. approach is the best one available.[9] The European Court of Human Rights, for example, has dealt with cases arising out of Turkey's often violent confrontation with the Kurdish separatist movement there. One, decided in 2000, involved a newspaper article by the president of a major labor union, in which the author said that "not only the Kurdish people but the whole of our proletariat must stand up against" the nation's anti-Kurdish laws and policies.[10] The Court wrote that "there is little scope [in the applicable international human rights law] for restrictions on political speech," but that governments could limit free expression when a speech

---

[8] Dennis v. United States, 341 U.S. 494 (1951) (the most recent version of the "clear and present danger" test in the United States); Brandenburg v. Ohio, 395 U.S. 444 (1968) (the "imminent lawless conduct" test).

[9] I return to the problem of sedition law in chapter 3.

[10] Ceylan v. Turkey, 30 EHRR 73 (2000), ¶ 8.

"incites to violence against an individual, a public official or a sector of the population."[11]

The law of personal libel provides a second example. Here the United States has adopted a notably stringent rule restricting the circumstances under which a person the Supreme Court calls a public figure can recover damages for the publication of a false statement that injures his or her reputation. The category of public figures is a large one in the United States, including leaders of large private corporations and prominent football coaches and celebrities as well as politicians.[12] Public figures can win only actual damages, which are usually relatively small, and even then only if they show that the false statements were made by someone who knew they were false or at least made a conscious decision to forgo any effort to find out whether they were true or false.[13]

Not surprisingly, other constitutional courts regularly confront libel cases brought by public figures. They have reached a range of conclusions, but none is nearly as restrictive of recovery as is the United States. For example, Australia uses a test of reasonableness. One major formulation was offered in a case brought there by a member of New Zealand's parliament who had been that nation's prime minister:

> [A] defendant's conduct . . . will not be reasonable unless the defendant had reasonable grounds for believing that the imputation [of something that damages reputation] was true, took proper steps, so far as they were reasonably open, to verify the accuracy of the material and did not believe the imputation to be untrue. Furthermore, the defendant's conduct will not be reasonable unless the defendant has sought a response from the person defamed and published the response (if any) made except in cases where the seeking or publication of a response was not practicable.[14]

Many in the United States find our domestic law of libel unsatisfactory.[15] Universalist scholars of comparative constitutional law suggest that looking at the solutions that other constitutional democracies have come up with would help us develop a better law of libel.

---

[11] *Id.*, ¶ 34.

[12] *See* Barbara Singer, "The Right of Publicity: Star Vehicle or Shooting Star?" 10 Cardozo Arts & Ent. L. J. 1, n. 1 (1991).

[13] The term the Supreme Court uses is that the false statements must be made with malice, but the decisions make it clear that the term refers not to some mental state like *having it in for the public figure*, but rather to knowledge of the statement's falsity or willful disregard of its truth or falsity.

[14] Lange v. Australian Broadcasting Corp., (1997) 189 CLR 520 (Aust. High Ct.) (opinion of Brennan, C. J.).

[15] *See* David A. Anderson, "Is Libel Law Worth Saving?" 140 U. Pa. L. Rev. 497 (1991); *see also* James Penzi, "Libel Actions in England, a Game of Truth or Dare? Considering the Recent Upjohn Cases and the Consequences of 'Speaking Out,'" 10 Temp. Imt'l & Comp. L. J. 211 (1996) (comparing English and U.S. libel laws).

The most controversial example involves the regulation of hate speech. Proponents of more extensive regulation of hate speech in the United States often refer to transnational constitutional norms—the existence of hate speech regulation in Canada,[16] the existence in some international human rights treaties of a *duty* to regulate hate speech[17]—in defending the proposition that hate speech regulation should not be treated as unconstitutional under the First Amendment to the U.S. Constitution.[18] They argue, quite rightly, that the fact that modern liberal democracies do in fact regulate hate speech without descending into totalitarian tyrannies where the government engages in extensive thought control shows that hate speech regulation in itself is compatible with a system that respects general norms of free expression. They conclude that hate speech regulation in the United States could be adopted without risking anything other than making the United States more like Canada—not, in their view, an obviously bad thing.

Again, this exemplifies the universalist use of comparative constitutional law. According to universalists, general principles of free expression and human dignity come into play when someone makes a speech castigating a racial, religious, or national group. Examining how a number of nations have worked out accommodations between those principles might be useful in developing the contours of any nation's domestic law dealing with hate speech.

The functionalist approach to comparative constitutional law is similar to the universalist one to the extent that it tries to identify things that happen in every constitutional system that is the object of study. So, for example, every democratic nation has to have a mechanism in place for going to war or for dealing with domestic emergencies that threaten the nation's continuing existence. But, the functionalist analysis goes, democratic nations should be careful about going to war, and about determining that a truly grave emergency exists. Functionalists believe that examining the different ways in which democratic nations organize the processes of going to war and declaring emergencies can help us determine which are better and which are worse processes.

As the example of war-making and emergencies suggests, functionalists tend to focus on issues of government structure. With respect to federalism,

[16] *See, e.g.*, Regina v. Keegstra, [1990] S.C.R. 697.

[17] International Covenant on Civil and Political Rights, art. 20(2) ("Any advocacy of national, racial or religious hatred that constitutes incitement to discrimination, hostility or violence shall be prohibited by law."); International Convention on the Elimination of All Forms of Racial Discrimination, art. 4(a) (States Parties "[s]hall declare as an offence punishable by law all dissemination of ideas based on racial superiority or hatred, incitement to racial discrimination").

[18] *See, e.g.*, Mari Matsuda, "Public Response to Racist Speech: Considering the Victim's Story," 87 Mich. L. Rev. 2320, 2341–48 (1989) (describing the development of international human rights law in connection with hate speech); john r. powell, "As Justice Requires/Permits: The Delimitation of Harmful Speech in a Democratic Society," 16 Law & Inequality 97, 147–50 (1998) (discussing *Keegstra*).

for example, a functionalist might ask: What forms of federalism best accommodate the diversity in a nation's regions? Can federalism be adapted to deal with diversities that are not tied closely to geography? Belgium's experiment with an incredibly complex set of federalist institutions—some geographic, some linguistic—layered on to each other might provide some insights into these questions.[19] Drawing on work by political scientists, functionalists consider whether presidential or parliamentary systems are better vehicles for achieving the goals a nation's people set for themselves.[20]

Both the universalist and functionalist methods are flawed, though. Put most generally, their difficulty is that they operate on too high a level of abstraction. We can assume that there *are* universal principles of liberty and justice, for example, but we can be reasonably confident that such principles are not fully captured in general terms such as *free speech* or *equality*. The free speech principle, whatever it is, is likely to be extremely complex, sensitive to the circumstances presented by particular problems. The law of freedom of expression must deal with forms of expression that involve words alone, words coupled with symbols, symbols alone, and actions whose social meaning is understood to be communicative. It must deal with expression that is thought to cause harm by persuading listeners of the rightness of the claims made, by structuring the environment in which listeners evaluate *other* claims, or by triggering responses without engaging a listener's cognitive capacities. It must deal with harms ranging from assaults on dignity to threats to national survival. And, of course, it must deal with political speech, commercial speech, sexually explicit speech, and many other varieties of expression. With so many variables going into the structure of the free speech principle, it may well be that a nation's experience with the cases thrown up in its own history will be substantially more illuminating of the underlying principle than other nations' experiences with their histories.

A parallel point holds for issues of government structure. Consider, for example, the question of going to war. Separation-of-powers systems might be leery of giving a president the power to initiate substantial military engagements, because, as William Treanor has pointed out (drawing on the views held by the framers of the U.S. Constitution), a single person may be reckless in seeking to obtain honor in military operations.[21] Members of the legislature,

---

[19] For a description, now somewhat outdated, see A. Alen, B. Tilleman, and F. Meersschaut, "The State and Its Subdivisions," in Treatise on Belgian Constitutional Law 123 (André Alen ed., 1992).

[20] Bruce Ackerman, "The New Separation of Powers," 113 Harv. L. Rev. 633 (2000). For an extraordinarily unpersuasive attempt to respond to Ackerman, flawed precisely by its failure to understand the functionalist approach, see Steven Calabresi, "Why Professor Ackerman Is Wrong to Prefer the German to the U.S. Constitution," 18 Const. Comm. 51 (2001).

[21] William Michael Treanor, "Fame, the Founding, and the Power to Declare War," 82 Corn. L. Rev. 695 (1995).

in contrast, gain little individually from authorizing military operations, and so may be more cautious than a president. Clearly, though, this argument depends on the precise structure of a nation's separation-of-powers system, and in particular on the relation between the president as party leader and the president as commander in chief.

CONTEXTUALISM AND EXPRESSIVISM

Contextualism, a third approach to comparative constitutional law, emphasizes the fact that constitutional law is deeply embedded in the institutional, doctrinal, social, and cultural contexts of each nation, and that we are likely to go wrong if we try to think about any specific doctrine or institution without appreciating the way it is tightly linked to all the contexts within which it exists. Contextualist comparative studies come in many forms—ethnographic and historical, for example. My concerns in this book lead me to present contextualism in a relatively thin way.

For present purposes, I limit my discussion of the contextualist approach to its focus on the *institutional* and *doctrinal* contexts of specific doctrines.[22] Constitutions combine substantive norms, such as commitments to free speech and equality, with institutional arrangements, such as federalism and parliamentary government. The substantive norms are implemented within the institutional arrangements, and particular institutional arrangements are sometimes more compatible with some interpretations of the substantive norms than with others.[23]

The hate speech issue provides a good example of why institutional contexts matter.[24] The arguments for hate speech regulation operate on the level

[22] For a somewhat more complete description of the effects of these contexts, see Mark Tushnet, "Interpreting Constitutions Comparatively: Some Cautionary Notes, with Reference to Affirmative Action," 36 Conn. L. Rev. 649 (2004), from which the next paragraphs are drawn.

[23] My thinking about this question has been influenced by my colleague Vicki Jackson, and in particular her argument that federalism might consist of discrete packages of institutional arrangements. *See* Vicki C. Jackson, "Narratives of Federalism: Of Continuities and Comparative Constitutional Experience," 51 Duke L. J. 223 (2001); Vicki C. Jackson, "Comparative Constitutional Federalism and Transnational Judicial Discourse," 2 Int. J. Con. L. 91 (2004). I emphasize that my observations are only influenced by her analysis, that she has not indicated whether she agrees with my observations, and that I actually disagree with aspects of her argument about federalism.

[24] As Daniel Halberstam has shown, failure to attend to institutional contexts is a major flaw in one of the important references to comparative constitutional law in U.S. adjudication, Justice Stephen Breyer's attempt in Printz v. United States, 521 U.S. 98 (1997), to enlist German federalism to explain why the U.S. Supreme Court's "anti-commandeering" principle is not compelled by the existence of a federal system. Daniel Halberstam, "Comparative Federalism and the Issue of Commandeering," in The Federal Vision: Legitimacy and Levels of Governance in the United States and the European Union 213 (Kalypso Nicolaïdis & Robert Howse eds., 2001).

of principle—free expression and equality. Those arguments typically overlook the institutional context within which hate speech regulations are implemented. One principle—among many—that (everywhere) guides the interpretation of constitutional protections of free expression is that those protections are designed to counteract a tendency on the part of government officials to overreact to perceived threats to order. Criminal law enforcement is much more highly centralized in other constitutional systems than it is in the United States. Great Britain's hate crime statute requires that prosecutions be authorized by the attorney general, a single official.[25] Even in Canada's federal system, criminal law enforcement is centralized in each province's attorney general.[26] The risk of abusive prosecutions for hate speech may be reduced by this centralization and the attendant responsibility for, and public visibility of, decisions to prosecute. Compare the United States, where thousands of local district attorneys have the power to initiate and carry prosecutions through.[27] The way the U.S. federal system is organized, that is, may increase the risk that clearly inappropriate prosecutions for hate speech will be brought. And, finally, that risk is relevant to determining whether a domestic constitutional provision protecting free expression should be interpreted to permit or prohibit criminal hate speech regulations. The institutional context of criminal law enforcement in the United States and elsewhere must be taken into account in determining how to interpret the *substantive* commitment to free expression.[28]

The doctrinal context matters as well. Here we can reconsider the earlier example of libel law. Cast in the most general terms, libel law provides the structure for accommodating interests in speech with interests in reputation, the latter an aspect of human dignity. Note, though, that in the United States the interest in speech is of constitutional magnitude, whereas the interest in reputation is merely one of policy.[29] The accommodation of interests in the United States *must* give greater weight to the interest in speech than to the

[25] Race Relations Act 1965, sec. 6(3).

[26] Constitution Act, 1867, § 92(14) (allocating criminal law enforcement to provinces); Can. Rev. Stat., ch. C-34 (1970) (giving provincial attorneys general primary law enforcement authority).

[27] In general, state attorneys general lack the power to displace local prosecutors except in highly limited circumstances.

[28] My argument deals with criminal enforcement of hate speech regulations. Other contexts involve much more decentralized decision making even in Canada and the United Kingdom—for example, in connection with hate speech regulations by school boards and government employers. It might be, then, that Canadian and British commitments to free expression might permit criminal hate speech regulation but ought not be interpreted to authorize noncriminal regulations.

[29] That is, as a matter of U.S. constitutional law, a state could abolish its tort of libel entirely, leaving people with no recourse whatever for damage to reputation caused by entirely false statements of fact.

interest in reputation. In contrast, in Great Britain and Australia, neither the interest in speech nor that in reputation is of constitutional magnitude. There the common law can develop in ways that give "appropriate" weight to both interests. And, finally, in Germany both the interest in speech and the interest in reputation as an aspect of human dignity are of constitutional magnitude. The balancing of interests in Germany will necessarily be different from that in the United States because the underlying constitutional provisions differ.

As I have described contextualism to this point, it simply insists on taking an appropriately wide view of the field in which constitutional law operates. Expressivism is a different, perhaps even more comprehensive version of contextualism. For an expressivist scholar, constitutional law—doctrines and institutional arrangements—are ways in which a nation goes about defining itself. Preambles to constitutions may be particularly useful for an expressivist. So, for example, the preamble to the Irish Constitution of 1937 is an especially rich text for these purposes. The preamble states:

> In the name of the Most Holy Trinity, from Whom is all authority and to Whom, as our final end, all actions both of men and States must be referred, We, the people of Ireland, humbly acknowledging all our obligations to our Divine Lord, Jesus Christ, Who sustained our fathers through centuries of trial, Gratefully remembering their heroic and unremitting struggle to regain the rightful independence of our Nation, And seeking to promote the common good, with due observance of Prudence, Justice and Charity, so that the dignity and freedom of the individual may be assured, true social order attained, the unity of our country restored, and concord established with other nations, Do hereby adopt, enact, and give to ourselves this Constitution.

The preamble's opening words and its later reference to Jesus Christ identify the nation with Christianity, and its use of the terms *final end* and *prudence, justice, and charity* show that the nation is specifically Roman Catholic. The document also looks backward in a powerful way, with its references to *centuries of trial* and a *heroic and unremitting struggle*. And, finally, the formulation "give to ourselves" states a relationship of self-donation and acceptance between the people of Ireland and their constitution that embeds the 1937 document in the nation's ongoing identity.[30]

An expressivist approach to comparative constitutional law would contrast the self-understandings found in the constitutional documents of different nations. For example, such an approach might point to the differences in self-understanding expressed in Canada's *Burns* decision and the *Stanford* decision

---

[30] One could engage in a similar analysis of the preambles to the constitutions of the United States and South Africa, and of the "post-amble" of the interim Constitution of South Africa, with its discussion of "national unity and reconciliation." Interim Constitution of the Republic of South Africa, Act 200 of 1993, ch. 15, final paragraphs.

in the United States. In the former, the Canadian Supreme Court significantly modified a prior holding to impose rather severe restrictions on the power of the national government to extradite a fugitive from the United States charged with a capital crime, unless the government obtained assurances that the death penalty would not be imposed.[31] The theme that the Canadian government had taken the lead in international discussions and implementation of human rights ran through the Court's opinion. So, for the *Burns* court, Canada's self-understanding as a leader on human rights *led to* the constitutional doctrine the court articulated. In *Stanford*, the U.S. Supreme Court applied a constitutional standard referring to "evolving standards of decency" in the context of the death penalty by insisting that the relevant standards of decency were those of the people of the United States, not those of the wider international community.[32] An expressivist analysis could use these cases to distinguish between the outward-looking self-understanding of Canada and the inward-looking one of the United States.

My discussion of what we can learn from comparative constitutional law offers some cautionary notes, not knock-down arguments against its use in domestic constitutional interpretation. Sometimes it is said that comparative law can bring to mind possibilities that might otherwise be overlooked or thought too utopian to be considered as part of a real-world constitution. Comparative law, the thought is, can help us rid ourselves of ideas of "false necessity," the sense we might have—grounded in our own experience because that is the only experience we have—that the institutions and doctrines we have are the only ones that could possibly be appropriate for our circumstances.

Combining contextualism with the insight that comparative study can raise questions about whether some arrangements that seem necessary to us are actually false necessities may have more subversive implications for the comparative enterprise than it might seem initially. The difficulty is that contextualism might lead us to see that the arrangements are indeed necessary, given the complete context within which they are set. The question is the extent to which the constraints imposed by a nation's legal institutions and arrangements, by its doctrinal history, by its legal culture, and so on down the list of constraining factors intersect in a way that reduces the set of choices (be they institutional, doctrinal, or whatever) to one—that is, to the one that is actually in place.[33] I doubt that this question can be answered

---

[31] United States v. Burns, [2001] 1 S.C.R. 283.

[32] Stanford v. Kentucky, 492 U.S. 361 (1989), *overruled by* Roper v. Simmons, 543 U.S. 551 (2005).

[33] Notice that this concern is entirely compatible with the proposition that no single set of constraints is all that constraining. Doctrine can be flexible and substantially open, for example, and institutional arrangements in themselves might not place strong limits on the possibilities. Rather, the concern is that adding one loose set of constraints to another, and to yet another, reduces the options substantially.

in the abstract, or generally.[34] I believe, though, that the comparative inquiry must be sensitive to all the contexts to which contextualism directs our attention.[35]

More precisely: contextualism in both its versions raises challenges to the idea that comparative study can help identify false necessities. The first version suggests that these institutions and doctrines might not be "false" in some strong sense because they may be so tightly integrated that no significant changes are possible. Expressivism suggests that a nation *has* a (single) self-understanding that its constitution expresses. Yet, these challenges should not be given more weight than they properly bear. Everything we know about the doctrines and institutions of law tells us that doctrines and institutions can accommodate much more change than we might think. We have discovered that we can tinker with a wide range of doctrines and institutions without transforming in the short run what we regard as constitutional fundamentals. And, as time goes on, our understanding of what those fundamentals are can itself change, sometimes in response to prior tinkering. This observation will play a large role in my discussion of forms of judicial review in chapter 3.

Similarly, it is a mistake to think that a nation has a single self-understanding. Doctrines and institutions might seem true necessities to an expressivist who says, "Well, this is the way we (or they) are." But, even within a nation's constitution and constitutional traditions, "who we are" is often—perhaps always—contestable and actively contested. In contrast to the inward-looking self-understanding articulated in *Stanford*, for example, there is another, outward-looking self-understanding that can be found in U.S. constitutionalism.[36]

---

[34] Although I must note that my intuition is that the answer will quite frequently be that the cumulative constraints are indeed quite substantial.

[35] And that many comparative exercises are not sufficiently sensitive to all those contexts.

[36] The currently favored way of making the point is to refer to the self-understanding expressed in the passage of the Declaration of Independence stating that, under some circumstances, "We the People of the United States" have a duty (perhaps prudential, perhaps principled) to show "a decent respect to the opinions of mankind" by explaining to the world the reasons for our actions. This view of the Declaration is reinforced when the Declaration is read in light of Scottish moral theory that was part of the Declaration's intellectual background, as to which see Garry Wills, Inventing America: Jefferson's Declaration of Independence (1978). Amartya Sen quotes a relevant passage from Adam Smith's *Theory of Moral Sentiments*:

> We can never survey our own sentiments and motives; we can never form any judgment concerning them; unless we remove ourselves, as it were, from our own natural station, and endeavour to view them as at a certain distance from us. But we can do this in no other way than by endeavouring to view them with the eyes of other people, or as other people are likely to view them.

Amartya Sen, "Elements of a Theory of Human Rights," 32 Phil. & Pub. Aff. 315, 350 (2004). For a slightly more extended discussion, see Mark Tushnet, "'A Decent Respect to the Opinions of Mankind': Referring to Foreign Law to Express American Nationhood," 69 Alb. L. Rev. 809 (2006).

Contextualism's challenge to the comparative enterprise, though serious, need not be fatal. The challenge does suggest that the study of the migration of constitutional ideas must be done with great caution—more caution, I think, than can be found in much of recent literature on "borrowing" constitutional ideas. Perhaps the true object of study should be the way in which those constitutional ideas that do migrate are transformed as they cross the border, or, alternatively, the way in which ideas that seem to have migrated have deeper indigenous roots than one might think, deeper even than the prevalence of citations to nondomestic sources would indicate.

CONCLUSION

I can begin to wind up this chapter by turning to an exchange between Justice Antonin Scalia and Justice Stephen Breyer. Justice Breyer has referred—probably mistakenly—to experiences with federalism in Germany to explain why it might be thought compatible with U.S. federalism to allow the national government to "commandeer" the executive resources of state governments to carry out national policy. Justice Scalia responded that Justice Breyer's approach, and perhaps reliance on comparative constitutional experience more generally,[37] was "inappropriate to the task of interpreting a constitution, though it was quite relevant to the task of writing one."[38] Justice Scalia's distinction between constitutional interpretation and constitutional design is not as sharp as he suggests, though. Consider the issue the next chapters take up—whether strong-form or weak-form institutions of judicial review better accommodate the competing interests in constitutionalism and self-government. That issue presents a question of constitutional design. Today, constitution drafters may well write provisions into their constitutions that make it clear that they have adopted a strong-form system or a weak-form one. The drafters of the U.S. Constitution did not include such provisions. Indeed, they did not write anything about judicial review into the

[37] Elsewhere Justice Scalia has relied on the claim that particular constitutional provisions do not license U.S. judges to refer to constitutional experience elsewhere. Stanford v. Kentucky, 492 U.S. 361, 369 n. 1 (1989) ("We emphasize that it is *American* conceptions of decency that are dispositive" of claims that imposing the death penalty on those who were under the age of eighteen when they committed their offenses was barred by the Eighth Amendment's ban on cruel and unusual punishment.). I think it a fair inference from Justice Scalia's position here and in other cases that he does not believe that the U.S. Constitution licenses judges to rely on comparative constitutional experience in any context, but he has not so stated in any of his opinions. In a speech to the American Society of International Law, Justice Scalia did state his "view that modern foreign legal material can never be relevant to any interpretation of, that is to say, to the meaning of the U.S. Constitution." *Quoted in* Anne Gearan, "Foreign Rulings Not Relevant to High Court, Scalia Says," Washington Post, April 3, 2004, p. A-7.

[38] *Printz*, 521 U.S. at 921.

Constitution. The design issue of how to structure judicial review, that is, is entirely a question of interpretation in the United States.

It is not out of the question, of course, that that design issue has been entirely resolved over the course of U.S. constitutional history. In theory, the Constitution's drafters may have understood that they were creating a strong-form or a weak-form structure. Or, equally in theory, an unbroken line of precedent might have resolved that structural question.

As it turns out, though, those possibilities are indeed only theoretical. The Constitution's drafters had diverse views about the structure of judicial review. Departmentalism, for example, was one widely held view. Thomas Jefferson was not, strictly speaking, a drafter of the Constitution, but obviously he was a person whose thinking about the Constitution was and remains important. Jefferson's version of departmentalism implied that judicial review, to him, had a structure quite similar to that of modern weak-form review.[39] Courts could express their views on what the Constitution meant, but the president and Congress were entitled thereafter to continue to act on their own views even if those views were different from the courts'.

Precedent is a somewhat larger barrier to reimagining judicial review in the United States as weak-form. The contemporary Supreme Court certainly regards judicial review as having the strong form, and much of the public appears to agree.[40] Exactly when we got strong-form judicial review is unclear, though. Something like strong-form review seems to have been the target of James Bradley Thayer's famous 1893 essay, "The Origin and Scope of the American Doctrine of Constitutional Law,"[41] but Thayer's position in support of a weaker version of judicial review continued to have substantial support in Congress, the presidency, and even the Supreme Court through the middle of the twentieth century. The modern articulation of strong-form judicial review is provided in *Cooper v. Aaron* (1958), where the U.S. Supreme Court described the federal courts as "supreme in the exposition of the law of the Constitution," and inferred from that a duty on legislatures to follow the Court's interpretations.[42] *Cooper v. Aaron*'s articulation of strong-form judicial review itself remains moderately controversial; contemporary conservatives continued to be attracted to some version of departmentalism, for example.[43]

---

[39] For a recent discussion of departmentalism, including some aspects of Jefferson's version, see Larry D. Kramer, The People Themselves: Popular Constitutionalism and Judicial Review 106–11 (2004).

[40] *See* chapter 2.

[41] James Bradley Thayer, "The Origin and Scope of the American Doctrine of Constitutional Law," 7 Harv. L. Rev. 129 (1893).

[42] 358 U.S. 1, 18 (1958).

[43] For example, Attorney General Edwin Meese provided a moderate departmentalist view in a widely noted speech in 1987. For citations to the speech and some reactions to it, see Kathleen Sullivan & Gerald Gunther, Constitutional Law 25–26 (14ᵗʰ ed., 2001).

In the end, I think the best assessment is that the question of what form the U.S. system of judicial review has is a design issue left incompletely resolved by the Constitution's text, by understandings about judicial review at the time of the Constitution's adoption, and by the precedents built up since then. If comparative constitutional law is relevant to designing the structures of judicial review, it is relevant to "interpreting"—really, figuring out—the structure of judicial review in the United States.[44]

Justice Louis Brandeis's observation, "If we would guide by the light of reason, we must let our minds be bold,"[45] may provide the best defense for doing comparative constitutional law. Or, as Claude Lévi-Strauss notably put it, ideas, like food, are "good to think."[46] For scholars, that probably should be enough. Those who address themselves to policymakers, including judges, and the policymakers themselves, should be appropriately cautious about what they believe they can learn from the study of comparative constitutional law.[47]

[44] The case for regarding the question of social and economic rights as equally open to interpretation illuminated by comparative constitutional law is more complex, and so I defer it until part 3.

[45] New State Ice Co. v. Liebmann, 285 U.S. 262, 311 (1932) (Brandeis, J., dissenting).

[46] Claude Lévi-Strauss, Totemism 89 (1963). I note that Lévi-Strauss almost certainly deliberately omitted the word "with" that most readers seem unconsciously to insert in his phrase.

[47] Konrad Schiemann, reflecting on his experience as a judge in England, observes, "Where I felt that the traditional approach led to a result which appeared to me unsatisfactory, I would turn to foreign law to see whether my hesitations found any echo elsewhere and whether some stimulus to my own thinking could be found." Konrad Schiemann, "A Response to *The Judge as Comparatist*," 80 Tulane L. Rev. 281, 283–84 (2005). This seems to me the appropriate stance to take to the comparative enterprise in which I am engaged here.

CHAPTER 2

Alternative Forms of Judicial Review

ONE DOES NOT have to read deeply in recent scholarship on the U.S. Constitution to find assertions to the effect that the U.S. constitutional system has been widely emulated in other nations.[1] Those assertions are plainly wrong when they refer to the constitutional system in the large. As political scientist Robert Dahl shows, the U.S. system is unique among the world's twenty-two long-standing and stable democracies.[2] Only somewhat more defensible is the assertion that the U.S. system of judicial review of statutes to determine whether they are consistent with constitutional limitations has been widely emulated. As the Canadian constitutional scholar Lorraine Weinrib has emphasized, there surely is a "post-war paradigm" of constitutionalism, a central feature of which is some form of judicial review.[3] Yet, even here the U.S. system of judicial review is hardly the dominant model. The German Constitutional Court probably has been more influential around the world than the U.S. Supreme Court. Many nations have created specialized constitutional courts on the German model, rejecting the older U.S. system of having the nation's highest court for ordinary law also serve as the highest court for constitutional law.[4] Few nations indeed guarantee judicial independence by conferring life tenure on their judges.

Here I focus on another, more recent development in systems of judicial review—the emergence of what I call weak-form judicial review. Understanding weak-form review's attractions requires a short detour into fundamentals of modern constitutionalism. Today, constitutionalism requires that a nation be committed to the proposition that a nation's people should determine the policies under which they will live, by some form of democratic governance.[5]

---

[1] For a representative example, see Lawrence G. Sager, Justice in Plainclothes: A Theory of American Constitutional Practice 3–4 (2004) ("Our constitutional practice is increasingly the object of admiration and emulation.").

[2] Robert Dahl, How Democratic Is the Constitution? (2001), ch. 3.

[3] Lorraine Eisenstat Weinrib, "The Postwar Paradigm and American Exceptionalism," in The Migration of Constitutional Ideas (Sujit Choudhry ed., 2006).

[4] Hans Kelsen, the jurisprude and constitutional scholar who designed and then served on the first Austrian constitutional court, argued that a specialized constitutional court would better understand the political component of constitutional law than would judges who dealt with ordinary (and in Kelsen's view, largely nonpolitical) law.

[5] As John Rawls and others have pointed out, nondemocratic, nonauthoritarian constitutionalism is a conceptual possibility, but not, I believe, a practical one under contemporary circumstances. For Rawls's presentation, see John Rawls, The Law of Peoples (1999).

Yet, constitutionalism also requires that there be some limits on the policy choices the people can make democratically. Those limits are set out in the nation's constitution.[6]

What if democratic processes produce policies that are arguably inconsistent with the constitution's limits? Two means of control were candidates from the early nineteenth century until the late twentieth century. The first was parliamentary supremacy—which allowed for democratic self-governance—surrounded by some institutional constraints on power-holders and many more normative ones. The second was judicial review, that is, the creation of a separate institution, removed from the direct influence of politics and staffed by independent judges charged with the job of ensuring that the legislature remained within constitutional bounds.[7]

In the system of parliamentary supremacy, political parties that competed for power in regular and reasonably fair elections placed some limits on what those currently holding power could get away with. Power-holders were expected to be drawn from social elites who had normative commitments to exercising power only within limits. Civil service bureaucracies implemented legislative policy but also helped shape it within the terms set by the bureaucrats' professional norms. The normative constraints on power-holders decayed over the course of the twentieth century. The democratization of politics reduced the prevalence of traditional social elites in leadership positions, and it also heightened the stakes of politics for both winners and losers in situations of real social tension. By the end of the twentieth century, only Australia and New Zealand among the world's major democracies remained seriously committed to parliamentary supremacy.[8]

---

[6] The constitution may be a single document, or a collection of documents understood to be constitutional in significance, some of which might be judicial decisions.

[7] There was actually a third mechanism of control. Much of what government officials do is to exercise discretion conferred on them by statutes that are not plainly unconstitutional. Discretionary decisions that violate fundamental rights can be controlled, and were controlled in systems of parliamentary supremacy, by a doctrine of ultra vires, that is, a rule that statutes conferring discretion were not intended to confer discretion to violate fundamental rights. The executive officer's discretionary action could then be found unauthorized, and appropriate legal remedies provided. A robust ultra vires doctrine means that important questions about tensions between judicial review and democratic self-governance arise only when legislatures clearly want to authorize an action that some judges will say violates fundamental rights. (I note that some collateral questions—in particular, about whether a robust ultra vires doctrine would itself interfere with legislative choice of policy—would still arise.) I discuss ultra vires rules in chapter 4.

[8] Australia has a written constitution enforced by its courts, but the Australian Constitution has few protections of fundamental rights, and its courts have interpreted those few quite narrowly. In the 1990s the Australian High Court toyed with the idea of inferring constitutionally protected fundamental rights from the Constitution's overall structure and commitment to republican government, but largely abandoned the experiment rather quickly. *See* Tony Blackshield & George Williams, Australian Constitutional Law and Theory: Commentary and Materials 1000 (3rd ed., 2002) ("The few civil and political freedoms that are expressly recognized in the Australian

The political developments I have sketched made judicial review more attractive. By the mid-1960s or so, most designers of modern constitutional systems concluded that some form of judicial review is the best means of ensuring that policies inconsistent with the constitution will not be implemented.[9] Yet, giving judges the power to enforce constitutional limitations can threaten democratic self-governance. The reason is that constitutional provisions are often written in rather general terms. The courts give those terms meaning in the course of deciding whether individual statutes are consistent or inconsistent with particular constitutional provisions. But as a rule, particular provisions can reasonably be given alternative interpretations. And sometimes a statute will be inconsistent with the provision when the provision is interpreted in one way, yet would be consistent with an alternative interpretation of the same provision.

Consider here a problem that the U.S. Supreme Court addressed in the late twentieth century. Sometimes a government will adopt a rule that has particularly severe effects on a class of religious believers. The rule might require all military personnel to wear only a military uniform, in the face of religious commands to wear distinctive headgear; it might ban the use of a psychoactive drug that plays an important role in a denomination's religious ceremonies; or it might deny unemployment benefits to those who are unable to locate jobs that would allow them to refrain from working on the day they observe as the Sabbath. Do such rules violate the Constitution's prohibition on

---

Constitution have infrequently been invoked in litigation, and when invoked have generally been given a restrictive interpretation by the High Court."). For the experiment and its limits, compare Australian Capital Television Pty Lid v. Commonwealth, (1992) 177 CLR 106 (Australia) (invoking an implied freedom of political communication to invalidate campaign finance regulations that gave significant advantages to incumbents), with Lange v. Australian Broadcasting Corporation, (1997) 189 CLR 520 (1997) (substantially limiting the scope of the implied freedom of political communication in a case involving the effects of constitutional principles on the common law of libel). Blackshield and Williams describe the cases leading up to Lange as an "abortive" effort to develop more substantial judicially enforceable liberties. Blackshield & Williams, *supra* at 1201.

[9] I note here, to put the matter aside for the remainder of my discussion, the possibility that a system-designer might rely on some supranational body to enforce limitations on democratic self-governance similar to those embedded in a nation's constitution. The best example of which I am aware is the Constitution of the Netherlands. That Constitution does identify substantive limitations on public policy. But it also provides, "The constitutionality of Acts of Parliament and treaties shall not be reviewed by the courts." Const. of the Netherlands, art. 120. The force of that provision is blunted by another provision, "Statutory regulations in force within the Kingdom shall not be applicable if such application is in conflict with provisions of treaties that are binding on all persons or of resolutions by international institutions." *Id.*, art. 94. One such treaty is the European Convention on Human Rights, to which the Netherlands has acceded, and which contains provisions that overlap substantially with those in the Dutch Constitution. In this book I focus almost entirely on domestic constitutional law; attempting to analyze the interaction between that law and the enforcement of treaty-based norms parallel to those in domestic law would require knowledge about the institutions of treaty-based enforcement, such as the European Court of Human Rights, which I lack.

restricting the "free exercise of religion"? In 1963 the Supreme Court held that they did, unless they were virtually the only way the government could promote important public purposes.[10] Almost thirty years later, the Court changed its mind, and held that such general rules were ordinarily perfectly constitutional, unless they were adopted with the specific aim of imposing harm on a religious denomination.[11] Now, suppose the decisions had come in the reverse order: first the Court adopts a doctrine that gives governments wide latitude, and later adopts one substantially limiting what governments can do. What if a legislature believes that the Court got it right the first time? We *know* that the constitutional interpretation favored by the legislature is not unreasonable: after all, the Supreme Court itself adopted it (for a while). No doubt, the Court's later interpretation is *also* reasonable. But why should the Court's reasonable interpretation prevail over the legislature's (also) reasonable one?

The example I have given is not esoteric. Indeed, experience has shown that people—that is, legislatures and courts—can disagree about what a constitutional provision should be interpreted to mean quite often, and that those disagreements can, again quite often, be entirely reasonable. The U.S. system of judicial review, which I call strong-form review, insists that the courts' reasonable constitutional interpretations prevail over the legislatures' reasonable ones. Courts exercise strong-form judicial review when their interpretive judgments are final and unrevisable. The modern articulation of strong-form judicial review is provided in *Cooper v. Aaron*, where the U.S. Supreme Court described the federal courts as "supreme in the exposition of the law of the Constitution," and inferred from that a duty on legislatures to follow the Court's interpretations.[12]

A contemporary version came in *City of Boerne v. Flores*,[13] which involved Congress' power to enact the Religious Freedom Restoration Act of 1993 (RFRA) pursuant to its power to "enforce" the prohibitions placed on state governments by Section 1 of the Fourteenth Amendment.[14] As we have seen, at the time RFRA was enacted the Court had held that states could enforce their general rules even against those whose religious views made it impossible or very difficult for them to comply with both their religious commitments and the state's law. RFRA rejected that approach, and required states to have strong justifications even for general laws that burdened religious exercise. And, again

---

[10] Sherbert v. Verner, 374 U.S. 398 (1963). I simplify the doctrine in this paragraph, for expository purposes.

[11] Employment Division, Department of Human Resources v. Smith, 494 U.S. 872 (1990). For an application of the ban on targeting denominations, see Church of the Lukumi Babalu Aye v. City of Hialeah, 508 U.S. 520 (1993).

[12] 358 U.S. 1, 18 (1958).

[13] 521 U.S. 507 (1997).

[14] 42 U.S.C. §§ 2000bb to 2000bb-4 (1994).

as we have seen, the rule enacted in RFRA was the one the Supreme Court itself had articulated for decades before it changed its approach.

The question for the Court was whether RFRA "enforced" Section 1. Analytically, one could take the position that the scope of Section 1 is open to reasonable alternative interpretations, the Supreme Court's prior interpretation being the first and Congress' more recent one the second. On that view, RFRA did enforce Section 1, *given* the congressional interpretation of Section 1. The Supreme Court took a different view. For the Court, the only rights that Congress could enforce were those the Court itself recognized. According to the Court, "legislation which *alters* the meaning of the Free Exercise Clause cannot be said to be enforcing the Clause." The opinion continued, "If Congress could define its own powers by *altering* the Fourteenth Amendment's meaning, no longer would the Constitution be 'superior paramount law, unchangeable by ordinary means.' "[15]

The deep assumption of strong-form review is found in the word *alter*. A proponent of some other version of judicial review might have written, "Congress has the power to specify the meaning of the Fourteenth Amendment, at least so long as its specification is reasonable, although different from the specification we ourselves would provide." Similarly, that proponent might have written:

> The Constitution defines the powers of Congress in broad terms; when Congress provides a reasonable specification of those terms' meaning in a particular context, courts should give considerable weight to that judgment. This does not allow Congress to "alter" the Fourteenth Amendment's meaning, but rather follows from the Constitution's allocation of interpretive power to both Congress and the courts.

Under a strong-form system like that emerging from the U.S. Supreme Court's decisions, the tension between judicial enforcement of constitutional limitations and democratic self-government is obvious. The people have little recourse when the courts interpret the Constitution reasonably but, in the reasonable alternative view of a majority, mistakenly. We can amend the Constitution, or wait for judges to retire or die and replace them with judges who hold the better view of what the Constitution means.[16]

---

[15] 521 U.S. at 519, (emphasis added), 529 (emphasis added) (quoting Marbury v. Madison, 5 U.S. (1 Cranch) 137, 1777 (1803)).

[16] There are, of course, other mechanisms of response: the Constitution authorizes impeachment of justices, and authorizes Congress to regulate, and thereby restrict, the courts' jurisdiction. Even more than constitutional amendment, these mechanisms have not been effective as tools for ensuring that judges interpret the Constitution as the people reasonably want it interpreted. At the start of the nineteenth century, Jeffersonians attempted to impeach Justice Samuel Chase, and their failure to remove him from office has been taken to establish the proposition that a judge should not be removed simply because Congress believes that he or she has made mistaken decisions. Some minor restrictions on jurisdiction have been enacted, but none going to central disputes over the correctness of the courts' constitutional interpretations. More interesting is the

Weak-form systems of judicial review hold out the promise of reducing the tension between judicial review and democratic self-governance, while acknowledging that constitutionalism requires that there be some limits on self-governance. The basic idea behind weak-form review is simple: weak-form judicial review provides mechanisms for the people to respond to decisions that they reasonably believe mistaken that can be deployed more rapidly than the constitutional amendment or judicial appointment processes.

In the remainder of this chapter I describe some systems of weak-form review and contrast them with strong-form review. Chapter 3 develops a number of deeper comparisons, asking such questions as, Are weak-form systems of judicial review likely to remain weak-form or, instead, turn into systems of either parliamentary supremacy or strong-form review? Before launching into those inquiries, though, I must restate a central proposition, because my experience is that students and colleagues are willing to give nominal assent to the proposition without really agreeing with it. The term *reasonable* plays a large role in the foregoing argument. It has two facets, both important. First, the argument acknowledges that *sometimes* disagreement about how a constitutional provision should be interpreted is unreasonable. The difficulty lies in refraining from expanding the category of unreasonableness so that it encompasses every position with which you disagree—or, worse, so that it encompasses every position a current majority on the Supreme Court rejects. So, second, one has to be comfortable with saying something like this: "I have worked through the relevant materials fully, and I believe that they establish that this constitutional provision should be interpreted to mean thus-and-so, from which it follows that the statute we are dealing with is unconstitutional. But, I know that you have done just as much work with the materials as I have, and you disagree with me about what the provision should mean. You are wrong, but I see this as a disagreement about something over which reasonable people can indeed disagree." This is not a position that many people are comfortable taking.[17] Even so, it should be clear that the interpretations proffered by any current Supreme Court majority are not the only reasonable ones available, because such interpretations are often met by dissent on the Court itself, offered by otherwise apparently reasonable people. That should

---

enactment of a statute only marginally different from the one invalidated. Legislators might hope that the Court would change its mind, or, more likely, distinguish its prior decision and uphold the statute, perhaps in part because the reenactment was understood by the justices as a rebuke, or threat.

[17] Common reasons offered in support of the conclusion that one's opponent is unreasonable are these. (1) Perhaps the opponent has not in fact worked through the materials as thoroughly as you have, and that, if he or she did, the opponent would discover that the only reasonable position was yours. (2) The opponent is simply not as smart as you are, and so does not draw the conclusions from the materials that an astute person would draw. (3) The opponent is not engaging in a good faith effort to determine what the provision means.

be enough to demonstrate that there is indeed a tension between strong-form judicial review and democratic self-government.

VARIANTS OF WEAK-FORM REVIEW

Weak-form systems of judicial review *are* systems of judicial review, thereby ensuring that the overall constitutional orders in which they are embedded satisfy the requirements of contemporary constitutionalism. But in weak-form systems, judicial interpretations of constitutional provisions can be revised in the relatively short term by a legislature using a decision rule not much different from the one used in the everyday legislative process.[18]

I discuss here the use of weak-form review in New Zealand, the United Kingdom, and Canada. I think it worth noting early on that these nations are reasonably well-functioning democracies in which civil liberties and civil rights are reasonably well protected—not perfectly, of course, according to whatever one's criteria of perfect enforcement are, but reasonably well. That observation is important for U.S. constitutionalists, who may be skeptical about claims that weak-form judicial review can even in theory be sufficient to protect fundamental rights. Perhaps one can mount theoretical objections to weak-form review, but its practice seems good enough—in the nations where it occurs.[19]

After describing several variants of weak-form review, I contrast them with strong-form review.[20] The discussion in this chapter is relatively abstract, with few references to how weak-form review has actually operated. The next chapter examines the real world of weak-form review, examining in more detail a theme that emerges from this chapter's description: legislatures in successful weak-form systems must sometimes, and not rarely, respond to judicial

---

[18] I insert the qualification "not much different" to emphasize that the strength or weakness of judicial review is linked inextricably to the decision rules employed in the constitutional amendment process. As the amendment process becomes easier, judicial review becomes weaker—and, conversely, as the legislative process becomes more difficult (with respect to specific issues, perhaps), judicial review becomes stronger.

[19] For reasons addressed in chapter 1, I do not mean by this observation to claim that weak-form review could be implemented in the United States without loss to fundamental rights (again, according to whatever measure of fundamental rights one has). I discuss some aspects of such a claim in chapter 3.

[20] Stephen Gardbaum, "The New Commonwealth Model of Constitutionalism," 49 Am. J. Comp. L. 707 (2001), was perhaps the first major article to identify the emergence of an alternative to strong-form review. As the article's title indicates, Gardbaum links the alternative to the nations in which it was first implemented. I suspect that he is right in seeing a connection between the preference for weak-form review and the strength of the tradition of parliamentary supremacy in the British Commonwealth. I believe that this connection is historical rather than conceptual, and so prefer the more generic term *weak-form review*.

interpretations by asserting their own, contrary understandings of the constitution, but they cannot do so too often, or routinely. The reason is that the system is effectively strong-form in the absence of legislative responses, and effectively parliamentary supremacy if legislative responses are too common.

The Interpretive Mandate

The New Zealand Bill of Rights Act, adopted in 1990, is in form an ordinary statute, which in theory could be repealed wholly or in part by any later legislative majority.[21] It enumerates a modern list of individual rights, such as freedom of expression and equality.[22] Those rights are not directly enforceable in the courts, though. The act specifically bars the courts from invoking its substantive provisions to hold that some statute has been repealed or is otherwise invalid, or to refuse to enforce the statute on the ground that the statute violates the act's substantive provisions.[23] Rather, the act is an *interpretive mandate*. Its key provision is this: "Wherever an enactment can be given a meaning that is consistent with the rights and freedoms contained in this Bill of Rights, that meaning shall be preferred to any other meaning."[24]

Why should a mere interpretive mandate be regarded as even a weak form of judicial review? Much turns on what we understand the mandate to require. The question of the mandate's meaning is more complex than it might seem. Initially, we can consider two scenarios in the courts. The judges begin by using the ordinary tools of statutory interpretation to determine what some provision means. They consult the statute's overall structure, its purposes, its legislative history, its relation to other statutes, various canons of statutory interpretation, and perhaps more (or less).[25] In the first scenario, the judges discover that some of the tools point in the direction of what they see as a rights-protective interpretation, others in a rights-restrictive one. The interpretive mandate urges or requires the court to adopt the rights-protective interpretation. That seems straightforward enough: The statute "can be" interpreted, without distortion, to be rights-protective, and the act tells the courts to adopt that interpretation. The second scenario is more difficult. Here all or nearly all of the ordinary tools of statutory interpretation point in

---

[21] *Id.* at 727, describes the political background that led to the act's adoption.

[22] There are some rights not commonly included in bills of rights, including a provision giving everyone a right "not to be subjected to medical or scientific experimentation without that person's consent," and a right to refuse medical treatment. New Zealand Bill of Rights Act 1990, §§ 10, 11, available at http://www.oefre.unibe.ch/law/icl/nz01000_.html (visited Jan. 19, 2006).

[23] New Zealand Bill of Rights Act 1990, § 4.

[24] *Id.*, § 6.

[25] There are national variations in the tools judges ordinarily use to interpret statutes, and I do not mean by the list in the text to assert that any specific court will use all of the techniques described.

the rights-restrictive direction. Does the act give the courts *another* interpretive tool, not simply a tiebreaker but overriding what "ordinary" statutory interpretation would yield?

This second scenario makes it clear that the pure interpretive requirement is a form of judicial review. The courts are saying, in essence, "The language of this statute tells us what you wanted to do, but if we did that you would be violating constitutional norms. You've also told us that you don't want to do that. So, we'll interpret the statute to be consistent with constitutional norms, even though that leads us to enforce a statute that does something other than what the statutory language says you wanted to do." Weak-form judicial review in the form of an interpretive mandate gives the courts an effect on policy that is different from the effect they have using their traditional methods of statutory interpretation.

The fundamental assumption behind weak-form review, that there can be reasonable disagreement over the meaning of constitutional provisions, complicates the picture even more. That assumption means that interpretations are not prepackaged as "rights-restrictive" or "rights-protective." Someone seeking to avoid a statute's burden will, of course, characterize the statute as rights-restrictive. The statute's defenders might reply that it is either neutral as to rights (correctly understood) or actually rights-protective. Libel law again provides a useful example: restrictions on the dissemination of false statements about a person restrict the right of free expression but promote a right to human dignity.

The interpretive mandate thus directs the courts to engage in *two* acts of interpretation: they must interpret the substantive rights protections, and then determine whether the statutory provision at issue can be interpreted in a manner consistent with their interpretation of the rights protections. It would not be surprising to discover that courts cannot readily disentangle the two interpretive steps. A judge who, going into the case, is troubled by a challenged statute will probably be inclined to think that one of the Bill of Rights Act's substantive provisions should be interpreted to cast some doubt on the other statute's policy, and then will probably be inclined to interpret *that* statute so that it does not violate the substantive provisions as interpreted—because, for example, it does not actually apply in the circumstances. Or, perhaps more interesting, suppose the judge thinks that all the ordinary tools of statutory interpretation point in the direction of a rights-restrictive interpretation. The judge could throw up her hands and say, "This statute violates substantive rights, but there's nothing I can do about it." Or the judge could say, "If we interpret the substantive rights properly, we will see that the statute does not violate those rights."

How judges use the interpretive mandate is, of course, an empirical question, some aspects of which I examine in the next chapter. Here I simply want to introduce another complication. How will *legislatures* respond to decisions invoking the interpretive mandate? Such decisions interpret statutes. Proponents of the interpretive mandate as a version of weak-form review hope that the judges' discussion of both the substantive rights and the questionable statute will induce legislatures to accept the court's rights-protective statutory interpretation. They hope that what the judges have to say will persuade the legislature that it actually does not want to adopt a rights-restrictive policy.

Suppose, though, that the legislature disagrees. A majority might think that the courts have adopted a mistaken interpretation of the Bill of Rights Act's substantive provisions.[26] Premised on that mistaken interpretation, the courts have distorted the other statute they are purportedly interpreting, and are thereby reducing the legislature's ability to pursue policies that it prefers and that are not inconsistent with substantive rights properly understood. What can the majority do? As far as it is concerned, the statute it already enacted was perfectly fine. Should it simply reenact the same statute, running the risk that the courts will once again distort it via "interpretation"? Should it reenact the statute, adding provisions that say in effect, "This time we really mean it"? We should note that one legislative response should *not* be available. The Bill of Rights Act is an ordinary statute, and its provisions can be amended by ordinary majorities. But the legislature should not be expected to amend the Bill of Rights Act. As far as the legislature is concerned, the act specifies substantive rights perfectly well. From the legislature's point of view, the courts have misconstrued the Bill of Rights Act.

Normatively, making the legislature correct the judges' errors by respecifying substantive rights gives the courts a larger role than they should have in a weak-form system. And, descriptively, amending the Bill of Rights Act in the face of a judicial decision interpreting a statute to avoid a rights-restrictive interpretation seems to me a quite unlikely outcome. The reason is that proponents of judicial review, whether in its weak or strong forms, expect that a judicial statement about what substantive provisions mean will carry important weight in the political process. The language of rights matters in politics, and we can expect people to be at a political disadvantage when their opponents are able to say, "Why do you want to take away the rights the courts have told us we have?" This political dimension of even the interpretive mandate, the weakest variant of weak-form judicial review, suggests that the difference between weak-form and strong-form review may not be as dramatic as it might seem at first.

The Augmented Interpretive Mandate

The British Human Rights Act 1998 (HRA) raises similar questions.[27] The HRA is an *augmented interpretive mandate*. Briefly: Like the New Zealand Bill

---

[26] Alternatively, the majority might agree that the statute is rights-restrictive, but want to implement a rights-restrictive policy. The questions about what sort of response such a majority might make are quite similar to those I discuss in the text.

[27] Human Rights Act 1998, 1998 ch. 42, available at http://www.opsi.gov.uk/acts/acts1998/19980042.htm (visited Jan. 19, 2006).

of Rights Act, the HRA directs courts to interpret statutes to be consistent with fundamental rights. It enhances their power, though, by authorizing them to issue a statement of "incompatibility." That is, if they are unable to interpret a statute to be consistent with fundamental rights, they can declare it incompatible with those rights. That declaration has no effects on anyone's legal rights. The statute remains in effect, and can be enforced or relied on in any legal proceeding. But the HRA's proponents expected—and asserted during the debates over its adoption—that Parliament would routinely respond by amending the statute to eliminate the incompatibility. Even more, the HRA allows the minister in charge of the legislation to place it on a fast track for amendment, bypassing some of the ordinary procedural hurdles to legislation proposed by one of the government's ministers. And if that is not enough, under the HRA a minister who finds that amending the statute is urgently required may do so by ministerial order rather than by legislation, subject only to subsequent ratification by Parliament.

The Human Rights Act emerged out of a conjunction of interests between the Labour and Conservative parties in the United Kingdom. Historically the Labour Party and its leaders had been strongly opposed to judicial intervention in politics.[28] Early in the twentieth century, the British courts had invoked common-law rules to interfere rather substantially with efforts to organize workers and parallel efforts to use economic force to compel employers to engage in collective bargaining. Labour Party leaders found the contemporaneous experience in the United States, where courts were invoking constitutional principles to obstruct the adoption of redistributive legislation, to confirm their suspicion that courts—staffed by upper-class professionals—would systematically disfavor Labour Party interests. In the 1970s a leading academic in Great Britain produced a skeptical study of the class backgrounds and, in his view, biases of sitting British judges that Labour Party leaders took to establish that things had not changed.[29]

What did change, though, was politics and international law. The long tenure of Margaret Thatcher and Conservative Party rule transformed the Labour Party. Among the things the party's leaders learned was that parliamentary supremacy could devastate the policy positions they favored, and they came to believe that judicial enforcement of entrenched rights could obstruct not the social democratic policies they favored but the strongly conservative policies they opposed. In addition, the United Kingdom was a party to the European Convention on Human Rights, and its policies across a wide range of matters, including free press and criminal procedure, were the subject of regular, and successful, challenges before the convention's enforcement

---

[28] This summary draws heavily on the account in Michael Zander, A Bill of Rights? (4th ed., 1997).

[29] John A. G. Griffith, The Politics of the Judiciary (1977). The book has gone through numerous editions, the latest to which I have access published in 1997.

body, the European Court of Human Rights in Strasbourg, France. These losses embarrassed the nation's political leaders, and—they came to think—properly so: Parliament had enacted, or at least failed to eliminate, intrusions on liberties the British cherished, and the European Court actually had done a good job of identifying such intrusions. And, on the most mundane level, Cherie Booth Blair, the wife of Labour Party leader Tony Blair, was a leading human rights lawyer in Great Britain.

Tony Blair's "New Labour" platform included a pledge to adopt some sort of Bill of Rights for the United Kingdom. And, after some nervousness, Conservative Party leaders accepted the idea. Political scientist Ran Hirschl suggests an explanation: They foresaw that they were likely to lose an election in the near future, and hoped that the courts would preserve some of the policy gains the Conservatives had achieved, through enforcing entrenched rights.[30]

Exactly what would the "Bill of Rights" for the United Kingdom be? The European Convention provided a reasonably good list of the fundamental principles that constitutionalists in the late twentieth century thought important. The Human Rights Act simply made most of the convention's rights enforceable as a matter of *domestic* rather than international law. Instead of losing in the British courts and then winning in the Strasbourg Court, a litigant could now "win" in the British courts.

But what would a victory mean? The HRA adopted the "interpretive mandate" model and then beefed it up a bit. As the HRA's supporters saw things, the pure interpretive mandate left judges with nothing to do when they confronted a statute that, in their view, *clearly* violated fundamental rights. In such cases, they simply could not interpret the statute rights-protectively. That seemed inadequate. But giving the judges the power to invalidate such a statute was too strong medicine in a nation where the tradition of parliamentary supremacy had deep roots and where there remained some discomfort with giving judges too much power. The HRA's solution was the declaration of incompatibility.

The HRA raises many of the same problems of interpretation that the New Zealand Bill of Rights Act does.[31] The declaration of incompatibility poses a few modest additional problems. From a litigant's point of view, a court that issues a declaration of incompatibility has *rejected* the litigant's claim—in the sense that the litigant walks away with his or her rights still impaired. What

[30] For Hirschl's argument, see Ran Hirschl, Toward Juristocracy: The Origins and Consequences of the New Constitutionalism (2004). Hirschl's argument about the reasons for adopting judicial review has been confirmed for a significant number of nations, and by theoretical models. See Tom Ginsburg, Judicial Review in New Democracies: Constitutional Courts in East Asia (2003); J. Mark Ramseyer, "The Puzzling (In)Dependence of Courts: A Comparative Approach," 23 J. Leg. Stud. 721 (1994); Matthew Stephenson, "Independent Judicial Review," 32 J. Leg. Stud. 781 (2003).

[31] For a discussion of interpretive questions about the HRA, see Geoffrey Marshall, "The United Kingdom Human Rights Act, 1998," in Defining the Field of Comparative Constitutional Law (Vicki C. Jackson and Mark Tushnet eds., 2002).

litigants will say is something like this: "My adversary relies on a statute to justify its actions, which actions make me worse off. If you construe the statute to mean X, my adversary could not rely on it to justify its actions, and the statute would not violate my rights under the European Convention. That's what I want." Now, how does the government respond? First, of course, it will say that the statute means Y, and that Y does not violate the European Convention. But its alternative argument is this: "Hey, it's all right with us if you find that construction Y violates the European Convention, because all you can do then is issue a declaration of incompatibility, and we can still do to the plaintiff what we want to do."

Three things inhibit the government from routinely rolling over on the question of incompatibility. The first, and almost certainly the most important, is that regularly conceding that its actions violate the European Convention would eventually become a political embarrassment. A government might occasionally get away with rolling over on that question when it could make a credible public case that the statute was really important. Try that too often, though, and the government's political standing is likely to fall.

Second, consider another aftermath of a declaration of incompatibility. The litigant walks out of the British court with nothing but the declaration in hand. Within Great Britain, that is just a piece of paper. But it might be more important in Strasbourg. That is, the litigant can go to the European Court of Human Rights, saying that the British government has violated his or her rights not under the HRA but under the European Convention itself. Of course, the Strasbourg Court might disagree with the British courts about what rights the convention confers. My guess, though, is that the judges on the Strasbourg Court are likely to think to themselves along these lines: "If British judges think that their government has violated the Convention, who are we to disagree? We're certainly not going to get in much hot water in Great Britain if we keep saying that we're just going along with what British judges have said."[32]

Third, as noted earlier, the general expectation is that governments will regularly respond to declarations of incompatibility by amending the statute. That expectation is likely to be satisfied, at least in the HRA's early years, when the same people who supported the act's adoption are in control of the executive government. If that is so, though, a government that wants to

---

[32] There is an additional complication. The Strasbourg Court has developed what it calls the "margin of appreciation" doctrine. *See* Handyside v. United Kingdom, 1 Eur. H.R. Rep. 737 (1976). According to that doctrine, the Strasbourg Court interprets convention provisions by giving member states a "margin of appreciation" to take account of distinctive local conditions and problems. *See id.* at 753–54 (referring to the fact that domestic authorities are in "direct and continuous contact with the vital forces of their countries"). The very fact that a domestic judge has found a violation of convention rights might count against a conclusion that the British government should be given a significant margin of appreciation with respect to the provision at issue. I discuss this and other aspects of the "margin of appreciation" doctrine in chapters 3 and 5.

advance a policy embodied in a challenged statute will have to defend the statute, that is, argue that it should be interpreted so as to be compatible with the European Convention. Otherwise it might win the individual case but then lose the policy by amending the statute.

Indeed, one might be more concerned about the creation of a regular practice of amending statutes in the face of declarations of incompatibility than with routine concessions of incompatibility. The degree to which that expectation is correct will provide a measure of the degree to which the HRA creates a weak or strong form of judicial review. The HRA system would be indistinguishable from strong-form review if statutes that courts declared incompatible with the European Convention were *always* amended to remove the incompatibility. Such a practice would belie the very premise of weak-form review: that there can be reasonable disagreement about what it is, exactly, that fundamental rights described in abstract terms protect and prohibit—or, equivalently, that courts will not always come up with the only reasonable interpretation of fundamental rights guarantees.

A "Dialogic" Mode of Review

The Canadian Charter of Rights, adopted in 1982, provides another version of weak-form review, notably labeled "dialogic" by the leading Canadian constitutional scholar Peter Hogg and one of his students.[33] As with the other documents I have discussed in this chapter, the Charter lists fundamental rights. Two provisions create weak-form review in Canada. Section 1 provides that the rights guaranteed by the charter are subject to "such limitations as are demonstrably justified in a free and democratic society."[34] Section 33 provides that Canadian legislatures can make statutes effective, for renewable five-year periods, "notwithstanding" their inconsistency with a large number

---

[33] Peter W. Hogg & Allison A. Bushell [now Thornton], "The Charter Dialogue Between Courts and Legislatures: (Or Perhaps the Charter of Rights Isn't Such a Bad Thing After All"), 35 Osgoode Hall L. J. 75 (1997). The Charter of Rights is the "Bill of Rights" portion of the Canadian Constitution. Formally, the Charter and the Canadian Constitution as a whole are enactments by the British Parliament. Constitution Act, 1867, 30 & 31 Victoria, c. 3; Constitution Act, 1982, (U.K.) 1982 c. 11. Hogg and Bushell argue that the Canadian experience shows that dialogue actually does occur; this aspect of their argument is challenged in Christopher P. Manfredi & James B. Kelly, "Six Degrees of Dialogue: A Response to Hogg and Bushell," 37 Osgoode Hall L. J. 513 (1999), and Christopher P. Manfredi, "The Life of a Metaphor: Dialogue in the Supreme Court, 1998–2003," 23 Sup. Ct. L. Rev. (2d) 104 (2004).

[34] Charter of Rights and Freedoms, § 1, enacted as Schedule B to the Canada Act 1982 (U.K.) 1982, c. 11. The Supreme Court of Canada outlined a multistage test for determining when a rights violation is "demonstrably justified" in R. v. Oakes, [1986] 1 SCR 103:

First, the objective, which the measures responsible for a limit on a *Charter* right or freedom are designed to serve, must be "of sufficient importance to warrant overriding a constitutionally protected right or freedom." . . . It is necessary, at a minimum, that an objective relate to

of important charter provisions.[35] These provisions license two kinds of legislative response to the constitutional interpretations offered by the courts.[36]

Consider a regulation of commercial expression—for example, a regulation of advertising for sweetened cereals, whose target audiences are children. Suppose the Supreme Court finds the regulation unconstitutional. The Court says that the goal of promoting health by diminishing children's consumption of sweetened cereals is a permissible one, but concludes that the regulation as enacted sweeps within its coverage too much expression that need not be regulated in order to accomplish a significant reduction in consumption.

How can the legislature respond? The Section 1 response is this: Bolster the record supporting the legislation so that it provides a better—a more "demonstrable"—justification for the statute's scope. For example, the legislature might compile evidence, if it can, showing that narrowing the statute's scope would make it much more difficult to administer effectively, by requiring regulatory agencies to draw lines that they are not competent to draw, or that any wording that would narrow the statute's scope to accommodate the Court's concerns would actually leave advertisements on the market that contribute significantly to the demands children make on their parents. Note, though, that the Section 1 response takes the Court's *interpretation* of the charter to be correct, and disagrees only with that interpretation's application to the statute.[37]

---

concerns which are pressing and substantial in a free and democratic society before it can be characterized as sufficiently important.

Second, once a sufficiently significant objective is recognized, then the party invoking s. 1 must show that the means chosen are reasonable and demonstrably justified. This involves "a form of proportionality test." Although the nature of the proportionality test will vary depending on the circumstances, in each case courts will be required to balance the interests of society with those of individuals and groups. There are, in my view, three important components of a proportionality test. First, the measures adopted must be carefully designed to achieve the objective in question. They must not be arbitrary, unfair or based on irrational considerations. In short, they must be rationally connected to the objective. Second, the means, even if rationally connected to the objective in this first sense, should impair "as little as possible" the right or freedom in question. Third, there must be a proportionality between the *effects* of the measures which are responsible for limiting the *Charter* right or freedom, and the objective which has been identified as of "sufficient importance."

Id. at ¶¶ 69, 70 (citations omitted).

[35] Voting, mobility, and language rights are excepted.

[36] Chapter 3 discusses whether the provisions have actually operated in the idealized manner I describe here.

[37] Kent Roach, The Supreme Court on Trial: Judicial Activism or Democratic Dialogue 8 (2001), describes what he calls "in-your-face" Section 1 responses. These responses involve what appear to be the simple reenactment of the invalidated legislation with relatively little done to bolster it. Roach treats these responses as involving decisions by Parliament that merely *purport* to accept the Court's interpretations, and argues that in such instances, Parliament should rely on the Section 33 response. *Id.* at 281. For additional discussion of in-your-face responses, see chapter 3.

The legislature attempts to show—"demonstrate"—that the violation the Court discerned is indeed justifiable given the Court's own understandings about what is needed to justify a violation. The Section 1 response, that is, does not involve a dialogue between courts and legislatures about the *meaning* of Charter provisions, but rather, and only, about how an agreed-upon meaning applies to the specific statute.

In contrast, the idealized Section 33 response does involve a dialogue about constitutional meaning. To continue the example, the Parliament might enact a Section 33 override of the Court's decision because, in the legislature's view, the charter's provisions dealing with freedom of expression are simply inapplicable to commercial speech.[38] This use of a Section 33 response would be predicated on a disagreement between the Court and the legislature over what the Charter *means*, not merely over how it should be applied.[39]

The institutional mechanisms used for judicial review in New Zealand, the United Kingdom, and Canada certainly seem to differ from judicial review in the United States. Perhaps, though, they are not that different. Chapter 3 takes up the possibility that, as implemented, these apparently weak forms of judicial review will actually be somewhat, perhaps even a great deal, stronger than one might think simply by reading their descriptions. Before engaging in that inquiry, I will describe the analytic (rather than empirical) differences between strong- and weak-form systems in more detail.

Contrasting Strong-Form and Weak-Form Judicial Review

Strong-form review is a system in which judicial interpretations of the Constitution are final and unrevisable by ordinary legislative majorities. They are not permanently embedded in the law, though. Judicial interpretations can be rejected by the special majorities required for constitutional amendment, and

---

[38] For an extended argument from a Canadian scholar that denying constitutional protection to commercial expression does not violate basic principles of freedom of expression, see Roger A. Shiner, Freedom of Commercial Expression (2003).

[39] I refer to an "idealized" version of the Section 33 response because Section 33 itself does not clearly distinguish between a legislative response that concededly is inconsistent with the legislature's own understanding of the Charter, and a response that is inconsistent only with the courts' understanding of the Charter. The language of Section 33 might have been clearer on what was being overridden. As written, Section 33 requires the legislature to say to the public, "We are making this statute effective notwithstanding what the Charter says." A better expression of weak-form review would allow the legislature to say, "We are making this statute effective notwithstanding what the Supreme Court has said the Charter says (or what we expect the Court to say the Charter means)." As Canadian constitutional scholars have pointed out to me, this point might be taken to demonstrate that the Charter actually establishes strong-form rather than weak-form review.

they can be repudiated by the courts themselves, either after new judges join the highest court or after some of the original judges rethink their position. For this reason, strong-form and weak-form review fit onto a time continuum: Strong-form systems allow the political branches to revise judicial interpretations in the longish run, weak-form ones in the short run.

In addition, strong-form systems differ from weak-form ones in the *normative* finality they give to judicial interpretations. Here I return to some questions I raised earlier about the precise language of the Canadian "notwithstanding" clause. A legislature can make a statute effective notwithstanding the fact that, without an override, the statute would violate rights protected by the charter. In this formulation the charter has normative finality. Contrast that with the more prevalent understanding that the notwithstanding clause allows a legislature to make a statute effective notwithstanding the fact that, without an override, the statute would be held *by the courts* to violate charter rights. On *that* understanding, the courts' decisions have normative finality, which is temporarily displaced by the override.

We can combine these distinctions between strong-form and weak-form systems by reverting to the idea of dialogue. Dialogic accounts of constitutional law treat the people, legislatures, executives, and the courts in conversation. The temporal continuum identifies the time frame over which the conversation occurs. The conversation ends when the participant whose decisions have normative finality signals that the conversation is over, at least for a while.

A standard political science model of the interaction between the U.S. Supreme Court and the political branches sees a dialogue occurring over a relatively long time frame. Originating with Robert Dahl in 1957,[40] and updated by Barry Friedman and others,[41] this model has the Court being brought into line with the constitutional views held by a political coalition that sustains itself in power for a suitably long period. The mechanism for alignment is the appointment process: As older judges die or retire, they are replaced by new ones who share the constitutional views of the dominant political coalition. Notably, in this model it is irrelevant whether the dominant coalition accepts or rejects strong-form review in principle or merely disagrees with the interpretations provided by a court that it does not (yet) control. In the end, the dominant coalition comes to live with strong-form review because it finds it pointless to argue the purely theoretical question of strong-versus weak-form review once it has taken control of the Court.

[40] Robert Dahl, "Decision-Making in a Democracy: The Supreme Court as a National Policy-Maker," 6 J. Pub. L. 279 (1957).

[41] *See, e.g.,* Barry Friedman, "Dialogue and Judicial Review," 91 Mich. L. Rev. 577 (1993); Barry Friedman, "The Importance of Being Positive: The Nature and Function of Judicial Review," 72 U. Cin. L. Rev. 1257 (2004); Robert W. Bennett, Talking It Through: Puzzles of American Democracy 101–4 (2003).

Scholars who emphasize the role of social movements in shaping constitutional law, such as Robert Post and Reva Siegel,[42] offer a model in which the conversation can take place over a shorter term.[43] According to this view, the people influence constitutional law by organizing social movements offering distinctive constitutional visions, typically oppositional to the vision dominant in the courts when the movements begin. Social movements influence constitutional law in two ways. One returns us to the political scientists' model: the movements affect electoral politics, which in turn affects the composition of the courts. But the social movement model offers an alternative mechanism: judges observing the social movement and its effects on society change their views about what the Constitution means. Unlike the political scientists' model, then, the social movement model does not depend on a change in the Court's composition for there to be a change in constitutional interpretation. Like that model, though, the social movement model takes the story to end when the courts come into line.

Bruce Ackerman has offered a model with an even shorter time frame. He develops a general account of constitutional transformation *within* an established constitutional system. The "switch in time" is important to that account.[44] The story, in outline, is this: A mobilized public and its political leadership enact legislation that faces constitutional challenges. The courts uphold those challenges, thereby obstructing the public's preferred policy agenda. The public and its political leaders turn their attention to getting control of the courts. Facing that opposition, the courts abandon their previous constitutional interpretations and adopt those offered by their conversational partners (here, more like adversaries). The interactions that produce the switch in time occur within a compressed time period.[45] Unlike the social movements model, here the mechanism of change is not persuasion but submission or fear that failure to change will produce severe adverse consequences for the Court. But, as in that model, the conversation ends when the Court comes to agree with its adversaries.

[42] *See* Robert C. Post, "The Supreme Court, 2002 Term—Foreword: Fashioning the Legal Constitution: Culture, Courts, and Law," 117 Harv. L. Rev. 4 (2003); Robert C. Post & Reva B. Siegel, "Legislative Constitutionalism and Section Five Power: Policentric Interpretation of the Family and Medical Leave Act," 112 Yale L. J. 1943 (2003); Reva B. Siegel, "Equality Talk: Antisubordination and Anticlassification Values in Constitutional Struggles over *Brown*," 117 Harv. L. Rev. 1470 (2004); Reva B. Siegel, "Text in Context: Gender and the Constitution from a Social Movement Perspective," 150 U. Pa. L. Rev. 297 (2001).

[43] Although it is not inherent in their model that it does.

[44] *See, e.g.*, Bruce Ackerman, We the People: Foundations 20 (1991) (providing a "five-stage process" including the switch in time); Bruce Ackerman, The Failure of the Founding Fathers: Jefferson, Marshall, and the Rise of Presidential Democracy 265 (2005) (describing "a recurring institutional dynamic," including a switch in time).

[45] This is, of course, consistent with Ackerman's metaphor of "moments," that is, short periods of time in which important political and constitutional developments take place.

Weak-form systems resemble Ackerman's model to the extent that both involve the possibility of what we might think of as "real-time" conversations between courts and legislatures. They differ, though, in two ways. In Ackerman's model, switches in time are rare, and mark the transition from one relatively large-scale organization of the constitutional order to another. In contrast, weak-form systems at least allow for the possibility of routine real-time constitutional conversations. In addition, Ackerman may implicitly give judicial interpretations normative finality, at least during the extended periods of normal politics that follow the switches in time. Weak-form systems treat constitutional interpretations offered by legislatures as normatively equal in weight to those offered by courts.[46]

"Weak-Form" Judicial Review within a Strong-Form System?

Once the structures of judicial review have been "continuumized," we are in a position to think about the possibility of blended systems. Perhaps there could be strong-form review with respect to some constitutional issues, weak-form review with respect to others.

The first problem with such a strategy is figuring out the basis for allocating issues to one mode of review rather than the other. One suggestive formulation points to both the possibilities and problems with *any* allocation strategy. We could use strong-form review for claims that a statute violates constitutional provisions expressing "substantive values . . . distinctively deserving of judicial protection,"[47] and weak-form review for claims that a statute violates other constitutional provisions. This formulation appeals to the intuition that some constitutional provisions simply are more important than others to preserving constitutionalism: protection of freedom of expression is more important than ensuring that the legislature periodically publish a "statement and account" of expenditures and receipts.[48]

The basis for that intuition is less obvious than one might think, and developing criteria for allocating issues to weak- and strong-form review that we could expect to be implemented reasonably well is particularly difficult. The difficulty arises because *all* the provisions we are dealing with are in the constitution. How, though, are we going to figure out which provisions "distinctively" deserve judicial protection and which deserve judicial protection

[46] For that reason, it is important in thinking about weak-form systems to consider whether legislative constitutional interpretations are likely to be normatively appealing. I take that issue up in part 2.

[47] Dan T. Coenen, "The Rehnquist Court, Structural Due Process, and Semisubstantive Constitutional Review," 75 S. Cal. L. Rev. 1281, 1283 (2002).

[48] The latter reference is to U.S. Const., art. I, § 9, cl. 7 ("A regular Statement and Account of the Receipts and Expenditures of all public Money shall be published from time to time.").

(remember, all the provisions are subject to judicial enforcement), but not "distinctively" so? Consider again the contrast between free expression and the "statement and account" clause. The latter is designed to ensure transparency in government action, not obviously less important than free expression. Even more, suppose a nation's people accepts the proposition that intrusions on freedom of expression are more important than violations of the "statement and account" requirement. That might support *more* aggressive judicial review of "statement and account" challenges than on free expression challenges: the people will be more alert to legislation that threatens free expression values than to legislation that raises "statement and account" problems, and so it is more likely that problematic "statement and account" legislation will get enacted under the radar of public attention. I believe that similar difficulties will attend any effort to distinguish among constitutional provisions for purposes of allocating them to one or the other form of judicial review.[49]

The second problem with any allocation strategy is this: the existence of strong-form review for some issues may induce the courts to abdicate their interpretive responsibilities with respect to the other issues, which is to say, to abandon weak-form review there in favor of rubber-stamping legislation, and—reciprocally—the fact that courts exercise strong-form review on some issues may induce legislatures to ignore what the courts have to say if they *do* exercise weak-form review on other issues.

The United States has a strong-form system of review. Yet, we can see some shadows of something like weak-form review in U.S. constitutional law and theory. Sometimes the Supreme Court uses a deferential standard of review, most notably with respect to what it calls legislation "[i]n the area of economics and social welfare."[50] This is a substantive standard of review, not a commitment to weak-form review in this area.[51] Sometimes scholars have advocated the adoption of something that initially looks like a substantive standard of review but that, on analysis in light of the development of weak-form review, is better understood as weak-form review. The scholars' approach,

---

[49] The most sustained discussion in U.S. constitutional law of which I am aware of drawing distinctions among constitutional rights in Supreme Court opinions is Justice White's assertion in *Bowers v. Hardwick*, that the "Court . . . comes nearest to illegitimacy when it deals with judge-made constitutional law having little or no cognizable roots in the language or design of the Constitution." 478 U.S. 186, 194 (1986). (*Bowers* was overruled by Lawrence v. Texas, 539 U.S. 558 (2003).) Yet, this assertion seems in serious tension with the Ninth Amendment's statement, "The enumeration in the Constitution, of certain rights, shall not be construed to deny or disparage others retained by the people." U.S. Const., amend. IX. Similarly, the assertion in Murdock v. Pennsylvania, 319 U.S. 105, 115 (1943), that First Amendment rights had a "preferred position," never received an extended defense. Indeed, any allocation strategy predicated on distinctions among constitutional rights seems to face the same Ninth Amendment difficulty.

[50] Dandridge v. Williams, 397 U.S. 471, 485 (1970).

[51] Part 3 discusses in detail how weak-form review might operate in that area.

which was given classic form in the late nineteenth century by law professor James Bradley Thayer, is particularly illuminating. I discuss deferential and Thayerian review in tandem rather than sequentially, to bring out their similarities and differences.

Thayer asserted the view that the Supreme Court should invalidate legislation only when the legislation was manifestly inconsistent with the Constitution: "[The court] can only disregard the Act when those who have the right to make laws have not merely made a mistake, but have made a very clear one—so clear that it is not open to rational question."[52] This formulation makes it clear that Thayerian review is predicated on the assumption that the legislature has indeed made a constitutional error in the court's eyes. But, according to Thayer, the Court should not set aside the legislature's erroneous judgment about what the Constitution permits unless that judgment was quite seriously wrong.

True Thayerian review should be distinguished from merely deferential review. In upholding a Maryland statute dealing with public assistance to the poor and distinguishing between such cases and those involving fundamental rights, the Court expressed its view that, by invoking a deferential standard of review, "We do not decide today that the Maryland regulation is wise, that it best fulfills the relevant social and economic objectives that Maryland might ideally espouse, or that a more just and humane system could not be devised."[53] Similarly, in sounding a "cautionary" note about the Court's decision upholding Texas's system of financing education primarily through the property tax, the Court asserted, "We hardly need add that this Court's action today is not to be viewed as placing its judicial imprimatur on the status quo. The need is apparent for reform in tax systems which may well have relied too long and too heavily on the local property tax."[54] These are claims that the statutes in question may be unwise, rather than claims that the statutes are unconstitutional yet nonetheless will be accepted by the Court.

True Thayerian review involves statutes that the court believes to be unconstitutional according to the judges' independent assessment of the constitution, but which the court nonetheless refrains from striking down. It is hard to discover opinions endorsing truly Thayerian review. In recent years, the only such opinion of which I am aware is Justice Souter's opinion concurring in the judgment in *Walter Nixon v. United States*.[55] The case involved a challenge to the constitutionality of the Senate's procedure for trying impeachments initially before a committee and then on a paper review by the Senate as a whole. Justice Souter did not find those procedures unconstitutional, but, he wrote, he

[52] James Bradley Thayer, "The Origin and Scope of the American Doctrine of Constitutional Law," 7 Harv. L. Rev. 129, 144 (1893).

[53] *Dandridge*, 397 U.S. at 487.

[54] San Antonio Indep. Sch. Dist. v. Rodriguez, 411 U.S. 1, 58 (1973).

[55] 506 U.S. 224 (1993).

could "envision different and unusual circumstances that might justify a more searching review of impeachment proceedings." These were circumstances in which "the Senate's action might be *so far beyond the scope* of its constitutional authority" that the courts should step in.[56] Justice Souter's formulation implies that the courts might refrain from intervening when the Senate acted beyond its constitutional authority, but not "so far beyond" that authority as to warrant judicial intervention.[57] This is indeed Thayerian review.[58]

Why do judges who understand the idea of deference in selected areas nonetheless rarely act as true Thayerians? As Justice Souter's formulation suggests, Thayerian review requires the creation of another continuum. Ordinarily, we think of constitutionality as a binary phenomenon: while it may sometimes be hard to figure out whether a statute crosses the line from constitutional permissibility into constitutional violation, we are confident that there is such a line. In Thayerian review, constitutionality is a matter of degree: unconstitutional, but not too unconstitutional; an error, but not a clear error. I suspect that strong-form review conduces to making this specific continuumization difficult. Quite often the courts will be invoking a binary vision of the Constitution because such a vision makes it easier to explain to legislatures and to the people why their choices cannot go into effect in the short run. That practice deprives the courts of opportunities to design the continuum of unconstitutionality.

[56] *Id.* at 253, 254 (emphasis added).

[57] Justice Souter's formulation resonates with my own understanding of Thayerian review. An alternative understanding treats Thayerian review as imposing an epistemic requirement on a judge's determination that a statute is unconstitutional. A judge finding a statute unconstitutional must, on this understanding, conclude not simply that the statute is unconstitutional (based on a full analysis of all the relevant considerations), but that this conclusion is clear to a high degree of certainty ("beyond a reasonable doubt," for example). Applying epistemic understandings of this sort to the operation of collective institutions like courts and juries is notoriously difficult. The standard question is, How can an individual judge have the required degree of certainty when others (dissenting judges, a minority of jurors, the majority in the legislature) not only do not have that degree of certainty but actually draw the contrary conclusion from their evaluation of the relevant material? The Supreme Court's decisions on the permissibility of nonunanimous jury verdicts, and on the requirement that juries be unanimous in finding aggravating circumstances in death penalty cases, illustrate the difficulties. *See* Schad v. Arizona, 501 U.S. 624 (1991) (upholding a capital conviction based on instructions that did not require jurors to agree unanimously on the defendant's state of mind); Apodaca v. Oregon, 406 U.S. 404 (1972) (upholding state laws allowing nonunanimous verdicts in criminal cases).

[58] A cousin of Thayerian review can be found in the Supreme Court's doctrine dealing with the circumstances under which a federal court can enjoin a pending prosecution under an unconstitutional statute. The Court has limited those circumstances quite severely, but it has at least held open the possibility that an injunction would be proper against a prosecution for violating a statute that was "flagrantly and patently violative of express constitutional prohibitions in every clause, sentence and paragraph, and in whatever manner and against whomever an effort might be made to apply it." Younger v. Harris, 401 U.S. 37, 53–54 (1971) (quoting Watson v. Buck, 313 U.S. 387, 402 (1941)).

In addition, true Thayerian review places judges in a difficult psychological position. A judge can put herself in the state of mind needed for merely deferential review relatively easily. All the judge needs to say is, "I would not vote for this were I a legislator, because I believe it is unwise policy, but—even as a legislator—I wouldn't think that the proposal is unconstitutional."[59] The state of mind of a Thayerian judge is harder to achieve. The Thayerian judge must say, "In my judgment this statute is unconstitutional, but—despite that, and despite the fact that I have the power to block the statute's enforcement— I think that this statute should go into effect because it is not *too* unconstitutional." Judges accustomed to acting on their judgments of constitutionality may find it hard to refrain from doing so on some occasions.[60]

A final reason for skepticism about the possibility of Thayerian review as an allocation strategy is related to the preceding one. Given the choice between exercising strong-form review and exercising Thayerian review, a judge might wonder what could be accomplished by doing the latter.[61] The Thayerian judge might think of his or her choice as tutelary: the judge might instruct legislators on their constitutional obligations by telling them that the statute they have enacted is unconstitutional and that they have to live with that unconstitutionality.[62] The state of mind of the Thayerian judge might be that of a wise parent, willing to let his or her children make decisions that the parent believes to be unsound so that the children will learn from experience how to make sound ones. (In my experience, parents have difficulty in achieving this state of mind.)

The difficulty with the tutelary view is obvious. Why should legislators who believe that the statute they enacted accomplishes valuable public purposes care that judges think that the legislature's action violates constitutional norms? Sometimes, perhaps, the legislators will have overlooked the constitutional problems the Thayerian court identifies. Having those difficulties pointed out, the legislature might reassess the overall wisdom of the statute,

---

[59] For a representative statement along these lines, see Lawrence v. Texas, 539 U.S. 558, 605 (2003) (Thomas, J., dissenting) ("If I were a member of the Texas Legislature, I would vote to repeal" the challenged antisodomy statute).

[60] I have a similar suspicion about the epistemic version of Thayerian review. That version will sometimes require judges to say to themselves, "I am convinced beyond a reasonable doubt that this statute is unconstitutional even though four of my colleagues, whose judgment is not always unreasonable, believe quite to the contrary, that the statute is entirely constitutional."

[61] It is clear enough what is accomplished by exercising strong-form review: an unconstitutional statute is not enforced.

[62] Mark Tushnet, "Thayer's Target: Judicial Review or Democracy?" 88 Nw. U. L. Rev. 9 (1993). There I argue that Thayer himself viewed Thayerian review as tutelary. I should note that even at the time this article was published, I was not convinced by my own argument, although I thought then and still do think that there were tutelary themes in Thayer's article. For present purposes, though, Thayer's own understanding is unimportant, as I am concerned here with problems Thayerian review poses for judges.

deducting the constitutional costs the court identified from the social benefits the legislature initially identified and, perhaps, concluding that, net, the statute does not actually advance the public well-being. And sometimes, perhaps, an aroused citizenry will become upset that their representatives have been faithful to the constituents' immediate desires, or perhaps faithful only to the legislators' immediate self-interest,[63] but unfaithful to the constituents' longer-term commitments as expressed in the constitution.

More likely, though, neither legislators nor constituents will think it necessary to respond to the Thayerian court's decision. I examine the reason for that in more detail in part 2. Briefly, though, the reason is that statutes often express a considered judgment by the legislature that the statutes are consistent with the constitution, and that such a judgment is (often) reasonable even if the judges disagree. Consider one of the well-known rhetorical tricks John Marshall used in justifying judicial review in *Marbury v. Madison*. Marshall asks readers to imagine a statute enacted by Congress that makes testimony by one witness sufficient to convict for treason, blatantly contradicting the constitutional requirement of two witnesses.[64] In such a case, Congress could not reasonably have thought that its action was consistent with the Constitution. But consider the statute at issue in *Marbury* itself, which the Court held unconstitutional because it altered the allocation of jurisdiction prescribed in the Constitution. It is a standard point in the *Marbury* literature to note that the Constitution could reasonably be interpreted to allow Congress to shift cases from the constitutionally identified category of appellate jurisdiction to the Supreme Court's original jurisdiction.[65] Most real-world cases are more likely to resemble *Marbury* than to resemble the hypothetical treason statute. And, in such cases, judges exercising Thayerian tutelary review will confront a legislature whose members can reasonably say to themselves, "We understand that the court's interpretation of the constitution is reasonable, and different from ours, but we also understand that our interpretation is a reasonable one too. Given the choice between two reasonable interpretations, we will adhere to our initial judgment—because it allows us to implement what we believe to be good public policy as well." In short, a Thayerian court may hope to teach the legislature a lesson about the legislature's constitutional obligations, but the students are likely to think the lesson unnecessary.

These problems with true Thayerian review suggest that courts will have difficulty pursuing a defensible strategy in which they allocate some issues to strong-form review and others to Thayerian review.

[63] On the assumption that the legislators' actions might not correspond to the constituents' immediate preferences because of agency problems.

[64] Marbury v. Madison, 5 U.S. (1 Cranch) 137, 179 (1803).

[65] *See, e.g.*, William Van Alstyne, "A Critical Guide to *Marbury v. Madison*," 1969 Duke L. J. 1, 31–32.

CONCLUSION

I have used this chapter simply to describe strong-form and weak-form judicial review, and to sketch their differences—and similarities. As institutions, they are different enough in terms of normative finality that we can treat them as binary alternatives. And, although they are located at points on a temporal continuum, the points are widely separated enough that it makes sense to think of them as distinct institutions. My descriptions have been rather general, and it might be that institutions that we can *describe* as quite different actually operate in practice quite similarly. The next chapter turns to an examination of how weak-form systems do—and might—operate in practice.

CHAPTER 3

The Possible Instability of Weak-Form Review and Its Implications

WEAK-FORM review purports to promote a real-time dialogue between courts and legislatures. Two literary allusions suggest skepticism about how that dialogue might actually proceed.

- Shakespeare: Responding to Glendower's claim that he could call the spirits from the vasty deep, Hotspur asks, "But will they come when you do call for them?"[1] The analogue: The courts try to get legislatures to respond to their constitutional interpretations, but the legislatures ignore them.
- Ring Lardner: "Are you lost daddy I asked tenderly? Shut up he explained."[2] The analogue: The legislatures try to get the courts to respond to *their* constitutional interpretations, but the courts ignore them.

In chapter 2 I suggested that weak-form review has the potential for both the Shakespearean degeneration into parliamentary supremacy and the Lardnerian one into strong-form review: the former when legislatures routinely invoke the override, for example, the latter when legislatures routinely amend statutes after a judicial declaration of incompatibility. There are other and more subtle possibilities, though, which this chapter examines. My discussions rely heavily on the more than twenty years of experience Canada has had with its system of judicial review, which I argue might be taken to exemplify the transformation of weak-form into strong-form review. I then qualify that argument by suggesting that the transformation, if it occurs, might arise not from some institutional dimensions of weak-form review but from the reflective choice of the people to shift their system from a weak-form to a strong-form one. The chapter concludes with a discussion of several examples of the way in which strong-form review might emerge organically from weak-form review over an extended period. Time might push weak-form review closer to strong-form review along the temporal continuum on which they differ.

---

[1] William Shakespeare, The First Part of King Henry the Fourth, act III, sc. 1.
[2] Ring Lardner, "The Young Immigrunts," in The Ring Lardner Reader 411, 426 (Maxwell Geismar ed., 1963).

Legislative Resistance to Judicial Interpretations

Dialogic accounts of judicial review have to allow for meaningful dialogue, that is, for legislative responses to judicial interpretations of the Constitution that reject or at least resist those interpretations. As I noted in chapter 2, routine resistance would restore parliamentary supremacy. Here I examine other forms of resistance, illustrating the process by what I have called the Section 1 response—provision by the legislature of additional reasons for enactment of a previously invalidated statute. Section 1 responses *can* preserve weak-form review, but there is some risk that some versions may undermine it.

Section 1 of Canada's Charter allows legislatures to respond to judicial decisions by showing that there is a better justification for the statute than the court thought in the first round of dialogue. Section 1 responses range from ones in which the legislature basically accepts the court's decision, but tinkers with some details, to what Canadian scholars call "in-your-face" statutes, where the legislature basically reenacts the invalidated statute but bolsters the justification by placing in a statutory preamble, for example, the points made by dissenting judges who would have upheld the statute in the first round.

The meaning of mere tinkering is ambiguous. One possibility, of course, is that the legislature agrees with the court's decision. In this circumstance, while the *present* legislature would not have enacted the invalidated statute, believing it to be unconstitutional at least after receiving the court's instruction, the legislature does not have the will to repeal it. Here the court rather clearly advances the interests of the current majority.

Another possibility is that the invalidated statute represented a momentary compromise among competing values, a compromise that might have been struck differently a few days or weeks later, and the new statute represents a compromise that *might* have been reached when the statute was initially enacted. The court has substituted its own balance of interests for the legislature's, but the court's substitute is politically acceptable. The result is not troubling to a democrat, because the court decision represents an outcome that a legislature might have reached, but it is not clear whether a true dialogue has occurred between legislature and court.

Perhaps more troubling to defenders of weak-form review as a valuable contribution to the institutions of constitutional democracy is a legislative response that grudgingly accepts the court's decision on the matters the court dealt with, but uses the opportunity to respond to the court as an occasion to expand other provisions in the statute in a direction that itself threatens rights.[3] Presumably,

---

[3] *See* Kent Roach, The Supreme Court on Trial: Judicial Activism or Democratic Dialogue 176–79 (2001) (describing legislative responses to Court decisions limiting police investigatory powers as accepting the precise holdings but expanding police authority in areas not touched on by the Court decisions).

the court can then respond by invalidating the new provisions too. But it may not do so. Judicial energy is limited, and the judges may be unwilling to revisit the statute too quickly. In addition, the judges may understand the legislature's actions as an expression of disagreement with the initial decision and may be willing to uphold the new provisions to accommodate an annoyed legislature— even though, had the provisions come to the court *before* its prior decision, the court might have found them unconstitutional. Upholding the provisions *after* the initial decision would not be inconsistent with that decision, after all, for that decision dealt with *other* aspects of the statute. In this scenario, the court's initial intervention might not lead to a net increase in liberty, once the legislature responds to the court and the court to the legislature, or even a net increase in actual compliance with the constitution as the court itself would understand it if all questions were considered at once.

Finally, there is the in-your-face response; that is, the reenactment of the challenged statute essentially unchanged. Here the question is, Why use the in-your-face response rather than Section 33? Professor Roach describes the override as "the equivalent of shouting to win an argument," while in-your-face statutes seem more like shouting back and forth, with no end to the argument in sight.[4]

Professor Roach gives two case studies of in-your-face legislation, in both of which Parliament adopted "the logic of the dissenting judges" in cases with which Parliament disagreed.[5] One of them began with *O'Connor v. The Queen*, which involved a prosecution for an alleged rape of four women in a residential school that occurred decades before the prosecution. The defendant demanded access to the records compiled during counseling sessions with the victims. The Canadian Supreme Court decided, by a vote of 5 to 4, that the defendant had an unqualified right to all records in the prosecution's possession, and that the defendant could get access to possibly relevant records in the hands of doctors and rape crisis counselors if the trial court determined they should be made available after balancing the defendant's right to present a defense against the victims' rights to privacy. The dissenters would have required the defendant to make a substantially stronger showing of need before gaining access to records in private hands.[6]

The Canadian Parliament responded to *O'Connor* with new legislation that, according to Professor Roach, "followed the dissent . . . by subjecting all records . . . to a two-stage process that balances the accused's rights against the complainant's privacy and equality rights and the social interest in encouraging the reporting of sexual assaults." And, like the dissent, the statute enumerated "ten allegations that, alone or together, were not sufficient to

---

[4] *Id.* at 176.
[5] *Id.* at 274–81.
[6] [1995] 103 C.C.C. (3d) 1 (Can.).

establish that a record was relevant."[7] The Canadian Supreme Court found that the new legislation satisfied the Charter.[8]

We can understand in-your-face legislation of this sort in one of two ways. The statutes may simply be temper tantrums, expressions of disagreement with the policy judgments the legislature imputes to the court. If so, the proper response is public education to show that the court's decisions are legal ones that make reference to, but are not determined by, policy judgments. Yet Section 1 itself may make this response unpersuasive, because policy judgments seem to pervade the Section 1 analysis of justification. Indeed, policy judgments—whether a less restrictive means would actually achieve the legislature's goals, for example—are just about all there is to a Section 1 analysis.

The second interpretation of in-your-face statutes that track dissenting opinions is that they exemplify weak-form judicial review. On this interpretation, the legislature is offering a reasonable alternative interpretation of the Constitution's meaning, whose reasonableness is demonstrated by the fact that one, two, or even four justices found it a better interpretation of the Constitution than the majority's. But then, the argument would go, why should a reasonable constitutional interpretation offered by five justices prevail over a reasonable constitutional interpretation offered by a legislative majority?[9]

In a dialogic system, the conversation does not end when the legislature responds to the court's actions. The courts themselves have to respond. What might they do? There are two possibilities: capitulation or resistance.[10] The Canadian Supreme Court's response to the medical information statute illustrates the former. Saving face when it upheld the legislative response, the Court characterized O'Connor as a common-law decision, not one resting on the defendant's rights under the Charter, and asserted that the new legislation was, like the court's earlier "common law" rule, a reasonable specification of the protected right to present a defense.[11] Professor Roach, a specialist in

---

[7] Roach, *supra* note 3, at 278.

[8] L.C. v. Mills, [1999] 139 C.C.C. (3d) 321, 339–40 (Can.).

[9] Here too we might see the difficulty of distinguishing between deferential review in a strong-form system, and weak-form review. The reasonableness of the legislature's position can be examined at the outset—that is, it can be the focus of the Court's consideration of Charter challenges. This would transform judicial review under the Charter from a relatively robust substantive review subject to revision through the override into review for reasonableness, which is typically regarded as the exemplary form of judicial restraint in a strong-form system.

[10] Resistance to in-your-face statutes is, of course, quite likely in strong-form systems. A strong-form court with an unchanged composition is likely to give the same answer when confronted with the in-your-face statute that it gave the first time. *See, e.g.*, United States v. Eichman, 496 U.S. 310 (1990), reaffirming Texas v. Johnson, 491 U.S. 397 (1989).

[11] *Mills*, 139 C.C.C. at 338–40, 353–54, 357-58, 390–91. If the initial decision was fairly described as a common-law decision, then the sequence of cases and legislation does not illustrate the operation of any form of judicial review at all, but only the ordinary and well-established practice of legislation consistent with the constitution displacing the common law.

criminal law and procedure, believes that the legislation was indeed inconsistent with *O'Connor*, and that it would have been better for the Court to say so and invite the legislature to use its power under Section 33 to override a judicial interpretation of the Charter.[12]

Resistance might occur in this way: Judges—like anyone—are unlikely to take seriously the claim that they overlooked or undervalued something so obvious that it produced an immediate in-your-face reaction. Rather, their response is likely to be, "We took it into account, and you lost already." More subtle, the judge's reaction to the in-your-face statute will be affected by what happens in the range of cases where the legislature on reflection comes to agree with the court. A judge is likely to think, "Well, I've gotten it right all those times when there has been no response, so the chances are pretty good that I've gotten it right this time despite the reaction I've provoked."

As the term itself suggests, at least within Canada the in-your-face response has a certain disreputable air. Professor Roach's position is typical, I think: use Section 33, not the in-your-face response. There are, however, two difficulties. Section 33 requires the legislature to say that it is making its legislation effective notwithstanding Charter provisions, when the fact of the situation is that the legislature does not think that its enactment is inconsistent with the Charter properly construed. And, perhaps more important, the preference for the Section 33 response, in a world where Section 33 is as a practical matter unavailable, is simply an unstated preference for strong-form review. The availability of the Section 33 response is my next concern.

LEGISLATIVE ACCOMMODATION OF JUDICIAL INTERPRETATIONS

Can weak-form review be sustained over a long term, or will it become such a weak institution that the constitutional system is, for all practical purposes, indistinguishable from a system of parliamentary supremacy or such a strong institution that the courts' decisions will be taken as conclusive and effectively coercive on the legislature? When legislatures routinely ignore judicial decisions, weak-form review is simply parliamentary supremacy in disguise. When legislatures routinely accede to those decisions, weak-form review is simply strong-form review in disguise. This section examines the latter possibility. As I have indicated, experience with weak-form systems is thin, but there is some evidence, from New Zealand, Great Britain, and even more forcefully from Canada, that weak-form systems do become strong-form ones.

The evidence seems to be that judicial interpretations generally "stick." That is, legislatures have the *formal* power to respond to a judicial interpretation with which its members disagree through legislation rather than constitutional

---

[12] Roach, *supra* note 3, at 279–81.

amendment, but they exercise that power so rarely that a natural inference is that the political-legal cultures in nations with weak-form review have come to treat judicial interpretations as authoritative and final.

The evidence of practice is hard to analyze, though. The basic problem lies in distinguishing between *agreement* with the courts' result and mere resigned *acceptance* of it. An example of the difficulty is provided by *Baigent's Case*, from New Zealand.[13] The case involved a search conducted by police relying on a warrant that had been issued based on false factual assumptions, where the police continued to search even after they knew that they were searching the wrong house. The targets of the search sued for damages, alleging that their rights under the New Zealand Bill of Rights Act had been violated. Their difficulty was twofold. The New Zealand act is a mere interpretive mandate and provides no remedies for violations of the rights it identifies. It seemed, then, that the plaintiffs had to rely on their common-law remedies against the police officers. But the second difficulty was that the police officers were immunized by a statute from liability under the common law. The Court of Appeal held in favor of the plaintiffs nonetheless. It held that the Bill of Rights Act authorized the courts to create a new "public law" remedy. Such a remedy was different from common-law remedies. In particular, the statutory immunity Parliament provided was, the court held, directed solely at common-law tort actions. As a result, the plaintiffs could pursue their new cause of action, and the police officers could not assert a statutory immunity from damages.

The government then asked the New Zealand Law Commission to consider whether a legislative response to *Baigent's Case* should be developed. The commission endorsed the Court of Appeal's analysis and told the government that it should not introduce legislation to eliminate the "public law" remedy, the contours of which, the commission said, should be fleshed out by further *judicial* action. The government agreed with that recommendation. *Baigent's Case* has been the object of substantial criticism—and admiration—in the New Zealand legal literature. At the end of the day, though, does the government's nonresponse represent agreement with the decision or simple acquiescence in it?[14]

Baigent's Case illustrates another way in which the difficulty of distinguishing between agreement and acceptance can arise. Weak-form systems have focused on human rights protections, as in the Canadian Charter of Rights and the British Human Rights Act. But human rights are *also* protected by international human rights norms, which are themselves sometimes enforceable coercively and which, in any event, have deep cultural resonances. As we

---

[13] Simpson v. Attorney-General [Baigent's Case], (1994) 1 HRNZ 42 (CA).

[14] My sense is that, in accepting the Law Commission's "do nothing" recommendation, the government at least came quite close to accepting the decision as an appropriate one.

have seen, one motivation for adopting the HRA was to reduce the embarrassment of routine reversals of domestic decisions by the European Court of Human Rights. To the extent that a weak-form court enforces a domestic right that tracks an international human rights norm, a legislature's failure to respond might result not from agreement with the court but from recognition that some international institution may enforce the international norm directly or from acceptance of the fact that the courts' invocation of international human rights norms creates a new political impediment to the enactment of purely domestic legislation.

In *Baigent's Case*, one judge referred to the International Covenant on Civil and Political Rights, which mentions the power of courts to "develop the possibilities of . . . remedy" as a justification for the creation of the public-law remedy.[15] He continued by observing that it would be "strange" to say that Parliament expected New Zealand citizens to be able to complain to the United Nations Human Rights Committee, as authorized by the government's agreement to the Optional Protocol authorizing individual complaints to the committee, but did not want the very same citizens to be able to get a domestic remedy under the Bill of Rights Act, which, he said, was one means of implementing the covenant.[16] But, with the threat of intervention from outside in the background, is the government's acquiescence in the case's outcome properly taken to represent acceptance of the Court of Appeal's approach to enforcing fundamental rights?

Weak-form systems that direct courts to interpret statutes in a manner consistent with fundamental rights present another difficulty. Recall that we want some system that recognizes that the general or abstract terms of the constitution can be specified in numerous reasonable ways. Legislatures might overlook constitutional values and might need to be reminded of them. But, once legislatures are so reminded, weak-form systems should conceptualize the legislature's action as offering an alternative specification of the meaning of the constitution's general or abstract terms. Interpretive mandates may not do a good job of embodying that conceptualization.

Interpretive mandates typically carve out an exception for statutes that cannot be fairly interpreted to be consistent with fundamental rights. So, for example, the British Human Rights Act reserves the possibility of a declaration of incompatibility for such statutes. The interpretive directive, though, is likely to induce judges to strive hard to find interpretations that make the statutes compatible with fundamental rights. In doing so, the judges will inevitably run the risk of opening themselves to charges that they are distorting rather than interpreting the statutes. The language of distortion versus faithful interpretation is

---

[15] *Baigent's Case*, (1994) 1 HRNZ 42, 72 (Casey, J.) (citing art. 2(3)(b) of the International Covenant on Civil and Political Rights).

[16] *Id.* at 74.

language that can obscure the underlying question, which is whether the courts are rejecting a reasonable specification of fundamental rights.

A recent British case offers an instructive example.[17] The case involved the process by which income support for asylum applicants would be terminated when their applications for asylum were rejected. The relevant regulation provided that support would be ended when the applicant ceased to be an asylum seeker, which occurred "on the date on which it is . . . recorded" by the secretary of state "as having been determined." The secretary of state rejected the application for asylum on November 20, and the rejection was recorded within the secretary's internal system on that date. The applicant did not receive notice of the denial for another four or five months. She claimed that she was entitled to income support for the period between the denial and her receipt of notice of the denial. One judge in the House of Lords thought that the applicant's claim was barred by the regulation's plain language: she ceased to be an asylum applicant when her application was denied and recorded, which occurred in November. The other Law Lords disagreed. Invoking what he called fundamental principles of the rule of law, Lord Steyn "interpreted" the regulation to mean that the denial had to be *properly* recorded, and that rule-of-law principles meant that the denial could not be properly recorded until the applicant received notice that her application had been denied. At the least, this is creative interpretation.[18]

More important for present purposes, calling what Lord Steyn did *interpretation* may obscure the more basic question: were the government's procedures for ending income support to those whose applications for asylum had been rejected a reasonable approach to providing fair procedures? Lord Steyn made a powerful case that they were not,[19] which suggests that decisions that purport to interpret statutes can openly address the underlying question. In other cases, though, the form of "interpretation" may make less apparent the disagreement between the courts and the government on what a reasonable specification of fundamental rights is.

A related conceptual difficulty arises from what might be called the myth of objective rights.[20] Suppose we have a political-legal culture in which two

---

[17] R. (on the application of Anufrijeva) v. Secretary of State, [2003] UKHL 36, [2003] All ER 827.

[18] James Allan & Grant Huscroft, "Constitutional Rights Coming Home to Roost? Rights Internationalism in American Courts," 43 San Diego L. Rev. 1, 25 (2006), quote observations made in Ghaidan v. Godin-Mendoza, [2004] UKHL 30, [2004] 2 A.C. 447, by Lord Nicholls of Birkenhead: "Even if, construed according to the ordinary principles of interpretation, the meaning of the legislation admits of no doubt, section 3 may none the less require the legislation to be given a different meaning."

[19] He wrote, for example, "There simply is no rational explanation for such a policy," *id.* at ¶ 24, and referred to Kafka in describing the system as one involving "hole in the corner decisions," *id.* at ¶ 28.

[20] Janet Hiebert suggested this line of argument to me.

beliefs are widespread: first, that there *are* objective rights (or, more generally, objective limits placed on government power in the constitution), and second, that courts have some comparative advantage over legislatures in specifying the content of general or abstract rights. In such a culture, one would expect legislatures never to override a court's invalidation, because legislators would believe both that there were rights and that the courts were more likely than they to identify what those rights are. That is, weak-form review does not make sense in such a culture. Perhaps the transformation of weak- into strong-form review, if it occurs, indicates only that the nations that have adopted weak-form review actually have political-legal cultures more suitable for strong-form review.

Yet, judicial review in any form makes no sense unless courts have *some* comparative advantage over legislatures in specifying the constitution's meaning. So, the two conditions for the stability of weak-form review seem to be these: First, the nation's political-legal culture accepts the possibility of a range of reasonable specifications of general or abstract rights. Second, within the legal culture the courts' comparative advantage over legislatures in specifying the constitution's meaning is thought to be relatively modest.[21] I have my doubts about whether the first condition can ever be satisfied. Many legal academics in the United States are comfortable with the idea of a range of reasonable specifications, but, I believe, most academics, judges, lawyers, and nonlawyers think that there are, in Dworkin's terms, right answers to questions about rights.

If my belief is correct, the dynamics of weak-form review's transformation into strong-form review are straightforward. The courts specify the meaning of the constitutional right. This is taken to identify the correct meaning of the right. The constitution authorizes legislatures to respond to that specification. But in the political-legal culture I am considering, the legislature can respond only by overriding not the specification on the ground that the legislature disagrees with the court's evaluation but the very right itself. Overriding a right, while authorized, is politically costly—beyond the political costs associated with the underlying policy. Legislators therefore must expend political capital to overcome the incremental cost of overriding a right. Doing so reduces the political capital available for other policy proposals.

Weak-form review affects public policy even if the cost of overriding a right is relatively small. It reorders the government's legislative priorities by taking political capital away from alternative proposals. Observing a legislature failing to respond to a weak-form invalidation thus tells us little about whether the legislature accepts the courts' decision on the merits. It could be that the legislature disagrees with the decision on the merits, but believes that expressing its

---

[21] The second condition matters because a weak-form system *properly* becomes a strong-form one when the courts' comparative advantage is large.

disagreement would preclude it from adopting some other policy that seems more important than the invalidated one.

And, if the cost of overriding a right is high, as I suspect it is likely to be, a legislative response is extremely unlikely. The cost of doing so would be too high, in terms of other policies forgone. At least in this case, which I think is likely to be the common one, weak-form review becomes strong-form review because of the political costs—not with respect to the invalidated statute, but with respect to other policies forgone—of invoking the mechanisms of response authorized by the Constitution.

So far I have examined mere interpretive mandates. As weak-form systems become somewhat stronger, the risk of conversion into strong-form review heightens. The Canadian story is instructive. To oversimplify: The national government has never invoked Section 33, and provincial use of the power to override Charter provisions has been quite rare and, even more important, almost completely discredited by the only significant invocations of the power during the Charter's lifespan. The effect has been the emergence of something close to a convention in Canada that Section 33 should never be invoked. But Canadian courts and scholars have defended vigorous exercises of judicial review in part because, they assert, Section 33 provides a safety valve for the expression of the democratic component of democratic constitutionalism. If the safety valve is blocked, that component lacks a means of expressing itself.

Section 33 was a last-minute addition to the Canadian Charter, inserted to allay concerns that the new Charter would undermine parliamentary supremacy. The Charter itself was the vehicle for a major constitutional reconstruction of Canada, designed by Prime Minister Pierre Trudeau to resolve persistent conflicts over Quebec's status within Canada by reconceptualizing Canada as a multicultural rather than bicultural nation, whose fundamental principles would be set out in a Charter of Rights rather than inferred from the competing traditions within the nation. To do so, Trudeau had to arrange for the "patriation" of the Canadian Constitution, that is, to free it from supervision by the British Parliament so that it would be an entirely domestic document. The Canadian Supreme Court held that the national government could request the British Parliament to relinquish control without unanimous support from the provincial governments, but that to do so without *substantial* provincial support would violate an unwritten constitutional convention.[22]

Trudeau therefore had to negotiate with provincial leaders over patriation and the wholly domestic constitution it would create. Provincial leaders had real concerns that the new Charter would erode their power. Saskatchewan's premier, a social democrat influenced by the traditional hostility toward entrenched bills of rights in the European and especially British left, suggested a legislative override provision. Trudeau accepted this, subject to a five-year

---

[22] *In re* Amendment of the Constitution of Canada, 125 D.L.R. 3d 1 (Can. 1981).

limit, allaying enough concerns so that the Charter was adopted in 1982, although Quebec refused to accede to it at least in part because Section 33 did not apply to language rights. The political setting in which Section 33 developed meant that its theoretical underpinnings were not well-developed.[23]

Section 33 reads, "Parliament or the legislature of a province may expressly declare in an Act of Parliament or of the legislature, as the case may be, that the Act or a provision thereof shall operate notwithstanding" specified Charter provisions.[24] Does this do what a provision creating a weak-form system should do? Recall that we want something that will induce legislative reconsideration of perhaps overlooked or underweighted constitutional values. The verbal formulation in Section 33 might actually interfere with this conceptualization, and possible restrictive interpretations that might have overcome the initial difficulty soon fell by the wayside.

Section 33 requires the legislature to declare that it wishes its legislation to take effect notwithstanding Charter rights. The notwithstanding clause has been invoked so rarely that I cannot provide a real example of the difficulty, but a stylized one can make the point. Parliament enacts a statute, which the Supreme Court of Canada finds to violate a Charter right. Parliament then invokes the notwithstanding clause, declaring that the statute should take effect notwithstanding the fact that it violates the Charter right. But, in Parliament's view, the statute does *not* violate the Charter right. What it wishes is that the statute take effect notwithstanding the Supreme Court's mistaken (though reasonable) specification of the Charter right's meaning. It is not hard to imagine that it is politically more difficult to enact a statute notwithstanding the fact that it violates the Charter than to enact one notwithstanding the views expressed about the Charter by the courts. In this way, the terms used in creating Canada's system of weak-form review make it more difficult to determine when legislative action consistent with the courts' decision expresses agreement with the courts or mere acquiescence in the near-inevitable.[25] As I have suggested, these problems may push parliaments in the direction of adopting in-your-face statutes rather than invoking Section 33.

Some ground might have been retrieved by reading Section 33 narrowly. Two limitations immediately suggest themselves. First, in a system in which judicial review is routine, one might naturally read the clause to require that

[23] For the political background, see Dale Gibson, The Law of the Charter: General Principles 130 (1986).

[24] Charter of Rights and Freedoms, § 33, enacted as Schedule B to the Canada Act 1982 (U.K.) 1982, c. 11.

[25] A parallel problem might emerge under the British Human Rights Act, although here it would depend on the language *courts* use in making declarations of incompatibility. In my view, British judges should avoid flat statements to the effect that legislation *is* incompatible with convention rights, and adopt more circumspect formulations, such as statements that legislation is "in my view" incompatible.

legislative overrides be retrospective. That is, the clause could be read to allow an override only with respect to a legislative provision that the courts had already held to be inconsistent with the Charter's rights–protecting provisions. Otherwise, the textual argument goes, the legislative provision does not operate "notwithstanding" the Charter's other provisions; where there is no prior declaration of unconstitutionality, the legislative provision operates, so far as the legislature knows, in a manner entirely consistent with the Charter.

Second, the clause rather naturally reads as if legislative overrides must be discrete. That is, in a single statute, a legislature can override only with respect to provisions of *that* very statute. The clause, after all, says that the legislature may declare "in *an* Act . . . that *the* Act . . . shall operate notwithstanding."

Further, these narrow readings seem to be consistent with the proposition that Section 33 was designed to accommodate entrenched rights and parliamentary supremacy. The narrow construction would mean that "the legislative decision to enact an override clause is taken with full knowledge of the facts, thereby encouraging public discussion of the issues raised by the use of such a clause."[26] The public would know, that is, that its legislature was about to deprive it or some part of it of entrenched rights, and as a result, political opposition to overriding those rights or political support for the group to be disadvantaged might be mobilized. As Paul Weiler put it, "[i]n a society sufficiently enamored of fundamental rights to enshrine them in its constitution, invocation of the *non obstante* [notwithstanding] phrase is guaranteed to produce a lot of political flak."[27]

The narrow interpretation of Section 33 links the entrenched rights directly to the political process. Consider the implications of interpreting Section 33 to require targeted and retrospective overrides. A proposal to invoke Section 33 would be tied to a single enactment, thus drawing public attention to the fact that the legislature proposed to enact a statute notwithstanding the individual rights provisions of the Charter. Further, the proposal would be a reaction to an authoritative decision specifying that its predecessor enactment did indeed violate one of those provisions. Section 33, on this account, might actually invigorate majoritarian politics by providing the people and their representatives with a way of engaging in direct discussion of constitutional values in the ordinary course of legislation.

As legislation and litigation proceeded under the Charter, Section 33 did not contribute substantially to the creation of weak-form review. The retrospective interpretation, which would have served to focus public debate on the invalidated policy and potential legislative override, was the first element

---

[26] Roger Tassé, "Application of the Canadian Charter of Rights and Freedoms," in The Canadian Charter of Rights and Freedoms 105 (Gérald A. Beaudoin & Ed Ratushny eds., 2nd ed., 1989).

[27] Paul C. Weiler, "Rights and Judges in a Democracy: A New Canadian Version," 18 U. Mich. J. L. Ref. 51, 81–82 (1984).

of the limited interpretation to go. A lower court held that the Charter's guarantee of freedom of association protected the right of public employees to engage in a strike. Before the country's highest court had expressed its view on that question, the Saskatchewan government enacted a back-to-work law ending a strike and used Section 33 to insulate the law from judicial review.[28] According to Michael Mandel, a leftist critic of the Charter, the government suffered no adverse political consequences from using Section 33 in this prospective manner.[29]

The reaction of the Quebec legislature, however, posed a more serious threat to the narrow interpretation of the clause. Nine weeks after the Charter was proclaimed, the Quebec parliament enacted a general "notwithstanding" statute. The technique was ingenious. The legislature repealed every statute in force and immediately reenacted them all, along with a statute that invoked Section 33 with respect to the entire set and indeed with respect to all statutes that it would thereafter adopt. The validity of this approach to Section 33 came before the Supreme Court of Canada in *Ford v. Quebec (Attorney General)*.[30]

The case involved one of the province's more sweeping attempts to preserve its francophone cultural identity: a statute, known throughout the litigation as Bill 101, requiring that all public signs and commercial advertising in the province be only in French. The Quebec legislature included an override provision in the statute when it was reenacted after the Charter's adoption. Businesses that wanted to post signs in French and English challenged the statute; Ford, the lead appellant in the Canadian Supreme Court case, ran a shop in which she sold wool and was told that she had to take down her sign that said "Laine—Wool" because it violated the statute. The challenge rested on Charter provisions guaranteeing the right of free expression, but such a provision would be unavailing if the override provision was upheld.

The plaintiff businesses argued that the override provision "did not sufficiently specify the guaranteed rights or freedoms which the legislation intended to override." Like other "clear statement" arguments, this one ultimately rested on the idea that when a legislature does something as serious as overriding otherwise applicable constitutional protections, it ought to follow procedures that are sufficient to bring into public view precisely what is at stake. In that way, the argument goes, the constitutional protections will be overridden only after the public duly considers precisely what is at stake.

The Supreme Court of Canada, however, rejected this argument, saying that Section 33 "lays down requirements of form only." The Court said that requiring the statute to specify the constitutional provisions to be overridden

[28] The courts a year later rejected the constitutional interpretation the provincial government feared. *See* Reference re Public Service Employee Relations Act, [1987] 1 S.C.R. 313 (Can.).

[29] Michael Mandel, The Charter of Rights and the Legalization of Politics in Canada 77 (1989).

[30] [1998] 2 S.C.R. 712 (Can.).

would amount to a substantive requirement. It suggested that requiring specificity would be unreasonable in situations, likely to be common, where the legislature could not reasonably be expected to anticipate which of the Charter's many provisions might be invoked to challenge its statute.

Because of some procedural aspects of the case that are irrelevant to my discussion here,[31] the Court went on to hold that the sign law did indeed violate provincial constitutional guarantees of free expression: freedom to use one's language was encompassed by the guarantee of free expression. The Court's analysis made it clear that the sign law would be unconstitutional under the Charter once the override's five-year term expired in February 1989, less than two months from the date the *Ford* decision was announced. Three days after the decision was announced, Quebec premier Robert Bourassa announced his government's intention to introduce a new sign law that would incorporate a notwithstanding provision.

The Canadian Supreme Court's decision would appear to be inconsistent with one part of the political account of Section 33 that I have offered, under which the point of the clause is to make it politically costly to override constitutional protections. Under the *Ford* decision, rather routine and indeed quite unfocused "notwithstanding" statutes satisfy the requirements of Section 33. At this point, though, it is important to distinguish between the political costs of using the Section 33 power and the political costs of adopting the substantive legislation. Even without constitutional protections of entrenched rights, some legislative proposals will be controversial on the merits because they infringe on the values that entrenched rights *would* protect if the system had such rights. If we add entrenched rights *and* the override power to the system, the same controversies will arise on the merits. The argument for Section 33 is that legislatures will incur some special costs, beyond those associated with adopting controversial legislation, when they use their power to override constitutional protections. Anglophones in Quebec and elsewhere in Canada objected to the sign law on the merits; indeed, three anglophone members of the Quebec government resigned to protest the new law. The degree to which the protests were directed at Section 33's invocation, as opposed to the statute's substance, though, is unclear.

Does the *Ford* interpretation of Section 33 undermine the argument that special political costs will attend the invocation of an override? Perhaps it does. A provincial legislature is unlikely to incur serious marginal costs within

---

[31] The court held that the sign law violated § 3 of the Quebec Charter of Human Rights and Freedoms, which states that "[e]very person is the possessor of the fundamental freedoms, including freedom of conscience . . . [and] freedom of expression." R.S.Q., ch. C-12, § 3 (1988) (Can.). The parallel provision of the Canadian Charter provides that "everyone has the following fundamental freedoms: . . . freedom of thought, belief, opinion and expression." Can. Const. (Constitution Act, 1982) Pt. I (Canadian Charter of Rights and Freedoms), § 2(B). An override provision did not protect the sign law against the provisions of the Quebec Charter.

the province for using its Section 33 power because it can do so with the ordinary low-level public attention that occurs in connection with every statute. Overriding court decisions may have been particularly easy in Quebec, which had its own judicially enforceable bill of rights nearly equivalent to the Charter. The people of Quebec thus could get almost all of the benefits of a bill of rights without feeling that one had been imposed on them from the outside.

Outside the province, however, the situation differed. Quebec's expansive use of the notwithstanding clause, and in particular its use to immunize the highly controversial sign law from Charter review, did draw public attention to the significance of overriding constitutional protections. It was not the Quebec public that noticed, though; it was the public in the rest of Canada.

Here the political context of the *Ford* litigation plays a central role. As the litigation proceeded through the courts, the Canadian national government attempted to reach a new accommodation with Quebec in what was known as the Meech Lake Accord, the key—though in many ways largely symbolic—provision of which would have embedded in the Canadian constitution the statement that Quebec "constitutes within Canada a distinct society."[32] By the time of the *Ford* decision, the national government, Quebec's legislature, and all but two provincial parliaments had agreed to the accord's provisions.

Some thought that under the "distinct society" clause, Quebec's sign law would be constitutional without regard to the Section 33 power. Under these circumstances, Quebec's use of a blanket override power, even if permissible under *Ford*, somehow seemed like a dirty pool. To those elsewhere in Canada who already had misgivings about the Meech Lake Accord, the override was just another example of Quebec's overreaching. The *Ford* decision and Bourassa's response affirmed that concern, and "from this point on 'there was virtually no chance that the Meech Lake Accord would be ratified.' "[33]

The Canadian provinces failed to adopt the Meech Lake Accord for many reasons, but one was surely that people elsewhere in Canada thought Quebec was pushing too hard for special rights. To the extent that its legislature's use of a blanket override was inconsistent with the expectations about how the power to override would be used, as expressed in the debates over the Charter's adoption, Quebec may indeed have incurred a distinctive political cost attributable to its use of override power, independent of the costs incurred by adopting the sign law itself. According to one observer, the invocation of Section 33 "undermined political support for the Meech Lake Accord outside Quebec, dealing a fatal blow to its chances for ratification."[34]

[32] Meech Lake Accord, § 2(1)(b), *reprinted in* Peter W. Hogg, Meech Lake Constitutional Accord Annotated 11 (1988).

[33] Peter Russell, "Canadian Constraints on Judicialization from Without," 15 Int'l Pol. Sci. Rev. 165, 167 (1994) (quoting Patrick Monahan, Meech Lake: The Inside Story 164 (1991)).

[34] Christopher P. Manfredi, Judicial Power and the Charter: Canada and the Paradox of Liberal Constitutionalism 202 (1993).

Perhaps the outcome of the experience with Section 33 was predictable, as positive political theory might suggest. Consider the sequence of decisions in constitutional adjudication: (1) A legislature adopts a statute by a majority vote. (2) A court decides that the statute is unconstitutional. (3) Some process—constitutional amendment or a Section 33 override—is available to override the court decision. If the decision-rule at stage 3 is no different from the decision-rule at stage 1 and—importantly—if there are no changes in preferences in the legislature between stage 1 and stage 3, we should expect that at the end of the day, the statute will be in effect; the same majority that enacted the statute in the first place will override the court's decision.

In contrast, if repudiating a judicial decision requires more than a majority, we can expect that some statutes that received a majority vote would not survive the supermajority requirement. The U.S. experience with anti-flag-burning statutes seems an obvious example. Substantial majorities in both the House of Representatives and the Senate voted for the Flag Protection Act of 1989. A proposal to amend the Constitution to override the Supreme Court's invalidation of the act secured more than a majority but less than the required two–thirds vote in the House of Representatives.

On closer examination, the flag-burning episode illuminates the Canadian experience as well. After the Supreme Court's first flag-burning decision, the Republican administration proposed not a new statute but a constitutional amendment.[35] The Democratic congressional leadership did not want to put the amendment to a vote and proposed a new statute as an alternative, holding out the possibility of a vote on an amendment if that proved necessary. Most observers believed that the Democratic leadership opposed a constitutional amendment but feared that, in the heat of the moment, it might receive the required supermajority. Apparently, the leadership hoped that by the time the Supreme Court rejected their proposed statute, if it did, passions would have cooled and the legislature would not adopt a constitutional amendment.

Why would the passage of time matter so much, though? Similarly, how could proponents of Section 33 believe that it could make a difference in outcomes, given that a majority could enact a statute overriding a court decision? The answer is obvious: in both situations, proponents hoped that preferences would change between stage 1 and stage 3. One source of preference change worth noting is the court decision itself. Certainly proponents of Section 33 believed that a court decision might educate the public in constitutional values, persuading some who supported the statute that it was indeed inconsistent with their commitment to more fundamental values. Similarly, in the flag-burning episode, the Democratic leadership may have hoped that passions would cool, not in the sense that other issues would displace flag burning, but

---

[35] Robert S. Goldstein, Saving "Old Glory": The History of the American Flag Desecration Controversy 205 (1995).

rather in the sense that the public would reflect on the values of speech and nationhood at stake and would conclude that their sense of national unity could be sustained without infringing so severely on the values promoted by the First Amendment. Here the change in preferences between stage 1 and stage 3 occurs *because of* what happens at stage 2.

Perhaps the language issue in Quebec was so important that even an endogenous preference change induced by the Canadian Supreme Court's decision invalidating the sign law could not shift enough votes to prevent enactment of a statute overriding the decision. Or, perhaps, the ability of a constitutional court to educate is smaller than proponents of Section 33 and other techniques of public education through judicial decision have hoped.

After the Meech Lake Accord failed, Canada's prime minister attempted to blame its failure not on Quebec but on Section 33 itself, the "fatal flaw of 1981, which reduces your individual rights and mine."[36] No longer seen as a way of avoiding problems of democratic debilitation, Section 33 came to be seen as inconsistent with the idea of judicially enforceable constitutional rights. In what political observers regarded as an act of political desperation, Canadian prime minister Paul Martin announced in 2006 that, if reelected, his government would propose to "strengthen" the Charter by eliminating Section 33.[37] Martin was defeated, so the proposal went nowhere. Yet, it seems significant that a leading politician believed that he and his party could retrieve a seemingly lost cause—their election campaign—by appealing to voters on the ground that Section 33 was a weakness in the Charter. Like the power to regulate jurisdiction in the U.S. Constitution, Section 33 may no longer be a significant part of the Canadian Charter. Something like a convention against its use may have emerged, precisely because the political costs of invoking the power turned out to be too great. Effectively, then, the Canadian system may include only the possibility of amending the constitution by a supermajority, not the possibility of majoritarian control of constitutional interpretation.

The reason for the apparent emergence of the convention in Canada may shed some light on broader issues at constitution making and the problem of democratic debilitation. As one commentator put it, "Canadians experienced a use of the notwithstanding clause that they found outrageous before they experienced a Supreme Court decision of equivalent political unpopularity."[38]

The political setting in which Section 33 emerged may mean that it did not become an element of Canadians' constitutional consciousness at all. It was inserted into the Charter as part of a compromise that papered over

[36] *Quoted in* Manfredi, *supra* note 34, at 202.

[37] *See* Daniel LeBlanc, "Martin's Charter Promise Easier Said than Done," Toronto Globe & Mail, Jan. 11, 2006.

[38] Manfredi, *supra* note 34, at 204.

arguably the most important issue in Canadian constitutional life—the status of Quebec. It was discredited, at least in part, because it was used in connection with precisely that issue.

Canada's experience with the notwithstanding clause suggests that institutions designed to address the problem of democratic debilitation by making it possible to deal with that problem visibly may fail *because* of their visibility. The characteristic that makes the institution attractive may make it impossible to function effectively. As Paul Weiler has noted,

> By taking the initiative ... before the Charter had time to put down roots in Quebec political life, and by making use of the *non obstante* formula a matter of legislative routine, the Parti Québécois [which enacted Bill 101, the initial sign law] was able to remove the political hazard of invoking the formula for particular laws, thus frustrating the entire scheme of the Charter.[39]

This "accident of history," as Christopher Manfredi puts it,[40] in the Canadian experience actually may be built into the institution of a non obstante formula in the following way. Constitutions in general consist of institutional arrangements designed to provide a framework for the resolution of political issues over the long term. The outlines of those long-term issues may be only dimly discerned when the constitution is adopted, and constitution makers do their best to put in place institutions that will do the best that can be done with whatever problems arise. Simultaneously, however, constitution makers face ordinary political problems in the present day, and frequently they may have to address those problems as a condition for securing the constitution's adoption. They have three strategies for dealing with such pressing problems. First, they may simply resolve them, adopting the kind of political solution already available through the use of existing political institutions. Second, they may relegate those problems to the new institutions they create, hoping that those institutions will do no worse in resolving them than the preexisting institutions did. Third, they may defer their resolution, in the hope that time will make those particular problems go away.

Consider here the U.S. Constitution. Article I, Section 9 bars Congress from exercising its enumerated power over interstate and foreign commerce to prohibit "the migration or importation of such persons as any of the States now existing shall think proper to admit" until 1808 but authorizes Congress to impose a tax of up to ten dollars on each such person. This compromise represents the third approach. The controversy over congressional regulation of the interstate slave trade was deferred until 1808, by which time, the Framers apparently hoped, the issue would have changed so that it could be resolved through ordinary political means.

---

[39] Weiler, *supra* note 27, at 90.
[40] Manfredi, *supra* note 34, at 204.

If the deferred issue does not change, as the slavery issue did not, or if it ends up not being deferred at all, as the language issue in Canada was not, the compromises on that issue, designed to secure adoption of the constitution, may well fail. A provision like a notwithstanding clause makes the overall process particularly vulnerable in dealing with those pressing political problems that have, under the second approach, simply been relegated to the new institutions. Such a provision allows politicians to take the issue *away from* the new institutions, leaving them to be handled by the process that did not resolve it in a satisfactory way before the constitutional revision.

If, however, the use of the notwithstanding power were delayed, a second problem would arise. As time passes, the notwithstanding clause or parallel institutions designed to address the problem of democratic constitutionalism would become less visible. Invoking them might seem contrary to understandings of constitutionalism that would have developed during the period when these institutions were not utilized.

The preceding suggestions may be too bleak, however. In Canada, the drafters of the Charter explicitly embedded ordinary politics within their fundamental constitutional arrangements, expecting that ordinary politics would interact with constitutional concerns in ways that would ultimately benefit the society overall. In one dimension, their expectations seem to have been defeated. Section 33 did affect the politics of constitutional arrangements, though not in the way the drafters seem to have anticipated. Yet, the text and history of Section 33 would have supported an interpretation different from the one the Canadian Supreme Court gave it in *Ford*. Had the court chosen a different interpretation, the course of constitutional development might have been different as well.

Despite claims made for it, the Canadian notwithstanding clause did not prove to be a means by which democratic discussion of constitutional norms could be promoted within a system also authorizing judicial review. Outside of Quebec, uses of Section 33 have been rare indeed.[41] Perhaps the most revealing indication of Section 33's real status was its invocation by Alberta's government to protect its "Marriage Amendment Act," which defined marriage as the union of a man and a woman, against an anticipated judicial decision that the Charter's equality provisions guaranteed gays and lesbians the same right to marry that heterosexuals had.[42] The only problem with this is that marriage and family law are regulated solely by national, not provincial, law in Canada. The Alberta "override" could have no legal effect at all. It expired

---

[41] For a then-comprehensive list of the invocations, see Tsvi Kahana, "The Notwithstanding Mechanism and Public Discussion: Lessons from the Ignored Practice of Section 33 of the Charter," 44 Canad. Pub. Admin. 255 (2001). The enumeration and analysis in this article are quite valuable, although I believe that Kahana overstates the importance of the invocations he identifies.

[42] Marriage Act, R.S.A. 2000, ch. M-5, available at http://www.canlii.org/ab/laws/sta/m-5/20051114/whole.html (visited Jan. 17, 2006).

in 2005 and was not renewed. The "override" was an expression of the Alberta government's opinion about gay marriage and the Charter, and of Section 33's practical insignificance.

Courts themselves can make decisions that reduce the incentives legislatures have to invoke Section 33. Return here to the *O'Connor* decision on medical privacy in rape prosecutions. The legislature having chosen not to invoke Section 33, the Court strategically retreated: instead of forcing the legislature to use Section 33, the Court found the new legislation constitutionally permissible. And, by doing so, the Court contributed to the disappearance of Section 33 from constitutional practice. More generally, courts might strategically retreat in the early years of a weak-form system, rather than forcing a confrontation, because doing so will lead to a long-term gain in judicial power as the system is transformed into a strong-form one.

I have argued that the absence of Section 33 responses to judicial decisions—or to anticipated decisions—indicates that Canada's weak-form system has been transformed into a strong-form one. But, putting aside for the moment the question of whether the Section 1 responses have been vigorous enough to sustain the system in a weak form, a defender of Canada's system might interpret the facts about Section 33 differently. She might say, "Of course there have been essentially no Section 33 overrides—because dialogue has worked the way it should. The courts' opinions educated the public, which on reflection concluded that its initial judgment about what the Charter meant was wrong, and that the courts were correct. Even a short dialogue—legislation followed by judicial review followed by a reconsideration that produces agreement with the courts' constitutional interpretation—is a dialogue, after all."

To begin our examination of this argument, note that the mere existence of the Section 33 power may strengthen judicial review. Michael Mandel, a severe critic of the Charter on the ground that it puts into legal form—and into the hands of lawyers—controversies that ought to be handled openly through politics, reported the comments of the clause's critics who begrudgingly acknowledged that "governments can be 'thrown out' for exercising" their powers under the clause and that invoking the clause "will be a red flag for opposition parties and the press . . . [which] will make it difficult for government to override the Charter."[43] Or, as phrased more generously by John Whyte, it "means, first, that what were once political problems have been transformed into legal problems but, second, that when political interests are sufficiently compelling these issues can revert to being resolved through political choice."[44]

A Charter enthusiast, in contrast, pointed out that the process has two faces. "It is probably true," according to Dale Gibson, "that a government

---

[43] Mandel, *supra* note 29, at 76 (citations omitted).
[44] John Whyte, "On Not Standing for Notwithstanding," 28 Alberta L. Rev. 347, 351 (1990).

would be taking a considerable political risk by introducing, in normal circumstances," overriding legislation, but the existence of the clause, particularly when it is interpreted narrowly, might strengthen judicial review by alleviating judicial concern about acting contrary to majority views. "[J]udges may safely assume . . . that their vigilance will not frustrate the democratic process," and they might therefore invalidate legislation more readily than they would if they knew that the only response available to the public was a constitutional amendment.[45] For one who admires the political process but who thinks that some rights deserve greater protection than they are likely to get in ordinary politics, Section 33 might seem to be a useful way of setting in motion an extraordinary sort of majoritarian politics in which the claims of the community and the claims of rights would both get their due.

Suppose a court invalidates a statute, and a legislative effort to override the decision fails.[46] The political culture then can take the failure to override as an indication of popular support for the court decision. To adapt a phrase from Thomas Reed Powell, the failure to invoke Section 33 is a way in which the people can be "silently vocal"; their inaction demonstrates their agreement with the court's decision.[47] Without the Section 33 power, the people have no way to express that agreement.

I agree that this might be so. Yet, there are instances where the legislative commitment to the invalidated statutes *seems* strong enough that one would expect to see serious consideration, at least, of invoking the override power. Kent Roach describes two prominent instances of this sort, and describes the failure to invoke Section 33 as the result not of the transformation of weak-form review into strong-form review but of "a failure of governmental and public will."[48]

His treatment of Alberta's failure to use the override in response to the Court's decision expanding Alberta's antidiscrimination statute to cover discrimination against gays and lesbians makes the point well.[49] Alberta's government was then one of the most conservative in Canada, particularly on social issues such as gay rights. Why didn't it try to override the Court's decision?

[45] Gibson, *supra* note 23, at 125–26.

[46] Peter Russell observes that after the Canadian Supreme Court invalidated the nation's criminal prohibitions on abortion, "the aroused and losing group went immediately to the parliamentary lobby to press for legislative redress" but there was no "inclination on the part of the politicians to use the override." Russell, *supra* note 33, at 171. Instead, the government proposed to amend the abortion statutes in a manner it contended would make them consistent with the Court's decision. It was not able to muster sufficient support for the new statute, however, and the Court decision stood unmodified.

[47] Thomas Reed Powell, "The Still Small Voice of the Commerce Clause," in 3 Selected Essays on Constitutional Law 931, 952 (Maurice Merrill et al. eds., 1938), *quoted in* Laurence Tribe, Constitutional Choices 34 (1985).

[48] Roach, *supra* note 3, at 175.

[49] *Id.* at 195–96.

On Professor Roach's telling, the story actually starts before the Court's decision, with a proposal by Alberta's government to use the override preemptively to protect against Charter challenges a statute that would have limited compensation to people who had been involuntarily sterilized. That proposal met with substantial public disfavor and the government abandoned it. Two weeks later came the antidiscrimination decision, and Alberta's premier pledged not to use the override without "intensive public consultation" and asserted that the Court's decision was "probably . . . right." Professor Roach concludes that the "use of the override . . . would have been almost as unpopular with Albertans as its proposed use against those the government had involuntarily sterilized."[50]

This account is persuasive, yet its force in the present context might be limited. The antidiscrimination statute had been enacted at a time when gay rights did not loom large on the political scene, and it is not clear that the exclusion of gays and lesbians from the statute's coverage reflected even then a deliberate decision by Alberta's legislators, much less that the continued exclusion expressed an existing majority's preferences. Professor Roach's second example does deal with the invalidation of a recently adopted statute, but here too the claim that the failure to consider a Section 33 override reflected deliberate choices is questionable. The case involved the Court's decision to strike down as violating free expression rights large parts of a statute regulating tobacco advertising. Professor Roach writes that "[t]he government bears a good share of the blame for not using the override."[51] The reason is politics, not deliberation about what free speech protections really should be. Tobacco interests were simply too strong for the government to use Section 33. The tobacco companies are rich multinationals that were able to secure significant postponements of the government's ban on sponsorship in part because of the millions they pump into cultural and sporting events.

The puzzle here is this: why were the tobacco interests able to block the adoption of an override statute when they had been unable to block the adoption of the regulations in the first place? Seemingly, because the Court decision had *independent* weight in the political process, giving the statute's opponents a new weapon—the Court's account of constitutional values—that they did not have before the decision. And that new weapon might be decisive.

But political explanations for failures to use the override do not really demonstrate that even a determined political majority can rein in the Court. The reason is that such majorities may find themselves unable to displace the Court's decision, at least if what the Court has done has the support of a substantial minority. I use formal models of the process in a separation-of-powers

---

[50] *Ibid.*
[51] *Id.* at 186.

system to illustrate the argument before extending it to a parliamentary system.[52] Consider a status quo with a "liberal" statute, a legislature that is liberal but slightly less so than the statute, a moderately conservative president, and a very conservative Supreme Court. What happens if the Court construes the statute quite narrowly, depriving it of any real liberal impact? The legislature may want to reenact that statute or, more likely, a slightly modified statute. But although the president might not have supported a statute as narrow as the one the Court has "created" through construction, he will veto any liberal or moderately liberal reenactment. In the end, the Court's conservative view prevails, even though the legislature has the formal power to override the Court's decision. Legislative inaction, that is, does not result from any failure of political will but rather from the structure of the legislative process in a separation-of-powers system.

Can the analysis be extended to parliamentary systems? Almost certainly, though with some modifications. The key point is to note that the "government" in a parliamentary system is rarely unified. Rather, the governing majority is a coalition of factions or interest groups *within* a single party. The executive must bargain with the various factions to ensure that the "government's" programs are adopted. In some circumstances, a minority faction within the ruling party can exercise the kind of veto that a president can in a separation-of-powers system.

Professor Roach's analysis of the failure to override the Court's abortion decision illustrates this structural characteristic of parliamentary systems. As Professor Roach recounts, "[A]fter five meetings with his caucus [that is, within the governing party], Prime Minister Mulroney announced . . . that a free vote would be held on abortion," resulting in "a procedural disaster." The most popular of five proposals was defeated by a vote of 118 to 105. The government then proposed its own bill, which passed the lower house by a small majority, "but only after party discipline was imposed on the Cabinet (*though not the back bench*)." In the Senate the bill was defeated by a tie vote, after which the government "somewhat gratefully allowed the bill to die and did not attempt . . . to appoint more senators or to strong-arm (or wheel in) the holdouts."[53] Perhaps one can construe this latter failure and the refusal to impose party discipline on backbenchers as failures of political will, but it seems to me more likely that they were responses to the strategic position of a minority faction within the governing party.

Treating legislative majorities as coalitions helps explain both why a Court decision might have independent weight, and why that fact might not show

[52] William N. Eskridge, Jr., & John Ferejohn, "The Article I, Section 7 Game," 80 Geo. L. J. 523 (1992); Lee Epstein, Jack Knight, & Olga Shvetsova, "The Role of Constitutional Courts in the Establishment and Maintenance of Democratic Systems of Government," 35 Law & Soc'y Rev. 117 (2001).

[53] Roach, *supra* note 3, at 194 (emphasis added).

that true dialogue has occurred. The core idea is that the Court's decision might change *some* minds, but not many. Suppose that getting a statute enacted actually requires support by 55 percent of the legislature, not a mere majority, because of the kinds of "veto points" I have described.[54] And suppose that the tobacco advertising statute just squeaked by with 56 percent support, with all the supporters believing that the statute was consistent with the Charter as they understood it. The Court's decision might change the minds of only a handful of legislators about what the Charter actually means, but that might be enough to make it impossible to invoke Section 33.

On this account, the public need not have accepted either strong-form review or any particular interpretation the Court offers for there to be no Section 33 overrides. The mere exercise of judicial review, coupled with some structural features of the legislative process, operates to block the use of the override power even though a majority rejects the Court's constitutional interpretation.

Emergent Strong-Form Review

So far I have offered a skeptical account of the apparent desuetude of the Canadian override provision. I turn next to defenses, not of the proposition that Canada has a weak-form system of judicial review, but of the proposition that strong-form review can evolve out of weak-form review in ways that a constitutional democrat can endorse because strong-form review *comes to have* popular support. It follows, of course, that the same might be true *ab initio*, that is, that constitutional designers might begin with strong-form review—as long as that institution had popular support in the ways exemplified by the evolutionary accounts that follow.

Popular Endorsement of Strong-Form Review in Specific Areas

Weak-form review invites repeated interactions between legislatures on courts over constitutional meaning. The fact of such interactions illustrates why weak-form review is sometimes called "experimentalist."[55] But sometimes experiments end when the community reaches the conclusion that it knows what the right answer really is.[56] Strong-form review might be appropriate in such circumstances, weak-form review appropriate when genuine uncertainty

---

[54] The precise number does not matter.

[55] *See, e.g.*, Michael C. Dorf & Charles F. Sabel, "A Constitution of Democratic Experimentalism," 98 Colum. L. Rev. 267 (1998).

[56] For a discussion of this phenomenon in the physical sciences, see Peter Galison, How Experiments End (1987).

exists in the relevant community about what some constitutional provision really means.

The history of free speech doctrine in the United States provides a good example. I provide a quick review of that history, and then connect the history to the idea of weak-form judicial review.

Standard accounts place the law dealing with speech critical of government policy at the heart of free speech doctrine. The place to begin is with Robert Bork's fundamental insight,[57] which can be put this way: Democratic self-governance means that the policy choices made by democratically elected representatives are entitled to be implemented as effectively as is practically possible, and speech critical of those policy choices reduces the likelihood of effective implementation to some degree. So, speech critical of government policies can be said to interfere with or undermine those policies, and in doing so to interfere with or undermine democratic self-governance.[58] Providing constitutional protection for such speech therefore interferes with or undermines democratic self-governance, and thereby illustrates the tension between self-governance and constitutionalism as enforced by means of judicial review.

Free speech law began by adopting an extremely generous standard of review of regulations aimed at speech critical of government policies. Such speech could be regulated, according to the Supreme Court's first rulings in the area, when legislatures made it a criminal offense to impede the implementation of substantive policies and properly instructed juries reasonably concluded that the speech at issue had a tendency to increase the likelihood that the policies would in fact be interfered with.[59] The Court also held that legislatures could impose criminal sanctions on a category of speech if it reasonably concluded that speech falling within the category had a general tendency to increase the likelihood that democratically chosen policies would be interfered with.[60]

Under pressure from powerful dissenting opinions written by Justices Holmes and Brandeis,[61] the Court revised its approach. Holmes and Brandeis

[57] Robert H. Bork, "Neutral Principles and Some First Amendment Problems," 47 Ind. L. J. 1 (1971).

[58] Geoffrey Stone et al., Constitutional Law 1061 (5th ed., 2005), deals with this aspect of free speech law under the heading "Speech That 'Causes' Unlawful Conduct." That characterization captures by far the largest part of the phenomenon, but probably not all: consider the possibility that speech critical of government policy will reduce the enthusiasm with which some citizens support the policy, and thereby reduce the civic resources available to implement it.

[59] This is a perhaps nonstandard but nonetheless accurate description of the holding in Schenck v. United States, 249 U.S. 47 (1919).

[60] Gitlow v. New York, 268 U.S. 652 (1925).

[61] Abrams v. United States, 250 U.S. 616 (1919) (Holmes, J., dissenting); Gitlow v. New York, 268 U.S. 652 (1925) (Holmes, J., dissenting); Whitney v. California, 274 U.S. 357 (1927) (Brandeis J., concurring on jurisdictional grounds).

argued that the "bad tendency" test was flawed as a standard for juries to apply because experience showed that juries were too ready to find a significant threat to the implementation of government policy in speech that actually was quite unlikely to impair government policy to any significant extent.[62] They made a similar point about legislative overestimation of the threat posed by speech falling within proscribed categories.

It took more than two decades for the Court to acknowledge the force of these arguments, with Chief Justice Vinson writing in 1951 that the Court's decisions in the intervening years "inclined toward the Holmes-Brandeis rationale."[63] When it did, the Court modified the standards in two ways. It eliminated the distinction between statutes aimed at protecting substantive policies from impairment by means of speech and statutes aimed at a specific category of speech. And, probably more important, it directed that juries be instructed that they could find liability only if they went through a calculation taking account of both the degree of risk and the magnitude of harm to the implementation of government policies.

Once again, experience placed this standard under pressure, and for the same reasons as before: Juries instructed as the Court directed in 1951 convicted defendants of violating the law when, as the Court came to see things, the risks to government policy were not large enough. The Court turned to a new strategy of controlling jury (and prosecutorial) overreaching. It would allow regulation of speech critical of government policy only when the speech itself has certain characteristics that the Court believed could be readily identified.[64] In doing so, the Court made it easier for judges to throw out erroneous convictions if they concluded that the speech at issue did not have those characteristics.

Brandenburg v. Ohio took the final step.[65] *Brandenburg* further refined the list of characteristics required before speech critical of government policy could be regulated: The speech had to use words that were an "incit[ement]" to "imminent lawless action."[66] Judges could examine the challenged speech and determine whether the words were a proscribable incitement. *Brandenburg* dealt with the role of juries as well. They were to be instructed that the defendant had to have acted with a specific mental state, and that the circumstances were such that lawless action was likely to occur: The Court's formulation was that the words of incitement had to have been "directed" at

---

[62] And, implicitly, that review of jury verdicts for unreasonableness was an inadequate check on such errors.

[63] Dennis v. United States, 341 U.S. 494, 507 (1951) (plurality opinion of Vinson, C. J.).

[64] *See* Yates v. United States, 354 U.S. 298 (1957) (allowing regulation only of speech advocating unlawful action, but not of speech advocating the doctrine that under some circumstances unlawful action was appropriate).

[65] 395 U.S. 444 (1969).

[66] *Id.* at 447.

producing imminent lawless action and had to have been "likely to . . . produce such action."[67]

Over the course of nearly fifty years, the Court revised free speech doctrine to reach a point that has remained stable for almost as long.[68] The decisions have several characteristics that resonate with aspects of the ideas underlying weak-form review.[69] First, the Court upheld the regulations at issue in the cases defining the core of First Amendment doctrine, until *Brandenburg*. Doing so gave the legislative and executive branches the opportunity to continue to develop regulations that would generate additional experience with the way in which governments actually went about regulating speech critical of government policy. Second, the Court regularly reviewed cases that allowed it to invoke collateral doctrines to invalidate speech restrictions without directly disparaging the core of existing doctrine.[70] Third, these cases also gave the Court information about how that core was actually working in practice. That experience repeatedly led the Court to revise that same doctrine. The stability of the *Brandenburg* revision can be taken as the consolidation of strong-form review in cases involving speech critical of government policy—the consolidation being shown by the fact that the Court *reversed* a conviction and thereby precluded the accumulation of additional experience.[71] We can describe the Court as allowing governments to experiment with speech restrictions, and ending the experiment when, in the Court's judgment, the experiment had yielded all the useful evidence it was going to yield. The doctrinal stability since *Brandenburg* shows that the Court's judgment on the disutility of additional experimentation was correct.

We should note several points about this general account of the transformation of weak-form into strong-form review:

• The analogy to experiments does suggest that the repeated interactions encouraged by weak-form review might be a good way of generating good constitutional doctrine.[72]

---

[67] *Ibid.* Formulated to deal with problems associated with decisions by prosecutors and juries, the *Brandenburg* test has been applied to cases in which private parties seek injunctions or damages from judges. *See, e.g.*, NAACP v. Claiborne Hardware Corp., 458 U.S. 886 (1982).

[68] Contemporary sedition convictions in terrorism-related cases have been based on jury instructions framed in the terms *Brandenburg* set, and on review the courts of appeals have relied on *Brandenburg. See, e.g.*, United States v. Rahman, 189 F. 3d 88, 114–15 (2d Cir. 1999) (rejecting a facial challenge to 18 U.S.C. § 2384, which prohibits seditious conspiracies to use force to overthrow the United States government).

[69] Only "resonate with," because the Court understood itself as exercising strong-form review.

[70] These are the "subsequent cases" referred to in *Dennis*, 341 U.S. at 507.

[71] An alternative account would be that the Court finally realized that its efforts to encourage legislatures and executive officials were not succeeding, and imposed its own restrictive rule. That account might be correct, but a full version would have to explain the timing of the Court's realization.

[72] The account resonates with pragmatic accounts of the process of lawmaking by judges. *Cf.* Oliver Wendell Holmes, Jr., The Common Law 98 (Mark De Wolfe Howe ed., 1963) (describing

• The account connects weak- and strong-form review. Recall that the basic difference between those forms is temporal: Weak-form review allows for legislative responses to judicial decisions over a shorter period than strong-form review does. But the accumulated force of weak-form decisions provides the basis for replacing that form with strong-form review. Weak-form review exercised over time becomes strong-form review—and properly so, as experience teaches us what the Constitution really means in a particular domain.

I have sketched a story about the evolution of weak-form into strong-form review in the United States. Eventually one might be able to tell a parallel story for Canada. The fact that Paul Martin's proposed repeal of Section 33 was a political nonstarter might mean not that Canadians are so attached to Section 33 that they cannot take its repeal seriously, but that they have become so attached to strong-form judicial review that no politician would actually invoke Section 33. Eliminating Section 33 would be like risky surgery to remove a vestigial organ that poses no threat.

At least one question with this account of free speech law remains unanswered. The account relies on the development of consensus *within the relevant community* that doctrine has reached a stable resting place—that is, a correct answer. Identifying that community may be more difficult than it initially seems to be. After all, free speech questions arise only when legislatures defend their regulations of speech as being consistent with the First Amendment. That very assertion might be taken as a demonstration that the needed consensus is lacking.[73] And, of course, the idea motivating weak-form review is that reasonable disagreement—that is, lack of consensus—over constitutional meaning is pervasive. I have no strong intuitions about how to resolve the problem of identifying when a consensus exists within the relevant community.[74]

Experience in Europe may suggest one approach to an answer here. The European Court of Human Rights (ECHR) enforces the European Convention

---

the transformation of repeated jury rulings into judge-made rules). We might contrast the development of First Amendment doctrine dealing with speech critical of government policy, which developed over an extended period, with First Amendment doctrine dealing with false statements that injure reputation, where the Supreme Court's first intervention, New York Times v. Sullivan, 376 U.S. 254 (1964), set a rather rigid standard, which many observers believe to be unsound.

[73] Federalism complicates the analysis even more with respect to state and local regulations, because one justification for federalism is that it allows individual communities to disagree with the normative (in this context, the constitutional) judgments made by even an enormous majority of other communities.

[74] The relevant community pretty clearly should include law professors who specialize in free speech and constitutional law, and perhaps for them (and even for everyone) the correct standard for identifying when a consensus exists is Justice Stewart's: we know it when we see it. *See also* text accompanying note 90 *infra* (arguing that the answer to a similar problem is likely to be sociological rather than legal). And it pretty clearly should not be confined to the Court itself, for that would reduce the process of experimentation to one of self-reflection.

on Human Rights, a set of fundamental rights. In 1976 the ECHR articulated the "margin of appreciation" doctrine.[75] According to that doctrine, each nation adhering to the convention can properly have its own understanding of how the convention's provisions apply to particular problems, and its understanding of what those provisions mean.[76] Variation in application and interpretation is allowed within a "margin of appreciation." As to the former, the ECHR referred to the "direct and continuous contact with the vital forces of their countries," which gave national governments a better sense than the ECHR of how it made sense to apply the convention in specific circumstances.[77] As to the latter, the ECHR referred to the "rapid and far-reaching evolution of opinions" on the content of human rights guarantees.[78]

The ECHR has implemented the margin-of appreciation doctrine in a manner consistent with my argument that weak-form review properly develops into strong-form review, and in a manner that accommodates concerns about the identification of the relevant community within which consensus should be sought. The ECHR's technique has been to narrow that margin over time with respect to specific interpretive problems as experience accumulates in the ECHR and in domestic courts, producing a more "Europe-wide" view—perhaps a consensus—on how to deal with those problems.[79] Although U.S. constitutional doctrine does not expressly invoke margins of appreciation, a full account of the emergence of strong-form review in First Amendment cases might profit from incorporating that idea.

Popular Endorsement of Strong-Form Review Generally

Perhaps, then, strong-form review can justifiably emerge out of repeated exercises of weak-form review in connection with a particular problem. The *popular* commitment to strong-form review in the United States suggests a related though broader possibility—that strong-form review can be *chosen* in a nation committed to constitutionalism and democratic self-governance. That choice might be deliberate or, as I think is true in the United States, it might emerge out of a nation's history. Here some recent discussions of constitutionalism by the German philosopher Jürgen Habermas and the U.S. constitutional scholar Frank Michelman point us in the right direction.

[75] Handyside v. United Kingdom, 24 ECHR (ser. A).

[76] I have formulated these points so as to evoke again the distinction drawn in chapter 2 between the "Section 1" and the "Section 33" response to a judicial interpretation of a constitution.

[77] *Handyside*, at ¶ 48.

[78] *Ibid.*

[79] For a discussion, see R. St. J. Macdonald, "The Margin of Appreciation," excerpted in Louis Henkin et al., Human Rights 564–66 (1999).

Addressing the question of how citizens can be motivated to support the political order in ways that reinforce its commitment to constitutional democracy, Habermas developed the idea of constitutional patriotism.[80] Habermas's interest in constitutional patriotism derives from two sources. The first is recent German history. Weimar constitutionalism failed, but the German Basic Law, with its commitment to "militant democracy,"[81] seems to have succeeded, and Habermas seeks both to account for and to sustain that success. The second source is the emerging constitution of Europe.[82] The very claim that there is such a constitution is controversial, because critics of the claim think that constitutions must be rooted in an ethnos of a sort that does not exist across Europe. Against that criticism Habermas offers the possibility of a constitutional patriotism, an allegiance to principles of liberal constitutionalism that, he believes, underlie the institutional arrangements endorsed throughout Europe.

Constitutional patriotism has two components. The first is a commitment to constitutional democracy. The second, and more important, grows out of the fact that constitutional democracy takes a variety of forms. Constitutional patriotism arises from critical reflection on a polity's particular history. It recognizes that "[o]ne's own tradition must in each case be appropriated from a vantage point relativized by the perspectives of other traditions."[83]

Yet, Habermas's position is weakened somewhat by his commitment to the idea of an emerging European constitution. So, for example, he describes a process in which "a common *political* culture could differentiate itself from the

---

[80] *Cf.* Jürgen Habermas, Between Facts and Norms: Contributions to a Discourse Theory of Democracy 499 ("The legally constituted status of citizen depends on the *supportive spirit* of a consonant background of legally noncoercible motives and attitudes of a citizenry oriented toward the common good."). *See* Sujit Choudhry, "Citizenship and Federations: Some Preliminary Reflections," in The Federal Vision: Legitimacy and Levels of Governance in the United States and the European Union 384–85 (Kalypso Nicolaïdis & Robert Howse eds., New York: Oxford University Press, 2001), for a summary of criticisms of ideas of citizenship as too weak to motivate adherence to the principles of constitutional democracy.

[81] That is, the view that government institutions—courts, ministries, and parliament—have a constitutional duty to ensure that the conditions for democracy are maintained.

[82] I use this term because I believe it to be accurate even after the rejection in France and the Netherlands of the proposed Treaty on the Constitution of Europe. The European constitution is *emerging*, and might not be embodied—at least in the coming decades—in a single document.

[83] Habermas, *supra* note 80, at 500. *See also id.* at 496 ("This idea of a self-determining political community has assumed a variety of concrete legal forms in the different constitutions and political systems of Western Europe and the United States."); 161 (referring to "the critical appropriation of tradition"); 281 ("Where political will-formation is presented as ethical discourse, political discourse must be conducted always with the aim of discovering, at a given point in time and within the horizon of shared ways of life and traditions, what is best for citizens as members of a concrete community."). Michelman puts it this way: "Habermasian constitutional patriots feel devotion to their country just because they perceive their country's concrete ethical character to be such as to make possible the credible pursuit in practice of a certain regulative political idea." Frank I. Michelman, "Morality, Identity and 'Constitutional Patriotism,'" 14 Ratio Juris 253, 254–55 (2001).

various *national* cultures," by which he refers to "traditions in art and literature, historiography, philosophy, and so on."[84] Here Habermas allows his critics to raise the question typically asked about liberal universalism: How can a commitment to universal liberal principles motivate citizens of concrete polities with particular histories? The term *patriotism* seeks to associate the emotional commitment usually connected to a particular nation with, instead, a general commitment to constitutionalism. In doing so, however, the term may fail to identify an attitude that can actually motivate in the way Habermas wishes.

The difficulty, I believe, is that Habermas's account of constitutional *patriotism* is too substantive, in contrast to the procedural orientation of his account of constitutional *democracy*.[85] Procedures are needed to resolve questions about the specification of abstract principles in particular settings. Similarly with constitutional patriotism: All liberal democrats share a commitment to liberal values stated abstractly, and can be patriotic about a constitution that expresses those abstract values. Particular constitutions will specify those values differently, however, in two ways. A constitution may itself specify what it means when it refers to "free expression," and it creates procedures by which the abstract values are specified in particular settings.

One can be a patriot with respect to a constitution that embodies a particular specification of constitutional democracy; that does not make one a constitutional patriot in Habermas's sense, but rather a national patriot.[86] More interesting, perhaps, is the problem of patriotism's relation to constitutional meaning as specified by the institutions created to do so. The whole point of creating such institutions is to create something that can resolve controversy over what the proper specification of constitutional meaning is. Michelman seems to me correct in asserting that the mere fact that the relevant institution has specified meaning in a particular way provides no reason for a proponent of one of the views rejected by the institution to abandon his or her antecedent

---

[84] *Id.*, at 507. For me, this amounts to saying that constitutional democracies are the same with respect to what makes them constitutional democracies, and different with respect to the things that tourists care about.

[85] Choudhry, *supra* note 80, at 381, treats Habermas's idea of constitutional patriotism as a variant of what Choudhry calls a "*civic* conception of citizenship," which is based on "an allegiance to shared principles of political justice flowing from a liberal political morality, and to a common set of political institutions through which those principles are realized." I am uncertain whether Habermas's concept does in fact incorporate ideas about institutions, but in any event the idea of constitutional patriotism that I find most interesting does (and substantially diffuses the focus on principles of political justice). Choudhry, *id.*, at 385–86, also mentions critics of Habermas who read him as identifying constitutional patriotism with "universalistic principles of political morality," which are "too general and abstract" to generate commitments to particular political communities. *See also* Arash Abizadeh, "Does Liberal Democracy Presuppose a Cultural Nation?," 96 Am. Pol. Sci. Rev. 495 (2002).

[86] *Cf.* Choudhry, *supra* note 80, at 394 ("Given that, on the civic conception of citizenship, it is the shared principles of political justice that lie at the foundation of political community, how can [one] also justify the reliance on specific projects or ends as part of the civic bond?").

views. Such a person, that is, could not take as a ground for his or her patriotism the fact that the constitution has the meaning specified by the institution.

The proceduralist move Habermas and Michelman endorse with respect to constitutional substance might be appropriate here as well. Constitutional patriotism might attach not to the varying substantive values produced by different systems of constitutional democracy, but to the varying institutional forms constitutional democracy takes. The critical reflection Habermas seeks occurs when participants in a particular political culture consider whether the institutional forms to which they have become accustomed best advance their views of constitutional democracy, and always have available to them the possibility of replacing the existing institutional forms with others.[87]

Now I can reintroduce the question of whether weak-form judicial review is a better institution than strong-form review in terms of the fundamentals of constitutional democracy. The primary question is whether the very existence of strong-form review somehow impedes submitting strong-form review to critical evaluation. The answer to that question will come from critical reflection on the history of a nation with strong-form review. So, for example, one can ask whether the U.S. system of strong-form review is *required* by the U.S. Constitution. As I suggested in chapter 1, I doubt that it is.[88] Of course, there are strong *cultural* barriers to shifting from the present system of strong-form review to a weak-form system.[89] Those cultural barriers do not impede critical reflection on strong-form review, of a sort that is actually now fairly common in law reviews. And, were those barriers overcome by a political movement dedicated to (among other things) replacing strong-form review with a weaker version, the legal arguments explaining why weak-form review was compatible with the existing Constitution would become plausible too.

Critical reflection on particular nations' histories may lead one to think that weak-form review is a better institution than strong-form review for Canada,[90] *and* to think that strong-form review is better for the United

---

[87] This is, I think, the identification in the context of constitutional patriotism of what critical reflection is. Choudhry, *supra* note 80, at 381, refers to a "celebration of the particular [that] is careful to remain open, tolerant, and inclusive."

[88] The obvious point to make is that the text of the U.S. Constitution does not create *any* form of judicial review. The judicial specification of strong-form review goes back a long way, but I doubt that there is good constitutional warrant for saying that the tradition that sustains strong-form review cannot itself be displaced by self-conscious political action.

[89] One can test the strength of those barriers by following through on my thought experiment and trying to imagine the contours of the system of judicial review that Congress would create after the Supreme Court declared it would no longer engage in judicial review. (My sense is that Congress would create a reasonably strong form of judicial review.)

[90] As noted earlier, during the 2006 parliamentary campaign in Canada, Liberal Party leader Paul Martin proposed that a Liberal government would immediately move to repeal the notwithstanding clause and thereby "strengthen" the Charter. *See* Daniel LeBlanc, "Martin's Charter Promise Easier Said than Done," Toronto Globe & Mail, Jan. 11, 2006.

States.[91] The explanation would lie in historical details, and I do not want to explore U.S. history here. My aim has been instead to suggest why strong-form review is compatible conceptually with constitutional democracy as it has developed in the United States.

CONCLUSION: REVISITING THE QUESTION OF WEAK-FORM REVIEW IN STRONG-FORM SYSTEMS

So far I have discussed the possibility that strong-form review can emerge out of weak-form review with respect to particular topics, and the possibility that strong-form review can be chosen by a nation's people as a result of the self-understanding they reach over time. The historically oriented analysis I have developed gives new purchase on a possibility raised in chapter 2: can there be islands of weak-form review in a system generally committed to strong-form review?[92]

Earlier I argued that we were unlikely to be able to identify principled bases for distinguishing areas in which strong-form review was appropriate and those where weak-form review was. So, for example, I have argued that the U.S. Supreme Court's approach to free speech over a rather long period can best be understood as an exercise in weak-form review, and that its current approach can best be understood as an exercise in strong-form review. The example can be generalized. At any particular time, courts might be exercising strong-form review in some areas, weak-form review in others. They would not have principled reasons—that is, reasons distinguishing the different areas on grounds that stand up to close rational scrutiny. But they might treat the areas differently because they simply have not accumulated enough experience to be confident that *their* specification of a constitutional provision's meaning is clearly better than the legislature's specification.[93]

Part 3 is devoted to a detailed examination of the foregoing argument with respect to judicial enforcement of social and economic rights. The U.S. courts exercise quite deferential review of legislation challenged on the ground that it violates social and economic rights. They have provided reasons for doing so, but those reasons are, I argue in part 3, inadequate. Instead, they should be exercising weak-form review in ways that invite dialogic responses from legislatures.

[91] *Cf.* Michelman, *supra* note 83, at 269 ("conditions then and there warrant a level of confidence that the struggle *over* corporate identity occurs *within* a corporate identity that is already incompletely, but to a sufficient degree, known and fixed. The answer is, in other words, a cultural contingency.").

[92] My discussion in chapter 2 of deferential review in some areas of constitutional law touched on this question, but as I argued there, deferential review is not really weak-form review.

[93] There might be other explanations for differential treatment, but again those explanations would be essentially historical or accidental.

Before reaching that point in the argument, though, I must address obvious questions about dialogic—that is, weak-form—versions of judicial review: Can legislatures usefully participate in constitutional dialogues? Will their responses be constitutionally informed and reasonable, or merely the expressions of unthinking partisan commitments? Part 2 takes up those questions.

PART II

Legislative Responsibility for Enforcing the Constitution

CHAPTER 4

Why and How to Evaluate Constitutional Performance

WEAK-FORM review clearly should enhance the role legislatures and executive officials play in constitutional interpretation and development. One of its premises is the recognition that people can reasonably disagree over the proper interpretation of a constitution's relatively abstract provisions. It follows from that premise that reasonable judicial interpretations have no intrinsic superiority to reasonable legislative and executive interpretations. And, it follows from *that* that weak-form systems are designed to give legislatures and executive officials an open role in constitutional interpretation. They can engage in "dialogue" with the courts, responding to—and, in some versions, even replacing—the courts' interpretations with their own. Or they can consider constitutional questions from the start, thereby diminishing the scrutiny the courts will give to the statutes that end up being enacted.

Those familiar only with strong-form judicial review, and particularly U.S. scholars of constitutional law, frequently express deep skepticism about the ability of legislatures to perform the task of constitutional interpretation well.[1] This chapter and the next examine whether legislatures are competent at constitutional interpretation. After explaining why some of the most common objections to legislative constitutional interpretation are mistaken, I develop what I call a constitution-based criterion for evaluating legislative performance. That criterion is quite generous in its toleration of a wide range of alternative and inconsistent interpretations of a single constitution, but, I argue, generosity of that sort is not only appropriate but necessary if we are to honor the commitments of constitutionalism itself. Chapter 5 then provides a number of case studies of legislative performance, most from the United States but with some glances toward Canada and Great Britain. I conclude that, applying the constitution-based standard as we should, we will find a fair degree of constitutional responsibility in legislatures, although not complete responsibility. But, I emphasize, the task is comparative, so that we must also ask whether constitutional courts are constitutionally responsible

[1] Because legislatures tend to be the focus of these discussions, not executive officials, and because repeatedly writing *legislators and executive officials* or *non-judicial officials* would become stylistically tiresome, I usually refer only to legislators and legislatures in this chapter. The analytic points, though, apply to executive officials as well, and some of the case studies in the next chapter deal with constitutional interpretation by such officials.

to any greater degree. My answer is that they probably are, but not dramatically so.

SKEPTICISM ABOUT LEGISLATURES' CONSTITUTIONAL COMPETENCE

The rhetorical moves expressing skepticism about legislatures are familiar. Critics list statutes the courts have found unconstitutional; they identify enacted statutes that are, by their own criteria, clearly unconstitutional; they point to one or two particularly egregious examples of patently unconstitutional statutes that were nonetheless enacted.

These rhetorical moves do not really show that legislatures are incompetent at the job of constitutional interpretation. The lists of statutes found unconstitutional could show only that the courts and legislatures *disagree* about what the constitution means. Yet, the premise of weak-form review is precisely that there will be disagreement, and often such disagreement rests on reasonable judgments made by both sides. Taking the lists of statutes held unconstitutional to reflect legislative incompetence is just to *assert* judicial superiority in constitutional interpretation, not to establish it against the claims of weak-form review.

Naming statutes the critic thinks unconstitutional does even less to establish that the place weak-form systems give legislatures in constitutional interpretation is unjustified. Sometimes the critic simply fails to make the necessary comparative judgment. The central issue in evaluating legislative performance is how well they perform relative to the courts. I might not think that some statute—a provision of the USA PATRIOT Act, for example—is constitutional, but if the courts uphold it against constitutional challenge, my criticism should be just as much a criticism of the courts as the legislature. More important, as I discuss in more detail later, the premise in weak-form systems of reasonable disagreement extends beyond reasonable disagreement over what the constitution means in connection with determining whether a particular statute is unconstitutional, to reasonable disagreement over how to determine what the constitution means. If my criticism of the USA PATRIOT Act rests on an originalist approach to constitutional interpretation, those who reasonably take a different interpretive approach, such as the functionalist one discussed in chapter 1, need not be bothered by the fact that Congress enacted a statute inconsistent with original understanding.

Explaining why the examples of egregiously unconstitutional statutes do not establish legislative incompetence at constitutional interpretation is a bit more complicated, although the basic point is simple. Such statutes are unconstitutional no matter what interpretive approach one takes. I can identify only two pieces of national legislation enacted over the past few decades that were, in my view, not consistent with any reasonable interpretive theory. One was Congress's effort to ban flag burning as a means of political protest.[2] The other was the Communications Decency Act, which would have had the effect of barring from the Internet and World Wide Web a large but vaguely defined category of "indecent" materials, a fair portion of which is plainly valuable when available to adults.[3]

Does the fact that Congress enacted these statutes, which for present purposes we can assume to be egregiously unconstitutional, show that it cannot be trusted to interpret the Constitution responsibly? The answer is no. The reason is that Congress enacted these statutes in a strong-form system, knowing that the Supreme Court was available to ensure that truly unconstitutional statutes would never go into effect. This *judicial overhang* affects how legislatures act in strong-form systems.[4]

The judicial overhang sometimes promotes legislative disregard of the constitution.[5] Legislators and executive officials may say to themselves, "Why bother to interpret the constitution at all, much less interpret it well, when the courts are going to end up offering the definitive interpretation anyway?" President George W. Bush provided a good example in his statement on signing the McCain-Feingold campaign finance statute. He said, "Certain provisions present serious constitutional concerns. . . . I . . . have reservations about the constitutionality of the broad ban on issue advertising, which restrains the speech of a wide variety of groups on issues of public import in the months closest to an election." His statement on this point concluded, "I expect that the courts will resolve these legitimate legal questions as appropriate under the law."[6] The Supreme Court upheld the provisions about which the president expressed

[2] Held unconstitutional in United States v. Eichman, 486 U.S. 310 (1990). I should note my uncertainty about whether even the anti-flag-burning legislation might be justified by a theory that allows for quite limited *ad hoc* departures from the conclusions compelled by all reasonable interpretive theories. For a brief discussion, see Mark Tushnet, "The Flagburning Episode: An Essay on the Constitution," 61 Colorado L. Rev. 39 (1990).

[3] The act was held unconstitutional in Reno v. ACLU, 521 U.S. 844 (1997). Michael Bamberger uses the CDA as the focal point of his opening narrative to demonstrate legislative irresponsibility. Michael A. Bamberger, Reckless Legislation: How Legislators Ignore the Constitution (2001), which offers several additional case studies, supplemented by a survey of state legislators' and executive officials' attitudes toward constitutional interpretation.

[4] It may be worth noting that the judicial overhang's effects are asymmetrical. Congress may enact statutes in full confidence that the courts will uphold them, even if someone might think that the statutes are as egregiously unconstitutional as those discussed in the text. But precisely because the courts will uphold these statutes, the judicial overhang has, as such, no effects on the laws that end up legally enforceable.

[5] For an examination of legislative behavior in light of the possibility of judicial review, see J. Mitchell Pickerill, Constitutional Deliberation in Congress: The Impact of Judicial Review in a Separated System (2004). Pickerill deals with modern federalism issues at pp. 98–131.

[6] Statement by the President, March 27, 2002, available at http://www.whitehouse.gov/news/releases/2002/03/20020327.html (visited Jan. 20, 2006).

reservations,[7] which suggests that the Court and the president might disagree about what the "appropriate" resolution was.

Political scientists include "position taking" among the motivations legislators have, distinguishing it from "credit claiming."[8] For a legislator to claim credit, something actually has to have happened, whereas legislators can take positions without being concerned about whether some policy gets implemented. Position-taking legislators may say to themselves, "I can get political mileage out of taking a position on this question, without worrying that anything actually will happen, because the courts will find the statute unconstitutional anyway."

Strong-form judicial review might encourage mere position taking. Enacting statutes that are sure be to held unconstitutional—because they are inconsistent with any reasonable approach to constitutional interpretation—is position taking. That legislators engage in this sort of position taking does not show that they affirmatively desire to have obviously unconstitutional statutes go into effect. True, this kind of position taking is a sort of legislative irresponsibility, but its existence flows from the existence of strong-form review. In itself, it does not show that legislators in weak-form systems are, or would be, incompetent constitutional interpreters.

The easy arguments about legislative incompetence should be set to one side. How should we conduct a serious inquiry into the capacity of legislatures to engage in constitutional interpretation? The first question is, Against what standard should we measure legislative performance? After describing the appropriate, constitution-based standard, I consider the motivations of individual legislators to do a decent job of constitutional interpretation, and then the criteria for evaluating the performance not of individual legislators but of legislatures as institutions. The chapter concludes with an explanation of my focus in the next chapter on a series of short case studies of the performance of national lawmakers as constitutional interpreters.

A Constitution-Based Standard of Evaluation

The easy arguments I have sketched try to evaluate legislative performance by reference to how courts interpret constitutions.[9] Such a court-based standard is

[7] McConnell v. FEC, 540 U.S. 93 (2003).

[8] For position taking, see David R. Mayhew, Congress: The Electoral Connection 61–73 (1974).

[9] See, e.g., Bamberger, supra note 3. Bruce G. Peabody, "Congressional Constitutional Interpretation and the Courts: A Preliminary Inquiry into Legislative Attitudes, 1959–2001," 29 Law & Soc. Inquiry 127 (2004) (reporting a study that asked members of Congress whether they should defer to the Supreme Court on questions of constitutional interpretation), indicates that a majority of respondents believed that members had the duty to arrive at a judgment independent of the Supreme Court's views.

inappropriate. I think it helpful to begin the inquiry into the proper evaluative standard by noting that even in strong-form systems, courts identify areas where legislative action is in fact regulated by the constitution but where the courts will not oversee legislative performance. The political questions doctrine in the United States, for example, marks out areas where the courts will not oversee legislative action to determine whether it is consistent with the limitations the Constitution places on Congress. The impeachment case of *Walter Nixon v. United States* provides a convenient illustration.[10] The House of Representatives impeached federal district judge Nixon after he was convicted of federal felonies. The case proceeded to the Senate for trial. Following rules it had adopted for impeachment trials of judges, the Senate convened a committee that heard testimony and reported to the entire Senate. Judge Nixon had no opportunity to present evidence to the Senate as a whole. The Constitution provides that the Senate has "the sole Power to try all Impeachments," and Judge Nixon contended that the Senate did not afford him a real "trial" as the Constitution required. In an analytically confused opinion, the Supreme Court held that Judge Nixon's claim presented a political question, meaning that the courts would not determine whether the procedure the Senate followed was a "trial" within the meaning the Constitution gave to that term.

The political questions doctrine does not mean that Congress is totally unconstrained by the Constitution in the areas it identifies. Rather, it means that Congress conclusively determines what the Constitution means in those areas. It follows that there are some areas in which the U.S. Congress does engage in constitutional interpretation. Yet, in the absence of judicial review, how can we evaluate Congress' performance? A court-based standard is plainly unavailable. That is, in examining the performance of nonjudicial actors in areas where there is no judicial review, we must develop some standard other than a court-based one. With such a standard in hand, we could identify the incentives legislators have *qua* legislators to interpret the Constitution well or badly.

The most promising candidate for a non-court-based evaluative standard is, not surprisingly, the constitution itself. Saying that, though, is only the beginning of the analysis. Suppose, first, that a particular evaluator/critic has a preferred interpretive theory, such as textualism or originalism. Such a person can readily determine whether legislators (and courts) are properly interpreting the constitution, by measuring their performance against what the interpretive theory demands. Legislative and judicial decisions consistent with the text are good ones, for example, while those inconsistent with the text are bad ones. And the evaluator can compare how well legislators do to how well judges do.[11]

---

[10] Walter Nixon v. United States, 506 U.S. 224 (1993).

[11] My own judgment, for what it is worth, is that judges do badly according to a standard that requires originalist interpretation, and indeed according to any standard other than one that allows judges to choose eclectically among interpretive approaches.

The difficulty, as I have mentioned, is that there is reasonable disagreement about the proper interpretive theory. Some believe that textualism is correct, others that the constitution should be interpreted with reference to moral standards, yet others that decision makers should be eclectic and exercise good judgment in choosing which interpretive method to deploy when specific constitutional questions arise. Adrian Vermeule has pointed out that we have no way of ensuring that the judiciary, considered as a collection of individuals, will adhere to any prescribed interpretive theory,[12] and the point is clearly true of legislators as well.

This reasonable interpretive diversity forces us to modify the evaluative standard. We still want a constitution-based standard, but it cannot be one that rests on a controversial choice among interpretive theories. One possibility is that we should evaluate performance by asking how often courts and legislatures make decisions that are not consistent with *any* reasonable interpretive theory. This is obviously an extremely weak standard, in the sense that we should expect to find few decisions indeed, whether by judges or by legislators, that are consistent with no reasonable interpretive theory. And, even if the aggregate behavior of courts and legislators differs, we are likely to be dealing with small absolute differences. Courts may come out better than other decision makers, but the margin is likely to be small, and probably not worth worrying about either way.

Another constitution-based standard might distinguish more effectively between courts and legislators. It begins by observing that interpretation is necessarily retrospective, and that nonjudicial policymaking and some aspects of judicial decision making have important, perhaps dominating, forward-looking components. It is at least plausible to presume, pending empirical inquiry, that the mix of retrospective and prospective components differs as between courts and legislators: Courts might primarily look backward—engage in interpretation—and give forward-looking policy considerations a secondary role, while legislators might be primarily concerned about the future and only secondarily about the past. On this view, the constitution-based standard leads us to ask whether, to what extent, and why decision makers engage in the backward-looking exercise of interpretation.

Once again, though, we must be generous in assessing what counts as looking backward, in light of the reasonable diversity of interpretive methods. One obvious backward-looking approach focuses on the constitution's text. Another, almost equally obvious such approach attends to prior decisions—judicial or nonjudicial—about the constitution's meaning. These approaches might be particularly appropriate with respect to questions about the structures of government, where alternative arrangements typically have few direct

---

[12] Adrian Vermeule, "The Judiciary Is a They, Not an It: Interpretive Theory and the Fallacy of Division," 14 J. Contemp. Leg. Issues 549, 553 (2005) (criticizing "the undefended assumption that sustained judicial coordination on a particular interpretive approach . . . is feasible").

implications for fundamental rights, and where it might be quite important to ensure that the resolution of one interpretive question does not gum up the works by interfering with the government's smooth operation.

Some nations, those whose nationhood is constituted by a constitution rather than by ethnicity or similar characteristics, have a third, somewhat less obvious backward-looking approach available. One would ask whether a proposal or practice is consistent with the aspirations of the nation's people as expressed in foundational documents.[13] These different approaches might perhaps be captured in a more general formulation of a constitution-based standard: "To what extent do decision makers orient themselves toward a nation's constitutional tradition?" I think it worth observing that, like the standard "inconsistent with all reasonable interpretive theories," this standard too is unlikely to identify many examples of legislative incompetence or irresponsibility, because it seems to me nearly inevitable that a very large proportion of all decision makers will be socialized into accepting the proposition that their actions ought to be oriented to the nation's constitutional tradition, at least in nations whose democratic systems are reasonably long-lived.[14] I develop the argument supporting the "orientation to tradition" criterion later in this chapter, though I sometimes refer to it before presenting the argument in its full form.

THE INDIVIDUAL LEVEL: LEGISLATORS' MOTIVATIONS

We can begin the examination of legislators' motivations by putting to one side what I believe is the most common, but erroneous, assumption about them. The point of a constitution is to place limits on legislators' natural inclinations to advance the interests of the majority at the expense of minority rights, and to adopt policies that give the decision makers short-term gains at the expense of long-term impairments of good government. I do not quarrel with this statement of the point of having a constitution, but it assumes, without independent support, that legislators have weak incentives to comply with the constitution's provisions.[15]

---

[13] Those documents would, of course, include the nation's constitution, but, for the United States, could include the Declaration of Independence, Lincoln's Gettysburg Address and Second Inaugural Address, Franklin Delano Roosevelt's "Four Freedoms" speech, and other similar documents. The French *Conseil Constitutionnel* has invoked the terse reference in the preamble to the nation's 1946 Constitution, endorsed in the currently applicable Constitution adopted in 1958, to "the fundamental principles acknowledged in the laws of the Republic."

[14] I have considered limiting the suggestion to nonjudicial actors who broadly accept the premises of democratic self-governance, so as to eliminate from consideration people like military officers who participate in antidemocratic coups d'état. My sense, though, is that even such actors claim, and I think often not disingenuously, that they intervene so as to preserve rather than transform the nation's constitutional traditions.

[15] Put another way, the legislators' "natural inclinations" might themselves be weak.

We must look more closely at constitutions themselves to see why this assumption is more questionable than proponents of the position I have described believe it to be. In the most general terms, constitutions contain two
kinds of provisions: precise ones and abstract ones. The abstract provisions
can be *specified*—that is, given meaning in real-world circumstances—in
different ways, all compatible with the provisions' language and purposes. In
addition, even precise constitutional provisions interact with each other.
Specification and interaction mean that, more often than one might initially
think, the constitution's meaning is underdetermined.

Sometimes a legislator uncontroversially violates the constitution's terms,
and in these cases we can profitably examine what induced her to do so. But,
notably, these cases are rare. As did Chief Justice John Marshall, we can describe a hypothetical case in which Congress enacts a statute violating the
precise constitutional provision requiring testimony by two witnesses to the
same overt act in treason prosecutions,[16] but we cannot overlook the fact that
the example is hypothetical. Legislators do not violate precise constitutional
provisions often enough for such violations to support a useful inquiry into
their motivations. Even more, legislators are likely to violate precise terms
only when they believe the nation to be facing a real crisis—in which case
constitutionalism more broadly is likely to come under pressure, in the courts
as well as the legislature.

More often, and more interesting, legislators enact statutes that *arguably* are
inconsistent with one or more specifications of the constitution's abstract provisions. But in such cases, the real issue is not *why* the legislature violated the
constitution but *whether* it did. The availability of different specifications of
abstract provisions means that under some specifications, a particular statute
will be unconstitutional while under others it will be constitutional.

The problem of specification arises even when rights are not directly at
stake. Consider, for example, the legislative veto controversy in U.S. constitutional law. That controversy involved statutory provisions that allowed one
or both houses of Congress to block the implementation of actions by presidential officials, acting pursuant to a broad delegation of authority, if a majority of the House of Representatives or the Senate (sometimes, majorities in
both houses) believed that the actions were inconsistent with the underlying
statute. The advocate of the view that constitutions are designed to counter
legislators' natural inclinations would be concerned that the legislature's disregard of the constitution's provisions (if there is such disregard) flows from its
placing more value on short-term considerations than on ensuring that the
long-term structure of government promotes good public policy. The alternative framing of the question is, however, obvious: Given the circumstances
of modern government, is the legislative veto a component of a long-term

---

[16] Marbury v. Madison, 5 U.S. (1 Cranch) 137, 179–80 (1803).

structure of government that promotes good public policy? Here too, that is, the constitutional controversy is *about* what best promotes constitutional values.[17]

The second characteristic of constitutions, the interaction among their provisions, raises the same question. Taken by themselves, two constitutional provisions might be clear or precise. But, taken together, they might generate ambiguity. Legislators can resolve that ambiguity by their decisions. And, in doing so, they do not disregard one or the other provision; they interpret the constitution as a whole.[18]

That alternative reasonable specifications of a constitution's provisions are available reproduces in the context of particular legislative decisions the problem posed by the availability of a range of reasonable interpretive methods. And, here as there, one cannot resolve the problem by stipulating what the constitution's abstract provisions mean[19] and then examining the incentives that lead legislators to "violate" the constitution.

So far I have simply tried to clear away some confusions that often attend discussions of legislators' incentives to comply with the constitution. The main concern about legislators' incentives is simple: They are *elected*. Their primary incentive is to retain their jobs. They will have incentives to comply with the constitution—defined for the moment as orienting their actions to the nation's constitutional tradition—only if doing so will make it more likely that they will retain their jobs. Is there reason to think that it will?

Bruce Peabody's recent survey of the views of members of the U.S. Congress indicates that its members do pay attention to the Constitution more often than academic skeptics think. And, interestingly, a fair number of Peabody's respondents take the view that Congress has the duty to arrive at a constitutional interpretation independent of the Supreme Court's interpretation.[20]

[17] My understanding of these issues has been decisively affected by Frank I. Michelman, Brennan and Democracy (1999).

[18] The recent controversy in the United States over the constitutionality of Senate filibusters of judicial nominations illustrates the problem identified here. There are two constitutional provisions. One would appear clearly to permit such filibusters when permitted by the Senate's rules. U.S. Const., art. I, § 5, cl. 2 ("Each House may determine the Rules of its Proceedings."). Another, though, makes it possible to argue that the Senate is required to vote on the merits of a nomination submitted by the president. U.S. Const., art. II, § 2, cl. 2 (the president "shall nominate, and by and with the Advice and Consent of the Senate, shall appoint . . . Judges of the supreme Court, and all other Officers of the United States").

[19] Or how its provisions, properly interpreted, interact.

[20] "[M]ore than 60% of the respondents refused to cede constitutional questions to the courts, believing instead that Congress should 'form its own considered judgment' on those issues." Peabody, *supra* note 9, at 146. The results of Peabody's survey are roughly consistent with others, such as Bamberger's and the survey reported in Donald G. Morgan, Congress and the Constitution: A Study of Responsibility (1966). In general, between two-thirds and three-quarters of respondents assert that legislators should form their own views on the constitutionality of legislation, that legislative discussions are reasonably well-informed about constitutional questions, and that discussions of constitutional questions influence legislators' votes.

That this view is so prevalent suggests that it would be profitable to speculate about why legislators might hold it, that is, why a person interested in retaining his or her job in an election might believe it proper to pay attention to the constitution.

From a purely self-interested point of view, legislators are interested in retaining their jobs until something better comes along. The latter qualification is important. Sometimes taking an action that is necessary if one is to retain one's job would make one worse off than leaving the job and going to the next best alternative. This constraint allows us to include in the analysis of incentives such things as the legislator's sense of himself or herself as a good person, or as a person doing a good job.[21] In addition, we have to remain attentive to the fact that the judicial overhang affects the incentives legislators have in strong-form systems.

Why might a legislator want to orient herself to the constitution? One answer is obvious: That might be what her constituents want. Of course we cannot rule out *a priori* the possibility that constituents will have such constitution-oriented preferences. Even more, on some important issues it seems quite likely that constituent preference is based on views in the constituency about the constitution's meaning. In the United States, for example, constituent preferences about the proper public policy on abortion are, I believe, almost certainly based on judgments about the rights of women and the rights of fetuses, judgments that—whether pro-choice or pro-life—are well within the range of reasonable specifications of the Constitution's meaning. A legislator whose interest in reelection leads her to cater to constitution-oriented constituent preferences is (indirectly) orienting her legislative activity to the nation's constitutional traditions.[22]

Second, a legislator can "vote her conscience" on matters about which the constituency is indifferent. Some constitutional issues—ones that involve technical constitutional questions, for example—may have this characteristic. In essence, constituents delegate their own ability to make constitutional judgments to their representatives. A representative can act according to her own constitutional judgments (if the legislator has them—a question I discuss later) on these matters without fear of adverse electoral consequences—at least within broad limits.

[21] The important empirical study of members of the U.S. House of Representatives, Richard Fenno, Home Style: House Members in Their Districts (1978), demonstrated that these legislators were indeed motivated by their desire to make good public policy within the constraints of retaining their positions.

[22] I believe it worth noting that standard examples of meanly self-interested constituent preferences, such as that of farmers for subsidies for their activity, involve legislation that, in the United States, receives rather limited substantive judicial review, and that aggressive judicial review occurs with respect to many issues, such as abortion, where constituent preferences seem to me likely to be constitution-oriented.

Those limits are important in thinking about a final possibility. Even on matters as to which constituents are largely indifferent, a legislator runs some risk of getting too far out of line, that is, of taking a constitutional position that will lead constituents to vote against the legislator once the position is brought to their attention.[23] The obverse of this point is equally important. Sometimes a legislator will have substantial freedom to adopt constitutional positions at odds with the views of his or her constituents on a matter not central to the constituents' overall views. Consider, for example, a constituency in which most voters care a great deal about getting direct benefits from government expenditures ("pork," pejoratively), and care a bit, but not all that much, about allowing prayer in public schools. Such a constituency will cut their representative some slack on the constitutional issue if the representative is very good is bringing home the pork. Of course, the more important the constitutional issue is to the constituency, and the more uncertain the representative is about how important the constitutional issue is to voters, the less slack the representative will have.[24]

So far I have discussed electoral incentives for legislators to orient their action to the nation's constitutional traditions. Of course, those incentives will not always operate. Constituents may be hostile to the nation's constitutional traditions, for example.[25] More important, the presence of *other* decision makers with responsibility for constitutional interpretation may give nonjudicial actors incentives to ignore the constitution in their actions.[26] Here again the judicial overhang plays a role, and I use it to illustrate the problem. But the difficulty arises because responsibility for constitutional interpretation may be divided among various institutions, including the executive branch.

I have already mentioned the possibility of (mere) position taking, which involves ignoring constitutional questions because the decision maker believes that some other actor will do so. A legislator may ignore constitutional questions because she believes the president will consider them in deciding whether

---

[23] A complete analysis would therefore have to include some assessment of the circumstances under which legislators have varying degrees of risk aversion.

[24] Again, though, I emphasize that the most potent examples of cases in which constituents may be unwilling to cut a representative some slack are cases in which the constituents' views reflect reasonable judgments about what the constitution requires or permits.

[25] Given the breadth of the range of reasonable specifications of a constitution's meaning, though, this possibility seems remote as a practical matter in reasonably stable democracies.

[26] I develop the argument by considering the effect of the existence of judicial review, but I believe (at least for now) that the argument holds whenever there is some decision maker who is the last mover in a process of decision making. Here *last mover* means a decision maker whose actions cannot be overridden by ordinary majorities. In the United States, the president is the last mover with respect to ordinary legislation because his or her veto cannot be overridden without a supermajority vote, and the Supreme Court is the last mover with respect to constitutional decisions because its decisions cannot be overridden unless a supermajoritarian amendment process is carried through to a successful conclusion.

to sign or veto legislation; a president may ignore constitutional questions because he believes that the courts will consider them in subsequent litigation. Mere position taking can be particularly troublesome when the final mover takes the position that its decision should incorporate some degree of deference to prior actors, because, in circumstances of mere position taking, the final mover may be deferring to a judgment that no one ever made.[27]

Mark Graber has identified another incentive legislators and executive officials have for refusing to address constitutional questions.[28] Graber notes that dominant political coalitions sometimes face policy issues that might divide the coalition if its leaders are forced to take a stand on the policy questions. Coalition leaders would therefore like to find some way to avoid taking a stand. Passing the questions off to some other decision maker—notably, the courts—is an attractive strategy if the policy questions have constitutional overtones.[29] If the courts find constitutional impediments to adopting the policy, coalition leaders can assuage the policy's supporters by blaming the courts, and can satisfy the policy's opponents by noting that the policy is in fact not going to take effect.[30]

Notably, these incentives to ignore constitutional questions exist because there is someone else to whom the buck can be passed. That fact, in turn, might have some implications for designing institutions to make it less clear who the last mover actually is. Weak-form judicial review blurs the line between the first and the last mover, perhaps to the point where the strategy of passing the buck will not be politically attractive. A Canadian legislator cannot hide behind that nation's Supreme Court, given the possibility of invoking the notwithstanding

[27] Justice Antonin Scalia rejects deference—at least when Congress has engaged in mere position taking—in this statement:

> My Court is fond of saying that acts of Congress come to the Court with the presumption of constitutionality. That presumption reflects Congress's status as a coequal branch of government with its own responsibilities to the Constitution. But if Congress is going to take the attitude that it will do anything it can get away with and let the Supreme Court worry about the Constitution . . . then perhaps that presumption is unwarranted.

Quoted in Ruth Colker & James J. Brudney, "Dissing Congress," 100 Mich. L. Rev. 80, 80 (2001) (quoting Antonin Scalia, U.S. Supreme Court, Address at the Telecommunications Law and Policy Symposium (Apr. 18, 2000)).

[28] Mark A. Graber, "The Nonmajoritarian Difficulty: Legislative Deference to the Judiciary," 7 Stud. in Am. Pol. Dev. 35 (1993).

[29] Provisions for advisory opinions from a constitutional court, such as the so-called reference jurisdiction of the Supreme Court of Canada, provide a ready institutional form for implementing this strategy.

[30] There is an asymmetry in this strategy: the coalition leaders still face a political problem if the courts say that adopting the policy would be constitutionally permissible. Graber's central examples are the controversy over slavery in the U.S. territories in the late antebellum period, and the controversy over abortion in the past thirty years; in both the courts held that a policy that one part of the dominant coalition wanted to implement was unconstitutional.

clause (or offering a stronger Section 1 defense of limitations on rights as demonstrably necessary). In that way, weak-form judicial review might *increase* the incentives legislators have to take their constitution seriously.

Brief consideration of legislators' incentives in parliamentary systems is appropriate here. In parliamentary systems with strong parties, individual legislators must retain the confidence of the parties' leaders if they are to remain in office. The majority party leadership is the nation's executive branch as long as it retains a majority, and—mostly—only legislation supported by the party leadership will be enacted. Accordingly, attention should be focused on whether and why the majority party's leaders would follow the constitution.

There are two qualifications. Party leaders may sometimes allow a free vote, that is, one in which members are allowed to vote their consciences without regard to the leadership's position. Free votes are rare in Canada and Great Britain, but they are said to occur on occasional "issues of conscience" that are not important to the majority party's platform.[31] Such matters are likely to be a (small) subset of constitutionally sensitive matters. Members of Parliament casting free votes, voting their consciences, are in the same position as the legislators in separation-of-powers systems whose incentives I have already discussed. In addition, the party leadership does not have complete control over whether a member remains in office. Some members have sufficiently strong support in the party, or in their constituencies, that they will remain on the party's election lists pretty much no matter what they do. These members too are like independently elected legislators in separation-of-powers systems.

COURTS AND LEGISLATORS

Evaluating legislative performance inevitably has a comparative component, which is sometimes submerged but deserves explicit attention, so I turn to comparing the capacities of legislators to those of courts. Constitution-based standards are retrospective. Legislation is largely forward-looking, putting in place policies that will guide the society in the future. Legislators enact forward-looking legislation to provide voters with a basis for assessing how much better the legislators have made the voters' lives. Put another way, legislators' incentives are not exclusively backward-looking.

Judges, in contrast, might be thought to look backward exclusively, examining the existing legal materials as a basis for determining what the law is. It might well be true that a large portion of judicial work is backward-looking, but it is not true that judges only look backward. And their forward-looking work resembles the kind of policy analysis that a forward-looking legislator

---

[31] Free votes have occurred in Canada and Great Britain on issues relating to abortion, capital punishment, televising parliamentary proceedings, and research on embryos.

might do. Put in terms of incentives, the desire to perform the judicial job well gives a judge an incentive to look forward with an eye to making good law— just as a legislator has an incentive to look forward with an eye to enacting good laws.[32] Judges do two forms of forward-looking work, one inherent in the job of judging in a hierarchical judicial system and the other part of one prominent interpretive theory.

Judges articulate rules one of whose purposes is to guide behavior, sometimes by judges below them in the judicial hierarchy, sometimes by executive officials implementing the rules the judges articulate. As Richard Fallon has emphasized, that fact means that good judging means articulating implementable rules.[33] A judge must look forward to determine whether a rule is implementable, anticipating how inferior judges and executive officials will respond to the rule. Concerned about implementation, judges will sometimes forgo articulating the rule that, in their judgment, best enforces the law in the backward-looking sense, because the second-best rule, when implemented by inferior judges and executive officials, will better achieve the goals revealed by an examination of the existing legal materials.[34] Being a good judge, that is, means looking forward as well as backward. The difference from legislators is one of degree, not of kind.

Implementability will be a concern no matter what the judge's interpretive theory is. Some interpretive theories are themselves quite forward-looking. The most obvious such theory is one that directs judges to interpret the constitution so as to balance rights appropriately against social goals.[35] General

[32] There is something of a play on words in this formulation. The laws a legislator has an incentive to make are good ones from the legislator's point of view because they increase the prospects of reelection by improving the lives of the legislator's constituents and thereby giving them reasons to reelect the legislator. The substantive goodness of the laws is only indirectly a matter of concern to the legislator. It is directly of concern to the judge seeking to do a good job. I should note that the literature on judges' incentives is extremely thin. The best of an unsatisfactory lot are Richard A. Posner, "What Do Judges Maximize? (The Same Thing Everybody Else Does)," 3 S. Ct. Econ. Rev. 1 (1993); Frederick Schauer, "Incentives, Reputation, and the Inglorious Determinants of Judicial Behavior" (The Robert Marx Lecture), 68 U. Cin. L. Rev. 615 (2000). I take these articles to argue that the only real incentives judges have are inner ones, such as the desire to do a good job, because, basically, there is nothing they could be asked to do that would make them worse off than they would be in their next best job. (Resignations of judges in the United States are rare, but sometimes occur because the judges find themselves unwilling to impose criminal sentences the law requires of them—and because such judges have decent alternative jobs available as practicing lawyers.)

[33] Richard H. Fallon, Jr., Implementing the Constitution (2001).

[34] In using the word *goals*, I do not mean to endorse a purely instrumental view of "the law." Alternative phrasings, though, make the sentence unwieldy. (The best alternative is something like "whatever it is that makes it good to follow the law.")

[35] I suppose the canonical text here is John Rawls's observation that a moral-political theory (and, inferentially, an interpretive theory) that does not take consequences into account is simply crazy. John Rawls, A Theory of Justice 30 (1971) ("All ethical doctrines worth our attention take consequences into account in judging rightness. One which did not would simply be irrational, crazy.").

limitations clauses such as Section 1 of the Canadian Charter of Rights embed such an interpretive theory in constitutional language, but the impulse to balance is so strong that balancing is an attractive interpretive theory even without a limitations clause.[36]

Consider, for example, the standard formulation of the appropriate way to think about constitutional rights in connection with law enforcement: We are told that the constitution should be interpreted to reach the right balance between liberty and security.[37] Reaching that balance requires the judge to consider the consequences for liberty and security of adopting alternative rules—that is, to make judgments about the effects in the future of adopting one rather than another interpretation of the relevant constitutional provisions. Balancing, as has been widely observed, is the exercise by judges of the kinds of judgments legislators routinely make.[38] Again, a judge who adopts balancing as an interpretive theory will often be looking forward in much the way that a legislator does. To that extent, the judge will have incentives similar to those of a legislator.

Undoubtedly, the judge's incentive to do the judicial job well induces a higher ratio of backward- to forward-looking deliberation than does the legislator's incentive to retain office. I suggest, though, that the difference in the ratios is not as large as is typically assumed.

Courts have different institutional characteristics from legislatures, of course, going beyond the fact that the ratio of their backward-looking to forward-looking focus is somewhat higher than that of legislatures. Conventionally, it is said that courts have an obligation to hear claims and arguments offered them by anyone with a case to make, and to provide reasons for their action or inaction, whereas legislatures get to choose the issues they deal with and have no duty to provide reasons for what they do. Further, the obligations to hear all cases and provide reasons are said to increase the likelihood that courts will reach correct results. These differences do exist, but, as with the issues I have already discussed, they are often described as larger than they really are.

The first point to note is that the conventional arguments rarely connect the normative claims about the duty to listen and provide reasons to descriptive claims explaining why judges have incentives to comply with the "duties," which are rarely if ever enforced by some other body that punishes judges who

[36] For complementary discussions, see David S. Law, "Generic Constitutional Law," 89 Minn. L. Rev. 652 (2005) (discussing balancing as a general approach to constitutional interpretation); David M. Beatty, The Ultimate Rule of Law (2004) (discussing proportionality review as a general approach to constitutional adjudication).

[37] See, e.g., David Cole, "Enemy Aliens," 54 Stan. L. Rev. 953, 955 (2002) (a strong civil libertarian's endorsement of the standard formulation: "In the wake of September 11, we plainly need to rethink the balance between liberty and security.").

[38] See, e.g., T. Alexander Aleinikoff, "Constitutional Law in the Age of Balancing," 96 Yale L. J. 943 (1987); Gerald Gunther, "In Search of Judicial Quality on a Changing Court: The Case of Justice Powell," 24 Stan. L. Rev. 1001 (1972).

do not provide reasons for their decisions. I have suggested that the incentives lie in the judges' desire to do a good job, where what counts as a good job is defined by the conventions about what judges ought to do. But, as I also suggested, legislators also want to do a good job in addition to wanting to be reelected. And there may well be conventions about what being a good legislator entails, conventions that I suspect include being willing to listen to complaints from constituents and to explain publicly, in newsletters, speeches, and the like, why the legislator does what she does.[39]

True, legislatures as institutions have no duty to provide reasons for what they do. Sometimes there are committee reports and the like, but sometimes not. And even committee reports are not actions by the legislature as a body in the way that judicial opinions are the actions of a court. Legislators often give their reasons in debates leading up to a statute's enactment, or afterward in public discourse about what the legislature did or did not do. It is not clear to me why it should matter that the *institution* gives reasons as long as individual members—that is, individual legislators—do.

The importance of a distinctive judicial duty to listen can also be exaggerated. First, not all constitutional courts are designed to entertain individual claims. Some require that constitutional complaints be submitted by a designated institution, typically the president, premier, the majority party in the legislature, or a minority—of some stipulated size, such as 40 percent—of the legislature. In France, for example, a group of sixty legislators can ask the Constitutional Council to assess the constitutionality of legislation before it goes into effect. When France adopted a law restricting the right of students to wear "conspicuous" religious symbols—aimed at young Muslim women wearing head scarves—the Constitutional Council did not have a chance to evaluate the statute, which obviously raised serious constitutional concerns, because only twenty legislators in one house and thirty-six in the other voted against the law. Other constitutional systems allow individuals to raise claims in lower courts, but give those courts some discretion in deciding whether to dismiss the claims or to forward them to the nation's specialized constitutional court. The duty to listen, that is, is not a characteristic of judges as such, but rather of judges in constitutional systems designed in a particular way. The duty to listen may not sharply distinguish judges from legislators in systems with other designs.

Further, systems where judges do have a duty to listen to all constitutional claims usually—and almost inevitably—give judges a variety of techniques to pay only the most cursory attention to those claims. In the United States, for example, the Supreme Court has nearly complete control over its docket, deciding in an entirely discretionary way which cases it wants to consider in

[39] It is an empirical question, on which there appears to be no information, about the strength of such conventions today.

detail. People say, "I'll take this to the Supreme Court," but if they do, there is no guarantee that the Supreme Court will listen. More formally, some courts, including those of the United States, have developed rules that screen out some cases as a matter of law. In 2004, for example, the U.S. Supreme Court invoked its doctrine of "standing"—the right to present a claim—to preclude Michael Newdow from continuing his case against the inclusion of the words "under God" in the Pledge of Allegiance. The reason was that Newdow's right to bring the claim had to rest on the fact that his daughter was enrolled in a school where, state and local law said, the Pledge had to be recited every day. But, the Supreme Court held, Newdow could not bring the claim because as a noncustodial parent he had no legal right under state law to control the environment to which his daughter was exposed.[40]

The real question about the duty to listen, in the present context, is once again comparative. Present the same claim to the courts and to the legislature, and then compare how seriously each one takes it. The example of Michael Newdow might be thought to show that courts will take claims more seriously. After all, he did get to the Supreme Court, where—before the Court dismissed his case—the justices listened to his arguments against having the words "under God" in the Pledge of Allegiance. In contrast, we can be confident that no one in Congress would have listened seriously to Newdow's claim that, as enacted into law, the Pledge of Allegiance violated the Constitution's ban on establishments of religion. The reason, though, is that members of Congress would have thought that Newdow's claim was obviously wrong on the merits, not that they should not be bothered to think about his arguments. The Newdow example and similar ones that could be generated about constitutional claims raised by criminal defendants and other unpopular groups are sometimes offered to show that courts are better at listening than legislatures. Most of the examples do not show that, though. Instead, they show that sometimes courts and legislatures disagree about what the constitution means, to the point where legislatures sometimes treat as silly some constitutional claims that courts think substantial. As I have observed, that sort of disagreement does not count against the capacity of legislatures to listen to constitutional claims.

Taking all these items together, I think the fair conclusion is this: There are surely differences between the conventional norms defining what a good judge does and what a good legislator does, but they are probably not night-and-day ones.

Two concluding points arise from the constitution-based standard I have identified as the right one to use. The constitution-based standard raises a question about the connection between the purported duties of judges and the likelihood that they will come up with correct answers to constitutional questions.

---

[40] Elk Grove Unified Sch. Dist. v. Newdow, 542 U.S. 1 (2004).

The duty to listen and give reasons might well increase the chance that judges will give a certain kind of answer—roughly, one that treats the constitution as a document embodying Reason. It is less clear, though, that the duty to give reasons, in itself, would increase the likelihood that a judge will correctly determine what the original understanding of a constitution's terms was. Put more generally, the claim about the relation between judges' duties and their ability to come up with correct answers must be that those duties will improve their ability to come up with the right answers, no matter what our criteria of rightness are. That claim seems to me quite implausible.

To see the next issue, consider a stipulated constitution-based standard, such as whether a decision maker adheres to originalist interpretation. What incentives do decision makers have to do so? Notably, we can ask that question about judges no less than about legislators. As far as I can tell, the only incentive a judge has to adopt any stipulated standard is internal to the judge; that is, judges are socialized into accepting that standard. Without a detailed examination of socialization processes, I would not reject the possibility that legislators are similarly socialized.[41] A much more important conclusion suggests itself once we put stipulated standards to one side, and consider whether the decision maker orients himself or herself to the nation's constitutional tradition. As I said earlier, in a reasonably stable democracy nearly everyone who becomes a legislator or a judge will almost surely have been socialized into doing so.

My conclusion from this comparison of judges and legislators is that there are indeed differences—hardly a surprising conclusion—but that the differences are probably not dramatic. If I am right, it might also well be that legislators can do a "good enough" job of constitutional interpretation—"good enough" relative to how well courts do the job.

The Institutional Level: Evaluating Legislative Performance

Legislatures are different from legislators. The processes through which legislatures aggregate the positions of individual legislators might make legislative outcomes either more responsive to constitutional concerns, or less so. Here I identify criteria we can use to evaluate legislative *outputs*, in contrast to the inputs I have dealt with in discussing legislators' incentives.

A modest way of beginning is this observation: Judges are (almost universally) lawyers. Legislators need not be.[42] Judges will have greater incentives to

[41] In particular, the lawyers among them seem to me likely to be exposed to roughly the same socialization institutions as judges are, and so might well accept internally the stipulated standard just as judges are said to do.

[42] For example, in Peabody's survey of members of the U.S. Congress, *supra* note 9, around half of the respondents were not lawyers. In the 108th Congress, 59 percent of the Senate and

orient themselves to a nation's constitutional traditions to the extent that legal training is valuable in allowing someone to do so. The ordinary processes of socialization—growing up taking civics classes, studying a nation's history in school, and the like—may induce those who are not lawyers to have a properly constitutionalist orientation, but for present purposes I will assume that being a lawyer increases the chance that a person has such an orientation because that assumption *weakens* my argument about the capacity of courts relative to legislatures and executives to take a constitutionalist stance.

Of course, nonlawyers can obtain assistance from lawyers. In the United States, the chief executive need not be a lawyer, but the Department of Justice provides legal advice to the president, including advice on constitutional questions. Peabody's survey of members of the U.S. Congress indicates that a large proportion of them do rely on lawyers "for help with constitutional issues."[43]

What incentives do legislators have for seeking assistance from lawyers on constitutional matters?[44] One important reason arises from the fact that legislators are involved in making and implementing *law*. They will often find it helpful to have legal assistance if they are to do so effectively. A legislator will want help in drafting legislation that, if enacted, would actually accomplish what the legislator wants to accomplish; an executive official will want assistance in figuring out what the legislature has directed her agency to do. The legislator's incentive is provided by the job itself: Creating a legal staff will help a legislator do the job of being a legislator, and whatever motivates a legislator to take and seek to retain the job also motivates her to create a legal staff.

Drafting and interpreting legislation does not inevitably entail interpreting the constitution. A legal staff created to help legislators do the job might therefore not actually give advice on constitutional matters. Yet, the staff itself—by assumption, lawyers—may *want* to do so, and might even give it unsolicited, in the course of performing its other duties. Legislators might not have direct incentives to get advice on constitutional matters, but they do have incentives to create legal staffs to advise them on the law. Constitutional advice from these staffs might then be a by-product of their creation.[45]

---

40 percent of the House of Representatives are lawyers. *See* Mildred L. Amer, "Membership of the 108th Congress: A Profile," CRS Report for Congress, *at* http://www.senate.gov/reference/resources/pdf/RS21379.pdf (last updated April 21, 2004). As of 2003, 61 percent of New York, 48 percent of California, and 30 percent of Missouri legislators were lawyers. *See* William M. Corrigan, Jr., "The Argument for Lawyers in the Legislature: A Proud History of Service," 59 J. Mo. B. 216 (2003), *available at* http://www.mobar.org/journal/2003/sepoct/prezpage.htm (visited Jan. 20, 2006).

[43] Peabody, *supra* note 9, at 151–53.

[44] I put aside the prudential concern for enacting legislation that will survive judicial review.

[45] I draw the idea of a by-product from Jon Elster, Sour Grapes: Studies in the Subversion of Rationality 43 (1983), but do not contend that constitutional advice is an essential by-product of creating a legal staff, either in the usual sense that it inevitably occurs once a legal staff is created or in Elster's sense that it cannot occur by intentionally seeking to obtain it.

Executive officials and legislators might also create legal staffs that special-ize in constitutional law itself. The reason, at least in separation-of-powers systems, is the ambition that James Madison said should be set to counter ambition.[46] A chief executive or a legislature out to aggrandize power might offer constitution-based as well as policy-based justifications for its actions. Its opponents in the legislature or the executive branch would be well advised to have constitutional arguments at hand in the political combat that will ensue.[47] The dynamics are clear: Once one side offers a constitution-based ar-gument,[48] the other side has an incentive to counter the argument. A good way of doing so is to develop a specialized staff.[49] And, once again, such a staff might take its professional mission to be attention to and advice about the constitution as a whole, not merely about separation-of-powers issues.[50]

Focusing on the incentives to create and rely on a legal staff weakens the force of a recent argument that the emergence in the past decade or so of strong party discipline in the U.S. Congress undermines the incentives legis-lators have to develop constitutional interpretations independent of those offered by the president.[51] Legislators create staffs that are, to some degree, in-dependent of their immediate control because they know, or fear, that they will not be in the majority forever, and might want to have some resources they can use when they lose control of the legislature. Among the staffs Congress has created are the Congressional Research Service, the Government Account-ability Office, and inspectors general in executive departments.[52] Even or per-haps particularly in a world of strong party discipline, these agencies provide resources for constitutional arguments by members of the legislative minority,

[46] The Federalist no. 51.

[47] Backbenchers, particularly permanent backbenchers, might be the moving force in parlia-mentary systems for the creation of this sort of legal staff, as I observe in Mark Tushnet, "Weak-Form Judicial Review: Its Implications for Legislatures," in Constitutionalism in the Charter Era (Grant Huscroft & Ian Brodie eds., 2005).

[48] Which, I emphasize, it need not always do. What matters is that the first step be taken.

[49] The Office of Legal Counsel in the U.S. Department of Justice (discussed in the next chap-ter) historically has taken its primary role to be defending the constitutional prerogatives of the presidency against what its staff regards as congressional intrusions. That the Madisonian ambi-tion only gives an incentive, but does not compel an outcome, is indicated by the fact that the U.S. Congress has not yet developed an equivalent specialized staff, although units like the counsel's offices in the House and Senate have the potential to become Congress's version. For a normative discussion, see Elizabeth Garrett & Adrian Vermeule, "Institutional Design of a Thay-erian Congress," 50 Duke L. J. 1277 (2001).

[50] One implication of this argument is that constitutional deliberations that affect legislators might occur behind the scenes, as legal staffs give advice to those actors. The fact that legislators do not, or only rarely, mention constitutional matters in their public discussions would then not be evidence that they have not already engaged in deliberation about the constitution.

[51] See Daryl Levinson, "Empire-Building Government in Constitutional Law," 118 Harv. L. Rev. 915 (2005).

[52] I put aside that these institutions already exist and were created before the emergence of real party discipline in Congress.

whose ambition certainly counters the ambition of the presidency.[53] Incentives do not guarantee performance, of course, and incentives can change: Professional staffs can become strongly politicized, for example, and their contribution to disinterested constitutional analysis thereby weakened. Again, though, those observations raise empirical questions, not analytical ones.

The legal staff is an *institutional* feature of legislatures, created in response to individual legislators' incentives. Our criteria for evaluating legislative performance should focus, similarly, on the legislature as an institution—composed, of course, of individuals, but producing outcomes that might not be directly responsive to any individual legislator's incentives or interests. Paying attention to institutional action suggests a number of evaluative criteria.

First, evaluation should focus on institutional performance, not individual behavior. It is trivially easy to compile a list of constitutionally irresponsible or thoughtless proposals legislators make as they engage in position taking. A member will shoot out a press release responding to some local outrage or put a bill in the hopper without taking any time to consider its constitutionality. Often these proposals result from the member's desire to grandstand, to do something that gets his name on the nightly news in the member's home district. They are not serious proposals for legislation, and the member has no real expectation that they would be enacted.

Noting grandstanding actions of this sort provides no basis for evaluating a legislature's performance of constitutional interpretation. What we need to examine are institutional actions, those that represent the outcome of a completed congressional process. Grandstanding proposals may count against assertions that members of Congress act in a constitutionally responsible manner, but the failure of such proposals to move through the legislative process should count in favor of assertions that Congress does so. Institutional actions proceed through a complex set of organizational structures. Those structures, designed for other purposes, may sometimes serve (imperfectly and as a byproduct) to screen out constitutionally irresponsible actions. (Institutional actions can, of course, consist of inaction as well. Failures to enact legislation that the constitution requires are irresponsible. Some constitutions do impose substantial affirmative duties on legislatures, but the conventional wisdom is that the U.S. Constitution is not among them. For that reason, I focus on actions in what follows.)

---

[53] According to its Web site, the American Law Division of the Congressional Research Service "responds to congressional requests for legal analysis and information involving federal and state statutory and case law. These inquiries span the range of legal questions that may emerge from the congressional agenda and representational needs of Members, from constitutional questions of separation of powers and executive-legislative relations to inquiries arising out of federal, state, and/or international law." *See* http://www.loc.gov/crsinfo/divwork/aldwork.html (visited Jan. 20, 2006). According to its Web site, the Government Accountability Office is "an independent, nonpartisan agency" that assists members of Congress with their inquiries about government operations. *See* http://www.gao.gov/about/history.html (visited Jan. 20, 2006).

Examining institutional actions, however, raises its own difficulties. Judges write opinions when they decide what the Constitution means. Legislatures usually do not. Enacted statutes typically become effective without an accompanying statement of the constitutional rationale on which the legislature relied.[54] Determining the constitutional basis for a completed action by a legislature requires us to examine a range of materials, such as committee reports, floor debate, and even newspaper stories, from which we can infer the constitutional basis on which the legislature acted. Such inferences will inevitably be open to question. The evaluation of a legislature's performance that results from such inferences will therefore often rest on a shaky foundation. Still, we should do the best we can.

In addition, legislators often might have varying rationales for their belief that a proposal is constitutional. Unlike judges, they need not sign an opinion giving a majority's position on the constitutional question.[55] Ultimately, each legislator must do no more than vote for the bill. But sometimes one constitutional rationale might be a good one and another bad. Imagine a statute adopted by a vote of 80–20. Sixty members of the majority may have thought about the constitutional questions the statute raised, and thought the statute justified by a rationale that, on detached reflection, one concludes was mistaken. But twenty members of the majority had a constitutionally good rationale for their votes. Without taking a position on the question, I simply observe that one reasonably could either challenge or defend the institutional action under these circumstances.

In addition to examining only completed actions, we should examine actions taken outside the shadow cast by courts in strong-form systems. At this point we can deepen the analysis of position taking and grandstanding. Judicial review provides an opportunity for the legislature as a body, not just individual legislators, to engage in grandstanding by enacting statutes that the legislators can be confident will be held unconstitutional. Consider a situation in which legislators have a choice: they can enact a splashy statute that directly attacks a problem, albeit in a way that the courts will find unconstitutional, or they can enact a boring one, full of obscure details, that might be a bit less effective in achieving the majority's policy goals but that would be

---

[54] One can design institutional mechanisms for supplying such rationales. For example, a "Committee on the Constitution" in each house could be given responsibility for preparing an authoritative statement on the constitutionality of every statute (or for stating that the committee could come to no conclusion on constitutionality). Whether such mechanisms would counter the political processes that lead people to agree on specific proposals without agreeing on their constitutional rationales, and, perhaps more importantly, would overcome the pressure that time places on legislators who need to do something, seems to me quite questionable. And, of course, one would have to examine the incentives legislators have for creating such a committee. I take up aspects of these questions in chapter 5.

[55] I leave aside here the fact that the Supreme Court sometimes issues opinions in which only a plurality of the justices accept a single rationale.

unquestionably constitutional. Presumably, enacting a statute that advances policy goals is attractive politically. Sometimes, though, enacting the splashy, but unconstitutional, statute may be even more politically attractive. Legislators then can take credit for trying to do something and blame the courts for the failure, even though the other statute might have been both constitutional and nearly as effective in achieving the legislators' policy goals. And, of course, they can then enact the constitutionally permissible statute, "fine-tuning" the original one after the courts' decisions.[56]

This behavior, which we might call anticipatory disobedience, is pretty clearly undesirable (except to the extent that it may be valuable as a vehicle allowing representatives to blow off steam before they get down to the serious business of legislating). Even if rather common, though, anticipatory disobedience might shed little light on the question of legislative constitutional performance. People will overeat if someone gives them free candy, but that fact says little about their actual desires regarding nutrition. To determine those desires, one would have to take people away from the setting in which they have access to free candy. Analogously, we can get a better sense of a legislature's actual constitutional capacity if we examine only cases in which the legislature cannot engage in anticipatory disobedience. The fact that legislators behave badly when they know that someone is around to bail them out tells us little about how they would behave were they to have full responsibility for their actions. Such cases do exist: the "political questions" cases where there is no realistic prospect of judicial review, so that legislators know that they have full and exclusive responsibility for arriving at a conclusion that, according to their oaths of office, must be consistent with the constitution.

A third criterion arises out of the premise of reasonable disagreement about a constitution's meaning and about interpretive method. One of the most serious pitfalls in evaluating legislative constitutional performance occurs when an analyst sets up a standard and asks whether the legislature's action conforms to the standard, when others might reasonably set up a quite different standard. The posited standard may be the analyst's own conclusion about the constitution's proper meaning, or it may be a standard drawn from Supreme Court decisions. Divergence from the standard nonetheless may tell us almost nothing about the legislature's constitutional performance.

Take, for example, the problem of campaign finance and the First Amendment. Suppose we take the U.S. Supreme Court's decisions in *Buckley v. Valeo* and *McConnell v. Federal Election Commission* as the standard by which we measure Congress's constitutional performance.[57] Undoubtedly, many existing proposals for campaign finance reform are inconsistent with the doctrine laid out in those cases. Assume that supporters of such proposals do not really

---

[56] *See* Pickerill, *supra* note 5, at 27.
[57] *Buckley*, 424 U.S. 1 (1976); *McConnell*, 540 U.S. 93 (2003).

expect that the Supreme Court will soon overrule those decisions. It seems to me quite wrong to say that these supporters are behaving in a constitutionally irresponsible manner. After all, many respected constitutional scholars, and even some Supreme Court justices, believe that the cases were wrongly decided. More generally, a legislature can act responsibly, in constitutional terms, even when it enacts statutes that the courts eventually hold unconstitutional as long as the constitutional position asserted by the legislature is a reasonable one.

This problem arises even outside the context of judicial review. Consider here the furious debate over whether President Clinton had committed an impeachable offense. The constitutional language was clear, but its meaning was not. Relying on their interpretation of the original understanding of the term "high crimes and Misdemeanors," some argued that a president could be impeached only for actions taken in his official capacity that posed a serious threat to the nation's political integrity.[58] Relying on a different interpretation of the original understanding and on some obvious functional considerations, others gave the example of a president who commits a murder for nonpolitical reasons and insisted that a president could be impeached for actions taken in his personal capacity, when such actions cast grave doubt on the president's personal integrity and on his ability to continue to represent the nation's people.[59]

The House voted to impeach the president, adopting a theory more like the second than the first.[60] The second theory may be wrong, but it is clearly a reasonable one: the standard is consistent with the Constitution's language, it makes functional sense, and it is consistent with at least some aspects of Congress's past practices in impeachment.[61] It seems clear to me that

[58] For a discussion of the competing interpretations of the constitutional term, see Richard A. Posner, An Affair of State: The Investigation, Impeachment, and Trial of President Clinton 98–99 (1999).

[59] Cass R. Sunstein, "Impeachment and Stability," 67 Geo. Wash. L. Rev. 699, 709 (1999) ("[A] President would be impeachable for an extremely heinous 'private' crime, such as murder or rape."); see also Frank O. Bowman III & Stephen L. Sepinuck, "'High Crimes and Misdemeanors': Defining the Constitutional Limits on Presidential Impeachment," 72 S. Cal. L. Rev. 1517, 1545 (1999) ("Criminal sexual misbehavior such as rape . . . would surely be an impeachable offense.").

[60] In saying that the House "adopted" a theory, I am aware of the problem of inference from behavior only, discussed earlier.

[61] The House Judiciary Committee refused to vote an article of impeachment against President Richard Nixon based on irregularities in his preparation of a tax return. For a discussion, see Laurence H. Tribe, "Defining 'High Crimes and Misdemeanors': Basic Principles," 67 Geo. Wash. L. Rev. 712, 721 (1999). The House did impeach Walter Nixon, former chief judge of the United States District Court for the Southern District of Mississippi, for actions taken at least arguably outside his official capacity, in connection with false testimony to a federal grand jury about telephone calls he made to a state prosecutor in exchange for payment. Nixon v. United States, 506 U.S. 224, 226–28 (1993).

opponents of the Clinton impeachment have no real ground for saying that the House acted in a constitutionally irresponsible manner in adopting the second theory.[62] Some expressed concern that the House did not "adopt" a definition of impeachable offenses,[63] but I find it hard to understand what the effect would be of a standard adopted by a majority vote in the House, prior to the vote on impeachment itself, on a House member who voted against the standard, even if that member believes that the first theory is the constitutionally mandated one.[64]

The more general point is that many constitutional questions admit of reasonable disagreement and that all sides in a dispute can take different positions while all remain faithful to the constitution. Take the problem in a different setting. The U.S. Supreme Court issues a constitutional decision. I may think that the Constitution pretty clearly means something else, and indeed three Supreme Court justices agree with me. I doubt that anyone could fairly charge me with being faithless to the Constitution were I to persist in holding the view I held before the Court acted.

Now, take the problem in the setting with which this chapter is concerned: A legislature acts in a way inconsistent with some stipulated standard, whether it be the critic's or the courts'. The mere fact that the legislature disagrees with the courts or with the critic does not establish that the legislature behaved in a manner demonstrating its inability to arrive at reasonable conclusions about the constitution.

Thus, a legislature may be wrong, from my point of view or from that of the courts. Its "errors" do not, however, show that the legislature is performing badly as a constitutional decision maker. At most, these errors show that the legislature disagrees with me, or the courts, about what the constitution means. Evaluations of legislative constitutional performance must therefore take account of the fact of reasonable disagreement over the constitution's meaning. The criterion an evaluator must apply is this: Did the legislature do something that is not at all oriented to the nation's constitutional traditions?

---

[62] As discussed in the next chapter, perhaps one can criticize the House of Representatives for failing to conduct a focused discussion of the definition of impeachable offenses until relatively late in the proceedings. A hearing exploring the question took place before a subcommittee of the House Judiciary Committee on November 9, 1998. *See generally* Background and History of Impeachment: Hearing Before the Subcomm. on the Constitution of the House Comm. on the Judiciary, 105th Cong. 230 (1998) (reporting the prepared statements of nineteen constitutional experts).

[63] *See, e.g.*, Susan Low Bloch, "A Report Card on the Impeachment: Judging the Institutions that Judged President Clinton," 63 Law & Contemp. Probs. 143, 150 n. 37 (Winter/Spring 2000) ("Unfortunately, neither the full Judiciary Committee nor the House as a whole ever articulated or agreed on a general standard.").

[64] At this point I am making no observation about whether President Clinton's behavior actually was inconsistent with the standard defined by this second theory. My concern is only with the adoption of the theory as the basis upon which to evaluate his behavior.

Obviously this criterion tilts the field of evaluation in the legislature's favor—setting a baseline that is truly a line rather than a point—because of the fairly wide range of reasonable positions available on nearly every constitutional question.[65] But, to me, it is the only criterion that makes sense.

Finally, evaluation of a legislature's performance must consider only situations in which the constitution actually provides guidance. Broadly described, constitutions create political structures and prescribe some particular outcomes. Across a wide range, constitutions say nothing about the outcomes that people operating within its structures must reach. To make the point obvious, the U.S. Constitution says nothing about whether the highest marginal rate should be 26 percent, 39 percent, or 54 percent in the income tax system, even if there is a constitutional requirement that tax rates not be confiscatory,[66] or whether there should be a time limit on eligibility for federally provided public assistance, even if there is some constitutional requirement that legislatures provide minimum subsistence for the needy. Clearly, one cannot evaluate the degree to which congressional action conforms to the constitution when the constitution gives the legislature unfettered discretion to act.

The income tax and welfare reform examples raise what we usually think of as ordinary policy questions. According to some respectable constitutional theories, some constitutional issues have the same analytic structure. According to these theories, constitutions establish structures giving participants incentives to respond to constitutional questions in position-specific ways and treat as constitutionally valid the outcome of the political process that operates according to those incentives. Herbert Wechsler's account of U.S. federalism is one example of such a theory.[67] According to Wechsler, the U.S. Constitution's structures gave political actors incentives to assert varying positions about the proper distribution of power between the national government and state governments. Whatever accommodation the political actors reach is what the Constitution means.[68] Jesse Choper offered a similar theory

[65] The evaluator must therefore be careful to ensure that he or she not unfairly label as "unreasonable" a constitutional position with which he or she disagrees. So, for example, while I believe that impeachment's opponents had the better case on what the standard for impeachment is, I believe as well that impeachment's supporters offered a reasonable, albeit erroneous, standard.

[66] In E. Enters. v. Apfel, 524 U.S. 498 (1998), four justices rejected the proposition that a tax scheme could never be an unconstitutional taking. Id. at 522 (O'Connor, J., writing for a plurality of herself and Justices Rehnquist, Thomas and Scalia); id. at 538 (Thomas, J., concurring) (agreeing with the plurality that the statute at issue violates the takings clause).

[67] See generally Herbert Wechsler, "The Political Safeguards of Federalism: The Role of the States in the Composition and Selection of the National Government," 54 Colum. L. Rev. 543, 546 (1954) (arguing that "the existence of the states as governmental entities and as sources of the standing law is in itself the prime determinant of our working federalism, coloring the nature and the scope of our national legislative processes from their inception").

[68] Id. at 559–60. Obviously, such accommodations change over time, and so the Constitution's meaning changes. But this is not anomalous with respect to the constitutional provisions addressed by theories like Wechsler's.

of separation of powers.[69] The Constitution gave members of Congress and the president political interests that would be served by preserving the power of their respective institutions, setting the institutions and their members at political odds over the distribution of power within the national government. The president would seek to maximize his or her power over officials within the national government, for example, while members of Congress would try to maximize their power over the very same officials. Political combat between Congress and the president will produce some outcome and, according to Choper, that outcome is what the separation of powers means.

The implication of such theories for evaluating legislative constitutional responsibility is clear: The concept of legislative constitutional responsibility is inapt with respect to provisions where the constitution does no more than create a political structure and incentives for the occupants of different positions. The constitution, according to theories of this sort, provides no standard whatever against which to assess congressional action.

Of course, constitutions do specify standards in many of their provisions. Further, theories like Wechsler's and Choper's are quite controversial, rejected by the Supreme Court and by many constitutional scholars.[70] The criterion that would allow us to select for examination only cases outside the range of orientation to the constitutional tradition suggests, however, that mere controversy is insufficient to disqualify a theory from the terrain. So, for example, a member of Congress who says openly that, as far as she is concerned, the Constitution places no limits on Congress's power to regulate state governments—a member, that is, who accepts Wechsler's theory—is acting in a constitutionally responsible manner.

One limitation on the scope of this final criterion deserves special note. Few legislators will, in fact, assert that the constitution places no substantive limits on what they may do. As a representative, Gerald Ford notoriously asserted that an impeachable offense "is whatever a majority of the House

[69] *See generally* Jesse H. Choper, Judicial Review and the National Political Process: A Functional Reconsideration of the Role of the Supreme Court (1980). Choper's theory differs from Wechsler's in a subtle but important way. Choper argues that questions of federalism and the separation of powers should be nonjusticiable, meaning that the courts should not resolve them. One can agree with that argument while also believing that the Constitution does in fact supply an answer to the questions: nonjusticiability means not that the Constitution defines the separation of powers questions as whatever allocation of power the political branches reach, but only that the courts will not specify the constitutionally required separation of powers.

[70] *See, e.g.,* United States v. Lopez, 514 U.S. 549, 578 (1995) (Kennedy, J., concurring) (referring to the absence of structural mechanisms to require members of Congress to consider the interests of states when they adopt legislation); INS v. Chadha, 462 U.S. 919, 942 n.13 (1983) (rejecting the proposition, implicit in Choper's approach, that "the assent of the Executive to a bill which contains a provision contrary to the Constitution . . . shields it from judicial review"); William P. Marshall, "Federalization: A Critical Overview," 44 DePaul L. Rev. 719, 728–32 (1995) (concluding that "the political checks that do exist do not go very far in assuring that federalism concerns are adequately protected").

[considers it] to be at a given moment in history."[71] As far as I can tell, this position had no purchase whatever during the Clinton impeachment. Impeachment's proponents and opponents alike produced standards for determining whether the president's actions constituted an impeachable offense; no one said, at least in public, that Ford had been correct and that the House could impeach the president simply because a majority wanted to do so. I suspect that the reason for this restraint is that members of Congress know that their constituents believe that the Constitution—in its impeachment provisions—means something, and that openly declaring that a constitutional provision (or arrangement, like federalism and the separation of powers) has no substantive content would demonstrate constitutional irresponsibility to the constituents, even if there is some theory of constitutional responsibility under which such a declaration is reasonable.

The criteria I have identified pretty clearly cut down on the number of cases we have for examining legislative constitutional performance with an eye to determining how well legislators do the job of constitutional interpretation. Still, I believe that using other criteria for selecting cases to examine would distort the evaluation we seek.

A Note on Executive Officials, and on State and Local Legislatures in the United States

So far I have written about legislators and legislatures generically, and occasionally about executive officials. But, of course, not all legislatures or officials are the same. High-level executive officials can get advice, often in real time, from lawyers. Police officers on the beat cannot. National legislatures may have more time to consider constitutional questions than city councils, and better advice when they do. It would be silly to contend that the incentives and institutional structures I have described affect *all* legislatures and executive officials to the same degree, and I do not. My focus is on national legislatures and high-level officials. There are reasons rooted in the structure of constitutional law for that focus. The most interesting questions of constitutional theory, those to which weak-form review is responsive, involve decisions by the highest lawmaking authorities in a nation. Nonconstitutional law can deal with actions by decision makers subordinate to those authorities.

The easiest place to begin is with low-level executive officials such as police officers or public social workers. Suppose a police officer beats a confession out of a suspect. Holding the officer liable for violating the constitution raises no issues of high constitutional theory.[72] Nations without judicially enforced

---

[71] 116 Cong. Rec. H11, 913 (daily ed. Apr. 15, 1970) (statement of Rep. Ford).

[72] The point was made in the United States in Charles L. Black, Jr., Structure and Relationship in Constitutional Law 90 (1969) ("Due process of law ought to be held to require that an

constitutions, such as Great Britain before 2000 and the Netherlands today, find it easy to deal with such cases. They start with the observation that the police officer has the authority to detain and question the suspect only because some statute gives him that authority. They continue by finding that the legislature that enacted that statute surely did not intend to authorize police officers to engage in unconstitutional actions. Of course, they say—sometimes implicitly, sometimes explicitly—the legislature *might* have the power to authorize the action, but until the legislature does so quite clearly, the courts will not assume that the legislature did so.

British courts have been particularly vigorous in implementing this approach, known as the *ultra vires* (meaning "beyond the power" granted) doctrine. A good example from another nation is the decision by the Supreme Court of Israel limiting the techniques the country's security service could use in interrogating prisoners suspected of aiding "terrorists."[73] The Court held that the nation's parliament had indeed authorized the security service to use normal investigative techniques, like those used by the ordinary police, but had not authorized them to use exceptional techniques such as sleep deprivation and extended periods in uncomfortable physical positions: "There is no statute that grants General Security Service (GSS) investigators with special interrogating powers that are either different or more significant than those granted the police investigator."[74] The Court's opinion observed, "Whether it is appropriate for Israel, in light of its security difficulties, to sanction physical means is an issue that must be decided by the legislative branch which represents the people."[75]

Invoking the ultra vires doctrine allows the courts to question executive actions while leaving it open to legislatures to decide that the constitution is not in fact violated by those actions. It can be a quite powerful doctrine for keeping executive behavior within constitutional bounds. The U.S. Supreme Court invoked the ultra vires idea, without using the term, in its decision invalidating President George W. Bush's policy of detaining so-called enemy combatants without giving them access to the courts.[76] One of the people detained was a U.S. citizen, Yaser Hamdi. A statute enacted in 1991 provides that "[n]o citizen shall be imprisoned or otherwise detained by the United States except pursuant to an Act of Congress." Forgoing analysis of the president's claim that he had inherent authority as commander in chief to detain citizens when he believed that such detentions would enhance the nation's

---

active judgment by the legislative branch, rather than by the police chief, on how much of our personal liberty and security we must surrender in the interest of a practicable administration of justice.").

[73] It is hard to come up with neutral language to describe what are politically contested facts, but I have done the best I can.

[74] Public Committee Against Torture v. State of Israel, HCJ 5100/94, July 15, 1999, ¶ 32

[75] *Id.* at ¶ 39.

[76] Hamdi v. Rumsfeld, 542 U.S. 507 (2004).

military operations, four justices concluded that Congress had in fact authorized the detention of citizens found in Afghanistan, for purposes of ensuring that they would not return to combat against the United States, when it authorized military operations there after September 11, 2003. Justice Sandra Day O'Connor was careful to refer to the "narrow category" of citizen-detainees with which her analysis dealt, thereby suggesting that the authorization of action in Afghanistan might not extend to detention of other citizens seized elsewhere.

As the *Hamdi* decision suggests, the ultra vires doctrine does not raise serious questions of constitutional theory because the legislature can always enact a statute authorizing the action and thereby expressing its view on what the constitution permits—a view that is, technically, not in conflict with the courts' prior action. The ultra vires doctrine allows my analysis to focus on legislative capacity to interpret the constitution responsibly.[77]

A doctrine similar in structure to the ultra vires doctrine allows me to focus on *national* legislative capacity, in federal nations. The ultra vires doctrine shifts attention from the executive official to the legislature that enacted the statute that was the source of the official's purported authority. A different doctrine, known as *preemption*, allows us to shift attention from a state or local legislature to the national legislature. The legislative authority of national governments and state or local governments often overlaps. The national government preempts state legislation when it enacts a statute that deals with some subject over which both levels have power, in a manner inconsistent with state-level legislation.[78]

Sometimes the national legislature will not have dealt with some subject over which both levels have power, but a state government will have done so, and in a constitutionally questionable manner. How could preemption doctrine come into play here? Courts could begin their analysis by noting that the national legislature had the power to deal with the subject. Its failure to do so, they could continue, reflected its judgment that state legislatures would deal with it in a constitutionally responsible manner. So, the courts could conclude, the national legislature should be taken to have preempted the state-level statute—that is, to have foreclosed the state from enacting the statute.

This use of preemption is not at all theoretical. In 1956 the U.S. Supreme Court barred the states from enforcing their laws against seditious activity directed at the United States.[79] Such laws, which obviously raise serious free

---

[77] Ordinary ultra vires doctrine controls what administrative agencies do. So, for example, the British Human Rights Act 1998 applies to acts of subordinate officials and lawmaking bodies, but not to primary legislation, again reflecting the point that real questions about the relationship between judicial review and self-governance arise only in connection with primary legislation.

[78] Fully spelled out, preemption doctrine gets quite complicated, and I provide only the outlines here.

[79] Pennsylvania v. Nelson, 350 U.S. 497 (1956).

speech questions, were preempted by the existing federal antisedition statute, the Court held. In another constitutionally sensitive area, the Court invoked the preemption doctrine to bar states from enforcing their libel laws against statements made in political broadcasts, holding that federal regulation of broadcasting preempted state libel laws even though there was no provision in federal law saying anything one way or the other about libel.[80]

A robust implied preemption doctrine could be quite important in federal nations where the national government has expansive powers even when those powers are not exercised. Courts could invoke the doctrine to overturn state and local legislation without raising questions about the ability of the nation's people to govern themselves by enacting national legislation on the very same subject. That point is driven home by another aspect of a well-designed preemption doctrine. Just as a legislature can expressly authorize an action that the courts find ultra vires because it is constitutionally questionable, so the national legislature can expressly authorize a state legislature to adopt a law the courts find constitutionally questionable.[81] The courts need not be taken to be confronting "the people" in any dramatic way when they invoke the constitution against state legislatures in areas where the national government has the power to preempt or permit state-level action. All they are doing is insisting that the *nation's* people focus on what the courts regard as a constitutionally questionable action. The tensions of judicial review, constitutionalism, and democratic self-governance arise only if the courts disagree with what the national legislature does once it has focused on the action.

I must note one final complication. The ultra vires doctrine is technically a doctrine of statutory interpretation: Courts should not construe statutes to authorize actions that the judges think are constitutionally questionable. Some constitutional courts lack the power to interpret statutes. Many European constitutional courts, for example, are supposed to do no more than interpret the constitution. Nearly every one, though, has developed some technique that allows it actually to interpret statutes. Some, for example, have taken upon themselves the power to say, "If this statute were interpreted thusly, it would be unconstitutional, and therefore we interpret it otherwise."[82] The U.S. Supreme Court is in a more difficult position with respect to actions by

---

[80] Farmers Educational & Cooperative Union v. WDAY, Inc., 360 U.S. 525 (1959).

[81] For the United States *see* In re Rahrer, 140 U.S. 545 (1891) (upholding as constitutional state legislation authorized by a congressional statute, after similar state legislation had been held unconstitutional).

[82] This technique has provoked some of the most persistent legal struggles in nations with specialized constitutional courts, that is, where one court is authorized to enforce the constitution while a different set of courts enforces ordinary law. The highest "ordinary" courts have not infrequently rejected the constitutional court's statutory interpretations on the ground that the constitutional court was not authorized to interpret statutes, but only to enforce the constitution. Most of these struggles have been resolved in favor of the constitutional courts' power, but some continue.

state executive officials, because the Court does not have the power, except in extraordinary cases, to interpret state law. If a state supreme court has said that its statutes authorize its police officers to act in a constitutionally questionable way, the U.S. Supreme Court is stuck with that interpretation, and can only decide whether the action is in fact unconstitutional.[83] The ultra vires doctrine can help a great deal in alleviating confrontations between courts and legislatures, but it cannot do everything.

A structurally similar problem arises in connection with preemption. Some federal systems simply deny the national government the power to preempt subnational legislation in some areas. The U.S. federal system does so in a quite small number of areas, the Canadian system in a larger number. In such systems, the question of legislative capacity to interpret the constitution in these nonpreemptible areas must be answered as to the state or provincial legislatures. My discussion of legislative incentives and structures would almost certainly need to be changed to address the modified question.[84]

CONCLUSION

The arguments in this chapter are driven by the fact that weak-form judicial review makes the job of constitutional interpretation in legislatures more important than it is in strong-form systems. I have developed reasons for thinking that the differences between courts and legislatures, with respect to the capacity to interpret the constitution, are not quite as stark as might be thought. Those reasons implicate the incentives legislators and judges have to do the job of constitutional interpretation well. The following chapter offers a number of case studies of legislative performance, as a way of seeing whether the confidence weak-form systems have in legislatures might be justified.

[83] Although some scholars contend that this limitation is rooted in the U.S. Constitution, the better analysis is that it arises because of the statutes Congress has enacted to regulate the Supreme Court's jurisdiction. Under that analysis, Congress *could* authorize the Court to interpret state law incidental to its power to consider the constitutionality of actions by state executive officials or by local governments.

[84] Because nonpreemptible areas in U.S. law are relatively small, it probably would not be either socially or constitutionally important were state legislatures to be constitutionally irresponsible in these areas.

CHAPTER 5

Constitutional Decision Making Outside the Courts

THE PREVIOUS chapter identified the criteria to use in evaluating constitutional decision making outside the courts. Studies using appropriate criteria to evaluate such decision making are rare. Here I offer several relatively informal case studies, with the hope of providing some information that will be useful in considering whether weak-form review's confidence in nonjudicial constitutional decision making is justified. I do not contend, of course, that these case studies establish that we *should* repose our confidence in such decision making. For one thing, I offer only a few case studies, whereas weak-form review implicates the entire range of constitutionally significant decisions that legislatures and executive officials might make. The case studies do go beyond the merely anecdotal accounts I criticized in the previous chapter. I believe that they are sufficient to place some burden on critics of the capacity of non-judicial decision makers to engage in good constitutional decision making—a burden of providing similar case studies showing that such decision makers do the job badly.[1]

In my judgment, the case studies show that broad-brush skepticism about nonjudicial decision makers is unwarranted. As we will see, there are some specific reasons to be skeptical about certain decision makers with respect to some decisions. For example, lawyers for executive officials might sometimes be overly protective of the executive's prerogatives. Still, the discrete skepticisms that might arise do not, I believe, seriously undermine the confidence in nonjudicial decision makers that weak-form review calls for. To that extent, they bolster the case for weak-form review.

The chapter begins by examining constitutional decision making in the U.S. Congress, and then turns to the U.S. executive branch. The chapter concludes with some examination of the way in which Canadian and British ministries, and their parliaments, have responded to the creation of weak-form review in those nations.

---

[1] In the interest of readability, I have eliminated much of the material identifying specific sources for many of my assertions. Full documentation, including some qualifications on the arguments not relevant here, can be found in Mark Tushnet, "Evaluating Congressional Constitutional Interpretation: Some Criteria and Two Informal Case Studies," 50 Duke L. J. 1395 (2001), and Mark Tushnet, "Non-Judicial Review," 40 Harv. J. on Legis. 453 (2003).

The U.S. Congress: Impeachment in the House

Congress's actions during the Clinton impeachment satisfy the criteria I identified needed to ensure a decent basis for assessing congressional constitutional performance. There was a completed congressional process, and the Walter Nixon case made it reasonably clear that no court would review any decision taken in the course of a presidential impeachment.[2] Although some important legal questions connected to impeachment have a wide range of reasonable answers, and there might be no legal standard available with respect to others, some interesting legal questions about impeachment have answers within a sufficiently narrow range that we can assess how well Congress did in answering them.

First, can Congress impeach and convict a president without removing him from office? The prospects for President Clinton's conviction and removal from office, never large, diminished as the impeachment process went on. Law professor Joseph Isenbergh suggested that the House and Senate could express their disapproval of the president's conduct by impeaching and convicting him but not removing him from office.[3] Isenbergh's argument began with the text. According to Article II, the president "shall be removed from Office on Impeachment for, and Conviction of, Treason, Bribery, or other high Crimes and Misdemeanors."[4] This is the Constitution's only reference to grounds for impeachment. Isenbergh read to be "a mandatory sentencing provision": if a president is impeached for and convicted of a high crime or misdemeanor, then the president must be removed. But, according to Isenbergh, this provision did not rule out another scenario: the president could be impeached for and convicted of something other than a high crime or misdemeanor, in which case removal from office was not mandatory but rather discretionary. In addition, Isenbergh noted that the category of high crimes and misdemeanors was well understood at the Framing to refer to offenses against the state and that removal from office of a person who committed such offenses plainly was appropriate. But, according to Isenbergh, the Framers (probably) anticipated that an official might commit misconduct, like murder, unconnected to office and yet deserving of public sanction. Impeachment for and conviction of such an offense, coupled with a sanction other than removal, is an appropriate response. Finally, Isenbergh suggested, this scenario made some functional

---

[2] *Nixon* made it only reasonably clear—not certain—that there would be no judicial review, because some aspects of that decision suggest that the Court refused to review Judge Nixon's challenge only because the justices concluded that Congress had adopted a constitutional interpretation that was, in the justices' view, a reasonable one. *See, e.g.,* 506 U.S. 224, 230 (1993) (referring to the "variety of definitions" of the word "try").

[3] The argument is set out in Joseph Isenbergh, "Impeachment and Presidential Immunity from Judicial Process," 18 Yale L. & Pol'y Rev. 53 (1999).

[4] U.S. Const., art. II, § 4.

sense, as the Clinton episode itself indicated. Presidents might engage in misconduct not severe enough to justify removal from office but sufficiently severe as to deserve the high degree of formal condemnation that impeachment and conviction would represent.

Isenbergh's proposal received some endorsement in the press but got nowhere in Congress.[5] The reasons are clear. First, and in my judgment, less important, the proposal did not actually serve the political interests of those supporting impeachment and conviction. As the impeachment wore on, it became clear that impeachment's proponents really did believe that the president should be removed from office and that to them any step short of removal was tantamount to approval of the president's conduct.

Second, and more important, Isenbergh's proposal, while not entirely insupportable, was wildly at odds with well-settled understandings about impeachment.[6] As far as I know, no serious consideration had ever been given to the possibility that civil officers could be impeached for and convicted of something less than a high crime or misdemeanor.[7] Isenbergh accurately noted that the Constitution's text made this possibility available. But text—and even modest functional sense—is not all that matters in constitutional interpretation. Practice and settled understandings matter as well. Here, practice and settled understandings were so firmly established that Isenbergh's proposal lay outside the bounds of reasonable interpretation. Nor did Isenbergh suggest why those settled understandings should be displaced in favor of an interpretation that, on his view, had always been available. Congress's inattention to the proposal demonstrated its ability to reject unreasonable constitutional interpretations.

A second issue that arose in the impeachment process was the standard of proof to be used in impeachment proceedings. House members had to decide not only what constituted an impeachable offense, but also what standard of proof they should require once they had settled on a definition. As the issue came to be framed in the House, two standards of proof (roughly speaking) were available. The first focused on facts alone, and was referred to as the

---

[5] For a discussion that reprints a series of exchanges over Isenbergh's proposal, see Akhil Reed Amar, "On Impeaching Presidents," 28 Hofstra L. Rev. 291, 317–41 (1999) (reprinting journalistic exchanges between Amar and Stuart Taylor, Jr., dealing with Isenbergh's proposal, among other topics). Taylor noted that "not one senator has warmed to" Isenbergh's proposal. *Id.* at 324. Senator Susan Collins (R-Me.) proposed a variant of Professor Isenbergh's proposal, in which the Senate would first vote on whether to find the president guilty of the impeachment charges and then on whether to remove him from office. See Lorraine Adams, "A Freshman with an Endgame Idea; As Unassuming Advocate, Collins Hopes 'Findings of Fact' Will Send Message," Wash. Post, Jan. 29, 1999, at A1.

[6] Amar correctly uses the term "mainstream" to refer to the position against which Isenbergh was arguing. Amar, *supra* note 5, at 332.

[7] Amar also asserts that Isenbergh could not point to a single Founder who expressed the Isenbergh view. *Id.* at 333.

"grand jury" standard: did the factual evidence provide a reasonable basis (probable cause) for concluding that the president had committed an impeachable offense? Some House members were attracted to the grand jury standard, because they drew an analogy between the House—which, in impeaching, acted like a grand jury preferring charges—and the Senate, which, in trying an impeachment, acted as a trial jury.[8]

The alternative standard of proof incorporated a normative conclusion: given what a majority of House members concluded the president did, would the president's action justify removing him from office? This second standard would build into the House action some of the judgments senators charged with the ultimate decision to convict would have to make. Applying the second standard, a House member would ask, "Should a senator, convinced to the degree that I am convinced of President Clinton's commission of the acts charged, vote to convict and thereby remove him from office?"[9]

The grand jury analogy supported the grand jury standard but, in my judgment, that standard was probably outside the range of reasonable interpretations.[10] One may criticize the House as an institution for failing to conduct a focused debate on the standard of proof even if the grand jury standard was a reasonable one. Of course each House member could decide independently what standard of proof should be required. But a process that allowed members to think clearly about the question was clearly desirable and did not take place.

The issue of standard of proof was obscured because it was easy to frame the issue as dealing solely with the standard of proof of facts, rather than as one implicating a political judgment about the ultimate decision on whether the president should be removed from office.[11] The House had a massive submission of facts from the Independent Counsel. It would have been ridiculous to plow the same ground again and, upon analysis, a factual inquiry was unlikely to alter a reasonable person's conclusions from the Independent Counsel's submission. The facts supporting the central charges could not be challenged reasonably. For those House members who thought that the standard of proof involved only the application of a standard to factual matters, it was reasonable to conclude that the grand jury standard—and, indeed, many standards more demanding than probable cause—was satisfied, given the factual record before the House. That is, the problem was not that the grand jury standard

---

[8] *See* The Consequences of Perjury and Related Crimes: Hearing Before the House Comm. on the Judiciary, 105th Cong. 14–15 (1998) (statement of Rep. Gekas).

[9] *Id.* at 133–34 (statement of Rep. Bryant).

[10] Posner agrees. Richard Posner, An Affair of State: The Investigation, Impeachment, and Trial of President Clinton 120 (1999) ("Because the trial of a President before the Senate is such a costly and disruptive process, it seems clear that the House ought to believe that the President is guilty, not merely that he may be, before it votes to impeach.").

[11] For statements showing how the question of the standard of proof was bound together with questions about whether the House should engage in a factual inquiry, see David E. Kendall, "Constitutional Vandalism," 30 N.M. L. Rev. 155, 168 (2000).

was correct or incorrect. Rather, the question was framed badly to the extent that it focused on facts alone and ignored the issue of the president's removal. Impeachment was designed to be a political process. It seems unreasonable to structure that process to render the House of Representatives, the body closest to the people, merely the processor of facts. The impeachment process should have clearly induced House members to exercise a political judgment, not simply a factual one, about whether the president committed acts that justified removing him from office.

Here, I think Congress can be faulted for failing to frame the issue clearly. The Independent Counsel's factual presentation made it too easy for the House to focus on facts rather than political judgment.[12] And, of course, politics played a role here as it did in other aspects of the impeachment. Some House members found it politically desirable to obscure the question of removal.[13] The interaction of politics and the Independent Counsel's factual submission led the House to act in a insufficiently responsible manner.

What, then, can be said about Congress's overall performance of the job of constitutional interpretation during the Clinton impeachment? "[G]reat cases like hard cases make bad law,"[14] and at the time, the impeachment seemed like a great case. Congress's performance under heightened political tensions may have been worse than would be true under more usual circumstances. Overall, though, I believe that Congress did not perform the job of constitutional interpretation badly during the impeachment.[15] Isenbergh's proposal was correctly rejected. The House should have come to a clearer conclusion about the validity of the grand jury standard as the basis for impeaching a president. Congress's underperformance is understandable, however, and does not, in my view, seriously undermine the claim that Congress can do a decent job of constitutional interpretation.[16] At the same time, though, it is important to keep in mind the role that politics played, not only in affecting substantive decisions but also in structuring the decision-making process.

[12] Some opponents of impeachment tried to insert political judgment into the process by arguing that a prosecutor convinced of a person's guilt might nonetheless exercise discretion in refusing to charge the person. This argument did not make much headway, in part because it was connected to arguments that still rested on factual matters, in this instance, whether a prosecutor exercising discretion should take into account the prospect that a trial would result in an acquittal.

[13] Among these members were those who, after voting in favor of the articles of impeachment, then stated publicly that they did not want the Senate to convict the president. *See* Posner, *supra* note 10, at 120.

[14] Northern Sec. Co. v. United States, 193 U.S. 197, 400 (1904) (Holmes, J., dissenting).

[15] Kendall offers a different evaluation, though of course from the partisan viewpoint of an attorney representing President Clinton. *See* Kendall, *supra* note 11, at 155 (charging that the House's institutional performance throughout the impeachment proceedings was "so abysmal as to amount to constitutional vandalism").

[16] Recall that decency is necessarily a comparative standard and one that, according to academics, the Supreme Court routinely fails to rise to as well.

The U.S. Congress: War Powers

Controversies concerning the constitutional allocation of the power to make war between Congress and the president come close to satisfying the criteria for evaluation of congressional constitutional interpretation. In addition, war-powers controversies have been common enough that they are almost routine. Although military commitments that put U.S. soldiers' lives at risk are clearly matters of great moment to members of Congress, I believe that such commitments are probably not perceived by those members as the kinds of great cases that might make bad law. Some important qualifications complicate the picture, though.

The first is the ambiguous status of the judicial overhang. Since the enactment of the War Powers Resolution, members of Congress regularly have sought judicial review of presidential decisions regarding the deployment of military force overseas.[17] The Supreme Court has never ruled directly on whether such plaintiffs are entitled (have "standing") to raise the issues they present. The Court of Appeals for the District of Columbia Circuit, where nearly all of these lawsuits have been heard, has developed a law of standing that first holds out the hope that someday some legislator will be found to have standing and then routinely denies standing in the court's exercise of equitable discretion.[18] The ambiguities generated by this law mean that members of Congress might think that they have judicial review available to them. This mistaken belief might distort the way in which members consider war-powers questions.

Second, there is a wide range of reasonable interpretations of the Constitution's allocation of power in this area. Some scholars take the view that Congress has the primary role in committing U.S. armed forces to relatively large-scale operations in which they might meet armed resistance.[19] Others

[17] For a comprehensive review, *see generally* Anthony Clark Arend & Catherine B. Lotrionte, "Congress Goes to Court: The Past, Present, and Future of Legislator Standing," 25 Harv. J. L. & Pub. Pol'y 209 (2001).

[18] *See, e.g.,* Campbell v. Clinton, 203 F.3d 19, 23 (D.C. Cir. 2000) (holding that a group of Congress members lacked standing to challenge the president's failure to abide by the War Powers Act in his deployment of U.S. forces to the former Yugoslavia because they had failed to exhaust their legislative remedies).

[19] *See, e.g.,* John Hart Ely, War and Responsibility: Constitutional Lessons of Vietnam and Its Aftermath 5–10 (1993) (rejecting the notion that the Constitution's requirements for the authorization of the use of force abroad have become obsolete or have been amended by subsequent practice); Louis Fisher, Congressional Abdication on War and Spending 183 (2000) (asserting that "it is not only unconstitutional but unwise to allow presidents to engage the country in war singlehandedly"); Louis Fisher, "Congressional Abdication: War and Spending Powers," 43 St. Louis U. L. J. 931, 1006 (1999) (calling for joint action by Congress and the president on war-powers issues and suggesting that unilateral actions by the president are "inherently unstable"). I emphasize that the concept of abdication comes into play only when one believes that the Constitution specifies some particular allocation of power between the president and Congress.

contend that the president has the primary power to initiate such operations, subject only to subsequent congressional control through the appropriations process.[20] It might be difficult to locate any completed congressional action inconsistent with some position within this reasonable range. A further complication is that one view, probably also a reasonable one, holds that the Constitution does not specify an allocation of power between Congress and the president and that the allocation of power depends solely on political interactions between the branches.[21]

Perhaps these difficulties can be avoided. Sometimes critics charge Congress with irresponsibility in exercising the war powers it has.[22] In the most general terms, the charge is that Congress fails to take any position regarding the allocation of war-making authority between it and the president. By doing so, critics assert, Congress positions itself to criticize the president if the military operation fails and to claim credit if the operation succeeds.[23]

Congress's action in connection with the 1999 military operation in Kosovo provides an opportunity to assess this criticism and thereby to see how

---

E.g., Fisher, *supra*, at xiv ("Abdication means to relinquish a right or power. . . . Abdication means giving to someone else something that belongs to you."); Douglas R. Williams, "Demonstrating and Explaining Congressional Abdication: Why Does Congress Abdicate Power?" 43 St. Louis U. L. J. 1013, 1014 (1999) (noting that Fisher's position requires "the elaboration of a constitutional theory of war powers . . . [that] would establish the constitutional baseline").

[20] *See, e.g.*, John C. Yoo, "The Continuation of Politics by Other Means: The Original Understanding of War Powers," 84 Cal. L. Rev. 167, 174 (1996) (insisting that the Constitution was "designed to encourage presidential initiative in war" and that Congress can "express its opposition to executive war decisions only by exercising its powers over funding and impeachment").

[21] It is important, I believe, to distinguish this position from others that find, in the accumulated weight of practice, criteria for determining the proper allocation of power between Congress and the president. *See, e.g.*, Peter J. Spiro, "War Powers and the Sirens of Formalism," 68 N.Y.U. L. Rev. 1338, 1355–65 (1993) (reviewing Ely, *supra* note 19). The latter position holds that, at any given time, the accumulated weight of practice determines the proper allocation of authority. It acknowledges that practice can change incrementally, leading to the conclusion that different allocations may be constitutionally commanded at different times. The former position, in contrast, is that there never is a constitutionally mandated allocation of authority, except in the sense that the Constitution creates a framework within which president and Congress contend for power. The allocation is not determined by text, nor determined by practice, but only by the outcome of political struggles over that allocation at particular moments in time. Not surprisingly, lawyers are uncomfortable with a position that finds nothing in the Constitution other than politics to determine so important a matter, and it is accordingly difficult to locate lawyers or legal academics making strong statements of this position.

[22] *See, e.g.*, Abraham D. Sofaer, "The Power Over War," 50 U. Miami L. Rev. 33, 55 (1995) ("Why is Ely not shocked at the irresponsibility of setting out, in advance and in a statute, the very untenable and scornworthy defense that legislators advanced during Vietnam: 'We approved and paid for it, but it's not our war?'"); Daniel N. Hoffman, "A Republic, If You Can Keep It," 82 Mich. L. Rev. 997, 1001 (1994) (reviewing Edward Keynes, Undeclared War: Twilight Zone of Constitutional Power (1992)) (referring to the phenomenon of "a Congress reluctant to challenge presidential initiatives for fear of being branded subversive, appeasing, or otherwise irresponsible").

[23] For a collection of quotations to this effect, see Williams, *supra* note 19, at 1036–37.

well Congress performed as a constitutional interpreter. The military operation began on March 24. On the previous day, the Senate, by a vote of 58 to 41, adopted a concurrent resolution authorizing the president "to conduct military air operations and missile strikes" against Yugoslavia. Almost a month later, the House rejected the concurrent resolution by a tie vote of 213–213. On the same day, the House rejected a declaration of war against Yugoslavia by the overwhelming margin of 2 in favor, 427 against. It also rejected a concurrent resolution directing the president to remove troops from Yugoslavia, by a vote of 139 in favor and 290 against. The House did adopt a bill prohibiting the use of ground forces in Yugoslavia, but the bill did not come up for a vote in the Senate. Finally, Congress approved an emergency supplemental appropriations bill to cover the Kosovo operation's costs.[24]

Congress's failure to adopt a clear position on the Kosovo operation might seem to exemplify irresponsibility. As Louis Fisher notes, the House took "multiple and supposedly conflicting votes" and "the Senate decided to duck the issue."[25] And yet, the example is not as clear as one might hope. First, as the title of a classic political science article puts it, "Congress is a 'They,' not an 'It.'"[26] This phrase resonates with the distinction drawn in chapter 4 between legislators and legislatures. Every single member of Congress might have a fully formed and defensible position on the allocation of war power between president and Congress, and, even so, the aggregation of those positions in a majority voting system might produce an outcome in which Congress as an institution takes no clear position on that allocation. Note, for example, that a clear Senate majority took the position that Congress ought to endorse the military operation, as did exactly half of those voting in the House.[27] Those opposing the military operation had reasons for their opposition as well. In the aggregate, "Congress" might be said to have abdicated its institutional responsibility to take a clear position on the constitutional question, but no individual member of Congress will have done so. In this way, the requirement of evaluating only completed actions makes it difficult to assess Congress's actions: each completed action, in each house, might be constitutionally responsible, but the series of actions taken together supports the charge of irresponsibility.

Beyond this, there is a bit more to be said. As noted earlier, one of the contending views of the allocation of the war power is that Congress's only role comes when it exercises its power to appropriate funds. Congress, as an

[24] Fisher, *supra* note 19, at 100–104 (describing these congressional actions).

[25] *Id.* at 102.

[26] Kenneth A. Shepsle, "Congress Is a 'They.' Not an 'It': Legislative Intent as Oxymoron," 12 Int'l Rev. L. & Econ. 239 (1992).

[27] The conclusion I seek to draw here may be obscured by the possibility that some members of Congress believed that the military intervention was a good idea but that Congress had no constitutional duty to endorse such an operation. These members could vote in favor of the operation without committing themselves to a view on the underlying constitutional question.

institution, played that role—and perhaps only that role—in connection with the Kosovo operation. In that sense, Congress did adopt a position within the range of reasonable options available on the question of the allocation of the war power.[28] In addition, if the Constitution says nothing about the allocation of war power between the president and Congress, leaving to the branches the political process in which to work out differences, the notion of congressional irresponsibility is inapt: Congress will do what it does and the president will respond, in part perhaps by charging Congress with irresponsibility. As the controversy proceeds, some accommodation will be worked out, or one side will prevail entirely. And that, according to the "political process" option, is all that the Constitution requires.[29]

Finally, and relatedly, I am unsure about the cogency of the charge of irresponsibility. War-powers decisions can be highly contested, and people can reasonably differ about the wisdom of any particular operation. What to one observer seems irresponsible might be characterized by another as an appropriate ambivalence about the proper course to pursue in a situation of ambiguity. Further, precisely to the extent that the critical observer can charge Congress with irresponsibility, so can constituents. The charge is that members of Congress may be trying to have their cake and eat it too, by taking positions that allow them to criticize an unsuccessful military operation and claim credit for a successful one. That is, irresponsibility can be politically beneficial. But constituents can notice the member of Congress's course of conduct just as readily as can the critic. Constituents can punish their representatives for perceived irresponsibility, thereby eliminating the purported political benefits of such behavior. To the extent that Congress behaves irresponsibly, its members may lose the electoral benefits thought to flow from irresponsibility. That, in turn, increases the likelihood that Congress acts responsibly.

I believe that the pattern Congress's response to the Kosovo military operation exhibits is typical: charges of congressional irresponsibility or abdication are made but, upon analysis, these charges turn out to be less cogent than initial reaction to Congress's actions suggests. On the whole, we can understand the actions of individual members of Congress as clear commitments on contested constitutional questions that are within the range of reasonable answers, and we can understand what Congress as an entity did to be consistent with at least two (and perhaps more) reasonable interpretations of the Constitution's allocation of power between the president and Congress.

[28] Obviously, a refusal to appropriate funds would also, on this view, have been a constitutionally responsible decision.

[29] But see Williams, supra note 19, at 1030 (arguing that the constitutional allocation of authority requires that Congress "politicize the question of constitutional war powers"). I believe that even if this is an accurate characterization of the general approach's requirements (rather than of Williams's own version of the approach), Congress necessarily politicizes the war-powers question by acting in whatever way it chooses.

The U.S. Senate: Motions Raising Constitutional Questions

A United States senator may raise a point of order regarding any bill under consideration. Ordinarily the Senate's presiding officer initially rules on points of order, with the possibility of appeal to the Senate as a whole. Senate precedent establishes, however, that points of order addressing the constitutionality of bills are automatically referred to the Senate for disposition by a roll call vote recording the votes of each senator.[30] Points of order are nondebatable under standard rules of parliamentary procedure. Ordinarily, senators therefore have to discuss the constitutional questions raised by the point of order *before* a senator raises it. Of course, a senator can lay out a constitutional argument prior to formally raising a constitutional point of order.[31] Debate on the merits of the constitutional issue is therefore possible both before and after the point is raised.

Formal constitutional points of order are rare.[32] Obviously, constitutional questions can be raised in the ordinary course of debate on the merits of proposals, as they were, extensively, in connection with the campaign finance legislation enacted in 2002. In such discussions, the integration of constitutional concerns and policy questions is present on the surface of the discussions. In contrast, the constitutional point of order at least purports to separate constitutional questions from policy ones.

Fewer than ten constitutional points of order have been raised since 1970.[33] One involved an objection to a proposed constitutional amendment that

[30] For a description of the procedure, see Louis Fisher, "Constitutional Interpretation by Members of Congress," 63 N.C. L. Rev. 707, 719–20 (1985). On the practice of submitting constitutional points of order to the Senate, *see* Floyd M. Riddick & Alan S. Frumin, Riddick's Senate Procedure 987 (Alan S. Frumin ed., 1992).

[31] *See, e.g.*, 131 Cong. Rec. S14,613 (daily ed. Nov. 1, 1985) (statement of Sen. Rudman (R-N.H.)). Senator Warren Rudman, after being recognized, opened his comments with the statement, "Mr. President, today I shall raise a point of order challenging the constitutionality" of a pending amendment. *Id.* After outlining the constitutional objection to the amendment, he formally raised the constitutional point of order. *Id.* Senate practice gives the presiding officer discretion to allow debate on a point of order, see Charles Tiefer, Congressional Practice and Procedure: A Reference, Research, and Legislative Guide 506 (1989), and one precedent indicates that constitutional points of order are debatable, see Riddick & Frumin, *supra* note 29, at 987.

[32] Constitutional issues are more often discussed in committee hearings, sometimes with testimony from constitutional "experts." In these hearings, however, the discussions are not dispositive because no votes are taken, as they are when a point of order is raised, and hearings are more obviously scripted than the discussions on the Senate floor. In addition, senators on the floor speak by themselves, with staff participating only in helping the senator prepare for the discussion. The point-of-order practice therefore provides a cleaner opportunity for assessing senators' performance than does the discussion of constitutional issues at the committee level.

[33] My research assistant Rachel Lebejko Priester located references to these motions in secondary literature, and the authors are cited with the relevant pages referenced in the Congressional Record.

would have provided for representation of the District of Columbia in Congress.[34] Senator Orrin Hatch (R-Utah) argued that the constitutional amendment would itself be unconstitutional because it would deprive other states of their equal representation in the Senate without their consent, contrary to the limitation built into Article V of the Constitution. Other senators disagreed that the proposed amendment would in fact contravene the requirement of equal representation, and after some procedural confusion was resolved, the Senate rejected the point of order and approved the resolution submitting the proposed amendment to the states for ratification. Another point of order raised an objection to an appropriations bill as a violation of the origination clause's requirement that "bills for raising Revenue shall originate in the House of Representatives."[35] The point of order was withdrawn when another senator pointed out that, under Senate custom, appropriations bills did not have to originate in the House.[36]

The other constitutional points of order raised various objections. Senators raised individual rights claims through constitutional points of order on bills that would ban federal financing of abortions for federal prisoners, that would impose tax liabilities for already completed transactions, and that would enact a new federal ban on flag burning in the face of a Supreme Court decision holding anti-flag-burning statutes unconstitutional.[37] Other constitutional points of order rested on separation-of-powers concerns, particularly that proposed legislation would violate the legislature's prerogatives. For example, a senator objected to provisions of the Civil Rights Act of 1991 that would, in his view, make the legislative branch subject to review by executive and judicial authorities.[38] Another senator objected that public financing of presidential elections would violate the constitutional requirement that federal expenditures be made through appropriations statutes.[39] Finally, an extensive debate occurred when a constitutional point of order was raised in 1984 against a proposal to authorize the president to veto particular items in appropriations bills.[40]

---

[34] 124 Cong. Rec. 27,249 (1978) (statement of Senator Orrin Hatch (R-Utah)), *cited in* Neil Kumar Katyal, "Legislative Constitutional Interpretation," 50 Duke L. J. 1335, 1378 n. 147 (2001).

[35] U.S. Const. art. I, § 7, cl. 1.

[36] *See* Tiefer, *supra* note 31, at 507 n. 107.

[37] *See* Stephen F. Ross, "Legislative Enforcement of Equal Protection," 72 Minn. L. Rev. 311, 360 n. 195 (1987); M. Bryan Schneider, Note, "The Supreme Court's Reluctance to Enforce Constitutional Prohibitions Against Retroactive Income Tax Statutes," 40 Wayne L. Rev. 1603, 1605 (1994); Charles Tiefer, "The Flag-Burning Controversy of 1989–1990: Congress' Valid Role in Constitutional Dialogue," 29 Harv. J. on Legis. 357, 378–79 (1992).

[38] 137 Cong. Rec. D1325–26 (daily ed. Oct. 29, 1991), *cited in* Nicole L. Gueron, Note, "An Idea Whose Time Has Come: A Comparative Procedural History of the Civil Rights Acts of 1960, 1964, and 1991," 104 Yale L. J. 1201, 1211 n. 86 (1995).

[39] *See* Ross, *supra* note 37, at 361 n. 198.

[40] *See* Fisher, *supra* note 30, at 719–22.

Plainly, many bills and enacted statutes raise constitutional questions that are never subject to a constitutional point of order. Senators have no obligation to use the procedure. This points to the difference between senatorial and judicial consideration of constitutional questions discussed in the previous chapter: subject only to justiciability requirements such as standing, courts *must* address constitutional questions litigants present to them, while senators have no obligation to raise a constitutional point of order. Conceding, then, that the constitutional point of order is not a substitute for judicial review, I examine the quality of the senators' discussions when they do deal with constitutional points of order.[41]

Debates on constitutional points of order contain several elements, the proportions varying with the subject matter and the political context. First, senators discuss whether a proposal is constitutional by referring to relevant judicial decisions. For example, Senator Warren Rudman (R-N.H.) relied on Supreme Court decisions about the government's responsibility for medical care of prisoners to explain his constitutional objection to a proposal that would deny the Federal Bureau of Prisons the authority to pay for federal prisoners' abortions.[42]

Second, senators supplement their use of court decisions by invoking the constitutional principles they believe underlie those decisions. Senator Slade Gorton (R-Wash.), objecting to a provision making tax increases retroactive, cited court decisions casting constitutional doubt on such increases.[43] Senator James Sasser (D-Tenn.) responded that "the Supreme Court has already ruled," referring to another set of decisions. Returning to the debate, Senator Gorton then elaborated on the underlying principle: a retroactive statute is unconstitutional when it is "harsh and oppressive . . . when it is imposed without notice, that is to say when it is imposed retroactively beyond the date in which the Congress and the President have given notice that they intend to pass a tax."[44]

Third, senators rely directly on the Constitution and basic constitutional principles without drawing in any significant way on court decisions. In a constitutional point of order debate raised against a proposal to enact a line-item veto, one senator mentioned a recent Supreme Court decision invalidating the so-called legislative veto on separation-of-powers grounds, saying that the

[41] Senators may well discuss constitutional questions in other forums, such as hearings at which they take testimony about a proposal's constitutionality. Only the constitutional point of order, however, requires each senator to take a recorded, formal position on a question of constitutional interpretation.

[42] *See* 131 Cong. Rec. 30,243–44 (1985).

[43] *See* 139 Cong. Rec. S19,751 (1993). Several months after the debate, the Supreme Court reversed one of the decisions to which Senator Gorton referred. United States v. Carlton, 512 U.S. 26 (1994).

[44] 139 Cong. Rec. S19,752, S19,757 (1993).

line-item veto was "merely a variation on the same constitutionally impermissible theme."[45] That, however, was a rare reference to the courts in the debate. Far more often, senators referred to "the simple language of the U.S. Constitution" and invoked general separation-of-powers principles.[46]

Finally, senators discuss whether they should even make their own independent judgments about the constitutionality of the proposals. In a sense, these debates are about whether a constitutional point of order is itself out of order. A supporter of the line-item veto proposal, for example, said, "I want to pass this amendment, send it to the House, have them pass it, have the president sign it, and let the Supreme Court decide whether it is constitutional to do this."[47] More often, and not surprisingly, senators assert their constitutional responsibility to interpret the Constitution on their own, sometimes referring to the oath of office they take to uphold the Constitution.[48] Perhaps the most dramatic example of a claim of independent senatorial responsibility was Senator Jesse Helms's (R-N.C.) position on the constitutionality of denying federal funding for abortions obtained by federal prisoners. Senator Helms argued in part that Supreme Court precedent supported the constitutionality of the proposal, but he also asserted indirectly, but reasonably clearly, that the proposal was constitutional because the Supreme Court's basic abortion decisions lacked an adequate constitutional foundation.[49]

The constitutional arguments made in these debates are usually quite truncated. They contain few quotations from cases or even the Constitution, and, of course, no citations. They are, after all, debates and not judicial opinions. In some ways, too, the debates are telegraphic, with senators making shorthand allusions to more elaborate arguments they do not develop fully. Taking these considerations into account, however, it seems that nearly all the debates

[45] 130 Cong. Rec. S10,855 (1984) (statement of Sen. Mark Hatfield (R-Ore.)).

[46] *See, e.g.*, *id.* at S10,857 (statement of Sen. Pete Domenici (R-N.Mex.)); *id.* at S10,858 (statement of Sen. John Stennis (D-Miss.)).

[47] *Id.* at S10,861 (statement of Sen. Alan Dixon (D-Ill.)). The Supreme Court eventually held a different Line Item Veto Act unconstitutional more than a decade later. *See* Clinton v. City of New York, 547 U.S. 417 (1998). An interesting variant on the argument that constitutionality should be addressed by courts occurred in the 1990 debate on adopting a constitutional amendment on flag burning. At the time of the Senate debate, the House of Representatives had already failed to adopt a constitutional amendment by the required supermajority. The Senate proceeded to consider adopting the amendment nonetheless. Senator Dale Bumpers (D-Ark.) proposed an amendment that would have enacted another anti-flag-burning statute. Senator Pete Wilson raised a constitutional point of order. 136 Cong. Rec. S15,548–49 (daily ed., 1990). In response, Senator Bumpers said, "[T]hat is not really a decision . . . for us to make," because, in light of the failure of all other efforts, his statute was "the only thing in the world [that has] a chance of getting before the Supreme Court." *Id.* at S15,549. The Senate upheld the point of order by a vote of 51 to 48 and proceeded to consider the constitutional amendment. *Id.*

[48] *See, e.g.*, 130 Cong. Rec. 10,861–62 (1984) (statement of Sen. Gorton).

[49] *See* 131 Cong. Rec. 30,244 (1985) ("I hope that Congress, and certainly the Senate, will not this day embark on a misinterpretation of the Constitution of the United States.").

contain the skeletons of decent constitutional arguments, and sometimes there is even a bit of flesh on the bones. Although there are no transcripts of the discussions at the closed conferences of Supreme Court justices, evidence from notes the justices take suggests that the Senate discussions of constitutional questions differ less than one might expect from the actual face-to-face discussions the justices have. If conference discussions set the standard for assessing when deliberation is sufficient—rather than, for example, published Supreme Court opinions—senators seem to do a decent job of constitutional interpretation.[50]

A skeptic might suggest, however, that these debates on constitutional points of order are no more than sideshows to the main stage: the consideration of the policy wisdom of the proposals before the Senate. The correspondence between votes on constitutional points of order and votes on the merits is extremely close.[51] The Senate accepted the point of order made against the proposed line-item veto by a vote of 56 to 34, but, as Louis Fisher notes, the constitutional point of order "was the simplest way to defeat an amendment [the majority] opposed on policy grounds."[52] Professor Stephen Ross's analysis of the votes on the abortion-funding point of order is similar. The Senate was equally divided over whether to adopt the amendment limiting federal funding of abortions for federal prisoners, which meant that the amendment remained on the table. The constitutional point of order was raised. A motion to table *that* point of order was defeated by one vote. Ross notes that "even though the vote on the motion to table represented a vote on the merits and the point of order vote supposedly involved constitutionality, of the Senators participating in both votes, only two . . . switched their votes between the two motions."[53] The amendment's supporters saw the handwriting on the wall, with one saying that "my thought is it is well to vitiate the yeas and nays. We have had a clear vote, though it is disappointing to me."[54] The supporters allowed the amendment to be defeated on a voice vote.

The constitutional point of order's distinctive function is to allow senators to put aside their views on the policy wisdom of the proposal at hand and to focus solely on its constitutionality. No procedural rule can guarantee that senators will in fact deal solely with the constitutional questions. The correspondence between senators' positions on constitutional points of order and

[50] Professor Beth Garrett suggested to me that, just as the justices exchange letters that flesh out their conference positions, so senators also distribute "Dear Colleagues" letters at times. To that extent, the analogy between floor debates and conference discussions might be strengthened.

[51] Professor Frederick Schauer has reported to me the preliminary results of a study of senators' views on campaign finance reform. According to Schauer, every senator who favored campaign finance reform believed it to be constitutional, while every senator who thought reform bad policy also believed reform to be unconstitutional.

[52] Fisher, *supra* note 30, at 721.

[53] *See* Ross, *supra* note 37, at 360.

[54] 131 Cong. Rec. 30,247 (1985) (statement of Sen. William Armstrong (R-Colo.)).

their positions on the merits suggests that the constitutional point of order does not in fact narrow the range of matters senators think about before they vote. It seems as if the constitutional analysis senators engage in actually does no independent work.[55] Senators take the position on the constitutional point of order that matches their position on the merits, and they do so because of their views on the merits.[56]

The suggestion, then, is that senators' votes on constitutional points of order simply reflect, without change, their views on the policy questions raised by the underlying proposals. This suggestion might be bolstered by two related observations. Senators rarely raise constitutional points of order even though many proposals could certainly be the subject of such points. Senators also advert to constitutional questions in ordinary debate without raising constitutional points of order.

Why, then, use the constitutional point of order when policy grounds would arguably suffice? The answer might be something like this: the appearance of identity between policy views and constitutional ones is misleading.[57] Actually, some senators believe that the proposal is *unwise* as a matter of public policy. They also believe that their constituents mistakenly believe that the proposal is a good one. The senators therefore fear adverse electoral consequences from voting according to their policy views. The senators believe as well, however, that their constituents will *not* punish them electorally for voting against a proposal that they believe to be unconstitutional.

Why might senators think that voting to uphold a constitutional point of order will insulate them from electoral harm? Consider two possibilities: *timing*

---

[55] One might note in response that at least sometimes the constitutional analysis drives the policy views. The testing points would be issues that do *not* raise serious constitutional questions; a senator who objects to one of these collateral provisions demonstrates that policy is his or her primary concern.

[56] It might be worth pointing out, however, that some political scientists believe that judges act in precisely this way as well. The so-called attitudinal model they favor holds that the correspondence between justices' views on the proper interpretation of the Constitution and their views on the policy wisdom of the matters they consider is also quite close. For a presentation of the attitudinal model, see Jeffrey Alan Segal & Harold J. Spaeth, The Supreme Court and the Attitudinal Model (1992).

[57] Professors Elizabeth Garrett and Adrian Vermeule invoke Jon Elster's idea of "the civilizing force of hypocrisy" to explain how constitutional arguments might have weight independent of a legislator's policy views:

> Even a wholly self-interested legislator cannot afford to take positions in constitutional argument that are too transparently favorable to his own interests. So legislators who want to invest in credibility will have to adjust their positions to disfavor or disguise their own interests to some degree.

Elizabeth Garrett & Adrian Vermeule, "Institutional Design of a Thayerian Congress," 50 Duke L. J. 1277, 1289 (2001) (citing Jon Elster, "Alchemies of the Mind: Transmutation and Misrepresentation," 3 Legal Theory 133, 176 (1997)).

and *responsibility*. Professor Nelson Lund's brief discussion of Congress's adoption of a flag-burning statute illustrates the timing explanation.[58] Congress had before it two proposals, a statute (largely supported by Democrats) that sought to conform a prohibition of flag burning to the Supreme Court's invalidation of a Texas flag-burning statute, and a constitutional amendment (largely supported by Republicans) that would have specifically authorized adoption of flag-burning legislation. By adopting the statute, senators deferred consideration of the constitutional amendment. The deferral would have been permanent had the Supreme Court upheld the new federal statute,[59] but even a temporary deferral might be valuable for senators opposed to anti-flag-burning legislation but facing a public demanding that something be done.[60] Deferral would be "a delaying tactic meant to divert attention away from a constitutional amendment until after popular interest in the matter subsided."[61]

The reason that timing might matter in this way needs elaboration. Electoral retaliation is always delayed until the next election. On Lund's account, the risk of electoral retaliation evaporates because senators believe that voters' preferences will change: voters who wanted an enforceable flag-burning statute in 1989 would care more about other things by 1990 or 1992, when they would consider whether to reelect a senator who voted for the statute but against the constitutional amendment. There are, however, several difficulties with the timing explanation. References to the desirability of letting things cool off pervade the arguments favoring the adoption of an anti-flag-burning statute over amending the Constitution.[62] Lund's language seems to suggest that a senator who voted for the statute simply to defer consideration of the constitutional amendment somehow behaved insincerely,[63] but it is hard to see why. Those senators, it might be said, voted in a way that assured the implementation of their constituents' *long-term* preferences rather than of their passing preferences.[64] That senators would gauge the intensity of preferences,

[58] Nelson Lund, "Rational Choice at the Office of Legal Counsel," 15 Cardozo L. Rev. 437, 471–72 (1993).

[59] It did not. *See* United States v. Eichman, 496 U.S. 310 (1990).

[60] *See* Lund, *supra* note 58, at 470 n. 75 ("*Even if one doubts that Senator Biden was sincere* in claiming that he favored legal protection for the Flag, it would not necessarily follow that he was insincere in suggesting that proponents of a constitutional amendment were engaged in 'opportunism.'") (emphasis added). This is not to suggest that no senator believed that adopting a flag-burning statute was bad policy but nonetheless voted for it because of electoral concerns.

[61] *Id.* at 471.

[62] *See* Robert J. Goldstein, Burning The Flag: The Great 1989–1990 American Flag Desecration Controversy 168–69 (1996) (collecting such statements).

[63] *See, e.g.,* Lund, *supra* note 58, at 472–73 n. 77 (referring to "a political strategy aimed at derailing a constitutional amendment that would have authorized statutory protection of the Flag").

[64] Perhaps alternatively, they implemented those of their constituents' preferences that are important enough to remain salient over a long term. That is, the constituents may still care about adopting a statute banning flag burning, but over time that preference becomes less significant relative to other issues on the constituents' agenda.

it might further be said, was one of the reasons the Framers gave senators six-year terms of office.

There is another reason to discount the timing explanation for the Senate votes in the flag-burning controversy. Notably, the timing explanation does not, by itself, explain why a senator would vote to *reject* the constitutional point of order and adopt a statute the senator believed would be held unconstitutional. The length of time between the vote on the constitutional point of order and the next election is the same no matter how the senator votes. What seems to matter is that the senator might be able to say to constituents, "I tried to get you a flag-burning statute, but the Supreme Court wouldn't let me." The possibility that the senator will also have to explain a vote against a constitutional amendment that would have authorized a flag-burning statute complicates the picture. The senator's response actually assumes that the constituents continue to desire the adoption of an enforceable flag-burning statute. The senator's challenger can point out that, by voting against the constitutional amendment, the senator did not try as hard as he or she could have to get constituents the flag-burning statute they wanted.

Perhaps the complication actually explains how the timing explanation works. The senator may not be able to explain to constituents why the existing Constitution—the one invoked in the constitutional point of order— makes it impossible to enact an enforceable flag-burning statute. The senator *might*, however, be able to explain to constituents why it would be a bad thing to amend the Constitution to authorize such a statute.

In the flag-burning case, senators were presented with two distinct questions: should they adopt a flag-burning statute if consistent with the First Amendment, and should they adopt a constitutional amendment that would ensure the constitutionality of flag-burning statutes. Lund treats these two questions as a single one about the desirability, as a matter of public policy, of having an enforceable flag-burning statute. They are not.

A senator who sincerely wanted a flag-burning statute might think that obtaining one by means of amending the Constitution would leave the nation worse off than it would be without a flag-burning statute.[65] The senator's concern might be twofold. An apparently narrow constitutional amendment directed solely at authorizing flag-burning statutes might be taken by future Congresses and Supreme Courts as expressing a broader policy about the basic principles of free expression, thereby authorizing larger incursions on free expression than the senator believes appropriate. The senator might also be concerned about setting a precedent—not about free expression but about amending the Constitution. The senator might believe that proponents of unwise constitutional amendments (as the senator sees the proposals) would be

---

[65] The argument is elaborated in Mark Tushnet, "The Flagburning Episode: An Essay on the Constitution," 61 U. Colo. L. Rev. 39 (1990).

emboldened were the Constitution amended to authorize flag-burning statutes. The cost of forgoing an enforceable flag-burning statute after constitutional amendment might be lower than the costs associated with amending the Constitution. Making sense of the timing explanation requires consideration of the possibility that a proposal will be made to amend the Constitution at the moment that the constitutional point of order is raised.

The *responsibility* explanation for invoking the Constitution rather than policy is that the constitutional point of order allows senators to shift responsibility for the proposal's defeat from themselves to the Constitution. Senator David Boren's (D-Okla.) statements in the line-item veto debate illustrate how the responsibility explanation might work. Many opponents of the line-item veto statute thought it was bad policy. Senator Boren, a former governor who had exercised a line-item veto over his state's budget, clearly did not. He expressed his willingness to cosponsor a constitutional amendment creating a line-item veto power. But, he said, "as much as I favor the line-item veto, I feel I have no choice but to vote that it does not comply with the Constitution of the United States."[66] This sense of compulsion makes the Constitution, and not the senator, responsible for the proposal's defeat.[67]

The discussion of legislators' incentives in the previous chapter suggests why senators' electoral incentives do not necessarily lead senators to ignore their own considered constitutional views when voting on a constitutional point of order. Possibility is not necessity, of course, and the coincidence between constitutional positions and policy positions might be suspicious. It may be wrong, though, to see votes on constitutional points of order as politically expedient reflections of underlying policy views. One might instead see the votes on the constitutional points of order as reflecting considered *constitutional* judgments, influenced but not dictated by policy views.[68]

Consider the following theory of constitutional interpretation. The Constitution should be interpreted in light of text, original understanding, accumulated

---

[66] 130 Cong. Rec. 10,863 (1984).

[67] Justice Anthony Kennedy alluded to precisely the same responsibility-shifting function of the Constitution in the Supreme Court's initial flag-burning decision. Justice Kennedy voted with the five-justice majority to find unconstitutional a state's ban on flag burning as a means of political protest. He observed that "sometimes we must make decisions we do not like" because "the law and the Constitution, as we see them, compel the result." Justice Kennedy suggested as well that this effort to shift responsibility can never be entirely successful: when "we are presented with a clear and simple statute to be judged against a pure command of the Constitution . . . , the outcome can be laid at no door but ours." Texas v. Johnson, 491 U.S. 397, 420–21 (1989) (Kennedy, J., concurring). Precisely the same thing could be said about senators who attempt to shift responsibility for the defeat of a proposal their constituents favor from themselves to the Constitution: the constituents could *still* lay responsibility at the senators' doors.

[68] Obviously this account cannot explain senators' votes with respect to amending the Constitution but only their votes on constitutional points of order against legislative proposals, which are necessarily predicated on the existing Constitution.

precedent, and fundamental principle. Often, and particularly in the most contentious cases, those sources will not conclusively establish that a proposal (or enacted statute) is constitutional or unconstitutional. If they do not, one can properly resolve the constitutional question by taking into account whether the proposal or statute would improve the functioning of the government as an ongoing operation. Sometimes senators holding this theory of constitutional interpretation will find themselves in precisely this situation of interpretive openness.[69] When they do, the coincidence between their policy views and their votes on a constitutional point of order indicates a fully responsible exercise of the senators' duty to vote on the constitutional point of order solely with reference to their theoretically informed view of the proposal's constitutionality.

Finally, it seems worth emphasizing that the constitutional theory described is a perfectly respectable one that judges could hold as well. In a sense, then, the Senate's practice on constitutional points of order *might* support the proposition that nonjudicial constitutional review can be little different from judicial constitutional review—if judicial review is understood in a specific way and if senators in fact adopt the theory of constitutional interpretation that could justify the apparent congruence between policy views and votes on constitutional points of order. The limited scope of the practice of the constitutional point of order may be important here as well: politicians who do reasonably well when they occasionally face up to constitutional questions directly might not do as well were they to confront such questions routinely.

The U.S. Executive Branch: The Department of Justice's Office of Legal Counsel

The Office of Legal Counsel (OLC) in the United States Department of Justice reviews legislative proposals for constitutionality as the executive branch's legal advisor, acting by delegation from the attorney general.[70] How well does the OLC do in ensuring that the executive branch does a reasonably good job in interpreting the Constitution? Here I examine some aspects of the OLC's operation, focusing on its task of vetting proposed legislation to advise the president on its constitutionality but looking occasionally at other aspects of the OLC's work.[71]

[69] Whether senators actually hold this theory is debatable, but the theory seems to me reasonably commonsensical, and one that a senator might well adopt.

[70] In addition to published materials, I rely on telephone interviews with Randolph Moss, former assistant attorney general, OLC (Jan. 21, 2001), Cornelia Pillard, former deputy, OLC (Sept. 21, 2001), and Martin Lederman, former attorney advisor, OLC (July 9, 2001).

[71] I note that obtaining information about OLC's operation is difficult because its staff members believe—in my view, erroneously—that their communications to the president are covered

The OLC is headed by an assistant attorney general nominated by the president and confirmed by the Senate.[72] The office staff includes several deputies, all of whom are political appointees. The staff lawyers are a combination of young attorneys, including those drawn to serve a particular administration— but who sometimes stay with the office for at least a few years after the administration they joined has departed—and career civil servants who provide long-term institutional memory.

The bill clearance process, which is only one part of the OLC's role as chief constitutional advisor to the executive branch, involves an attempt to screen *all* legislative proposals for constitutionality. Typically, as bills arrive, a deputy assigns the bill to a staff lawyer, sometimes on the basis of the lawyer's expertise, but sometimes simply because the lawyer is available to do the analysis. The assignment may also include some guidance about the administration's initial reaction to the proposal, and the staff attorney and a deputy may interact as the comment develops.

Assignments based on expertise are not always possible or accurate. There are two relevant kinds of expertise. A lawyer can be an expert in some substantive statutory area, such as pension law or employment law, or the lawyer can be an expert about some general constitutional area, such as religious freedom or economic liberty. Assigning a bill to a staff lawyer based on subject matter may have no relationship to the lawyer's constitutional expertise. The more common practice of assigning a bill based on constitutional expertise, however, may be equally problematic. A proposal may raise red flags with respect to one constitutional question that, on analysis, turns out to be insubstantial, while containing in its details an entirely different and more substantial constitutional question with which another staff lawyer may be more familiar.[73]

In theory, the OLC should clear proposals at every stage, from introduction to modification in committee to amendment on the floor. Often, however, the legislative process moves too quickly for the OLC to offer its views on every new

---

by the attorney-client privilege. (My view is that the OLC's lawyers are lawyers for the United States, not the president, which means that they are lawyers for the people of the United States. Some of their communications to the president might be covered by the substantially narrower executive privilege.)

[72] The degree to which the assistant attorney general in charge of the OLC regards himself (no women have held the position as of yet) as an essential part of the president's policy team has varied, as has the president's interest in making constitutional law an important component of his policy agenda. Douglas W. Kmiec, The Attorney General's Lawyer: Inside the Meese Justice Department (1992), describes Kmiec's service in the OLC in an administration that did take constitutional law to be an important element in its policy agenda. Kmiec's account is from the perspective of one who saw himself playing a large role on the constitutional policy team.

[73] Collegial interactions within the office obviously alleviate this difficulty, but time pressures may limit the extent to which such interactions occur.

development. In practical terms, bills and occasional committee modifications are all that the OLC can actually consider,[74] except for the possibility of screening bills when they reach the president's desk for signature or veto. Turnaround times are typically short, ranging from hours to a few days, with a seven-day deadline being unusually long. In the vast majority of cases, the OLC concludes that the bill raises no constitutional concerns, and indicates that it will have no comment on the bill.[75] Of the remainder, bills likely to move through the legislative process receive more attention than proposals that are not likely to advance.

As a matter of form, the OLC considers the constitutionality of a bill before deciding whether to recommend that the president veto the bill if it is adopted by both houses of Congress. After the staff lawyer responsible for a bill comes to a conclusion and drafts a comment, a deputy assistant attorney general examines and approves the comment. That comment is then sent to the department's Office of Legislative Affairs (OLA), which has responsibility for advancing the administration's legislative agenda. That office, in turn, compiles the constitutional comments from the OLC and policy-based comments from other components of the Department of Justice, such as the Civil Rights Division or the Criminal Division, whose activities would be affected by the bill. The OLA writes a letter to the Office of Management and Budget (OMB), which, after receiving comments from *all* affected departments, compiles and transmits the administration's comments to the relevant congressional committees. The OMB letter is the only one that is released outside the administration, and the OMB sometimes omits the OLC's constitutional comments from its letter.[76]

OLC comments aim to determine the constitutionality of legislative proposals on a blend of assumptions about constitutional interpretation, and the mix varies over time. Some administrations have distinctive agendas regarding the Constitution and its proper interpretation, and bill clearances will be shaped by those agendas. Other administrations accept Supreme Court doctrine as generally controlling. Even in the former case, however, the OLC's professional orientation appears to be shaped in significant part by judicial doctrine. The OLC can defend its judgments on constitutionality against

[74] The OLC can process modifications made in committee if the committee staff members are willing to continue to notify and work with the Department of Justice regarding significant developments. The OLC also occasionally has the opportunity to comment on floor amendments, depending on the pace of the legislative process and the importance the OLC and the Office of Legislative Affairs (OLA) attach to the floor amendment.

[75] Of course, talented lawyers can always gin up constitutional challenges to any legislative proposal so that the no-comment decision then presumably rests on a judgment that the proposal raises no substantial constitutional questions.

[76] *See* Douglas W. Kmiec, "OLC's Opinion Writing Function: The Legal Adhesive for a Unitary Executive," 15 Cardozo L. Rev. 337, 338–39 (1993) ("OMB cannot always be relied upon to fully divulge OLC's legal thinking to Congress.").

challenges from policy-oriented members of the administration by pointing to the Supreme Court as the source of the OLC's interpretation.[77]

The labels the OLC has developed to give its conclusions suggest its reliance on judicial doctrine. The weakest label for a proposal that raises constitutional questions is that the proposal raises a "litigation risk," which means, roughly, that a reasonable judge *might* but probably would not find the proposal unconstitutional if adopted. Stronger labels are that the proposal raises "constitutional concerns" or "serious constitutional concerns." Here a second element of constitutional interpretation can enter, with the OLC offering a constitutional perspective independent of that developed in Supreme Court opinions. Finally, the OLC may assert that the proposal, if enacted, would be unconstitutional, which ordinarily amounts to an OLC recommendation that the president veto the proposal if enacted in its present form.[78]

Each OLC label functions both as a prediction about possible future action, whether in courts or by the president, and as a marker in negotiations over the bill's language and content. Either through the OLA or, with White House permission, by direct contact with a member of the congressional staff, OLC attorneys may suggest revisions that would achieve the drafter's primary goals without presenting even a litigation risk. Of course, the more serious the OLC's constitutional objections, the more leverage it has in these discussions because of the possibility of a veto recommendation.[79]

Of primary interest here, the OLC's constitutional analysis occurs within an executive department by subordinate officials in an administration with its own political agenda. That the OLC is part of a specific administration means that the OLC's constitutional comments might be affected by the administration's interest in moving its agenda through Congress. That it is part of the executive branch means that the OLC typically defends the president's prerogatives against what its attorneys see as threats to the presidency as an institution.

---

[77] Cornelia T. L. Pillard, "The Unfulfilled Promise of the Constitution in Executive Hands," 103 Mich. L. Rev. 676, 737–38 (2005), observes that OLC may have a culture of relying on judicially developed doctrine because of its role in providing advice when requested by other executive branch entities. Because requesting such advice is optional, Pillard observes, OLC can bolster the credibility of its advice, and so induce agencies to request it, by pointing to some body of law external to OLC as the basis for its positions.

[78] A provision the OLC regards as clearly unconstitutional may be embedded in omnibus legislation, and the OLC may think it inappropriate to recommend a veto of such a bill merely because it contains an unconstitutional provision. The OLC may then develop a statement for the president to issue when he signs the bill, in which the president will note the provision's unconstitutionality and indicate that the administration will not treat it as binding. *See, e.g.*, Kmiec, *supra* note 76, at 345–46 (noting that "it has fallen to [the OLC] to set forth in a draft signing statement how the unconstitutional feature will be handled").

[79] Lund argues that the OLC comments serve as veto threats, but that the credibility of the threats does not depend on the quality of the OLC's arguments, primarily because members of Congress are accustomed to receiving OLC comments containing "very aggressive advocacy of the interests of OLC's client." Lund, *supra* note 58, at 466–67.

Observers suggest that the latter effect is more substantial than the former. The controversy in 2004 over the so-called torture memo produced by the OLC, which I discuss in more detail later, illustrates that proposition.

Staff attorneys will usually know the administration's position on major proposals important to the administration. The OLC will interact with the White House in developing the proposals to avoid constitutional difficulties. Sometimes, however, the staff attorneys drafting comments on a particular bill might not be aware that the administration has a position on the proposal. Even more often, the attorneys will sometimes fail to know the politics of a proposal—for example, whether it comes from an ally of the administration or is being pushed by someone whose vote the administration needs on other issues. Finally, as a matter of interpretive methodology, courts have often said a great deal about substantive constitutional questions raised by legislative proposals. Judicial decisions as a source for constitutional interpretation thus may weigh against the incumbent administration's policy positions.[80] The OLC's bill comments may therefore be reasonably disinterested relative to the specific legislative agenda of the administration in office.[81]

The OLC has good strategic reasons for being reasonably disinterested. As former assistant attorney general Randolph Moss observes, "Congress is less likely to take seriously a constitutional objection to proposed legislation if that objection, or the general approach of the Office is seen as policy—as opposed to legally—driven."[82] An administration that seeks political cover by obtaining a statement from the OLC that some proposal is unconstitutional will hardly be helped if the perception becomes widespread that OLC comments simply use constitutional terminology as a way of advancing the administration's policy agenda. Yet, similar to the congruence between senators' constitutional and policy positions, principled constitutional analysis often leaves ample room for policy considerations. Where it does, OLC comments will be consistent with both existing doctrine and the administration's policy agenda.

The flag-burning episode illustrates how the OLC's legal analysis might conflict with an administration's legislative agenda.[83] The OLC's position was

[80] Disinterestedness may be reinforced by the OLC's focus on determining constitutionality according to current judicial criteria, because the courts—depending on their composition— need not be assumed sympathetic to a particular administration's legislative agenda.

[81] The OLC may, of course, be disinterested when its analysis leads to a conclusion that an administration proposal is constitutional, but one can identify the independent effect of disinterestedness only by examining situations in which the OLC analysis conflicts with the administration's legislative program.

[82] Randolph D. Moss, "Executive Branch Legal Interpretation: A Perspective from the Office of Legal Counsel," 52 Admin. L. Rev. 1303, 1311 (2000).

[83] For another example, see Elizabeth Garrett, "Harnessing Politics: The Dynamics of Offset Requirements in the Tax Legislative Process," 65 U. Chi. L. Rev. 501, 536 n. 134 (1998) (describing a decision by the first Bush administration to forgo changing the tax rate on capital gains by executive order, after receiving legal advice that such an action would be unconstitutional).

that Supreme Court doctrine clearly indicated that no anti-flag-burning statute would be held constitutional. As a result, the Bush administration supported adopting a constitutional amendment. The OLC's stance may actually have weakened the administration's position because it allowed opponents to make the argument that it was unwise to amend the Constitution.[84]

The line-item veto controversy provides another example of how OLC legal analyses might conflict with an administration's agenda. The Reagan administration believed that it could gain greater control over fiscal policy if the president had the power to veto specific items in appropriations bills. The Constitution provides that the president shall have the opportunity to sign or veto "every Bill which shall have passed" both houses of Congress.[85] Conservatives argued that the practice of packaging a large number of unrelated appropriations in a single statute transformed that statute from a single constitutional "Bill."[86] They argued that each subunit within these larger packages was a "Bill" within the meaning of the Constitution, and therefore could be vetoed individually. However, Charles Cooper, the OLC head, concluded that the Constitution could not be read in this way.[87] The OLC's legal analysis conflicted with the administration's policy agenda, supporting the proposition that the OLC *can* offer legal advice in a reasonably disinterested way.[88]

Administration proposals are likely to be vetted by the OLC for constitutionality before they emerge in the public eye. The OLC's participation in drafting legislation allows it to trim away the most constitutionally problematic features, modifying legislative proposals—thereby altering the administration's initial (politically driven) agenda—in the service of a more disinterested view of the Constitution's requirements.[89]

---

[84] One can perhaps locate a political motive for the administration's position: decision makers oriented to politics might have thought that Democrats would be more vulnerable the longer the issue persisted on the national agenda and that allowing Democrats to pursue an unconstitutional statutory remedy to be followed by consideration of a constitutional amendment would hurt Democrats. *But see* Lund, *supra note* 58, at 470 ("The Bush administration had no obvious motive for overstating the vulnerability of the proposed bill to constitutional challenge.").

[85] U.S. Const. art. I, § 7, cl. 2.

[86] For a collection of essays discussing this position, see Pork Barrels and Principles: The Politics of the Presidential Veto (1988).

[87] 12 Op. Off. Legal Counsel 128, 159 (1988).

[88] As with the flag-burning controversy, one can offer a more political account, in which the administration might not have been politically unhappy over being unable to exercise a line-item veto. By keeping the issue alive, the administration was able to place responsibility for fiscal excess on Congress, and by having no line-item veto power, the administration was not forced to take responsibility for particular appropriations decisions.

[89] As Randolph Moss puts it, "[O]n almost a daily basis, the Office of Legal Counsel works with its clients to refine and reconceptualize proposed executive branch initiatives in the face of legal constraints." Moss, *supra* note 82, at 1329. This "provides a means by which the executive branch lawyer can contribute to the ability of the popularly-elected President and his administration to achieve important policy goals." *Id.* at 1330. Yet, here too another complication arises. The OLC

When embodied in concrete proposals, an administration's agenda may raise few constitutional red flags within the OLC.[90] In addition, many legislative proposals do no more than pose a "litigation risk," in the OLC's terms, and disinterested advice to that effect is likely to do little to impede the progress of an administration proposal. At the same time, modifying proposals to take into account the OLC's constitutional concerns almost inevitably reduces the degree to which the proposal, if enacted, will advance the administration's policy goals.

I discuss later in this chapter the concern expressed by some students of the Canadian Charter of Rights, that constitutional concerns expressed by civil servants will lead the executive branch to modify its proposals more extensively than is strictly required by the Charter. A similar question arises in the OLC. Risk aversion can be a problem when legally oriented civil servants advise policy-oriented cabinet members. Civil servants may be less attentive to the administration's policy goals, and the cabinet member may not realize that the civil servant is overestimating the risk that the legislation will be held unconstitutional. The OLC's organization, a combination of civil servants and legally trained political appointees, reduces the chance of distortion of the administration's policy agenda. Nonetheless, it is likely that some degree of risk aversion remains and may reshape an administration's legislative proposals.

Further, proposals adversely affecting the prerogatives of the presidency as an institution are different from other legislation. With respect to such proposals, the OLC protects the presidency, not the incumbent president.[91] In fact, protecting the presidency sometimes means *opposing* the incumbent.[92] The incumbent may have a different view of the Constitution than the view taken by the OLC,[93] or the president may have political reasons for accepting legislation the OLC regards as incursions on the office, in exchange for what

---

interacts with other elements in the Department of Justice, such as the Civil Rights Division; the "White House"; and other parts of the administration. As a proposal is reshaped in response to OLC concerns, those other institutions may contact the OLC and attempt to change the position the OLC has taken, either by directly changing the OLC's views or by downgrading an evaluation from "serious constitutional concern" to "litigation risk." The OLC sometimes resists these concerns, sometimes accommodates them, and occasionally is persuaded on the merits that its initial evaluation was incorrect.

[90] It therefore seems worth noting that the specific line-item veto proposal that the OLC addressed was raised initially *outside* the Reagan administration, by its conservative allies.

[91] As always, the degree to which the OLC advances a view in defense of the institutions of the presidency in tension with the views of the incumbent administration will vary somewhat across administrations. In general, however, the career lawyers will defend the institution of the presidency and the deputies will offer resistance to varying degrees.

[92] Obviously, opposing here means something like "forcefully advocating an alternative position within the administration."

[93] A president who had been a senator, for example, might think that the institution of the presidency had fewer prerogatives against congressional investigation than the OLC might believe.

the president regards as more important immediate policy goals.[94] In short, the OLC provides advice that is more interested than disinterested when the presidency's prerogatives are in question.[95]

The OLC's pro-presidential bias was demonstrated dramatically in the so-called torture memo issued under the signature of Jay Bybee, then OLC's head, in August 2002.[96] The memorandum addressed, among other things, whether the Constitution allowed Congress to limit the president's choice of interrogation methods by prohibiting him from using torture as incident to his power as commander in chief. The memo concluded that existing statutes should be interpreted not to limit the president's discretion, because an interpretation purporting to restrict his power would raise serious constitutional questions. According to the memo, "the President enjoys complete discretion in the exercise of his Commander-in-Chief authority and in conducting operations against hostile forces."[97] Several paragraphs later, the memorandum said, "As our Office has consistently held during this Administration and previous Administrations, Congress lacks authority under Article I to set the terms and conditions under which the President may exercise his authority as Commander in Chief to control the conduct of operations during a war."

As many commentators observed at the time, this was a remarkable statement because nowhere in the memorandum did its authors indicate that a leading Supreme Court precedent provided some significant support for a contrary conclusion.[98] An influential concurring opinion in that case by Justice Robert Jackson observed that the president's power was "at its lowest ebb" when the president purported to rely solely on the powers inherent in the office in refusing to follow a statute in which Congress "set the terms and conditions" for his actions.[99] Two defenders of the memo suggested that the document was simply "standard lawyerly fare," and that the memo's principal author was part of an emerging group of constitutional theorists who believed

---

[94] Negotiations over proposals can be particularly complex when the president's prerogatives are at stake. Sometimes the OLC's constitutional analysis functions as a bargaining chip, but it may seem peculiar to all participants for the president to offer to accept something the OLC asserts is unconstitutional.

[95] An analysis predicated on institutional interests is compatible with some aspects of fundamental constitutional theory. As Madison wrote in The Federalist, in a system of separation of powers, "the interest of the man must be connected to the constitutional rights of the place." The Federalist No. 51, at 322 (C. Rossiter ed., 1961). A president whose staff provides disinterested interpretation of the president's powers will be at a disadvantage when Congress and the courts interpret the Constitution to advance their institutional interests.

[96] Available at http://www.washingtonpost.com/wp-srv/nation/documents/dojinterrogationmemo20020801.pdf.

[97] The conjunction *and* seems important here because it indicates that the OLC believed that some of the president's actions as commander in chief might not involve operations against hostile forces.

[98] Youngstown Sheet & Tube Co. v. Sawyer, 343 U.S. 579 (1952).

[99] *Id.* at 637 (Jackson, J., concurring).

that the Court's decision was fundamentally erroneous.[100] Yet, good lawyers ordinarily do what they can to mention and distinguish cases that seem to undermine their position—even if they disagree vehemently with those cases.[101] The torture memo's failure to discuss the Supreme Court decision reflected both the author's views about the Constitution's meaning and, more important in the present context, the OLC's traditional commitment to strong pro–executive branch interpretations of the Constitution.

Judicial guidance on questions regarding the institutional presidency is less available than it is with respect to other constitutional questions. When courts have addressed such questions, the OLC has regularly given "cases unfavorable to executive branch prerogatives vis-à-vis Congress a far more limited reading than cases in other areas and, conversely, given favorable cases a very broad reading."[102] Historic practice plays a more important role in interpretation. The president may wish to give up some aspect of the presidency's prerogatives for reasons of policy or principle. Because constitutional precedent is often set by the executive's course of conduct in this area, relinquishing a constitutional position to gain some other policy advantage undermines the presidency in two ways. It directly sets a precedent about what counts as a permissible incursion on the presidency, and it demonstrates that the presidency can survive and continue to function after a particular prerogative has been limited. Thus, the OLC's position as defender of the institution of the presidency may bring it into conflict with the policy objectives of the president it serves.

Professor Douglas Kmiec describes one example in which the conflict between the OLC's defense of the presidency's prerogatives clashed with the president's political agenda.[103] The Civil Service Reform Act of 1978 created a "Special Counsel" to receive and investigate complaints by federal employees who believed that they had suffered retaliation for disclosing government mismanagement. Under the act, the presidentially appointed Special Counsel could be removed by the president only for "inefficiency, neglect of duty, or malfeasance in office." In 1986, Congress began to consider revising the act and expanding the Special Counsel's authority by giving the Office of Special Counsel the power to sue executive branch agencies. The OLC objected to both the limitations on the president's power to remove the Special Counsel

---

[100] Eric Posner & Adrian Vermeule, "A 'Torture' Memo and Its Tortuous Critics," Wall St. Journal, July 6, 2004.

[101] For example, the memorandum could have noted that saying that the president's power is "at its lowest ebb" in certain circumstances does not mean that the president has *no* power.

[102] John O. McGinnis, "Models of the Opinion Function of the Attorney General: A Normative, Descriptive, and Historical Prolegomenon," 15 Cardozo L. Rev. 375, 431 (1993).

[103] Kmiec, *supra* note 76, at 340–44. Kmiec's account seems colored by his disdain for political considerations that, in other contexts at least, seem entirely defensible. Kmiec, *supra* note 72, at 60–63, provides a somewhat more restrained account.

and to the new litigating authority. The OLC regarded the Office of Special Counsel as a subordinate component of the executive branch subject to presidential direction and the presidency, not the courts, as the location for resolving disputes within the executive branch. For what Kmiec regards as political reasons, the OMB "muffled" the OLC's objections, and Congress adopted the new Whistleblower Protection Act of 1988, leaving the OLC "appalled." In the end, the OLC's views prevailed when President Reagan pocket-vetoed the legislation. [104] Notably, the veto occurred during a presidential campaign, but President Reagan was not running for reelection and therefore did not bear any direct political costs arising from his failure to indicate earlier his—or the OLC's—opposition to the legislation.

Despite anecdotal illustrations of the OLC's effects, precise and systematic information about the OLC's bill clearance practice is thin. Nevertheless, several conclusions seem justified. First, the OLC probably presents constitutional analyses as disinterested as those of the courts when it assesses proposals that OLC staff attorneys and deputies do not believe to be part of an incumbent administration's legislative program. That class may be larger than one might initially think because those accustomed to thinking about legislative politics may assimilate proposals by administration allies with administration proposals, while OLC attorneys and even deputies will not. The fact that OLC staff attorneys are civil service bureaucrats weighs against the fact that they also serve particular administrations. Additionally, the disinterestedness of OLC analysis arises in part because the attorneys assess constitutionality with existing court decisions in mind.

Second, OLC analyses of core administration proposals will certainly be slanted to favor the administration's position. The OLC will help shape the proposals to avoid severe litigation risks. It is important to note that the aim is to ensure that the legislation, if enacted, would survive constitutional attack, not to ensure that the legislation actually is constitutional according to a disinterested approach to constitutional interpretation. (That the most common evaluation expressing constitutional concern is phrased in terms of litigation risk may generate a cast of mind that operates to offset the pro-administration bias somewhat.) Further, interactions between the OLC and other parts of the administration may affect the OLC's constitutional evaluations. Courts do not engage in such interactions.

Third, OLC analyses of proposals that its attorneys believe will undermine presidential prerogatives aggressively support the presidency, again because of the OLC's self-identified bureaucratic mission to defend the presidency's prerogatives. As noted earlier, the relevant constitutional law in this area is largely made by practice and much less so by judicial decision. This has two implications. There rarely exist independent criteria by which to assess

[104] See Kmiec, *supra* note 76, at 340–44.

whether the OLC's position is "correct" in some ultimate sense. Nevertheless, the near absence of judicial intervention renders difficult, if not impossible, a direct comparison of the OLC's performance as an interpreter of the Constitution with that of the courts. All that may be said is that in this particular area the OLC has incentives that push it away from disinterestedness.[105]

THE BRITISH EXECUTIVE: RESPONDING TO THE HUMAN RIGHTS ACT

The British Human Rights Act 1998 makes many provisions of the European Convention on Human Rights enforceable in the British courts. The act contains a provision not directly connected to judicial review, on which I focus here. Section 19 of the act requires that a minister in charge of a legislative proposal "make a statement to the effect that in his view the provisions of the Bill are compatible with the Convention rights ('a statement of compatibility'); or . . . make a statement to the effect that although he is unable to make a statement of compatibility the government nevertheless wishes the House to proceed with the Bill."[106] I call the latter type of statement an "inability statement."

The point of these provisions for "rights vetting," as political scientist Janet Hiebert calls the process, is clear.[107] Just as judges are supposed to interpret statutes to make them consistent with the convention, ministers are supposed to submit bills to Parliament that are, in their view, consistent with the convention. The problem, as one supporter of the HRA puts it, is that "governments are rarely, if ever, prepared to own up to violating fundamental rights."[108] How are the statements of compatibility supposed to make governments more likely to do that?

The answer combines political and bureaucratic elements. The ministerial statement of compatibility itself can be brief, but members of Parliament might use the statement as a predicate for questions about the reasons the

---

[105] It seems worth noting that a *more* politically oriented OLC might be more disinterested because, on occasion, the incumbent administration's political interests could offset to some extent the OLC's bureaucratic commitment to protecting the office of the presidency. For example, imagine a situation in which a disinterested analyst would conclude that the president did not have a privilege to resist disclosure. A politically oriented decision maker might conclude that political circumstances should lead the president to waive the privilege, when the OLC might seek to strengthen the privilege by resisting disclosure.

[106] Human Rights Act, 42 Pub. Gen. Acts and Measures, § 19(1) (1998) (Eng.). These "statements of compatibility" or the inability to make such a statement "must be in writing and be published in such manner as the Minister making it considers appropriate." *Id.* § 19 (2).

[107] Janet Hiebert, "Rights-Vetting in New Zealand and Canada: Similar Idea, Different Outcomes," 3 N.Z. J. Pub. & Int'l L. 64 (2005).

[108] Francesca Klug, Values For a Godless Age: The Story of the UK's New Bill of Rights 166 (2000).

minister has for believing the legislative proposal to be compatible with the European Convention.[109] Further, a minister who introduces a proposal accompanied by an inability statement might be embarrassed at having to face charges of violating fundamental rights (where the proposal is thought to be incompatible with convention rights) or of incompetence for being unable to do part of the job, that is, to determine compatibility.

Ministers will rely on their departments' civil servants, or on some general "Human Rights Act Compliance Unit," to provide the detailed justifications that they can expect other members of Parliament to demand.[110] The civil servants charged with determining whether a minister can make a statement of compatibility will be committed to ensuring adherence to the European Convention because that is their job. As Francesca Klug indicates, the requirement "has the potential to get the slumbering beast of Whitehall moving in terms of humans rights scrutiny of policies and legislation in the way nothing else ever has."[111] She notes that civil servants have asserted that they already paid attention to the European Convention, but she suggests that this is only out of concern for "risk management," that is, simply to avoid having legislation found inconsistent with the European Convention by the European Court of Human Rights.[112] The idea is that civil servants' charge had been to ensure that ministers avoid the embarrassment of having legislation criticized by the European Court but that now the charge to civil servants is a positive one—to ensure that ministers can make accurate statements of compatibility.[113]

One design feature of the rights-vetting process deserves specific mention. As my discussion of the OLC suggests, *where* the vetting takes place might matter. Whoever is charged with the task will be more sensitive to claims that legislative proposals might infringe on rights than pure policymakers, because, as students of bureaucracy have emphasized, what you see depends on where you sit. But the rights vetters could be located in a ministry with a substantive mission—in the Ministry of Housing, say—or in the Ministry of Justice, whose mission is "law" quite generally. Rights vetters located within substantive ministries, or drawn from such ministries' staffs, are likely to give somewhat greater weight to policy considerations relative to rights ones, compared to rights vetters located in a central unit.

---

[109] *See generally id.* at 171 ("Although this has got off to a slow start, it is hard to believe that even the more robotic tendency among backbenchers will not use this opportunity in time.").

[110] The Department for Constitutional Affairs has a Human Rights Team, one of whose functions is "responsib[ility] for the human rights act law and policy." Human Rights Team, *at* http://www.lcd.gov.uk/hract/unit.htm (visited Sept. 27, 2006).

[111] Klug, *supra* note 108, at 170.

[112] *Id.* at 170–71.

[113] It is not clear that Klug's description of the pre-HRA practice carries with it some critical sting, as she appears to think: civil servants *should* advise ministers to develop policies that minimally comply with the convention.

Klug suggests that the requirement of statements of compatibility "has a farcical element," because ministerial statements will become as routine "as a cry of 'order, order,' from the Speaker, making its value appear somewhat dubious."[114] The problem goes deeper than that, however. Accurate and sincere statements of compatibility and inability statements may both be so easy to issue that they may not place much constraint on a government's ability to advance whatever legislative agenda it has.[115] The reason that inability statements may be easy to make is that a statement that a minister is *unable* to make a statement of a proposal's compatibility with the European Convention is not a statement that the proposal *is* incompatible with the convention. Actual incompatibility is, of course, one reason a minister might have to make an inability statement, but it is not the only reason. As Geoffrey Marshall points out, a minister can make an inability statement for a variety of other reasons—for example, because, in the minister's view, there is insufficient time to determine whether it is possible to make a statement of compatibility, but there is a pressing need for the legislation.[116] A minister might say, in effect, that the question of the proposal's compatibility with the convention is a quite difficult one, which the minister has been unable to resolve in the time available. Alternatively, the minister might refrain from making a statement of compatibility on the ground that the complex issues are better explored in debate in the House of Commons.[117] Marshall suggests the possibility of ministers taking a position similar to that taken by some senators. The minister might defend an inability statement by referring to the possibility of judicial consideration of compatibility after the proposal is adopted.[118]

Inability statements may not have the political effect hoped for because they need not be public statements of the government's willingness to violate convention rights. Further, with the stick of political discipline taken away, civil servants may have less power, and therefore less bureaucratic reason, to insist that only legislation that they can draft statements of compatibility for move forward.

---

[114] Klug, *supra* note 108, at 170.

[115] An additional difficulty, which the Section 19 procedure shares with judicial review, is that the very making of a statement of compatibility may lull potential opponents into believing that there is no basis in human rights law for challenging the legislation. For a comment to this effect, see Helen Fenwick, Civil Rights: New Labour, Freedom and the Human Rights Act 345 (2000) (suggesting that the Regulation of Investigatory Powers Act 2000 "might not have been put before a Commons dominated by Labour MPs had [it] not been shrouded in human rights rhetoric and accompanied by a statement of [its] compatibility with the European Convention on Human Rights").

[116] Geoffrey Marshall, "The United Kingdom Human Rights Act, 1998," in Defining the Field of Comparative Constitutional Law 110 (Vicki C. Jackson & Mark Tushnet eds., 2002).

[117] Stephen Grosz et al., Human Rights: The 1998 Act and the European Convention 30 (2000).

[118] Marshall, *supra* note 116, at 110.

Statements of compatibility may be easy to make as well. First, similar to bill clearance at the OLC, the largest portion of proposed legislation will raise no substantial questions under the convention. Second, and more important, the Home Office has announced the sensible policy that the mere existence of arguments supporting the conclusion that a proposal is compatible with convention rights is insufficient to justify issuing a statement of compatibility. Such a statement will be issued when "the balance of argument supports the view that the provisions are compatible" with convention rights.[119] The convention simultaneously defines rights at a relatively high level of abstraction and incorporates in the definition of particular rights qualifications suggesting that rights are not violated when a government pursues valuable social objectives. Under such provisions, it will not be difficult for a minister to conclude that the "balance of arguments" supports a statement of compatibility.

Third, and probably most important, the HRA directs that convention rights are to be interpreted by referring to decisions by the European Court of Human Rights in Strasbourg. The Strasbourg Court has developed a doctrine of deference that gives nations a "margin of appreciation" in their actions alleged to violate the convention.[120] The "margin of appreciation" doctrine gives civil servants even more space within which to find proposals compatible with convention rights. The doctrine has two components. The first is ordinary deference to administrative or executive judgment. British human rights lawyers assert that British courts should not invoke this component of the "margin of appreciation" doctrine in applying the Human Rights Act.[121] Whether or not courts should invoke this component, civil servants attempting to determine compatibility should not. It is simply incoherent for a civil servant to invoke a doctrine of deference to administrative discretion because the question for the civil servant is precisely whether to exercise discretion in a way that violates the convention as the civil servant sees things.

The "margin of appreciation" doctrine's second component, however, can play a large role in the civil servant's deliberations. The European Court developed the doctrine because it recognized that it was an international court

[119] Hansard 83540 (statement of Home Minister Jack Straw, May 5, 1999), *available at* http://www.parliament.the-stationery-office.co.uk/pa/cm199899/cmhansrd/vo990505/text/90505w02.htm#90505w02.htm_sbhd0.

[120] *See* Handyside v. United Kingdom, 1 Eur. H.R. Rep. 737 (1976). For another implication of the "margin of appreciation" doctrine, see chapter 2, note 32.

[121] *See, e.g.*, Rabinder Singh, Murray Hunt & Marie Demetriou, "Current Topic: Is There a Role for the 'Margin of Appreciation' in National Law After the Human Rights Act?" 4 Eur. Hum. Rts. L. Rev. 16 (1999); Michael Fordham & Thomas de la Mare, "Identifying the Principles of Proportionality," in Understanding Human Rights Principles 27, 82 (Jeffrey Jowell & Jonathan Cooper eds., 2001) ("What the domestic judges should not do is to 'read-across' the 'margin of appreciation' *as applied by the Strasbourg Court* in individual cases."); Keir Starmer, European Human Rights Law: The Human Rights Act 1998 and the European Convention on Human Rights 190–91 (1999).

with authority to review legislation adopted by numerous states with distinctive cultures facing varying problems. The court felt these elements should be taken into account in determining whether a particular statute violates convention rights.[122] The civil servant determining whether a proposal is compatible with convention rights can sensibly ask, "Does this proposal lie within that portion of the margin of appreciation arising from distinctive national problems and characteristics?"[123] Ministers and their governments always have good reasons, from their own points of view, for proposing new legislation. A good lawyer will find it relatively easy to find in those reasons some distinctive national characteristics or problems that place the proposal within the margin of appreciation.[124]

Examining several instances in which ministers made statements of compatibility reveals additional problems. The Human Rights Act 1998 had an effective date of October 2, 2000, but the British government announced that it would issue statements of compatibility even before that date.[125] Two skeptics about the utility of statements of compatibility point to the rapid enactment of the Criminal Justice (Terrorism and Conspiracy) Act in 1998 to show how politicians can "brush[] aside concerns about . . . patent breaches" of convention rights. The act was the government's response to a terrorist bombing in Omagh, Northern Ireland, in August 1998. The provisions the critics questioned modified rules of evidence in terrorism cases. Senior police officers can be treated as expert witnesses who can give their opinion that a defendant is a member of a terrorist organization without providing direct evidence of membership, although such an opinion cannot be the sole basis for a conviction.[126] In addition, a defendant's guilt may be inferred from his

---

[122] See *Handyside* at 753–54 ("By reason of their direct and continuous contact with the vital forces of their countries, state authorities are in principle in a better position than the international judge to give an opinion on the . . . 'necessity' of a 'restriction'.").

[123] Domestic courts cannot invoke the second component of the "margin of appreciation" doctrine in reviewing civil servants' and ministers' assessment of the nation's distinctive characteristics and problems because the courts are part of the overall domestic system for determining what the nation's distinctive characteristics and problems are. See Starmer, *supra* note 120, at 190. The possibility of a judicial declaration of invalidity might temper the civil servants' use of the "margin of appreciation" doctrine. This sort of risk assessment would work *in favor* of stricter interpretation of convention rights, in contrast to the kind of risk assessment Klug thinks inadequate.

[124] It is worth noting that this can be true even with respect to proposals to adopt legislation essentially identical to legislation of another nation held by the European Court to violate convention rights. The European Court of Human Rights has held, however, that the margin of appreciation may be narrow indeed when "there is a general consensus in Europe about how particular issues are to be dealt with." Starmer, *supra* note 120, at 189. In a narrow class of cases, this provides a real limit to a minister's ability to make a statement of compatibility.

[125] See Clive Walker & Russell L. Weaver, "The United Kingdom Bill of Rights 1998: The Modernisation of Rights in the Old World," 33 U. Mich. J. L. Reform 497, 558 (2000).

[126] Criminal Justice (Terrorism and Conspiracy) Act 1998 c. 40 (U.K. 1998), *available at* http://www.hmso.gov.uk/acts/acts1998/98040—a.htm.

or her failure to mention a material fact after being given the opportunity to consult a lawyer.

The European Court of Human Rights has held that legislation affecting an accused person's right to remain silent may violate the convention's provisions guaranteeing a presumption of innocence and a fair trial. The court assesses the impact of inferences from silence on the particular trial: "The Court must . . . concentrate its attention on the role played by the inferences in the proceedings against the applicant and especially in his conviction." [127] Under this sort of balancing test, applying the provisions of the Criminal Justice (Terrorism and Conspiracy) Act "may, at least under certain circumstances, contravene rights" under the convention. [128]

This does not mean that the legislation contemplates "patent breaches" of the convention and that a statement of compatibility necessarily must "brush aside" such concerns. Drawing on concepts familiar in United States constitutional law, it can be said that the proposal, as applied, might be unconstitutional. The statement of compatibility, however, refers to the proposal's facial validity. Distinguishing between facial validity and "as applied" unconstitutionality clarifies why a minister might find it easy to make a statement of compatibility. It seems unreasonable to deny ministers the opportunity to make such statements merely because one can identify some circumstances under which applying the proposal would violate convention rights. It follows that it then becomes easier to issue a statement of compatibility in the face of well-founded arguments that the proposal might be applied in a way that violates convention rights. The minister can reasonably assert that the balance of arguments favor facial validity even though critics are unquestionably right in spinning out scenarios where the proposal would violate convention rights.

The statement of compatibility issued in connection with another statute illustrates the way in which interaction between facial validity and the statement of compatibility might work to reduce the constraint imposed by requiring such a statement. The 1999 Immigration and Asylum Act gives ministers broad authority to transmit or receive personal information about asylum seekers and other immigrants to or from other nations. [129] Article 8 of the European Convention creates a "right to respect for . . . private . . . life," which has been interpreted to cover informational privacy. [130] The authority

[127] Murray v. United Kingdom, App. No. 18731/91, 22 Eur. H.R. Rep. 29 (1996), at 61.

[128] Clive Walker, "The Bombs in Omagh and Their Aftermath: The Criminal Justice (Terrorism and Conspiracy) Act 1998," 62 Mod. L. Rev. 879, 888 (1999).

[129] Immigration and Asylum Act 1999, c. 33 (U.K. 1999), *available at* http://www.hmso.gov.uk/acts/acts1999/19990033.htm. The act and the statement of compatibility are discussed in Helen Mountfield, "The Concept of a Lawful Interference with Fundamental Rights," in Understanding Human Rights Principles 23 (Jeffrey Jowell & Jonathan Cooper eds., 2001).

[130] European Convention on Human Rights, art. 8; Z. v. Finland, App. No. 22009/93, 25 Eur. H.R. Rep. 371 (1997) (involving the disclosure of personal medical records in a criminal trial).

given ministers might be exercised in a way that violates Article 8. The minister in charge of the legislation made a statement of compatibility, asserting that "those using the Act would not use or disclose information in a way which was incompatible with . . . Article 8 of the Convention."[131] The minister avoided possible facial invalidity by making a commitment to principles of implementation. It would seem easy enough for a minister to assert, with respect to any proposed statute, that it would not be implemented in a manner that violated convention rights.[132]

A ministerial practice allowing a statement of compatibility to be made despite a serious possibility that the statute would authorize many violations of convention rights, as long as the statement is supplemented by representations about enforcement, cannot be a serious constraint on ministers. Civil servants will be asked to draft statements of compatibility and the enforcement representations rather than drafting statutes that avoid the underlying questions about rights violations. Just as the statutes would be written with an eye to substantive convention rights, so the enforcement representations would be written with an eye to avoiding a challenge that the statute and representations do not satisfy the convention requirement that limitations on convention rights be prescribed by law.[133]

The process by which the 2001 Anti-Terrorist, Crime and Security Act was adopted illustrates yet another method by which statements of compatibility can be made without serious impact on the government's agenda. The European Convention on Human Rights allows governments to derogate from its requirements—that is, to eliminate their legal obligation to comply with the convention—"in time of war or other public emergency threatening the life of the nation . . . to the extent strictly required by the exigencies of the situation."[134] The Human Rights Act allows ministers to announce a derogation in anticipation of introducing legislation inconsistent with convention rights (and therefore otherwise incompatible with the Human Rights Act's requirements).[135]

After the terrorist attacks in the United States on September 11, 2001, Prime Minister Tony Blair's government wanted to introduce legislation against terrorism. One of the proposed provisions would have authorized indefinite detention of some alleged foreign terrorists who, the government believed, could not be tried expeditiously, deported to a nation where they would be safe while restrained from continuing terrorist activities, or released

---

[131] Mountfield, *supra* note 129, at 23.

[132] In some circumstances the minister could later issue binding guidance on enforcement, but it is doubtful that any assertions made in support of a statement of compatibility would themselves be binding.

[133] *See* Mountfield, *supra* note 129, at 23–24.

[134] European Convention on Human Rights, art. 15.

[135] Human Rights Act, 42 Pub. Gen. Acts and Measures, § 14 (1998) (Eng.).

in the United Kingdom.[136] Such indefinite detentions, the government agreed, would violate the convention because detention in contemplation of deportation is permissible only where deportation would occur within a reasonably limited time.[137] On November 11, David Blunkett, the home secretary, issued an order derogating from the applicable provision of the European Convention.[138] The next day the government introduced its antiterrorism legislation. Blunkett made a statement of compatibility, taking the position that, the government having derogated from the convention provision with which the bill's provisions would be inconsistent, the legislation was now compatible with the convention.[139]

As the antiterrorism bill quickly moved through Parliament, questions arose about other provisions in the bill. Some critics argued that the derogation itself should be subject to judicial review. The House of Lords adopted an amendment specifying that it would be, but the House of Commons removed the amendment, and the act was adopted without a specific provision dealing with the reviewability of the derogation order.

The Law Lords, sitting as the nation's highest court, citing among much other material the Reports of the Parliamentary Joint Committee that scrutinizes legislation for compatibility with the convention, found that the statute was inconsistent with the convention. The government had derogated only from the provisions dealing with detention, not those dealing with discrimination. The statute discriminated against aliens who posed no different threat to national security than some British citizens. Further, because it was not "strictly required by the exigencies of the situation," as required by the terms of the law authorizing derogations, indefinite detention was a disproportional response: "the choice of an immigration measure to address a security problem had the inevitable result of failing adequately to address that problem . . . while imposing the severe penalty of indefinite detention on persons who . . . may harbour no hostile intentions towards the United Kingdom."[140] The government responded by abandoning its program of indefinite detention. It substituted a system of "control orders" that allowed the former detainees to return to their communities, with curfews, close surveillance, and severe restrictions on movement. Eliminating the discrimination the House of Lords

[136] See Mountfield, supra note 129, at 23–24.

[137] See Chahal v. United Kingdom, App. No. 22414/93, 23 Eur. H.R. Rep. 413, 465 (1996) (interpreting Article 5(1)(f) of the Convention on Human Rights).

[138] Human Rights Act of 1998 (Designated Derogation) Order 2001, (2001) S.I. 3644, available at http://www.legislation.hmso.gov.uk/si/si2001/20013644.htm (visited Sept. 27, 2006).

[139] See Mountfield, supra note 129, at 23–24. It is worth noting that, given the public attention to the process, it seems unlikely that anything would have been different had the minister issued no derogation order and then made an inability statement.

[140] A. v. Secretary of State, [2004] UKHL 56 (Dec. 16, 2004) (judgment of Lord Bingham of Cornhill), available at http://jurist.law.pitt.edu/gazette/2004/12/ruling-on-indefinite-detention-of.php (visited Sept. 27, 2006).

criticized, the government expanded the scope of its program to include British citizens as well.[141]

So far I have discussed statements of compatibility. Inability statements have their benefits as well. Notably, they can be the vehicle for a reasonably clear statement by the government that a proposal it favors is compatible with fundamental rights even though it may be incompatible with the European Convention on Human Rights as interpreted by the European Court.[142] So, for example, the first inability statement made in support of government legislation occurred in 2002, in connection with a proposed statute that continued in effect an existing ban on paid political advertising on television and radio. Despite a European Court decision suggesting that such a broad ban violates the convention,[143] Tessa Jowell, the minister responsible for broadcast regulation, argued that the ban promoted rather than interfered with democratic decision making by limiting the influence of powerful and well-funded groups to dominate or distort public debate.[144] This is in effect a statement that the legislation should be regarded as consistent with fundamental rights, an expression of disagreement with one interpretation of the European Court's position. As such, it advances the project of weak-form systems of protecting fundamental rights by identifying a specific example of legislation about which there can be reasonable disagreement over its consistency with fundamental rights. Minister Jowell went on to say that the government would "mount a robust defence" of the statute if it were attacked, and there certainly are grounds for distinguishing the case the European Court decided from a challenge to the British statute. Yet, even so, the minister indicated that the government would "reconsider" its position and revise the legislation if the *British* courts rejected the government's defense (and would certainly do so if the European Court ruled against the government), once again indicating that the Human Rights Act might give the courts a larger role than it seems on the surface.

I have argued that ministers and civil servants will have little difficulty in making and drafting inability statements and statements of compatibility, but

[141] Prevention of Terrorism Act 2005 (effective March 11, 2005).

[142] Technically, a minister facing European Court jurisprudence that the minister believes to interpret the convention wrongly could make a compatibility statement that explained why the legislation was compatible with the convention properly interpreted. The form of an inability statement—that the minister is unable to state that the legislation is compatible with the convention—actually might enhance its value by emphasizing that the legislation takes a position as to which there can be *reasonable* disagreement.

[143] Vgt Verein Gegen Tierfabriken v. Switzerland, application no. 24699/94, June 28, 2001. The decision did acknowledge the possibility that a more targeted ban on paid broadcast political advertising might be consistent with the convention. *Id.* at ¶ 75.

[144] Minister Jowell's statements are in Hansard vol. 395, part 313, Dec. 3, 2003, cols. 787–89, available at http://www.publications.parliament.uk/pa/cm200203/cmhansrd/vo021203/debtext/21203-15.htm.

I do not mean to imply that the Human Rights Act strategy for securing non-judicial enforcement of fundamental rights must fail. The reason is simple. The statements of compatibility are just that: statements that the proposal is in fact compatible with convention rights. The arguments about how easy it may be to make such statements are not arguments that the statements are inaccurate. Ministers will, in fact, be complying with fundamental rights when they conclude that the balance of arguments support a statement of compatibility. The problem is not that ministers and civil servants will disingenuously evade their obligation to determine whether a proposal violates convention rights. The problem, if there is one, is that the European Convention defines fundamental rights in a way that may be insufficient.

CHARTER PROOFING

Janet Hiebert has identified one process—Charter proofing—that might push ministers to propose legislation that is so clearly within constitutional bounds that their statements of compatibility will be obviously correct. The term is derived from practice in Canada under the Charter, but the phenomenon—on the analogy to "weatherproofing"—can exist in any weak-form system.

Charter proofing has two components, one attractive from the point of view of advocates of weak-form review, the other less so. Both components arise from bureaucratic risk aversion, in the form of a desire to avoid public embarrassment for the minister whom the civil servants assist. Public embarrassment has two forms. The first results from criticism in the press and by the public. Here risk aversion can offset to some degree the ease with which almost any legislative proposal can be accommodated to the requirements of modern constitutions, with their general and abstract descriptions of protected rights. To avoid public criticism, civil servants will take care that draft legislation falls well within constitutional bounds.

This sort of bureaucratic caution is not cost-free. It might lead to the sacrifice of some of the minister's policy goals, as proposals are trimmed back, and thereby made a bit less effective, to keep them away from the constitutional boundaries rather than pressing up against those boundaries. Avoiding public embarrassment, though, has benefits too, particularly in eliminating controversy that might impair the government's ability to pursue *other* parts of its policy program. Charter proofing of this sort seems to me no different from bureaucratic risk aversion based on fear of public criticism on the ground that the proposal goes somewhat too far as a matter of policy.

The second form of public embarrassment arises from weak-form judicial review itself, and, as Hiebert stresses, undermines the very case for weak-form review. In this version, civil servants Charter-proof legislative proposals by predicting what the courts will say about them. They do not want their minister to be embarrassed by a judicial declaration of incompatibility or unconstitutionality, particularly after the minister made a statement of compatibility in introducing the legislation. Yet, one of the virtues of weak-form review is that it makes transparent the fact that constitutional provisions can be given competing, reasonable interpretations. In the eyes of defenders of weak-form review, the interpretations offered by courts in such systems should be given no special weight simply because they are offered by courts rather than by ministers. Charter proofing with the courts in mind, though, does give the courts' interpretations special weight. As Hiebert puts it, when this sort of Charter proofing occurs, "Parliament is not really contributing to judgment about the reasonable reconciliation of Charter conflicts."[145] It is simply predicting—and perhaps not very well—what the courts will do when the legislation is brought before them.

Hiebert suggests, albeit tentatively, that the bad form of Charter proofing has become prevalent in Canada. In part this may result from the important role generalist lawyers in the Department of Justice play in Charter proofing. That department has a Human Rights Centre that centralizes the vetting process, and also provides the lawyers for the ministries' legal units, who intervene early in the process of developing legislative proposals. Lawyers from the generalist department may be less sensitive than ministry lawyers to the impact that risk aversion might have in impeding the government's ability to advance its legislative policies. Hiebert notes that no Canadian minister has ever made a statement that a legislative proposal was inconsistent with the Charter (as it might be interpreted by the courts), suggesting that the rights-vetting process is quite risk averse.[146] If so, one might raise questions related to those developed in part 1 about the stability of weak-form review. Charter proofing of this sort reduces the benefits of independent judgment that are part of the case for weak-form review. One might then think that strong-form review should replace the now seemingly pointless weak-form system.

Against that skepticism, Hiebert offers the experience of New Zealand, which has a similar rights-vetting process. There over thirty reports of inconsistency between proposed legislation and that nation's statutory bill of rights have been made, including eighteen on legislation introduced by the executive government itself. The structural reason for this is clear: reports in New Zealand are prepared by the attorney general, a member of the executive cabinet who nonetheless by tradition operates with substantial independence from the prime minister. Strikingly, though, Hiebert's account of the occasions on which reports of inconsistency were made includes a high proportion of cases where there seems to have been a reasonable disagreement between the attorney general and the executive government on how to proceed. Fully

---

[145] Janet L. Hiebert, Charter Conflicts: What Is Parliament's Role? 55 (2002).
[146] Hiebert, "Rights-Vetting in New Zealand and Canada," *supra* note 107.

50 percent of the reports, for example, identified violations of equality norms in connection with legislation modifying statutes providing benefits to married partners and long-term opposite-sex cohabitants without giving equivalent benefits to gay couples. The government basically conceded that the new legislation was indeed inconsistent with equality norms, but asserted that it made more sense to deal with the issue of benefits for same-sex couples in comprehensive legislation rather than piecemeal—which it did within a few years. My own evaluation of the other cases is that nearly all of them, and indeed perhaps all of them, involved legislative proposals where people could reasonably disagree on whether they violated fundamental rights. Hiebert is troubled by only two statutes on which reports were made, one authorizing twenty-four-hour electronic monitoring of child sex offenders, including those convicted before the statute took effect, and another allowing government appeals of acquittals in some criminal cases where a "perversion" of the justice system occurred. It is not clear to me that either proposal violates fundamental rights.[147]

Avoiding the second form of Charter proofing—the anticipation of judicial reactions—may be quite difficult. Advocates of weak-form review insist on the beneficial effects of embarrassment in shaping a culture of rights. They favor weak-form review rather than mere press criticism because they believe that experience has shown the inadequacy of the latter as a tool to control government. For them, courts should become another source of judgments that might embarrass ministers. The difficulty lies in creating a culture in which the courts' statements have *some* weight, but only because people believe that the courts' institutional characteristics increase the likelihood that the constitutional interpretations they offer are more reasonable than the reasonable ones offered by the government. If courts' judgments have more weight than that, one might as well adopt strong-form judicial review. As I said in part 1, experience with weak-form judicial review is too recent to support confident judgments about the possibility that weak-form systems will indeed create such cultures.

Parliamentary Responses to Weak-Form Review

As British civil rights activist Francesca Klug indicates, advocates of weak-form review hope that it will affect the legislative branch in parliamentary systems. Yet, over the past century, parliamentary systems have become systems

---

[147] The U.S. Supreme Court has upheld special provisions requiring sex offenders' names to be distributed against *ex post facto* challenges, Smith v. Doe, 538 U.S. 84 (2003), and has allowed states to hold in custody sex offenders after they completed the period for which they were criminally sentenced (because the custody was not punishment), Kansas v. Hendricks, 521 U.S. 346 (1997). A number of democratic systems authorize government appeals of acquittals in some cases.

of executive government. The party or coalition with a majority in parliament selects a prime minister and a cabinet. Those executive officials propose legislation, which is almost automatically endorsed by the parliamentary majority.[148] When parliamentary government becomes executive government, as it typically has, how can the legislative branch play a role in constitutional interpretation?

The answer is, "Through special parliamentary committees charged with assessing the constitutionality of legislative proposals." Standing alone, though, that answer is insufficient. Committees representative of the parliament would have majorities from the governing party or coalition. We need to know why such committees would not be simple rubber stamps for the executive ministries.

Again, experience is too recent to know the answer to that question. Australia lacks a constitution with substantial individual rights provisions enforceable in the courts. It does have a standing committee in the Senate, one of whose tasks is to evaluate proposed legislation to determine whether it would "trespass unduly on personal rights or liberties," or otherwise intrude on fundamental values.[149] The committee, which always includes members of the opposition, emerged as an important institution in a period when the Senate sought to develop a legislative role independent of the executive government. Its staff prepares an "Alert Digest" identifying possible problems with proposed legislation, and forwards the alerts to the appropriate minister. The committee then publishes any responses it receives. According to Allison Martens, Australian legislators believe that the committee has indeed induced some changes between draft and final legislation that are responsive to concerns about fundamental rights, although she describes the committee's overall record as "mixed"—a judgment, though, that does not seem to take account of the possibility of reasonable disagreement over what modifications are needed to bring proposed legislation into line with fundamental rights.

In suggestive preliminary work, Hiebert has examined the operation of the British Joint Committee on Human Rights.[150] The committee operates by sending letters to ministers, asking for more information on particular questions or for clarification of the justifications the ministry has for an apparent

[148] The executive government also obstructs significant legislation offered by members of parliament outside the government. The majority party or coalition will sometimes divide over a legislative proposal, but when the proposal is an important one, the consequence is that the government falls and new elections take place. Concern over losing those elections places severe constraints on the willingness of backbenchers—members of the majority party or its coalition partners—to oppose significant legislative proposals by the ministries.

[149] I draw on Allison M. Martens, "Reconsidering Republican Institutions as Guardians of Rights: Lessons from Australia," prepared for presentation at the 2003 Annual Meeting of the American Political Science Association, Aug. 28–31, 2003.

[150] Janet L. Hiebert, "Parliament and the Human Rights Act: Can the JCHR Help Facilitate a Culture of Rights?" 4 Int'l J. Con. L. 1 (2006).

rights violation. Typically, the ministry does elaborate, but rarely changes its proposal in response to the committee's inquiry. Ordinarily the committee does not repeatedly press the minister for answers. Instead, it describes the exchange in a subsequent report, in which the committee may, as it puts it, bring its concerns "to the attention" of the full parliament.

The committee has twelve members, six from the House of Commons and six from the House of Lords. The committee has never had a majority of its members from the majority party, but only because of a perhaps transitional feature: seats on the committee are allocated in rough proportion to party membership in *each* House, and because the House of Lords remains disproportionately Conservative—pending further reforms—there are equal numbers of Conservative and Labour members from the House of Lords. Accidentally, then, the existing Joint Committee might be somewhat independent of the executive ministries. Still, that accident might last long enough for the committee to develop a culture of independence that would have some effect.[151]

More important, perhaps, are the Joint Committee's size and role. It is a small committee drawn from a very large parliament. The smaller the committee, the less representative can it be of the parliament as a whole—which means the less likely it is that its membership will have views that coincide with those of the majority party or governing coalition as a whole. In addition, small numbers mean large variance. The random or quirky views of an individual member on a particular subject may carry the day in a small committee when they would have no impact in a larger body.

In addition, the Joint Committee's role is structurally to be skeptical about government proposals. Who, though, might want to serve on such a committee? Not someone who imagined herself a team player who might eventually become a minister herself. Rather, membership on the committee seems likely to attract the permanent backbenchers, people who are loyal to their party but who have no hope of becoming ministers someday. Their lack of prospects for advancement *within* the executive government might make them particularly willing to cast a skeptical eye on government proposals. In this connection it may be significant that, according to one study, the "nucleus of compliance-culture is the House of Lords," because that House is not typically a hotbed for members ambitious to serve in the executive government, and because "peers do not have to kowtow as much as MPs either to the electorate or to their party leaderships."[152]

The experience of the Joint Committee in dealing with the British antiterrorism legislation indicates some of the possibilities, and some of the limits,

---

[151] Hiebert quotes Lord Lester, a respected member of the Liberal Democrats, as emphasizing that "getting off to a consensual start was very important for the committee, which 'is working really well now and I hope that we will create a culture that will outlive us.'" *Id.* at 17.

[152] Danny Nichol, "The Human Rights Act and the Politicians," 24 Legal Stud. 451, 472 (2004).

on the committee's ability to vet proposals for constitutionality. The committee heard evidence from the home secretary two days after the legislation was introduced and issued a report two days after the hearing.[153] Hiebert notes that an effective parliamentary committee must have sufficient time to consider constitutional questions carefully. The scrutiny given the antiterrorism legislation shows that the British committee can move extremely quickly when speed is required.

Hiebert's study of the Canadian parliamentary process indicates that such expedition may be unusual. Both houses of Canada's parliament have standing committees charged with evaluating the constitutionality of proposed legislation.[154] Time pressures sometimes make serious evaluation impossible. Hiebert provides a case study of the enactment of a statute aimed at responding to a surprising court decision limiting the power of police to search a person's house.[155] The Supreme Court suspended the effect of its decision for six months when it became clear that existing legislation left a huge gap in the ability of police officers to conduct plainly appropriate searches. Unfortunately, there was no effective government in place for much of that period. The government had already been dissolved when the Court issued its suspension order, and elections were held two weeks later. It took time for the new justice minister to consult with police officials and develop a legislative proposal that, in her view, acceptably balanced privacy and crime investigation concerns. The Supreme Court's suspension order was to expire on November 27, 1997. Corrective legislation was introduced on October 30. The Supreme Court extended its suspension order on November 19, for another month. The legislation was passed on December 17, just as the extended order was to expire. The justice minister pressed the relevant committees to vet the new legislation, and they did. But no one seems to think that the committees had enough time to do the job well. The House of Commons Committee's report referred to the "accelerated consultation," which limited the information the committee received from witnesses, and one member complained that the expedited procedure contributed to an "alarming emasculation of Parliament as an institution."[156]

The steps in the British antiterrorism legislation's enactment that followed those described earlier illustrate another feature of parliamentary consideration of constitutional matters. The Joint Committee's initial report emphasized the committee's view that the government had not shown that an emergency existed threatening the life of the nation and that several provisions in the proposed legislation were incompatible with convention rights.

---

[153] Joint Comm. on Human Rights, Second Report (2001), *available at* http://www.publications. parliament.uk/pa/jt200102/jtselect/jtrights/037/3702.htm.

[154] Hiebert, *supra* note 145, at 16.

[155] *Id.* at 147–54.

[156] *Quoted in id.* at 157, 158.

Using its standard locution, the committee drew these "matter[s] to the attention of each House."[157] The government made some modifications in the bill, which was then the subject of another report by the Joint Committee a few weeks later.[158] Again the government made a few modifications in the bill, which was then approved by the House of Commons.

The bill faced more problems in the House of Lords, which rejected ten provisions in the bill, an extraordinary action. The bill was sent back to the House of Commons, which insisted on retaining the provisions. The legislation returned to the House of Lords, which acceded to the House of Commons on all but one of the provisions, a section extending hate-crime laws to cover religion. Its continued insistence on deleting that provision might have provoked a constitutional crisis by making it impossible for the government to get the legislation adopted promptly,[159] but the government receded, withdrawing the provision and proposing to submit it separately.[160] The Joint Committee's actions seemed to have some effect on the proposals as they moved through the legislative process, but its inability to obstruct legislation—coupled with the similar inability of the House of Lords—limited what the committee could accomplish.[161]

The antiterrorism legislation was extraordinary legislation, and the lessons to be drawn from the process of its enactment must be limited ones. Hiebert observes that the committee's reports have played a role in parliamentary debates—although, she says, they are cited more often by the opposition than by the government's supporters. Another observer of the process offers a similarly tempered judgment: "[I]t is hard to say whether or not all this would have happened even without a Human Rights Act, but at very least, the rights formulation proved helpful in framing the discussion as one in which it was necessary to seek to balance freedom and security, rather than to allow an entirely blank cheque to the latter."[162] At the moment, I suspect that all one can fairly

[157] Joint Comm. on Human Rights, Second Report, *supra* note 153, at ¶ 37.

[158] Joint Comm. on Human Rights, Fifth Report (2001), *available at* http://www.publications.parliament.uk/pa/jt200102/jtselect/jtrights/51/5102.htm (visited Sept. 27, 2006).

[159] The House of Lords cannot permanently block legislation adopted by the House of Commons, but it can delay its enactment—except in the case of the budget bill—for up to one year.

[160] For the statement by the home secretary doing so, see http://www.publications.parliament.uk/pa/cm200102/cmhansrd/vo011213/debtext/11213-36.htm (visited Sept. 27, 2006). *See generally* Andrew Evans, "Terror Bill Clears Lords," Press Ass'n, Dec. 11, 2001; Amanda Brown, Joe Churcher & Andrew Evans, "New Setback as Peers Reject Religious Hatred Offence," Press Ass'n, Dec. 13, 2001; Ian Craig, "Lords Pass Anti-Terror Law," Manchester Evening News, Dec. 14, 2001, at 4; Michael Zander, "The Anti-terrorism Bill—What Happened?" 151 New L. J. 1880 (2001).

[161] For additional examples of the JCHR's work and effects, see Hiebert, "Parliament and the Human Rights Act," *supra* note 150, at 31–35; Janet L. Hiebert, "Parliamentary Review of Terrorism Measures," 68 Mod. L. Rev. 676 (2005).

[162] Conor Gearty, "11 September 2001, Counter-terrorism, and the Human Rights Act," 32 J. L. & Soc. 18, 27 (2005).

say is that weak-form review might improve the attention legislators pay to constitutional questions even in parliamentary systems. But, as Hiebert stresses, the conditions under which that will occur are reasonably stringent ones, and the effects might well be small.

A Note on "Reading Up" and Unconstitutionality by Omission

Cases in Canada and the United States dealing with one aspect of equality jurisprudence illustrate another way in which legislatures can be responsive to constitutional values. The problem here arises when the courts find that a statute conferring benefits on one group is unconstitutional because it does not extend those same benefits to another. Analytically, equality could be achieved in one of two ways: eliminate the benefit to the favored group, or extend it to the disfavored one. When should the statute be "read up," as the Canadian Supreme Court puts it, to extend the remedy? Typically, the answer involves some guess by the courts about what the legislature would prefer had it known that it had to choose between eliminating the benefit for all or extending it to some.[163]

The courts might guess wrong, of course, or the legislature sitting at the time of the decision might disagree with the enacting legislature's preferences. The legislature would then have to decide for itself whether to eliminate the benefit for all or to appropriate the funds required to ensure that the previously excluded group gets the benefit. Legislatures typically go along with courts that "read up" a statute. The reason is clear enough: those receiving the benefit want to keep getting it, and exercise their political power to block its withdrawal, leaving the legislature only with the possibility of extending the benefit.[164] In this way, politics supports one of the options the constitution makes available to the legislature.

Portugal's post-fascist constitution adopted in 1976 contains a provision even more dramatically relying on the legislature to enforce constitutional norms. The country's president can ask the Constitutional Court for an advisory opinion on the question, "Has the legislature failed to enact legislation necessary to implement the constitution?" The Constitutional Court in turn is to "communicate" the fact of unconstitutionality by omission, as the doctrine is called, to the legislature.[165]

[163] *See, e.g.*, Beverley McLachlin, "Charter Myths," 33 U.B.C. L. Rev. 23, 32 (1999) ("The aim in each case is to fashion the remedy that will bring the law into harmony with the Constitution and preserve the legislators' intent to the greatest degree possible."); Califano v. Westcott, 443 U.S. 76, 89–90 (1979) (summarizing prior cases).

[164] Heckler v. Mathews, 465 U.S. 728 (1984), drives home the point. There Congress enacted a statute conferring a *new* benefit on a group, and expressly provided that, were the courts to find that the statute unconstitutionally discriminated, the group that was to receive the benefit would be "deprived" of it. (The Court ultimately found that the statute did not discriminate.)

[165] Constitution of Portugal, art. 283.

The Portuguese Constitutional Court has found unconstitutionality by omission in a handful of cases.[166] An early decision held that the legislature violated the constitution by failing to enact a consumer bankruptcy statute. More recently it held that the legislature could abolish the guarantees of job security given to public employees, but found unconstitutionality by omission when the abolition failed to include a provision for unemployment compensation for the discharged civil servants (previously unnecessary because of their job guarantees). The number of cases is small because the Constitutional Court's doctrine allows it to find unconstitutionality by omission only when the constitution creates an affirmative duty to *legislate* on a particular subject, not merely a duty to promote various goals.

Obviously the doctrine of unconstitutionality by omission places responsibility on the legislature, without any serious enforcement mechanism.[167] Its enforcement, that is, comes solely through politics, and in particular through the sense legislators might have that the Constitutional Court's identification of a constitutional violation deserves respect. And, indeed, the Portuguese parliament has regularly repaired its omissions, usually within a few months (although the civil service problem remained unsolved for more than two years, perhaps because of its fiscal implications).[168]

Compliance with judicial decisions reading up an expansive remedy and finding unconstitutionality by omission shows that legislatures *can* be responsive to constitutional imperatives even in situations that might seem to push to the limits of the judicial role. Sometimes ordinary legislative incentives operate, but to some extent a sheer interest in complying with the constitution seems to matter.

CONCLUSION

My own assessment of these case studies is simple, and mundane. Legislative and executive officials charged with interpreting a constitution can do an

---

[166] The following account relies on an interview with Paulo Mota Pinto, a judge on the Constitutional Court, on May 19, 2005.

[167] Conceptually, one could construct a doctrine under which an individual would be entitled to compensation from the government on the basis of harms caused by failure to enact required legislation, but the Portuguese Constitutional Court has not yet done so.

[168] The Colombian courts have developed a doctrine according to which a "state of affairs" can be unconstitutional. According to one account, between 1997 and 2004 the court found "grave regulatory and policy failures" in connection with matters ranging from failure to pay pensions to failures in the administration of prisons, and ordered both the appropriation of funds and the development of plans to ensure compliance. Manuel José Cepeda Espinosa, "The Judicialization of Politics in Colombia: The Old and the New," in The Judicialization of Politics in Latin America 94–95 (Rachel Siederr, Line Schjolden & Alan Angell eds., 2005). The article does not discuss the degree to which these orders have been complied with.

"OK" job, and sometimes that is what they do. Particular officials sometimes have incentives to skew their interpretations, although rarely are the incentives strong enough to push the interpretation outside the (wide) range of interpretations that are reasonable ones. More important, I suspect, many officials often have incentives to avoid interpreting altogether, although some of those incentives occur because of institutional structures that allow the officials to pass the buck.

The previous chapter noted that evaluating the performance of legislators and executive officials in interpreting the constitution is inevitably a comparative matter. In making comparisons with judges, I think it quite important to avoid being romantic about judges while being realistic—or cynical—about legislators and executive official. As a general matter, judges do an OK job of constitutional interpretation, too. And, finally, the word *too* is important. Considered realistically, the performance of legislators and executive officials in interpreting the constitution is not, I think, dramatically different from the performance of judges. To that extent, the confidence weak-form systems of judicial review have in their nonjudicial officials may be justified.

PART III

Judicial Enforcement of Social and Economic Rights

CHAPTER 6

The State Action Doctrine and Social and Economic Rights

CONSIDER the following cases: (1) A man employed by a private college informs his employer (in response to an inquiry) that he is gay. The employer fires him. The former employee sues the college, claiming that the college's action violates the nation's constitutional requirement that everyone be treated equally. (2) A hearing-impaired person seeks medical care from a hospital, which indicates its willingness to provide the care on the condition that the patient provide, and pay for, a sign language interpreter to assist in the delivery of the medical care. The patient sues the hospital, claiming that its refusal to provide service violates the constitutional norm of equality. (3) A group of farmworkers organizes itself and approaches the workers' employer, seeking to bargain collectively over wages, hours, and conditions of labor. The employer refuses to bargain. The union sues the employer, claiming that the refusal to bargain violates the workers' constitutionally protected right of association.[1]

Now consider these cases. (1a) The college employee files a complaint with the local antidiscrimination commission. The commission rejects the claim, explaining that the statute creating it authorizes it to remedy discrimination based on race, gender, age, and other categories, but not sexual orientation. The employee files an action in court seeking to force the commission to consider his claim on the merits, arguing that the exclusion of sexual orientation from the statute violates the nation's constitutional requirements requiring equal treatment for all. (2a) The hearing-impaired person files a claim with the nation's health care system seeking reimbursement for the cost of a sign language interpreter. The system denies the claim, pointing out that the legislation creating the system does not allow it to cover those costs. The hearing-impaired patient files an action in court, arguing that the system's refusal to cover the costs of sign language interpreters violates the nation's constitutional norms of equality. (3a) The farm workers file a complaint with the nation's labor relations board, asking that it conduct a representation election and afterwards use the legal tools it has to require that the employers engage in collective bargaining with their union. The labor relations board dismisses

---

[1] These examples are drawn from cases decided by the Canadian Supreme Court, and discussed in detail in chapter 7.

the complaint, saying that the legislation creating it specifically excludes farm workers from coverage. The farmworkers file an action in court, arguing that the exclusion of farmworkers from coverage violates the nation's constitutional guarantees of freedom of association.

The first lawsuit in each pair of cases involves a claim by one private party against another. U.S. constitutional lawyers say that the issue in the first set of cases is "state action"; constitutional lawyers elsewhere say that the issue is whether the constitution has direct horizontal effect. The "state action" doctrine is one of the most difficult in U.S. constitutional law, and has been almost as difficult in other constitutional systems.[2] The issues in the second set of cases, in contrast, present straightforward questions of substantive constitutional law—perhaps difficult to resolve on the merits, but no more so than many other substantive issues. Yet, it should be clear that nothing distinguishes the two sets of cases other than the nominal defendants—private parties in the first set, government agencies in the second.[3] Or, put another way, the state action issue is, on careful analysis, merely a question, sometimes difficult, of what the substantive requirements of a nation's constitution are.

This chapter lays out the basics of the state action doctrine in U.S. constitutional law. I focus on the United States, to the exclusion of other constitutional systems, to bring out some of the doctrine's complexities, which would be obscured were we to move to comparative analysis too quickly. Relying on two major U.S. constitutional cases—one uncontroversial, the other quite controversial—I explain that the state action doctrine is, in the end, about application of constitutional norms to what I call the background rules of

[2] One indication of the doctrine's difficulty is the location of materials dealing with the doctrine in leading U.S. constitutional law coursebooks. Two place it very late in the course, after substantial discussions of substantive constitutional issues; a third places it only slightly earlier in the book. See G. Stone et al., Constitutional Law (5th ed., 2005) (materials in the final chapter); Kathleen M. Sullivan & Gerald Gunther, Constitutional Law (15th ed., 2004) (materials at pp. 888–926, after discussion of equal protection law); Jesse H. Choper et al., Constitutional Law (9th ed., 2001) (materials at pp. 1415–86 of a book with 1,542 pages).

[3] Laurence H. Tribe, Constitutional Choices 255–56 (1985) (suggesting that litigants should often sue the government officials "who possess the power, by virtue of the state rules at issue, to put 'private' actors in a position to inflict injury"), argues—in my view, unnecessarily—that the difference in nominal defendants should have large doctrinal consequences. With some government agency as defendant, the litigation might produce an injunction against the agency's enforcement of the unconstitutional rule, thereby depriving the private party (soon to become a defendant) of any defense that its action was authorized by state law. (Note as well that when the private actor's power arises from what I call background rules of law, the relevant government officials are judges, and structuring a lawsuit with judges as defendants is conceptually awkward.) With a nominally private party as defendant, the litigation would be this: The defendant relies on some authorization from state law. That authorization is void because it is unconstitutional. The outcome would be an order directing the defendant to act pursuant to whatever background rule the constitution mandates. There is, in my view, no significant difference between these litigation structures.

law—property law, contract law, tort law.[4] With that explanation in hand, we can see that the results under the state action doctrine, or—equivalently—the application of constitutional norms to the background rules, amount to the enforcement (or not) of constitutional social welfare rights, which I define as rights to such matters as health care, jobs, housing, and the like. So, for example, finding state action in the sign-language interpreter case is the same as finding that the hearing impaired are entitled to health care without paying themselves for sign language interpreters.

Chapter 7 then looks at the treatment of the issue of horizontal effect in other constitutional systems. I rely on comparative constitutional law as a source of insight into the structure of domestic constitutional law. I argue that some structural features of the U.S. constitutional system obstruct our vision of the equivalence of the state action doctrine and the constitutional protection of social and economic rights, but also that solutions to the state action problem are easier to come by in constitutional systems more comfortable with social democratic premises.

The final chapter takes up objections to the judicial enforcement of social and economic rights (or, again equivalently, to an expansive state action doctrine). Many of the most cogent objections rest on the assumption that judicial enforcement must occur through strong-form judicial review. The development of weak-form systems of judicial review opens up the possibility that social and economic rights can be enforced in court without raising the problems identified by those who object to constitutional protection of such rights. Cases from the South African Constitutional Court and several U.S. state supreme courts illustrate that possibility, but also suggest that weak-form systems of judicial review may not provide a stable solution to either the state action problem or the question of enforcing social and economic rights in court.

SOME EASY CASES AND A HARD CASE

In 1960 the *New York Times* published a paid advertisement headed "Heed Their Rising Voices."[5] The advertisement supported the civil rights activities of Martin Luther King, Jr., in Montgomery, Alabama, describing how the police had reacted to protests. The advertisement said that student leaders were expelled from school after singing "My Country, 'Tis of Thee," that "truckloads of police armed with shotguns and tear-gas ringed the Alabama State College Campus," and that "[w]hen the entire student body protested to state authorities by refusing to re-register, their dining hall was padlocked in an attempt to starve them into submission."

---

[4] I will simply call these the background rules in most of what follows.

[5] A rich description of the background and the Supreme Court's decision is Anthony Lewis, "Make No Law": The Sullivan Case and the First Amendment (1991).

L. B. Sullivan was the city commissioner in Montgomery who had responsibility for the police department. He sued the *Times* for libel. He said that the advertisement's references to the "police" would be read as referring to him, and that several factual statements in the advertisement were false. Which they were: the students had sung the National Anthem, not "My Country, 'Tis of Thee," some students had not protested the expulsions, the dining hall was never padlocked, and, although large numbers of police officers were sent to campus three times, they never "ringed" the campus. Sullivan claimed that these (trivial) factual misstatements damaged his reputation. An Alabama jury agreed, awarding him $500,000. The jury applied the usual standards in libel cases at the time: false statements were libelous per se if—as these statements did—they "tended" to injure a person's reputation, and the jury could award both "general" and punitive damages.

The U.S. Supreme Court held that the libel award violated the First Amendment's protection of freedom of expression because it "failed to provide the safeguards" the Constitution required.[6] The details of the First Amendment holding are not my concern here. The first section of the Court's opinion is. It addressed and rejected Sullivan's claim that the First Amendment was irrelevant because it was "directed against State action," whereas his libel claim was made in a lawsuit by one private party against another. The Court devoted little time to rejecting Sullivan's argument. True, the Court said, the case was a civil lawsuit between private parties, with the legal standard based on "common-law" rules—that is, those developed over centuries by judges, rather than rules enacted by a state legislature. But, the Court said, the "test" was whether state power had been exercised. A judicial order directing the *New York Times* to pay a half million dollars was, the Court held, an obvious exercise of state power. Based on that conclusion, the Court then held that the state's common-law rules had to conform to the requirements of the First Amendment.

As a state action decision, *New York Times v. Sullivan* is entirely uncontroversial. State action exists when state courts enforce common-law rules, and the only interesting question is what substantive limits the Constitution places on those rules. That statement, while accurate, is misleadingly simple. The reason arises from the interaction among several other propositions. First, the entire edifice of markets in society is erected on the background rules of property, contract, and tort law. (Libel law is a species of tort law.) Second, ordinarily the background rules treat the parties as interchangeable: sometimes a person is a buyer, sometimes a seller, and the background rules are the same no matter who the buyer or seller is. The usual terminology for this proposition is that the background rules are *neutral* as between the parties, promoting market transactions without systematically favoring one side or the other.

---

[6] New York Times v. Sullivan, 376 U.S. 254 (1964).

Third, sometimes the Constitution *requires* that the state put a thumb on the scales in favor of one side—that is, requires departures from neutrality. The really interesting question is, when does it.

Here is an example of a case where the Constitution requires a departure from neutrality.[7] Sometimes members of a church decide that one of them has so departed from church tenets that the rest should no longer have any social dealings with him or her. The person who is "shunned" retains strong emotional commitments to the church and to the other members, and also experiences great distress at being shunned. Sometimes he or she sues the other members, claiming that they should be held liable for the tort of intentional infliction of emotional distress. The defendants respond that holding them liable would violate their right to free exercise of religion under the First Amendment.

Courts regularly, and properly, ignore the state action issue, entertain the First Amendment defense on the merits, and find for the defendants.[8] Why? The plaintiff in a shunning case invokes a rule of tort law that is neutral on its face as to questions of the religious or nonreligious sources of the infliction of emotional distress. The substantive law of the free exercise clause, though, requires (to oversimplify) that states depart from neutrality by reasonably accommodating religiously motivated actions.[9]

The cases I have described are "easy" state action cases. *Shelley v. Kraemer*, in contrast, is usually treated as a difficult state action case.[10] *Shelley* was a constitutional challenge to racially restrictive covenants, which are (or were) provisions in deeds of sale of housing that purported to bar any person buying the house from reselling it (ever) to a person of a specified race. Restrictive covenants were used to keep neighborhoods all white, by allowing white home owners to sell their houses only to white buyers. *Shelley v. Kraemer* arose when an African American family bought a house with a racially restrictive covenant from a white seller, and the neighbors sued to enforce the covenant by keeping the Shelleys from moving into their new house.

Had the case arisen after *New York Times v. Sullivan*, the state action issue would seem trivial. As Chief Justice Fred Vinson put it in *Shelley*, judicial

---

[7] The analysis that follows is drawn from Mark Tushnet, "*Shelley v. Kraemer* and Theories of Equality," 33 N.Y.L. Sch. L. Rev. 383 (1988), which provides more complete citations.

[8] *See, e.g.*, Paul v. Watchtower Bible & Tract Soc., 819 F.2d 875 (9th Cir.), *cert. denied*, 484 U.S. 926 (1987).

[9] The oversimplification is that the Court's most recent decision sharply limits the degree to which accommodations are constitutionally required. Employment Division, Oregon Dept. of Human Resources v. Smith, 484 U.S. 872 (1990). After *Smith*, the accommodation claim would have to be recast in more complex terms, for example, as a claim that the government cannot interfere with internal governance of a church, even by means of the background rules of tort law, or that the church members are invoking their constitutional right of (non)association as well as their free exercise rights.

[10] 334 U.S. 1 (1948).

enforcement of a common-law rule finding racially restrictive covenants lawful was plainly action of an arm of the state government. *Shelley* is controversial not because judicial enforcement of the covenants should not be treated as state action, but because it is not at all clear that, under modern constitutional doctrine, the rule authorizing the enforcement of the restrictive covenants was unconstitutional.

How can that be so? The problem starts with trying to identify the background rule the state courts were enforcing. Restrictive covenants in general are not uncommon. Some modern subdivisions include covenants restricting what changes home owners can make on their front lawns, for example. As a general matter, property law is not hostile to restrictive covenants, viewing them as ways in which communities can ensure that houses have the greatest value to the community as a whole. Property law treats covenants restricting the power of an owner to sell his or her property differently, though. Such covenants are called "restraints on alienation." Property law is suspicious of restraints on alienation because they limit the size of the market for housing, restricting the number of people who can buy a house. That is bad for buyers as a class, but it is also bad for sellers as a class, even if some sellers are happy to accept a restraint on alienation at the time they buy their houses: fewer potential buyers means a thinner market for houses, with more variation in what a seller can expect to get for the house.

Property law's hostility to restraints on alienation generated a rule about restrictive covenants: They were permissible—would be enforced—if they did not restrict the market for housing too substantially, impermissible if they did. So, for example, a covenant restricting sales to the descendants of a subdivision's developer would not be enforceable because that class was too small. The issue in *Shelley* can be recast: what is unconstitutional about a background rule of property law saying that a covenant restricting property transfers on the basis of race does not limit the class of potential purchasers too severely, and therefore is enforceable by the courts?

Note that the background rule is not, "No one can sell property to African Americans." That would be obviously unconstitutional, as a rule singling out African Americans for treatment that harms them. Rather, the background rule is, "We will enforce all restrictive covenants that do not limit the class of purchasers too severely." That rule is not cast in racial terms at all. What is wrong with it?

Chief Justice Vinson suggested that the state courts really were enforcing a race-specific rule. He was skeptical about the claim that the state courts would have enforced a covenant barring home owners from selling their houses to *whites*. Perhaps so, but would that have been because the courts were enforcing a race-specific rule? Not obviously: given the racial composition of the United States in the 1940s, a "no whites" rule would have restricted the market for housing severely, when a "no African Americans" rule would not. That is, the state courts might have enforced a race-neutral rule that had the effect of allowing the restrictive covenants in *Shelley* while prohibiting the "no whites" covenant Chief Justice Vinson had in mind.[11]

Chief Justice Vinson relied more heavily on what he called "more fundamental considerations." Those considerations were embodied in the doctrine that equal protection "is not achieved through indiscriminate imposition of inequalities." The thought here is that, for some reason, there is something constitutionally wrong with a rule that imposes equal disadvantages on African Americans and whites. Chief Justice Vinson's assertion anticipates the Supreme Court's holding in *Brown v. Board of Education*, that segregated education was unconstitutional—even though whites were just as much barred from attending schools with African Americans as African Americans were from attending schools with whites. The best explanation for the "no indiscriminate imposition of inequalities" rule is that it serves the goal of preventing the actual subordination of African Americans. In practice, school segregation perpetuated subordination, as did racially restrictive covenants, no matter what one might say about the theoretical equal imposition of inequalities.

On analysis, the hard case of *Shelley v. Kraemer* confirms what the easy case of *New York Times v. Sullivan* establishes. The state action doctrine does no independent work. It is one way of posing the question, "What constitutional norms apply to the rule of law invoked in this case?" Sometimes state action cases are thought to be difficult because we do not clearly understand that constitutional norms apply to the background rules of property, contract, and tort in the same way they apply to innovative statutory requirements. Sometimes, though, state action cases are genuinely difficult because we do not clearly understand what the content of substantive constitutional law is—and because sometimes our intuition about the proper result in *Shelley* runs up against the implications of invoking the substantive rule applied there in other circumstances.

---

[11] L. Tribe, *supra* note 3, at 260, suggests that the state rule was not neutral for a different reason. He argues that the issue is whether the state may choose to automatically enforce racially restrictive covenants "while generally regarding alienability restraints as anathema." As stated, this appears to be inaccurate, because background property law in the 1940s tolerated a wide range of restraints on alienation, those that were reasonable and did not restrict the market for housing too severely. And, more technically, some racially restrictive covenants would not be enforceable if they were not "suitable" for the neighborhoods in which the houses were located.

An additional possibility is that the background property rule could be regarded as "race-sensitive," in the sense that it dealt with a subject that was of particular interest when race was involved. The U.S. Supreme Court's treatment of race-sensitive rules is complex. Under one view of the cases, rules dealing with race-sensitive subjects require compelling justification. *See, e.g.,* Loving v. Virginia, 388 U.S. 1 (1967) (holding unconstitutional state laws barring marriages between persons of different races). The difficulty with this doctrinal area lies in identifying which rules are race-specific in the relevant sense, a matter on which the Supreme Court has given little guidance.

STATE ACTION, BACKGROUND RULES OF LAW, AND SOCIAL WELFARE RIGHTS

The antisubordination analysis supports yet another approach to *Shelley*, one that makes clear why the case remains controversial. Equal enforcement of racially restrictive covenants has a differential impact on whites and African Americans, and in practice is distinctly unfavorable to African Americans. That is, the background property rule in *Shelley* may have been neutral on its face between whites and African Americans, and may not have fallen into a special category of rules on "race-sensitive" subjects, but it had a disparate adverse impact on African Americans. We could then extract from *Shelley* the substantive constitutional doctrine that background rules with a racially disparate adverse impact are unconstitutional unless they have a strong justification. Decades after *Shelley*, the Supreme Court rejected that doctrine in *Washington v. Davis*.[12] And the reason is revealing: a doctrine treating rules with racially disparate adverse impacts would be incredibly "far-reaching and would raise serious questions about, and perhaps invalidate, a whole range of tax, welfare, public service, regulatory, and licensing statutes that may be more burdensome to the poor and to the average black than to the more affluent white."[13]

That statement refers only to statutes. The background rules of law might be even more significant. They are the rules that create the legal framework for distributing wealth between the poor and the more affluent. If *such* rules are subject to a doctrine suspicious of racially disparate impact, the state action doctrine—that is, the doctrine that constitutional norms must be applied to the background rules of law—would transform American society.

Consider two chestnuts of state action theory.[14] (1) A person moves into a new house and invites his neighbors to a housewarming party. But, being a racist, he refuses to invite his African American neighbors. One of them shows up anyway, and the home owner calls the police to arrest the "intruder" for trespass.[15]

---

[12] 426 U.S. 229 (1976). The case left open the possibility that disparate impact, when coupled with other evidence, might support an inference of the discriminatory intent that it held the Fourteenth Amendment made a predicate for unconstitutionality. Perhaps, in retrospect, we could reconstruct *Shelley* by locating additional evidence to support such an inference. For example, the Restatement of Property, published in 1944, stated the general rule that restrictive covenants were permissible if the excluded class was not too large, but then specifically exempted from that rule racially restrictive covenants when such covenants were "reasonably appropriate." This exemption might support an inference that the disparate impact of enforcing restrictive covenants was intended.

[13] 426 U.S. at 248.

[14] Much of the analysis in the remainder of this chapter was developed in conjunction with Gary Peller, and published in Gary Peller & Mark Tushnet, "State Action and a New Birth of Freedom," 92 Geo. L. J. 779 (2004).

[15] Charles L. Black, Jr., "The Supreme Court 1966 Term—Foreword: 'State Action,' Equal Protection, and California's Proposition 14," 81 Harv. L. Rev. 69, 101 (1967), described the "social trespasser" hypothetical as entirely theoretical, which it is. Yet, it serves as a useful introduction to the worries that underlie concern about an expansive state action doctrine.

(2) A person lives in a house on a street corner. Neighborhood children walk across his lawn in a shortcut to school. But, being a racist, the home owner—though not bothered when white children use the shortcut—objects when African American children do, and calls the police to arrest African American trespassers. Most commentators have thought that the police officers commit no constitutional wrong if they enforce the racist wishes in either case. Yet, the analysis the Court has used pretty strongly indicates that *something* unconstitutional has happened. An arrest is state action under any definition. The rule the police enforce—the general law against trespass, which makes it an offense for someone to remain on a person's property without permission—is not cast in racial terms. But, in the circumstances, the law of trespass is being invoked for intentionally discriminatory reasons—the home owner's, of course, not the police's reasons. Even so, a rule that authorizes the police to intervene without concern for the property owner's reasons has a racially disparate impact, similar to that in *Shelley*.

The difficulty can be seen as well in Laurence Tribe's translation into substantive terms the Court's state action holdings in more recent cases. One involved a "warehouseman's lien."[16] These liens arise when a person rents space in a self-storage facility and then fails to pay the rent. The warehouseman gets a lien on the property stored there. New York had a statute saying that the warehouseman could sell the property without notifying the owner, to cover the unpaid rent. Mrs. Brooks argued that selling the property like that violated her right to "due process of law." The Supreme Court held that there was no state action when the warehouseman sold the stored property. To Tribe, the issue in this case was whether "the state rules . . . put 'private' actors in a position to inflict injury—for example, by delegating governmental or monopoly power to private entities."[17] But, what is the "delegation" here? The warehouseman is simply *selling* property in its possession; the "delegation" lies only in the definition of the relative rights of Mrs. Brooks and the warehouseman.

Has anything gone wrong with the analysis? I agree with the controversial proposition that "private" property is actually a delegation of power from the state,[18] but many commentators find that characterization troubling. For example, Frank Goodman writes that "the . . . assertion that individuals engaged in ordinary activities on their own behalf . . . are wielding the power of the state . . . merely because their conduct is not prohibited by state law or protected by the Constitution, is a notion disquietingly totalitarian [and] conspicuously artificial."[19] Writing from an Australian perspective, Greg Taylor

---

[16] Flagg Bros. v. Brooks, 436 U.S. 149 (1978).

[17] L. Tribe, *supra* note 3, at 255.

[18] *See, e.g.*, Robert Hale, "Coercion and Distribution in a Supposedly Non-Coercive State," 38 Pol. Sci. Q. 470 (1923).

[19] Frank Goodman, "Professor Brest on State Action and Liberal Theory, and a Postscript to Professor Stone," 130 U. Pa. L. Rev. 1331, 1338 (1982).

describes the state action doctrine as resting on an ideology of individual autonomy that undergirds the background rules "by permitting everything [the common law] does not expressly prohibit," and that neutral rules reflect "indifference in the interests of freedom."[20]

This misunderstands the underlying claim, which is not that individuals are wielding state power in the circumstances, but that the state's undoubted wielding of its own power—in defining the background rules in one way rather than another—is being questioned. And yet, the concern for totalitarianism is not entirely misplaced. The substantive constitutional law hidden inside state action doctrine could have large implications for the content of the background rules, to the point that adjustments in the background rules to ensure that they conform to substantive constitutional norms could indeed transform the market basis of the U.S. economic order.

Consider here *why* there was a disparate impact in *Washington v. Davis.* The case involved a test for police officers on which whites performed substantially better than African Americans. Without venturing anything like a complete answer, we can say that there was a disparate impact because of the effects of educational backgrounds, family life, and experiences outside the police department. Suppose the test had been held unconstitutional. The government could respond to that holding either by abandoning the test or—more interestingly—by intervening to rectify disparities in educational background and family life. That is, it could intrude on the private sphere in ways that seem totalitarian.

The conventional analysis of the state action doctrine avoids this difficulty by advocating a balancing test that allows the courts to weigh the promotion of substantive constitutional norms such as racial equality against the intrusion on the privacy interest in preserving a sphere of unregulated action.[21] Erwin Chemerinsky puts it clearly: The key to the analysis is that courts would balance "the infringer's freedom" against "the alleged violation."[22] So, for example, the "social trespasser" case is thought easy because the racist home owner's privacy interest—which may have a constitutional dimension—outweighs the neighbor's interest in racial equality.

Yet, the conventional analysis has its own difficulties. For one thing, striking the balance is not always easy. My experience in teaching the state action doctrine has led me to shift away from the "social trespasser" example, because it seems to me that today's students do not find obviously outrageous a requirement that the police refuse to enforce the racist preference in the social

---

[20] Greg Taylor, "Why the Common Law Should Be Only Indirectly Affected by Constitutional Guarantees: A Comment on Stone," 26 Melbourne U. L. Rev. 623, 628, 638 (2002).

[21] For examples, see Robert J. Glennon & John Nowak, "A Functional Analysis of the Fourteenth Amendment 'State Action' Requirement," 1976 Sup. Ct. Rev. 221; Louis Henkin, "Shelley v. Kraemer: Notes for a Revised Opinion," 110 U. Pa. L. Rev. 473 (1962).

[22] Erwin Chemerinsky, "Rethinking State Action," 80 Nw. U. L. Rev. 503, 506 (1985).

trespasser case. To make the same point, I now have to use examples of race-based exclusions in a young person's search for someone to date and possibly marry. And even those examples do not work all that well for me.

A further and perhaps more important difficulty is that the balancing approach rests on an unanalyzed concept of the "private" sphere. Here the shortcut case provides a useful entry point. The home owner has the right to exclude people from his property because of the background law of property. But, it would not take much to recharacterize the home owner's actions in property law terms: He has given an easement to white children to use the shortcut, but has refrained from giving such an easement to the African American children. *Shelley* itself might show that a background rule of property law that enforced easements arising from racist preferences is unconstitutional.

Even the social trespasser case is subject to this analysis. Every exercise of "private" rights depends on the potential exercise of state power to prevent other private actors from interfering with the rights holder. We can see this by asking what would happen if an actor attempted to use self-help to change an existing state of affairs. A "private" realm only exists to the extent that the state would interfere neither with an initial exercise of rights, nor with self-help by one unhappy with the right holder's choice. If the rejected house-warming "guest" appears at the dinner party anyway, the host depends on state enforcement of trespass law to defeat the self-help attempted by the rejected guest. If the state refuses to protect the host, and instead protects the uninvited "guest" from being ejected, the state has recognized a different legal entitlement vis-à-vis the home of the host. In either case, the state is acting.[23]

An additional example brings the point home, almost literally. Consider the problem of homelessness. Ordinarily scholars think about government sponsored housing programs, supported by taxes, as implementing a right to housing. There is an analytically easier (but in practice unrealistic) solution. Suppose a homeless person simply locates a mansion owned and occupied by a single recluse, and moves in. The recluse calls the police, of course, demanding that they use force to eject the intruder. The homeless person says that the recluse is underusing the property, and that he can live in one or two rooms without seriously disrupting the recluse's life. So, the homeless person says, the property rights the police will enforce should be defined to distribute the entitlement to live in the mansion between him and the recluse.[24]

These examples show that the very point of the state action doctrine is to bring into question the background rules that themselves *constitute* the private

[23] Only if the state refused to protect both the host and the uninvited attendee would there be no state action. The parties would be left to an unregulated state of nature—a realm virtually impossible to imagine in a legal system with rules against physical violence.

[24] The example is not entirely unrealistic. The South African case, Government of the Republic of South Africa v. Grootboom, 2000 (11) BCLR 1169 (CC) (S. Afr.), discussed in detail in chapter 8, arose after homeless people moved into unoccupied property designated for later development.

domain. Substantive constitutional norms might require that property law be defined so as to refuse to give effect to racist preferences in transferring property, as in *Shelley*, or creating easements. One cannot *balance* a preexisting private property interest against some constitutional interest when the question at hand is, What is the proper scope of the background rules in light of constitutional norms?

For these reasons, the persistence of a state action doctrine is something of a puzzle, as is the suggested doctrinal resolution. After setting out the intellectual background against which the modern state action doctrine developed in the United States, the remainder of this chapter examines the doctrine in U.S. constitutional law from two perspectives. The first takes what I called in chapter 1 an *expressivist* approach to the question. It sets the state action problem in the particularities of U.S. constitutional history and ideology. The second takes off from the observation that the state action doctrine is about *judicial* rather than legislative definition of the effects of constitutional norms on the background rules of property, contract, and tort. It argues that concerns about the state action doctrine are, at base, concerns that courts might end up enforcing social welfare rights by defining the background rules in light of constitutional norms, and that courts are particularly inappropriate forums for doing so. This second argument recapitulates and deepens the analysis I have already provided of *Shelley v. Kraemer*.

The second argument returns us to issues associated with strong- and weak-form review and so to comparative constitutional law. The argument relies heavily on the assumption that judicial review takes a strong form. Weaken that assumption, and the argument weakens as well.

The Demise of the State Action Doctrine in the Wake of *Lochner*

The state action doctrine was established as a matter of equal protection law in the *Civil Rights Cases*.[25] The Court there held that Congress had no power under the Fourteenth Amendment to address discrimination that did not flow from state action. This fit well with the reigning conception of constitutional law, which was organized around a sharp distinction between private liberty and public power. *Lochner v. New York* invalidated a state statute limiting the hours bakers could work, because—among other reasons—bakers were fully competent to enter into contracts with their employers on whatever terms the parties were able to agree on.[26] During the era when this view held sway— conventionally given the label *the Lochner era*—the Court viewed its liberty of contract decisions as necessary to protect the private liberty of individuals

---

[25] 109 U.S. 3 (1883).
[26] 198 U.S. 45 (1905).

from the collective power of the state.[27] Seen in this way, the *Civil Rights Cases* and *Lochner* were based on the same analytic grounds: just as the protection of private economic liberty to choose employment terms entailed the constitutional nullification of maximum hour legislation, the protection of private liberty to choose contractual partners entailed the constitutional nullification of antidiscrimination laws that would take this choice out of private hands.

In the *Lochner* context, the private realm was identified according to the background law of property, contract, and tort, which was taken to establish a neutral realm of private liberty the judiciary would protect against legislative encroachment. The comments of Professor Goodman and Mr. Taylor quoted earlier in this chapter reflect the continuing force of this idea. Working the idea out in more detail, the Court took standard common-law rules as a baseline but acknowledged that *some* departures from the baseline were constitutionally permissible.[28] Legislatures could modify the common law by adopting legislation fitting within the categories of the government's police powers—health, safety, and morality. In addition, courts could modify the common law through the usual processes of common-law development. And, finally, legislatures could mimic the courts in modifying the common law, and perhaps go a bit further than the courts themselves would because legislatures were less bound by the doctrine of precedent. Yet, in all these areas the Court insisted that there were limits to the degree to which courts and legislatures could modify the common-law baselines.[29] The categories of the police power were broad but not unlimited, and some judicial modifications of the common law went beyond development into transformation. It was for the courts deploying constitutional norms to enforce the limits on the degree to which legislatures and courts could modify the common law.[30] In a sense, the Court constitutionalized the common-law rules—or rules derived and not departing too much from them—by using those rules as the baseline from which to identify public regulation. Thus, in *Lochner* itself, the Court contrasted New York's maximum hour legislation with the liberty of the employer and employee as identified by common-law doctrines. Because there was a freely chosen offer and acceptance of contractual terms "between persons who are *sui juris*" and (equivalently) because bakers "are in no sense wards of the State," the legislation, according to the Court, invaded the private liberty of individuals.[31]

[27] *See* Gary Peller, "The Metaphysics of American Law," 73 Cal. L. Rev. 1151, 1193–1219 (1985).

[28] *See, e.g.*, NY. Cent. R.R. v. White, 243 U.S. 188 (1917) (upholding a workers' compensation statute).

[29] *See, e.g.*, Adkins v. Children's Hosp., 261 U.S. 525, 561 (1923) (stating that "there are limits to the power" of the state to interfere with the liberty of the individual and that "when these have been passed, it becomes the plain duty of the courts in the proper exercise of their authority to so declare").

[30] For a discussion of the *Lochner*-era Court's decisions upholding departures from the common law, see David E. Bernstein, "*Lochner's* Legacy's Legacy," 82 Tex. L. Rev. 1 (2003).

[31] 198 U.S. at 54, 57.

In *Lochner*, the Court's equation of constitutionally protected liberty with common-law rights was merely implicit; in the *Civil Rights Cases*, the link was explicit. The Court struck down the Civil Rights Act of 1875, a federal public accommodations antidiscrimination law, on the ground that Congress could not provide such a remedy under its Fourteenth Amendment enforcement power, without a prior violation of the Fourteenth Amendment. Such a violation required "state action" because the amendment's prohibitions are directed to the states. According to the Court, an individual's decision to discriminate was simply a "private" wrong:

> If not sanctioned in some way by the state, or not done under state authority, [the injured party's] rights remain in full force, and may presumably be vindicated by resort to the laws of the state for redress. An individual cannot deprive a man of his right to vote, to hold property, to buy and to sell, to sue in the courts, or to be a witness or a juror; he may, by force or fraud, interfere with the enjoyment of the right in a particular case . . . but unless protected in these wrongful acts by some shield of state law or state authority, he cannot destroy or injure the right; he will only render himself amenable to satisfaction or punishment; and amenable therefore to the laws of the state where the wrongful acts are committed.[32]

According to the Court, wrongs would be identified by reference to the laws of the state; no constitutional violation existed unless those laws were themselves racially discriminatory. The Court's somewhat confusing suggestion that the discrimination victim's "redress is to be sought under the laws of the State"[33] did not mean that the Court believed that the common law generally forbade racial discrimination, or that states had an affirmative obligation to enact antidiscrimination legislation. Instead, the Court incorporated existing common-law distinctions as the baseline from which to determine if the state had acted. The Court's reference to the special duties of innkeepers and public carriers makes this clear:

> Innkeepers and public carriers, by the laws of all the states . . . are bound, to the extent of their facilities, to furnish proper accommodation to all unobjectionable persons who in good faith apply for them. If the laws themselves make any unjust discrimination, amenable to the prohibitions of the fourteenth amendment, congress has full power to afford a remedy.[34]

If the state protected a discriminatory decision by an ordinary private party not to enter into contractual relations with an African American, the state was not discriminating because it was neutrally enforcing its racially neutral common-law rule that anyone can choose with whom to contract. An

[32] 109 U.S. at 17.
[33] *Id.* at 24.
[34] *Id.* at 25.

individual's decision not to do business with an African American did not constitute interference with common-law rights to "buy and sell" because no one had the right at common law to force other private parties into contractual relations. Further, the common-law distinctions between parties who were at liberty to choose contracting partners and those who were not would set the baseline for the analysis of state action under the Fourteenth Amendment. If the state protected the same discriminatory act by an innkeeper or common carrier, state action would exist because such a result would depart from the ordinary common-law rule that such "public" parties had a duty to contract rather than a liberty to decline.[35]

Scholars in the early twentieth century systematically criticized the "liberty of contract" line of decisions.[36] Critics sought to show that the common law of contracts, torts, and property on which the Court's constitutional decisions were based was not really private, but rather incorporated public policy decisions.[37] The modifications the *Lochner* Court thought permissible within the constraints it articulated were, according to these arguments, indistinguishable from the ones the Court thought impermissible, given the Court's own reasons for allowing departures from the common law. Legislative regulation of economic relations, for example, did not introduce public power into the private marketplace because the common-law rules themselves already constituted a form of collective regulation of market actors.

One line of attack on the liberty of contract doctrine was to challenge the formalist boundaries of traditional common-law doctrine. Of course, the common law placed some restrictions on the exercise of the private rights it conferred. Contracts were void if they resulted from force or fraud, for example, and one could not use one's property so as to create a nuisance. The *Lochner*-era Court believed that the categories of *force*, *fraud*, and *nuisance* were well defined and narrow. Critics challenged that belief. Taking the criteria that the Court used to identify a case of force or fraud, the critics demonstrated that

---

[35] State antidiscrimination laws would have been a testing ground for the *Lochner*-era Court's approach. The Court could have allowed state legislatures to expand the protections of nondiscrimination requirements beyond the common law's limits—to encompass theaters as well as inns, for example. And perhaps the Court might have allowed legislatures to impose similar requirements on all businesses "affected with a public interest," understood to be a reasonably limited category. Cf. Barry Cushman, Rethinking the New Deal Court: The Structure of a Constitutional Revolution 47–60 (1998) (discussing the Court's use of the concept of "affected with a public interest" in cases involving price and wage regulation). But, as the Court did with wage and hour regulation, it almost certainly would not have permitted legislatures to designate all businesses to be affected with a public interest. See id. at 56 (noting the importance of the public/private distinction in *Lochner*).

[36] Holmes had arguably presaged the entire Realist deconstruction of the public/private dichotomy decades earlier. See Oliver Wendell Holmes, Jr., "Privilege, Malice, and Intent," 8 Harv. L. Rev. 1, 3 (1894) (arguing that common-law entitlements rested on social policy judgments).

[37] For excerpts from the literature, see American Legal Realism 76–97 (William W. Fisher III et al. eds., 1993).

force and fraud could be found in a far wider range of circumstances than the *Lochner*-era judges believed.[38]

The Court's eventual rejection of the liberty of contract doctrine incorporated, at least rhetorically, many of these arguments. For example, in *Miller v. Schoene*, the Court rejected a takings challenge to a state law requiring the destruction of cedar trees threatening to infect nearby apple trees with cedar rust.[39] The Court reasoned that no compensation was required because, even in the absence of legislation, a policy choice had been made by the application of common-law rules. The common law of property either would have found the cedar trees to constitute a nuisance, entitling the apple tree owners to compensation and possibly an injunction, or would recognize a privilege on the part of the cedar tree owners to inflict damage on the apple tree owners without paying compensation: "It would have been none the less a choice if, instead of enacting the present statute, the state, by doing nothing, had permitted serious injury to the apple orchards."[40] In short, the common-law rules could not provide a neutral baseline of private rights because they necessarily benefited some and burdened others, and no neutral principles could dictate which way such distributive consequences should run.

The overruling of the *Lochner*-era liberty of contract cases provided constitutional authority for the large-scale economic regulation adopted during the New Deal. As a conceptual matter, the constitutional permissibility of economic regulation rested upon the notion that social relations that were conducted against the background rules of the common law did not constitute a realm of private liberty, as the *Lochner* ideology presented it, because enforcement of the background rules constituted a particular form of public regulation, not the absence of regulation altogether. The critics' analysis of the "private" common law provided the intellectual basis for rejecting the pretensions of the *Lochner* Court that it was protecting individual liberty against collective power.

These developments made it possible, at least conceptually, to reject the state action doctrine as articulated in the *Civil Rights Cases*: the new constitutional understanding rejected the notion that enforcement of background entitlements could ever be neutral, and acknowledged that such enforcement necessarily constituted a form of public regulation, ideas incompatible with the premises of the state action doctrine.[41] But, even while its analytic justifications

---

[38] This was one strategy deployed in Hale, *supra* note 18.

[39] 276 U.S. 272 (1928).

[40] *Id.* at 279.

[41] The Court may have started down that road. As Charles Black argued in 1967, the Court had found state action in every case presenting the question since 1906. Black, *supra* note 15, at 85. Black's argument on this point should not be taken to prove that much, however, given the Supreme Court's limited jurisdiction, the prevalence of state action dismissals in the lower courts, and the more general limitation that lawyers would likely have been hesitant to bring

were rejected in the realm of economic and social legislation, the ideology reflected in the state action doctrine not only survived but became central to the postwar consensus regarding the proper way to understand American constitutional law.[42] After the fall of *Lochner*, constitutional law was reconceptualized on a basis that was analytically incoherent but perhaps ideologically satisfying to its architects.

The Persistence of the State Action Doctrine in U.S. Constitutional Law

Why has the state action doctrine persisted in U.S. constitutional law? I examine two possibilities here. First, the state action doctrine expresses something important within U.S. legal culture, no matter whether the doctrine is analytically sustainable. Second, the doctrine captures something about the strong form of judicial review in the United States. The second discussion provides the basis for the examination in the following chapters of the possibility of enforcing social welfare rights through weak-form judicial review.

In the U.S. legal culture, the concern, already mentioned, that an expansive state action doctrine has totalitarian overtones plays an important part. The underlying intuition is that there is something more problematic, more threatening to liberty, from government action than from action by private parties. The government might be more threatening because it can inflict *more* harm than private actors, or because it can inflict a different and more troubling *kind* of harm. On examination, though, neither argument seems particularly strong, suggesting that an expressive analysis of the doctrine provides greater insight than alternatives.

One strand of U.S. doctrine assimilates private action to government action—when the private actor exercises the same kind or degree of power the government does. *Marsh v. Alabama* held that the proprietors of a company town—the company that owned the land and employed essentially all of the residents—could not invoke ordinary trespass laws to exclude people from the town center.[43] The state action doctrine does not insulate private actors who are in a position to inflict the same degree of harm that governments ordinarily could. In addition, "worst case" scenarios of government power involve

---

cases ill-fitting conventional state action doctrines. Still, a fair reading of *Shelley v. Kraemer* could lead one to conclude that the Court ruled that enforcement of the background rules did constitute state action, which would leave nothing outside the ambit of the Fourteenth Amendment.

[42] I here avoid the question of why American constitutional law understandings developed as they did, in favor of a description of what happened. For some speculation on the former, see Louis Michael Seidman & Mark V. Tushnet, Remnants of Belief: Contemporary Constitutional Issues (1996); Gary Peller, "Neutral Principles in the 1950's," 21 U. Mich. J. L. Reform 561 (1988).

[43] 326 U.S. 501 (1946).

totalitarian regimes that do indeed seem to exercise power orders of magnitude greater than the power any private actor can exercise. And, finally, people subject to abuses of private power in a market economy can take their business elsewhere. The existence of an "exit" option in market transactions reduces the ability of private actors to inflict harm. Indeed, another strand in U.S. state action doctrine responds to this: the argument for imposing constitutional norms on a private actor has a stronger intuitive appeal when the private actor has a monopoly than it does when the person claiming to be harmed has clear options available.[44]

Each of these arguments has weaknesses. At the most general level, I doubt that one could sustain the claim that *all* governments are in a position to inflict greater harm than *any* private corporation. The Supreme Court of Argentina, in a case presenting a version of the state action question, observed that "basic rights" could be violated by "unions, professional associations, and large enterprises," which "almost always wield enormous economic power, often rivaling that of the state."[45] Governments are constrained by politics, which—however imperfectly democratic—nonetheless places some limits on what they can do. A corporation with a large local presence can disrupt a person's life at least as much as a politically constrained city government can. Consider, for example, the relative risk to life and limb posed to ordinary residents by well-regulated police departments and that posed to workers by loosely regulated chemical manufacturers. Beyond injuries to life and limb are the disruptions of daily life that plant closings can inflict.[46] Justice Douglas expressed this insight when, decades after the decision, he characterized *Shelley* as a case involving "zoning"—done by private actors, to be sure, but with the same social effects as zoning by city governments.[47]

The exit option for those who object does not distinguish private actors from government ones either. Part of the theory of federalism is that people can "vote with their feet" to avoid harms inflicted by local and even state governments, and that the threat of such exit constrains governments from acting oppressively. One counter to this argument relies on the practical difficulties many people face in relocating. Yet, similar problems can afflict many people who find themselves oppressed by private actors: it is not easy for everyone to give up a job where the boss is a sexual harasser and to find another job.

[44] As the Court put it, "It may well be that acts of a heavily regulated utility with at least something of a governmentally protected monopoly will more readily be found to be 'state' acts than will the acts of an entity lacking these characteristics." Jackson v. Metropolitan Edison Co., 419 U.S. 345, 350 (1974).

[45] Samuel Kot, 241 F.C.S. 291 (Sept. 5, 1958) (Argentina), translated in Angel Oquendo, Latin American Law (2006).

[46] It might even be that there are parallels between the worst-case scenarios of government oppression and worst-case possibilities of private oppression. The case of Karen Silkwood offers one classic example of the latter.

[47] Bell v. Maryland, 378 U.S. 226, 328 (1964) (Douglas, J., concurring).

Indeed, a large body of scholarship examines the ways in which strategically minded private actors can take advantage of employees' "firm-specific" investments of human capital to extract more from them (exploit them) more than they could if the employees could relocate costlessly.[48] Indeed, *Flagg Bros. v. Brooks* might exemplify this problem. Mrs. Brooks did not herself place her goods in the Flagg Brothers warehouse. Rather, when she was evicted from her apartment, "the city marshal arranged for Brooks' possessions to be stored" at the Flagg Brothers warehouse. The sense in which Mrs. Brooks had an exit option here is quite attenuated: she could have taken her goods out of the Flagg Brothers warehouse and stored them someplace else, but only after satisfying Flagg Brothers' demands for storage and rental fees, and her dispute with them was precisely over those fees.[49]

The Court's treatment of the monopoly argument is equally weak. According to the Supreme Court, a private actor subject to extensive government regulation does not engage in state action with respect to matters the government has chosen to leave unregulated.[50] *Jackson v. Metropolitan Edison Co.* involved a claim by Mrs. Jackson that Metropolitan Edison, which had a monopoly in supplying power to Detroit, failed to give her notice that it was terminating her service for failure to pay the electric bills.[51] Metropolitan Edison was highly regulated, but Michigan's regulators had not imposed any relevant regulations governing termination of service. Recall here the "nonetheless a choice" language the Court used in the cedar tree case. There the government made a decision to cut down infected trees, but that was just as much a choice as would a decision to let the losses lie where they fell, on the apple trees that would be harmed by cedar rust. The implications for the Jackson case are obvious: Regulating prices but not procedures for termination is a choice that must conform to constitutional norms. More generally, in a highly regulated world—which is to say, in the contemporary world generally—a decision to leave something unregulated is just as much a choice as the decision to develop any particular regulation. The equivalence of the state action doctrine and substantive constitutional law emerges once again.

The magnitude of harm that governments inflict does not seem categorically different from the magnitude of harm that private actors can inflict. What of the *type* of harm? Justice John Marshall Harlan argued that "the types of harm which officials can inflict when they invade protected zones of an

---

[48] *See, e.g.*, Kent Greenfield, "The Place of Workers in Corporate Law," 39 B.C.L. Rev. 283, 314 (1998).

[49] Alternatively, we could see Mrs. Brooks's exit option as leaving the city, the threat of which constrains the terms on which the city marshal would enter into an agreement with Flagg Brothers. Again, the exit possibility here does not seem particularly robust.

[50] The clearest statement of this aspect of the doctrine comes in Rendell-Baker v. Kohn, 457 U.S. 830 (1982).

[51] 419 U.S. 345 (1974).

individual's life are different from the types of harm private citizens inflict on one another."[52] What might this mean?

Consider first the subjective experience of the people harmed. I doubt that people feel much different when their power or water supplies are cut off pursuant to the summary procedures adopted by a private utility, as in the Jackson case, than when the same supplies are cut off pursuant to equally summary procedures used by a city-owned utility.[53] My sense of popular discourse, too, is that procedural unfairness emanating from any source is described as, roughly, a denial of due process. (Think of the kinds of interactions people have with unresponsive consumer service departments of mail-order or Internet suppliers.)

Perhaps Justice Harlan's point was that state actors inflict a distinctive kind of injury. Private thugs and police officers can break down doors, but the police—when they act unconstitutionally—betray the trust of the citizenry, provoking indignant cries like, "You're supposed by on my side!" Yet, this amounts to a claim that illegal actions by police officers are more harmful than illegal actions by private thugs because they betray trust in addition to damaging property.

Sometimes the harms seem to differ, but again because of the substantive constitutional norms to which government action must conform. I could not claim that my constitutional rights are violated when my neighbors erect a crèche on their lawn. Litigants do claim that their constitutional rights are violated when cities erect crèches, and sometimes prevail.[54] The difference arises from substantive constitutional law: the establishment clause, on a view the Court has accepted, is designed to ensure that some citizens do not receive signals—of a sort that perhaps only the government can emit—that they are not full members of the political community.[55]

The propositions that governments systematically inflict more or different types of harm than private actors do cannot stand up to close scrutiny. But, the cases I have described do indicate where the intuitions behind those

[52] Bivens v. Six Unknown Named Agents of Federal Bureau of Narcotics, 403 U.S. 388, 408 (Harlan, J., concurring).

[53] Memphis Light, Gas & Water Div. v. Craft, 436 U.S. 1 (1978), held that municipal utilities did have to follow constitutionally mandated procedures before terminating service.

[54] Compare Lynch v. Donnelly, 465 U.S. 668 (1984) (finding that erection of a crèche by a city did not violate the establishment clause when the crèche was evaluated in its setting), with County of Allegheny v. ACLU, 492 U.S. 573 (1989) (finding a constitutional violation where a nativity scene was the sole display on the main staircase of a county courthouse).

[55] Lynch, 465 U.S. at 697 (O'Connor, J., concurring). I do wonder about the proper response to a claim that a city's "power elite" erected a crèche on the plaza in front of city hall, or even on a plaza in front of and owned by the city's largest bank. Cf. Capital Square Review and Advisory Board v. Pinette, 515 U.S. 753 (1995) (finding that it would not violate the establishment clause for the Ku Klux Klan to erect an unattended cross on the public plaza surrounding Ohio's statehouse, and that excluding the cross violated the free speech clause).

propositions come from—the very place the analysis began. Consider the Jackson case. Mrs. Jackson put her case this way: Metropolitan Edison violated my rights when it terminated service without letting me know in advance. She could have put it differently: Michigan violated my rights when it failed to require that Metropolitan Edison let me know before it terminated my service—or, equivalently, that Michigan had an affirmative duty to require Metropolitan Edison to adopt procedures that would let me know before it terminated my service.

The *Lochner* era was characterized by a suspicion that government had any affirmative duties at all. The New Deal replaced that suspicion with a set of what Cass Sunstein calls "constitutive commitments" to social welfare rights, commitments that Sunstein argues have achieved constitutional status as the expression of Franklin Roosevelt's Second Bill of Rights.[56] The modern government *is* one of affirmative duties—at least until (and if) the United States abandons its system of social provision. We have repudiated *Lochner* in its core applications, and yet it remains with us in the state action doctrine. The reason is that Americans accept the modern regulatory state, which is why we have repudiated *Lochner*, but we are not entirely comfortable with it, which is why we retain the state action doctrine. The state action problem is a difficult one in the United States because Americans have only uneasily committed themselves to a social democratic state, a proposition supported by the comparative analysis in the next chapter.

THE STATE ACTION DOCTRINE AND THE JUDICIAL ROLE

There is another way to see the state action doctrine: as a way of allocating the regulatory power of the modern state between legislatures and courts. The alternative formulation of the claim in *Jackson* is that Michigan had an affirmative duty to regulate Metropolitan Edison. No one disputes that the state legislature or the agency that regulates utilities *could* have required Metropolitan Edison to follow state-prescribed procedures for terminating service. Mrs. Jackson said, in effect, that the government as a whole had an obligation to act, and that the courts had to discharge that obligation when legislatures or regulatory agencies failed to act. The state action doctrine thus serves to carve out areas in which legislative action is permissible—which is what the repudiation of *Lochner* and the creation of the modern regulatory state are about—from areas in which judicial action is required when legislatures have not acted. Seen in this way, the state action doctrine serves democratic decision making, at least in a setting where courts exercise strong-form judicial review.

---

[56] Cass R. Sunstein, The Second Bill of Rights: FDR's Unfinished Revolution and Why We Need It More Than Ever (2004).

Return to the development of the state action doctrine as classical constitutional theory decayed. The classical liberal state dealt with concerns about the level and distribution of important goods primarily in private law, secondarily in public law. In private law, the background rules of contract, tort, and property incorporated sub-rules—sometimes understood as exceptions or qualifications—responsive to concerns about the level of goods that people obtained in market transactions. These were the rules of force, fraud, nuisance, and the like. A distribution of goods that resulted from a seller's fraud on a buyer was normatively unacceptable within classical legal theory, without regard to any supervening constitutional norms. But, of course, classical legal theory defined the sub-rules narrowly. Narrow definitions were needed, in the first instance, because broadly defined sub-rules would displace market outcomes across too wide a range to be acceptable to classical liberals. They were needed, in the second instance, to ensure that common-law judges would not impose pre-liberal norms regarding the acceptable level of goods by finding fraud or coercion whenever the level or distribution of goods seemed unacceptable to the judges. Narrow exceptions, that is, resulted from a combination of substantive and institutional concerns. The substantive concerns disappeared, but the institutional ones remained important as classical constitutional theory was transformed into modern constitutional theory.

Two public law doctrines responded to concerns about the level and distribution of goods. Legislatures could modify background rules of contract, property, and tort by exercising a police power. That power was narrowly defined, like the sub-rules in private law, and for similar reasons.[57] The scope of the police power in classical theory can best be understood, I believe, as resulting from essentially institutional considerations. Courts agreed that legislatures might properly be concerned that courts in common-law litigation could not accurately identify all the occasions on which fraud, coercion, and the like actually occurred, and so allowed legislatures to exercise a police power targeted at fraud, coercion, and the like, but hitting somewhat more broadly than the courts themselves would. In addition, courts developed a constitutional doctrine directly limiting *legislative* distribution of goods. Classical theory condemned as class legislation laws that *intentionally*, not incidentally, deprived people of the share of goods they could obtain on the market or, derivatively, through securing legislation within the scope of the police power.

In private law, a critique of formalism accompanied the rise of the activist state.[58] That critique undermined the narrow definitions of the "exceptional" doctrines of fraud, coercion, and the like. A stylized account of the development follows: Courts began with the narrow definition of coercion, sharply

---

[57] Here I describe the police power in classical legal theory. The actual scope of the police power, as interpreted by U.S. courts through the nineteenth century, was significantly broader. *See* William J. Novak, The People's Welfare (1996).

[58] *See* Morton G. White, Social Thought in America (1976).

distinguishing it from freedom. But, in some cases, the plaintiff's freedom seemed significantly constrained, although not as severely constrained as it had been in the cases initially defining coercion. The courts treated these new cases as involving coercion as well. At some point, it became clear that coercion, as the courts had defined it, was not a category sharply distinguished from freedom but simply a particular location on a continuum of varying degrees of freedom. The critique of formalism was that drawing a line anywhere along this continuum was an arbitrary choice, not guided by any defensible liberal theory of freedom and coercion. Once the ideas of fraud, coercion, and nuisance expanded in the activist state, the way was open for private law to accommodate concerns for the level and distribution of important goods, by correcting market-based outcomes through the use of expansive versions of the classical sub-rules. The public law of the activist state expressed concern for the level and distribution of goods more directly. If market transactions resulted in outcomes where people did not have "enough," according to prevailing norms, those outcomes certainly could be changed by legislation, and sometimes had to be changed pursuant to constitutional command.

The state action doctrine is an imperfect substitute for the techniques by which classical theory protected a domain of private decision making immune from the demand for public justification that the Constitution requires of government action. It is imperfect because the state action doctrine does not in fact preserve such a domain, as a substantive privacy doctrine might. In the cases of interest here, there is no question that *legislatures* could require the private actor to comply with state-determined regulations, subject only to some sort of privacy-related constitutional doctrine. Consider, for example, a legislature's ban on racially restrictive covenants. Only a privacy argument, perhaps in the form of a claim under constitutional provisions barring governments from changing the terms of contracts retroactively or from taking property without compensation, could be raised against such decisions.

The state action doctrine thus protects not a domain of private decision making, but rather the value of allowing the state's law making processes—typically although not always expressing the values of a majority within the state—to regulate private decisions as they choose. Yet, seen as an aspect of lawmaking and majoritarianism, the state action doctrine seems redundant: the relationship between lawmaking and the Constitution is, in this aspect, fully described by identifying the substantive rights the majority may not invade.[59]

---

[59] At its origin, the state action doctrine operated as a limitation on *Congress*'s power to enforce the guarantees of the Fourteenth Amendment, leaving room open for lawmaking action at the state level. *See* the Civil Rights Cases, 109 U.S. 3 (1883). That function of the doctrine is captured in the word *federal* in this modern formulation: "Careful adherence to the 'state action' requirement preserves an area of individual freedom by limiting the reach of federal law and federal judicial power." Lugar v. Edmondson Oil Co., 457 U.S. 922, 936 (1982). Yet, I believe, today the

A reformulation might retrieve something useful. Perhaps we should distinguish among three types of interests: Some may not be restricted by any agency of government; others may be restricted, but only by legislatures; still others may be restricted by any agency of government, including the life-tenured federal judiciary. The first type goes by the name "rights." The state action doctrine identifies the second type. The difficulty then is apparent: We have no real account, outside of the state action doctrine itself, of how to give content to this second type of interest. Consider, for example, *Moose Lodge No. 107 v. Irvis*, where the Court found no state action in a decision to exclude African Americans made by a private club with a state-issued liquor license. The interest here must be one subject to legislative regulation. Is that interest one in private property, in making discriminatory choices, in personal association, in making discriminatory choices in the course of personal association, in making such choices in exercising one's rights over property, or something else? Which of these characterizations is the right one—*right* here meaning "a characterization that does not identify a constitutionally protected interest of the first type and that also does not identify an interest that is regulable by any lawmaking authority"? Constitutional theory has not developed the resources to answer that question.

There is an additional difficulty with treating the state action doctrine as dealing with legislative rather than judicial regulation. Here consider not a legislative ban on racially restrictive covenants but a state court's decision to refuse to enforce such covenants because they are inconsistent with the state's public policies as expressed in the judge-made common law. The cases make it clear that nothing in the state action doctrine stands in the way of such a common-law decision.[60] To be coherent, the state action doctrine must place state courts acting in their lawmaking capacities on the same level as state legislatures, while insisting that courts (state or federal) acting in their capacities as interpreters of the national constitution somehow must be more constrained. Consider in this connection *PruneYard Shopping Center v. Robins*.[61] There the California Supreme Court construed its state constitution to require that a shopping mall make its property available for protest activities. The U.S. Supreme Court upheld that decision in the face of the mall's argument that limiting its use of its own property in that way was a taking for which it had to be compensated. Notably, in other cases the U.S. Supreme Court held that the state action doctrine meant that, where state law was

---

rhetorical force of that statement comes from the phrase "area of individual freedom," rather than from the word "federal."

[60] Indeed, the *Civil Rights Cases* can easily be read as resting at least in part on the judgment that the discriminatory acts Congress sought to prohibit were already prohibited by state common-law rules, or at least could be so prohibited without constitutional objection.

[61] 447 U.S. 74 (1980).

different, shopping mall owners did not violate the Constitution in barring protestors from their property—or, to use the terms developed earlier in this chapter, that the background rule of property law giving property owners that right did not violate the Constitution.[62]

We might be willing to assimilate courts acting in their lawmaking capacities to legislatures because common-law lawmaking, at least, is subject to ordinary legislative revision,[63] whereas interpretations of the national Constitution are not. To sustain this distinction, we would have to develop a category of constitutionally relevant common-law interests, mirroring *Lochner*'s similar attempt, albeit this time so as to authorize either legislative regulation *or* judicial regulation subject to legislative revision.

The state action doctrine thus turns out to be a doctrine whose coherence depends on distinguishing between courts (acting in their federal constitutional capacity) and other lawmaking institutions. Constitutional theory after the decay of classical theory centered on coming up with such a distinction. It did not do so, which leaves the state action doctrine anchored only in a vague sense that somehow it protects individual freedom. The so-called doctrine is the expression of U.S. constitutional values, not an analytically defensible legal rule.

Distinguishing between Courts and Legislatures

The central dimension of the new understanding that emerged in constitutional law after the decay of classical theory divided constitutional issues between social and economic issues, sometimes called second-generation rights, and personal and civil rights, the first-generation rights. With respect to second-generation rights, the critical analysis of the distinction between public law and private action—the revaluation and expansion of "exceptions" to the common-law rules—was accepted as the premise for judicial deference to legislative judgment. The judiciary essentially abandoned the field to legislatures because social and economic issues ultimately rested on policy judgments not amenable to resolution pursuant to anything resembling legal reasoning. First-generation rights were, it was thought, different. The vision of a sharp distinction between public and private was embraced and articulated in the state action doctrine.

The doctrine's attempt to distinguish between courts in their constitutional capacities and legislatures and courts in their general lawmaking capacities resonated with the dominant legal ideology in this period—the Legal Process school, which aimed to turn attention away from substantive political or

---

[62] *See, e.g.*, Lloyd Corp. v. Tanner, 407 U.S. 551 (1972).

[63] It may be worth noting that the California Constitution can be amended by simple majorities acting by initiative, which makes that state's constitutional provisions somewhat more like ordinary majoritarian legislation than constitutional provisions elsewhere are.

social theory in favor of a tight focus on procedure and on the comparative competence of legal institutions.[64] The critical analysis of classical theory was taken to demonstrate the inevitably political character of judicial decision making. As applied to the common law and to constitutional law as well, this analysis threatened core notions about the rule of law, and the Legal Process school responded by simultaneously accepting the critical conclusions and limiting their relevance.[65] The strategy was to confine the critical analysis, developed with respect to the background rules of property, contract, and tort, to matters of social and economic rights.

The Legal Process school accepted the conclusion that all substantive legal decision making inevitably rested on policy judgments. But while substantive issues were taken as inevitably political, decisions about what procedures would be best suited to resolve various kinds of substantive conflicts, and jurisdictional decisions about which institutions were best suited to address particular kinds of substantive questions, could—it was said—be made in a neutral and principled fashion. According to the process theory reconstruction, the rule of law could be rescued by limiting the central insights to substantive issues of social life, such as issues about social and economic policy. The process theorists, in a variety of different formulations, argued that issues about *process*, including judgments about the relative competence of various institutions to decide questions of social policy, could be resolved neutrally. Process theorists thereby offered a reformed way to understand an apolitical rule of law by placing it on proceduralist grounds, the neutrality of which they defended by pointing out differences in the institutional characteristics of the decision-making bodies that were to decide questions of substance. Specifically, judicial decisions had to be principled in a way that legislative ones did not. From this the conclusion was obvious: Critical analysis had shown that the choice between free markets and economic regulation was political and therefore not amenable to principled resolution. Courts could not impose on the background rules any constitutional norms because doing so would be a choice about what sort of market regulation the society should have, which was a political not a legal matter.

Eventually it became clear that the attempt to salvage constitutional theory from the critical insights by preserving a domain of principled judicial action with respect to civil and other fundamental rights could not succeed. Specifying what those rights were was no more—but no less—principled than specifying constitutional limits on the background rights of property and

---

[64] For the intellectual context, see the discussion in William N. Eskridge & Philip P. Frickey, Introduction to Henry M. Hart, Jr., & Albert M. Sacks, The Legal Process: Basic Problems in the Making and Application of Law (1994).

[65] My sense is that the critical bite of the analysis of the common law as political was lost somewhere in the 1960s, but the threat to rule-of-law ideals posed by the critical analysis of constitutional law remained a matter of real concern at least through the 1990s.

contract. Process theory could lead to the kind of broad judicial discretion it purported to eliminate.

Constitutional problems arise when some people think that the Constitution permits one course of action and other people think that the Constitution prohibits it.[66] As constitutional theory was reconstructed, it had to provide rational arguments that would bring together those who initially disagree. The standard account is that such arguments must have two related components: an account of how "the law," properly interpreted, required (or, perhaps more accurately put, did not rule out) the results one's moral commitments commended, and an explanation of why courts were at least among the proper institutions for reaching those results.

Jan Deutsch, in two important articles, addressed each of the requirements the legal academy imposed on constitutional scholarship at the time. "Precedent and Adjudication," published in 1974, demonstrated why the first requirement—that the law require (or at least not rule out) the results one's moral commitments commended—was empty, in the sense that it could always be satisfied.[67] "Neutrality, Legitimacy, and the Supreme Court," published in 1968, demonstrated that existing accounts of law and politics failed to support claims of important differences between legislatures and courts as institutions for implementing moral or political choices.[68]

"Precedent and Adjudication" combined long extracts from various cases, some obviously related to the others, others seemingly unrelated, to show what Deutsch understood constitutional law to be. The article articulates a distinction between administration, which involves acting pursuant to "detailed and comprehensive rules," and adjudication, which involves "only precedent."[69] This distinction immediately called into question claims that judges, too, acted according to rules; for Deutsch, the rule of law could not be a law of rules.[70] What, then, was precedent? Deutsch stated his conclusion: "The choice among competing grounds of decision is . . . a choice about the kind and scope of the precedent being created."[71] Against the common view that judges looked backward at the precedents to find out what those precedents meant for the problem at hand, Deutsch said that judges *create* the precedents they rely on in the very act of relying on them. As he put it in the last line of "Precedent and Adjudication," "relevant precedent is nothing more and nothing less than both perceived as a rational solution to a set of issues occurring at a given time

---

[66] Obviously there are variants: some could believe that the Constitution requires a course of action, while others believe that it either prohibits or merely permits that course, and so on.

[67] 83 Yale L. J. 1553 (1974).

[68] "Neutrality, Legitimacy, and the Supreme Court: Some Intersections Between Law and Political Science," 20 Stan. L. Rev. 169 (1968).

[69] 83 Yale L. J. at 1566.

[70] The reference here is to Justice Scalia's famous article, Antonin Scalia, "The Rule of Law as a Law of Rules," 56 U. Chi. L. Rev. 1175 (1989).

[71] 83 Yale L. J. at 1583.

and a development perceived as a significant contribution to a just future."[72] Deutsch's contention that precedents did not exist as precedents until a court relied on them was a fundamental challenge to then-prevailing ideas that the manner in which law constrained judges was different from the ways in which legislators were constrained (or unconstrained).

"Neutrality, Legitimacy, and the Supreme Court" argued that constitutional decision making was continuous with "ordinary" politics. The article is a relentless attack on the idea that constitutional theory can sensibly distinguish between law and politics through criteria that allocate some issues to legislatures and others to courts. Deutsch began by taking seriously the Legal Process demand for principled decisions. He worked through the Legal Process arguments supporting that demand, concluding that the real basis for requiring neutrality was a demand for *generality*. He then asked why generality mattered. Deutsch's analysis of the arguments offered by Legal Process theorists in favor of the generality requirement led him to conclude that a court's decision was sufficiently general when it yielded what the judges believed to be acceptable answers to existing and reasonably foreseeable (litigated) cases. But, he continued, acceptability was measured by the society in which the question of neutrality arose. To generate a neutral opinion, then, the courts would have to engage in a social and political analysis of their own historical context.[73]

That activity, though, was continuous with, and indistinguishable in principle from, what legislators and executive officials do as they calculate how to achieve their preferred policies against existing opposition. To Deutsch, the courts were simply one political actor among many in the institutional universe. They had institutional needs that differed from those of Congress, and, perhaps more important, the public on which they relied for support (as did all political institutions) believed that courts had a distinctive mission. That meant that courts had to "satisfy both craft pressures and the needs of its symbolic role," if they were to be effective participants in politics.[74] However,

---

[72] *Id.* at 1584. The antecedent of the word *both* in this sentence is quite unclear, but appears to be the context of the decisions referred to as precedent and the context of the decision currently being made.

[73] 20 Stan. L. Rev. at 195 ("A neutral principle becomes one that is perceived as adequately general in the context in which it is applied" and referring to "that degree of generality perceived as adequate by the very society that imposes the requirement of adequate generality to begin with"). Deutsch sketched one interpretation of the contemporary context, *id.* at 222–25, but whether his interpretation was correct or not, it demonstrates the *kind of* analysis Deutsch thought required by Legal Process, properly understood as requiring political analysis.

[74] *See, e.g., id.* at 216 ("Nor is this a limitation peculiar to the judicial branch, for in the last analysis, obedience over the long term even to congressional statutes can be enforced neither by the sword nor by the purse."), 213 (referring to the Court's "institutional needs"), *see also id.* at 185 (discussing political calculations of Senator William Fulbright), 238 ("The Court is charged with the function of upholding the symbol of an evenhanded Government."), 243. By "craft pressures" Deutsch meant the normative standards prevalent in the legal profession at the time a decision is made, defining acceptable behavior.

these craft pressures and this symbolic role did not make courts different in kind from other politicians; internationalist southern Democratic senators had to think about *their* distinctive positions in politics too, which affected the calculations they made in determining what positions to take to maximize their political effectiveness. What judges had to take into account may vary over time, just as it may for elected politicians.

It is important to emphasize that Deutsch worked his way to this conclusion from *within* the premises of Legal Process. His argument was that judges attempting to act according to neutral principles *had to* engage in a political analysis of their environment if they were to succeed in acting according to neutral principles. That is, Deutsch demonstrated that we could make sense of the distinction between law and politics central to the Legal Process construct only by concluding that courts had to engage in (sophisticated) political analysis. The distinction could be sustained intellectually only by transforming it in a way that eliminated its utility within Legal Process theory.

The state action doctrine, then, appears to require a distinction between adjudication and legislation that its premises cannot sustain. Its persistence in U.S. constitutional law can be understood best by treating it as an expression of the values embedded in U.S. law more generally.

Applying the Analysis to Social and Economic Rights

The critical analysis that undermined classical constitutional theory demonstrated that background rights of property, contract, and tort all can be defined differently, with different consequences for the distribution of wealth and power. Without a natural law basis for deciding to recognize one entitlement, and not another, or one particular contract rule as compared to its alternative, or one or another property rule, the setting of each of the background entitlements is a result of state power that could have been exercised differently—that is, the result of policy and politics.[75] Accordingly, the state is responsible for the distribution of wealth, not only in the *ex post* decision whether to redistribute, but also in the *ex ante* ways that wealth is created by recognizing certain interests and not others as worthy of protection. The state is complicit in creating the distribution of wealth in society whether it "acts" affirmatively or whether it does nothing but enforce the background rules of property and contract law.[76]

These arguments make it impossible to sustain objections to the recognition of social and economic rights. *Lochner*-era constitutional doctrine rested

[75] *See* Duncan Kennedy, "Distributive and Paternalistic Motives in Contract and Tort Law, with Special Reference to Compulsory Terms and Unequal Bargaining Power," 41 Md. L. Rev. 563, 580–83 (1982).

[76] The *locus classicus* of this point is *Miller v. Schoene*, discussed earlier.

on the notion that economic life was conducted in a private realm of liberty to be protected against state regulation. The contemporary social welfare state implicitly incorporates the critique of the idea that the economic realm is free from state power by *permitting* social welfare redistributions. However, the contemporary liberal objection to *mandated* social welfare rights remains in the shadow of *Lochner* because it holds that questions regarding the distribution of wealth are among the most political and controversial and thus must be left to democratic processes for their resolution.

The contemporary understanding also echoes *Lochner* in the way in which it defends the distinction between judicially enforceable fundamental rights on the one hand and social and economic rights on the other. The defense takes the form of insisting that fundamental rights are those that ensure that the legislature is in fact democratic, and therefore entitled to deference. The courts should closely examine laws that impose burdens on rights deemed necessary for democratic legitimacy, or on groups unable to protect themselves in majoritarian interest group pluralism.[77] Close judicial scrutiny in these matters is warranted because it is necessary to ensure the ultimate democratic character of the legislature.

This familiar modern accommodation is analytically unstable. Under this view, stricter judicial scrutiny for free speech rights, for example, is triggered only by affirmative governmental action, not by inaction, and significantly, not by the burdens to free speech rights that are the consequence of background entitlements. To the extent that the enjoyment of rights to free speech is a precondition to democratic self-rule, the application of a state action limitation to the identification of free speech rights makes no sense. Larry Alexander has made this point in his analysis of the law dealing with content-neutral regulations of speech, sometimes called "Track Two" regulations.[78] These regulations deal with restrictions on the time and place where expression may occur in public. Sometimes these regulations are held unconstitutional because they too severely restrict the speakers' ability to disseminate their messages. The

---

[77] The source of this argument is United States v. Carolene Products, 304 U.S. 144, 153 n. 4 (1938):

> It is unnecessary to consider now whether legislation which restricts those political processes which can ordinarily be expected to bring about repeal of undesirable legislation, is to be subjected to more exacting judicial scrutiny under the general prohibitions of the Fourteenth Amendment than are most other types of legislation. . . .

> Nor need we enquire whether similar considerations enter into the review of statutes directed at particular religious, or national, or racial minorities . . . whether prejudice against discrete and insular minorities may be a special condition, which tends seriously to curtail the operation of those political processes ordinarily to be relied upon to protect minorities, and which may call for a correspondingly more searching judicial inquiry.

[78] Larry Alexander, "Trouble on Track Two: Incidental Regulations of Speech and Free Speech Theory," 44 Hastings L. J. 921 (1993).

courts evaluate laws that restrict free expression incidentally to their other goals by applying a standard of either reasonableness or heightened scrutiny.[79] But, Alexander points out, *all* general laws—including the background rules of property and contract law—have incidental effects on the ability of speakers to disseminate their messages.[80] If free speech is denied to an individual by "private" actors—exercising their background rights to exclude speakers from their property, say, or to impose speech restrictions as a condition of agreeing to employ someone—then a speech opportunity has been burdened, regardless of the source of the burden. And so, according to Track Two analysis, the courts should apply heightened scrutiny to the background rules of property and contract law to see if they are reasonable means of accomplishing social goals in light of their (incidental, if the word matters) impact on free expression.

The problem is that contemporary notions of the judicial role preclude courts from pursuing such a mode of review. The issue is whether such burdens, in light of other free speech opportunities that remain, are substantial enough that one should conclude that such a society is in fact undemocratic. This would require judgments about speech distribution, the degree of restriction, the availability of alternatives, and an evaluation of the significance of particular restrictions—precisely the kinds of judgment that Deutsch said courts had to make. Such judgments would require resolution of highly controversial issues about the nature of our social lives and the distribution of social power. Ordinarily, the political character of such issues implies deference to the legislature. Here, though, the judiciary cannot coherently defer to the legislature despite the inherently controversial nature of such judgments, because the legislature's own legitimacy—the premise of judicial deference—depends on the resolution of these issues. The determination of the reasonableness of the distribution of wealth and economic power (or the application of heightened scrutiny to such issues) is precisely what the rejection of constitutionalized social and economic rights says is beyond the competence of courts. And yet, if the identification of restrictions on democratic self-rule is to be conducted meaningfully, the process-based settlement *requires* that courts make such judgments.

Judicial determination of these issues would, of course, run afoul of the dominant postwar notions about the limits of the judicial role, but to the extent that such limits are themselves derived from the notion that the legislature is democratic, we are left in a conceptual house of mirrors. This incoherence is solved by application of the state action doctrine. In its evaluation of free speech, for example, the judiciary limits itself to a *Lochner*-ian concept that people have free speech liberty unless the state has burdened free speech

---

[79] *See id.* at 923–24.

[80] *See id.* at 927 (concluding that "the entire body of laws" is subject to Track Two First Amendment analysis).

through affirmative governmental acts. The effects of background entitlements on the exercise of free speech rights are immunized from constitutional
challenge. Or, to put it another way, application of the state action doctrine
to the identification of burdens on free speech assumes that free speech opportunities exist in the social field to such a degree that one can conclude that
democratic self-governance exists, as long as the legislature has not "affirmatively" acted to restrict such opportunities but merely "tolerates" restrictions
that arise from the background rules of property and contract.

A similar analysis applies to the general issue of the effect of the distribution of wealth on free speech rights, and on the democratic character of the
legislature. To the extent that the exercise of effective free speech depends to
some degree on the possession of wealth—as property, or as contractual bargaining power, for example—the evaluation of the democratic character of
the legislature analytically would require the judiciary to determine whether
the distribution of wealth in society was consistent with fair opportunities for
different people to influence the polity. Consider, for example, the proposition
that the background rules incidentally affect the ability of people to disseminate their views. Some people have the resources (derived from their activities in the "private" sphere pursuant to the background rules) to buy time on
television or to rent a hall at which a speech can be delivered; other people
lack such resources. According to Track Two analysis, the courts should determine whether the incidental effects of the background rules on the ability to
disseminate one's views are justified. Track Two analysis requires the courts to
determine whether the guarantees of free speech require the provision of resources to some people or, put another way, whether the First Amendment
constitutionalizes some social welfare rights. Treating such economic distributive issues as beyond the scope of the judicial role in determining whether the
legislature is sufficiently democratic makes sense only if one concludes that
any distribution of wealth, no matter how lopsided and uneven, is consistent
with democratic self-governance.

This discussion leads to a specific way to see the link between the state action doctrine and social and economic rights. Once one abandons the state
action limitation on the identification of free speech rights, the constitutional
determination of the adequacy of free speech opportunities leads to a constitutional evaluation of the consistency of democratic self-rule with the given
distribution of wealth.[81] Such an analysis may conclude that great disparities
in wealth threaten democratic self-rule because of their effect on the abilities
of different groups to communicate and organize. That in turn may imply
that the First Amendment free speech guarantees, when applied without the

---

[81] For present purposes it does not matter whether the standard the courts should apply is reasonableness or heightened scrutiny. All that matters is that courts necessarily have *some* role in
assessing the constitutionality of the background rules.

limitation of the state action doctrine, mandate a roughly egalitarian distribution of wealth in American society. Or, more modestly, that democratic self-rule requires that everyone have the minimal means to participate meaningfully in the marketplace of ideas and political life generally—and therefore that the Constitution guarantees minimally adequate food, shelter, medical care, education, and clothing—as preconditions to concluding that the legislature has democratic legitimacy.

Equal protection analysis leads to the same conclusion. To the extent that the Constitution requires stricter judicial scrutiny for burdens on discrete and insular minorities, removing the state action limitation leads to judicial evaluation of the distribution of economic power. Again, minorities can be burdened not only by affirmative governmental acts but also by governmental failures to act—that is, by racially distributive consequences of the exercise of background entitlements. The state action doctrine, often appearing in the equal protection context as a limitation of constitutional review to *de jure* governmental action, serves to immunize the effect of background entitlements on racial minorities by placing those entitlements beyond the scope of constitutional review. As we saw earlier, the Court recognized the point in *Washington v. Davis*, describing the "far-reaching" effects of close judicial review of background rights when they produced a racially disparate distribution of wealth. The Court's examples—tax, welfare, licensing—all involved affirmative governmental actions with a disproportionate impact on racial minorities. But without the state action limitation, constitutional scrutiny would include the entire social field, whether the result of the state affirmatively "acting," or simply the result of the exercise of background entitlements granted to nongovernmental actors.

The premises that support nondeferential review of de jure burdens on discrete and insular minorities support similar review of *de facto* burdens. If the inability of discrete and insular minorities to protect themselves in the legislative arena justifies special judicial scrutiny, that same obstacle exists with respect to de facto burdens on such groups. If the majoritarian processes of the legislature cannot be trusted when the legislature acts explicitly with respect to the interests of discrete and insular minorities, there is no reason to think that these processes are more trustworthy when the failure to act disproportionately impacts such groups. Or, equivalently, whatever makes us suspect that legislatures will not attend to the interests of racial minorities when they enact statutes should lead us to suspect that similar problems will attend the setting of background rights as well.

The state action doctrine rests on the view that the background, prelegislative state of affairs is a kind of neutral norm that needs no critical review; if the legislature has done nothing affirmative to change the relative social circumstances of discrete and insular minority groups, it is assumed that their position is not at risk from the majoritarian process. But if the judiciary has a special warrant for protecting discrete and insular minorities, such protection should extend to inaction as well as action, or, stated differently, to government enforcement of facially "neutral" background entitlements as well as to affirmative governmental acts.

Were the judiciary to apply equal protection norms without the state action limitation, it would review the distribution of wealth in all its guises to evaluate whether discrete and insular minorities had been discriminated against. Given the correlation that Justice White recognized between race and economic class, the application of equal protection on a de facto basis would, like the similar analysis of free speech rights, require critical evaluation of the disparate economic power of racial minorities. Like the free speech analysis, such an evaluation may conclude that equal protection requires a roughly egalitarian distribution of wealth to ensure that minorities are not discriminated against. Or, more modestly, such an evaluation may conclude that guarantees of minimally adequate social welfare rights to racial minorities is all that is required by a commitment against racial discrimination. By removing the state action limitation, the enforcement of norms against racial discrimination leads to the conclusion that the Constitution requires social and economic rights. Again, the only conceptual barrier to this result is the embrace of the discredited view that the Constitution does not reach such de facto effects because the state is not responsible for them.

Conclusion

I end this chapter with seemingly the most modest proposition about constitutionalized social and economic rights, but one that makes the most important point about the state action doctrine. The analysis I have presented does not establish what content we must give to the Constitution's protection of social and economic rights. In particular, it might be that, on full analysis, libertarians are correct in their belief that a market regulated only by narrowly defined doctrines of fraud, coercion, and nuisance provides the largest benefits to the poor and needy by encouraging the expansion of national output generally, which, they argue, ultimately benefits the poor and needy. The point, though, is that this is a *substantive* argument about social and economic rights, not a pre-theoretical proposition about government neutrality. It must be argued for—just as social democratic positions must be argued for.

The state action issue is equivalent to the question of constitutionalized social and economic rights because the background rules of property and contract affect (albeit perhaps indirectly) the interests remitted to the courts under process-based arguments that are the foundation of modern constitutional law. To say that the state action *question* is the same as the question of whether the Constitution protects social welfare rights does not answer the latter question affirmatively. Elimination of the state action question simply brings the question of constitutional protection of social and economic rights to the fore.[82]

The next two chapters develop and deepen the argument of this one. Chapter 7 examines Canadian constitutional law in some detail, to bring out additional dimensions of the problem of distinguishing between legislative modification of the common law (always permissible no matter what its extent) and judicial modification of the common law, sometimes impermissible because too extensive. It also develops the connection between the state action doctrine and social democratic ideology. That analysis provides the grounding for a more elaborate examination in chapter 8 of judicial capacity to enforce social and economic rights, particularly by means of weak-form review.

[82] For a similar analysis, albeit one less explicit about the implications of eliminating the state action doctrine (and reluctant to do so expressly because of what the author believes to be the conventional understanding of the consequences of that elimination), see John Fee, "The Formal State Action Doctrine and Free Speech Analysis," 83 N. Car. L. Rev. 569 (2005).

CHAPTER 7

Structures of Judicial Review, Horizontal Effect, and Social Welfare Rights

CONSTITUTIONAL systems around the world have confronted the state action problem. The terminology differs. The doctrine takes its name in the United States from the specific wording of the Fourteenth Amendment, which prefaces its substantive provisions with the phrase "No State shall." Elsewhere the problem is labeled *horizontal effect*. A constitution operates vertically when it regulates the relations between a government (usually envisioned as "on top") and citizens, residents, and the like. It operates horizontally when it regulates the relations between private parties. The concerns that animate U.S. discussions—about avoiding conceptions of government that have totalitarian implications, about the proper role of the courts and legislatures—have been expressed elsewhere. For example, in the leading South African case, a dissenter referred to "an egregious caricature . . . that so-called horizontality will result in an Orwellian society in which the all-powerful State will control all private relationships."[1]

Yet, constitutional courts outside the United States seem to have solved the state action problem more easily than the U.S. Supreme Court has. The German Constitutional Court's decision in the case of Erich Lüth has been enormously influential. I discuss the case in more detail later, but for present purposes it is enough to note that the Constitutional Court in that case *rejected* the proposition that Germany's Constitution, known as the Basic Law, directly regulated relations between private parties and simultaneously *created* a doctrine known as "indirect horizontal effect." Under that doctrine, courts charged with construing and developing nonconstitutional law must take constitutional values into account as they do so, and constitutional courts will oversee them to determine whether they have been sufficiently respectful of those values. Constitutional courts around the world have followed the German Constitutional Court in solving the state action problem by using the doctrine of indirect horizontal effect.

---

[1] Du Plessis v. De Klerk, 1996 (5) BCLR 658 (South African Constitutional Court), ¶ 120 (Kriegler, J., dissenting). The case was decided under South Africa's interim Constitution, which provided, "This Chapter shall bind all legislative and executive organs of state at all levels of government." Constitution of the Republic of South Africa, Act 200 of 1993, § 7 (1). The majority interpreted this provision as establishing that the Constitution did not apply to decisions of the courts in their lawmaking capacity.

The distinction between direct and indirect horizontal effect operates in this way: Consider an employee who alleges that her employer fired her because she would not accede to her supervisor's sexual demands. Assume that the nation's constitution bans discrimination on the basis of sex, that the employee's claim describes an example of such discrimination, and that there is no applicable antidiscrimination statute. Under a constitution with direct horizontal effect, the employee would have a claim against her employer based directly on the constitution.[2] Under a constitution with indirect horizontal effect, the employee would have a claim founded on contract law against the employer. The courts charged with developing contract law would be required to apply standard doctrines against wrongful discharge with an eye to the constitution's ban on sex discrimination. The nation's constitutional court would then examine the resulting law of wrongful discharge to determine whether it was appropriately sensitive to the nondiscrimination requirement.

I argue in this chapter that other constitutional systems have found it easier to solve the state action problem for two reasons. The first arises from the *structure* of constitutional review in those systems. Briefly: Those systems have one of two structures that facilitate the adoption of the doctrine of indirect horizontal effect. Some have an integrated judicial system in which the court charged with ultimate interpretive authority over the constitution is also charged with developing nonconstitutional law. In such systems, the high court can freely choose between direct and indirect horizontal effect, and high courts prefer indirect horizontal effect because it avoids some of the conceptual problems associated with direct horizontal effect. Other constitutional systems have a specialized constitutional court that is authorized to supervise the operation of courts charged with applying nonconstitutional law. (I will usually refer to the latter courts as the "ordinary" courts; they include courts that specialize in administrative law, labor law, and the like, as well as courts that deal with general contract and tort law.) In such systems, the constitutional court *must* use the doctrine of indirect horizontal effect to control the ordinary courts. The only question in such systems is the closeness with which the constitutional court will scrutinize the law developed by the ordinary courts. Overly aggressive supervision would undoubtedly provoke resistance on the part of the judges on the ordinary courts. Those judges may be in a position to resist effectively because they handle more business than the constitutional court can review closely.[3] The result has been that the constitutional

---

[2] South Africa's final Constitution provides, "A provision of the Bill of Rights binds a natural or a juristic person if, and to the extent that, it is applicable, taking into account the nature of the right and the nature of any duty imposed by the right." Const. S. Afr., § 8 (2). This is the Constitution's effort to capture the idea of direct horizontal effect.

[3] In central and eastern Europe after the fall of Communism, constitutional and ordinary courts engaged in what some called a "battle of the courts," as the ordinary courts resisted impositions from the constitutional courts. In the end, the constitutional courts prevailed essentially

courts combine the doctrine of indirect horizontal effect with a significant degree of respect for a domain of discretion within which the ordinary courts can continue to develop the law.

The structure of judicial review in the United States makes it extremely difficult to develop a doctrine like that of indirect horizontal effect. The U.S. system of federalism commits to state courts the development of the background rules of property, contract, and tort that are the domain of the state action doctrine.[4] The Supreme Court held in 1875 that the statutes regulating its jurisdiction did not authorize it to review and modify state court decisions determining the content of the background rules.[5] The Court has treated this holding as rooted in fundamental constitutional principles of federalism, and—except in some extraordinary cases—abjures the power to determine whether state court interpretations of the background rules ignore or undervalue constitutional values. True, those extraordinary cases, and some others, provide hints that a Supreme Court that wanted to do so could develop a doctrine like that of indirect horizontal effect. But, as yet, the Supreme Court has not been so inclined.

The second reason for the relative ease with which other constitutional systems have solved the state action problem arises out of the connection between the state action doctrine and social and economic rights. Again briefly: The more extensive a nation's commitment to social welfare values in its legislation, the readier that nation's courts will be to utilize an expansive doctrine of state action/indirect horizontal effect. The reason is simple. The state action doctrine is, at bottom, *about* social and economic rights. The more comfortable a system is with such rights, the less problematic will an expansive state action doctrine be.

I develop the argument just sketched through a detailed examination of the Canadian Supreme Court's confrontation with the state action problem. Initially rejecting the proposition that Canada's Charter of Rights applied directly to judicial decisions (and so to the background rules of property, contract, and tort), the Canadian Supreme Court spent two decades developing its version of the doctrine of indirect horizontal effect. By the twentieth anniversary of the Charter's adoption, Canada's constitutional law recognized a

---

everywhere. I do not know enough about these battles in detail to be sure, but I suspect that the constitutional courts prevailed at least in part because they retreated from overly aggressive modes of supervision. For a hint that this was so in South Africa, see Lynn Berat, "The Constitutional Court of South Africa and Jurisdictional Questions: In the Interest of Justice?" 3 Int'l J. Con. L. 39, 62 (2005) (suggesting that "friction" between the Constitutional Court and the ordinary courts explains the Constitutional Court's failure to "develop the common law" in a specific case).

[4] *See* Greg Taylor, "Why the Common Law Should Be Only Indirectly Affected by Constitutional Guarantees: A Comment on Stone," 26 Melbourne U. L. Rev. 623, 643 (2002) (noting the implications of the U.S. Supreme Court's inability to develop the common law).

[5] Murdock v. City of Memphis, 87 U.S. (20 Wall.) 590 (1875).

wide range of social welfare rights by means of the doctrine of indirect horizontal effect. Following my discussion of the Canadian cases, I examine German law more briefly, primarily to develop the argument about structures of judicial review.

SETTING THE STAGE IN *DOLPHIN DELIVERY*

To a scholar of U.S. constitutional law, perhaps the most remarkable thing about the first Canadian case to grapple with the state action issue, *Dolphin Delivery*,[6] is that the Supreme Court of Canada decided to adopt a position that U.S. scholars knew was impossible to sustain. The literature on the state action doctrine in the United States was extensive by 1986, and there was nearly universal agreement with Charles Black's characterization of the doctrine as a "conceptual disaster area."[7] In holding that the Charter applied to the common law in some sense, but did not apply in litigation between private parties, the Canadian Court walked into the northern version of the same area.[8] It has spent much of its time in later cases digging its way out of the hole that is the state action problem. How it has done so is my concern here.

Dolphin Delivery arose out of a labor dispute in Ontario and British Columbia. A union representing workers locked out of their jobs by Purolator, a courier service in Ontario, wanted to place economic pressure on Purolator. Dolphin Delivery had a contract with Purolator to deliver items Purolator sent to it in British Columbia. The union believed that establishing a picket line at Dolphin Delivery's office would hurt Purolator's ability to promise timely delivery in British Columbia. Dolphin Delivery went to court, seeking an order barring the union from putting up the picket line. It relied on established common-law doctrine that this sort of secondary picketing is a tort, that of inducing a breach of contract: the common-law view was that such picketing unjustifiably makes it more likely that Dolphin Delivery would fail to honor its contract with Purolator. The lower courts issued the injunction, relying on the common-law doctrine, and the union appealed to the Canadian Supreme Court.

The first important point in the Court's holding is a distinction the Court drew among areas of the common law. To say that the Charter applies to the common law but not in private litigation is to distinguish within the common law, because, obviously, the courts apply common-law rules in private litigation. The areas of the common law to which the Charter applied would be exercises of power by legislatures and executive officials that were not

---

[6] [1986] 2 S.C.R. 573.

[7] Charles L. Black, Jr., "Foreword: 'State Action,' Equal Protection, and California's Proposition 14," 81 Harv. L. Rev. 69, 95 (1967).

[8] For citations to Canadian criticisms of *Dolphin Delivery* and its progeny, see David Beatty, Constitutional Law in Theory and Practice 178 n. 109 (1995).

premised on specific statutory authority—roughly speaking, areas of preroga-tive power.[9] Later the Court extended this conceptualization of areas of the common law to apply the Charter to some acts by courts themselves. A court could violate the Charter's ban on unreasonable delay in bringing a defendant to trial, for example.[10] The judicial acts subject to Charter scrutiny did not re-sult, however, from any rules of law the courts developed pursuant to the com-mon law. They were, in this sense, similar to exercises of prerogative power.

In contrast, *Dolphin Delivery* concerned subjecting the background rules of tort, contract, and property to Charter review. The Court noted the possibil-ity that it could adjust the common-law rules about tortious interference with contractual relations to take account of Charter values, but—probably because of the case's peculiar litigation posture—declined to do so.[11] Instead, it constructed a doctrine that necessarily, though not explicitly, did place some of those rules under constitutional scrutiny. The difficulty arises from the Court's endorsement of the result in *Re: Blainey*.[12] There a young woman asked the local human rights commission to find that a hockey association violated her right to equal treatment when it refused to allow her to play on a boys' hockey team. The commission rested its refusal on the scope of its ju-risdiction as defined in the human rights statute. That statute banned dis-crimination based on sex but exempted athletic clubs from the ban when "membership in an athletic organization or participation in an athletic activ-ity is restricted to persons of the same sex." *Dolphin Delivery* described the case as one in which the hockey association "acted on the authority of a statute," referring to the exemption, which "removed the case from the pri-vate sphere."[13] The sense in which the hockey association "acted on the au-thority of the statute" is quite obscure. Obviously, the statutory exemption did not direct the association to discriminate. All it did was leave in place the hockey association's antecedent—that is to say, common-law—right to select team members.[14] In approving the result in *Re: Blainey*, then, *Dolphin*

[9] *See* Taylor, *supra* note 4, at 627 (noting some aspects of prerogative power).

[10] *See, e.g.*, R. v. Rahey, [1987] S.C.R. 588. I note that one might have conceptualized the speedy trial problem as one resulting from failures by executive officials to bring the cases to trial promptly, although that would not deal well with cases where the prosecution pressed for trial and the courts declined the prosecution's urgings.

[11] At the court of appeal, the parties agreed to withdraw from consideration the question of *whether* the Charter applied to the common law. At the Supreme Court, the parties briefed only the question of whether a common-law ban on secondary picketing violated the Charter's guar-antee of freedom of expression. At the oral argument, the Supreme Court's justices indicated that they wanted to hear argument on the state action question. The parties prepared their positions overnight, and both took the position that the Charter did apply to the common law.

[12] 26 D.L.R. (4th) 728 (Sup. Ct. Ont. 1986).

[13] Dolphin Delivery, [1986] 2 S.C.R. at 602, 603.

[14] *But cf.* Timothy Macklem, "*Vriend v. Alberta*: Making the Public Private," 44 McGill L. J. 197, 205–6 (1998–99) (asserting that the statute in *Re: Blainey* "invoke[ed] a ground of distinc-tion that was a prohibited ground of discrimination"). Macklem seems to believe that the "ground

Delivery necessarily held that the Charter modified the background rules to some undefined extent.

Distinguishing among "Public" Actors: Making the Hole Deeper

The notion of "acting on the authority of a statute" played a significant role in the Court's initial elaborations of *Dolphin Delivery*. In *Dolphin Delivery* the Court asserted that "the Charter would apply to many forms of delegated legislation," including "regulations of . . . creatures of Parliament and the Legislatures." It also endorsed Professor Peter Hogg's argument that the Charter would apply when private parties exercised powers "granted" them by legislation, meaning presumably powers beyond those they would have from the common law alone.[15]

With *Dolphin Delivery* behind it, the Supreme Court had a number of paths to take, though none would be analytically satisfying. Its initial choice was to distinguish between entities that were "the government" and those that were not, even though they had some degree of connection to the government.[16] *McKinney v. University of Guelph* was a challenge to mandatory retirement policies for faculty at public universities.[17] The Court held that such universities were not government actors subject to the Charter. Justice Gerald La Forest's opinion for three justices focused on the degree of autonomy the university's board of governors had from control by the legislature and the executive. While acknowledging that the university's policies *could* be "limited by regulation"—presumably, regulations applicable to other nongovernmental entities—and that the universities depended on government funding for the bulk of their operating expenses,[18] Justice La Forest argued that the university's independence with respect to the policies at issue meant that those policies could not be regarded as actions pursuant to government direction.

Justice La Forest's analysis in *McKinney* had three strands. The first was a *formal* analysis of the relation between the legislature and the executive on the one hand, and the university's board of governors on the other. Here Justice La Forest pointed out that a majority of the board of governors was not *directly* appointed by a government official; the other members were "officers of

---

of distinction" invoked was gender, but it actually was *sporting activities*, which is not a prohibited ground.

[15] [1986] 2 S.C.R. at 602.

[16] In the most general terms, these entities are quangoes or parastatals.

[17] [1990] 3 S.C.R. 229.

[18] *Cf.* Rendell-Baker v. Kohn, 457 U.S. 830 (1982) (finding no state action in decision by a school that received almost all of its funding from public sources to discharge a teacher for disagreeing with school policies, where the school did not rely on any standard required by the government in deciding to fire the teacher).

the Faculty, the students, the administrative staff and the alumni."[19] The second strand relied on the proposition that the mandatory retirement policies at issue were adopted by the universities acting as autonomous actors, that is, not under direction from any other government agency, and were presumably in the service of the universities' overall goals rather than in service of particular employment policies dealing with discrimination against the aged: "There is nothing to indicate that . . . the universities were in any way following the dictates of the government. They were acting purely on their own initiative."[20] The third strand was a negative one. The position most forcefully urged in favor of finding the universities to be state actors was that they performed public functions. But, Justice La Forest said, a public-function test was "fraught with difficulty and uncertainty,"[21] and would sweep too broadly, because many private corporations could fairly be described as performing public functions too. So, adopting a public-function test would go far toward eliminating the distinction *Dolphin Delivery* drew between public and private action.

The formal strand turned out to be dispositive in the companion case of *Douglas/Kwantlen Faculty Ass'n v. Douglas College*, which held that community colleges *were* government actors because the provincial minister of education controlled their boards of governors.[22] It must immediately be said that any doctrine that produces a distinction between public universities and public community colleges is not obviously attractive. For, just as in *McKinney*, in *Douglas College* high public officials did not direct the board of governors to adopt the challenged policies. Put another way, in both cases the boards of governors acted without direct control by higher officials—the minister of education in *Douglas College*, the legislature and the executive in *McKinney*—in adopting the challenged policies. And in both cases, higher officials had the power to require the universities or community colleges to adopt particular policies. That is, both cases involved *omissions* or failures to regulate by public officials with power to regulate. Yet, the results in the cases were diametrically opposed.

I must say that I do not see much in the policies relevant to the state action doctrine that commends a distinction between community colleges and universities in their exercise of ordinary property and contract rights. The Court repeatedly emphasizes the importance of sustaining a private domain to avoid a situation in which the courts would "strangle the operation of society and . . . 'diminish the area of freedom within which individuals can act.' "[23] Recall,

---

[19] [1990] 3 S.C.R. at 273. *Cf.* Lebron v. National Railroad Passenger Corp., 513 U.S. 374 (1995) (holding that Amtrak is a state actor because the United States owned all of Amtrak's preferred stock, and the president appointed, directly or indirectly, a majority of Amtrak's board of directors).

[20] [1990] 3 S.C.R. at 269.

[21] *Ibid.*

[22] [1990] 3 S.C.R. 570.

[23] *McKinney*, [1990] 3 S.C.R. at 262.

though, the discussion in chapter 6 of the difficulty in distinguishing among legislators, judges developing the common law, and judges interpreting the constitution. Once the Court concedes the power of the *legislature* to regulate, the relation between "strangling the operation of society" and a narrow state action doctrine is not at all obvious. The rhetoric of freedom sits uneasily in a world with expansive legislative power. Rather, as we will see, the state action doctrine must have something to do not with freedom itself but with the capacity of courts to implement restrictions on freedom that legislatures can more effectively implement. That is, the concerns that necessarily animate a state action doctrine disappear where the courts can easily regulate private activity with no greater difficulties than legislatures can.

Starting to Dig Out of the Hole by Analyzing Failures to Regulate

Perhaps the distinction between community colleges and universities, with respect to policies not commanded by high political officials, is that in the former case the legislature and executive have gone quite a long way toward dictating policy comprehensively (although not so far as to dictate the policy under scrutiny), while in the latter case those officials had not gone quite that far. When a community college's policy is challenged, the challenge is to a *failure* to regulate when regulation is possible and, with respect to many other matters, is actually done. At this point, the interesting question is, When what is inevitably at issue is a failure to regulate, why does it make a difference that government has gone quite far in regulating some entities but not others? The answer appears to be that sometimes a government's decision to move part of the way into a field imposes on it a constitutional duty to move farther.

The issue of when partial occupation of the field triggers a constitutional obligation to occupy much more of the field arises in two important post–*Dolphin Delivery* cases, *Eldridge* and *Vriend*. A stylized version of *Eldridge* is this: Hospitals are private entities under the definitions of *McKinney* and *Douglas College*.[24] Though they receive essentially all of their financing from government reimbursements and perform public functions, their boards of governors are not appointed or controlled by high public officials, and they set many policies without direction from such officials. One such policy is that they will make many services available to patients but will require patients who choose to use the services pay, unless the government reimburses the hospitals for the services. So, for example, a hospital might deliver newspapers to patients, but charge for the delivery service, or they might provide five-star meals but charge for the extra costs. Hospitals treat sign language interpreters for the

---

[24] Eldridge v. British Columbia (Attorney General), [1997] 3 S.C.R. 624.

deaf as one of these fee-based services. Until 1990, however, no deaf patient actually had to pay for the service, because a private charity provided it. The charity stopped doing so because it ran out of money. It asked the Ministry of Health to pick up the cost. The ministry administered the government's system under which hospitals received reimbursement for providing medically necessary services. The ministry declined to assume the costs because "it would strain available resources and create a precedent for the funding of similar services for the non–English speaking immigrant community."[25] Deaf patients sued, claiming that the failure to provide free sign language interpreters violated the Charter's equality guarantee.

Justice La Forest's opinion for the Supreme Court took an extraordinarily tortuous route to its holding that the hospitals had to provide free sign language interpreters. As Justice La Forest saw the problem, it involved the exercise of discretion by a decision maker—the hospital—to whom the legislature had delegated discretion. Parliamentary legislation stated that the purpose of the reimbursement system was to provide "comprehensive" medical care, defined as including "medically necessary services." According to Justice La Forest, the legislation gave hospitals the task of defining which services were medically necessary. The hospital's decision to treat some services as medically necessary but not provision of sign language interpreters was subject to Charter scrutiny.

All this seems straightforward, except for the fact that the hospitals were concededly private entities under *McKinney*. The question then arises, How do hospitals differ from all other private corporations, which receive charters from the government because, in the government's view, what they do benefits the public? Why are not all private corporations recipients of discretion delegated to them to perform so as to benefit the public? And, of course, if they are delegees of that sort, their exercises of discretion—that is, everything they do—should be subject to Charter review. Justice La Forest's answer was to distinguish among a private corporation's activities. Some activities were purely private, advancing only the private corporation's goals (and thereby, but indirectly, the government's goals in chartering the corporation). Other activities, however, were "in furtherance of a specific government program or policy. In these circumstances, while it is a private actor that actually implements the program, it is government that retains responsibility for it."[26] And, according to Justice La Forest, hospitals were indeed implementing government policy in deciding to provide some services at no charge while charging for sign language interpreters. The government's policy was to provide "a complete range of medically required hospital services," and "[t]he provision of [sign language interpreters] is not simply a matter of internal hospital

---

[25] *Id.* at ¶ 4.
[26] *Id.* at ¶ 42.

management; it is an expression of government policy."[27] Justice La Forest concluded, "while hospitals may be autonomous in their day-to-day operations, they act as agents for the government in providing the specific medical services set out in the Act."[28]

The problem with this analysis should be obvious. Justice La Forest says that the hospitals are implementing a government policy, and it refers to "specific medical services set out" in general legislation. But, of course, the general legislation does not refer to any specific medical services; that is what makes it general legislation. One might have thought that, after considering the request to pay for sign language interpreters, the Ministry of Health set the specific government policy of nonpayment. Justice La Forest, however, treated the general policy of medical care provision as the "policy," not the specific one dealing with sign language interpreters. In fact, no matter how hard one reads it, one cannot find in the relevant legislation either a requirement that the hospital charge fees for providing sign language interpreters or, more relevant in *Eldridge*, a ban on charging fees for doing so. That is, the hospital's choice resulted from its exercise of its background rights of property and contract. If there was any "delegation" from the government to the hospital, it resided in those background rights, not in the medical care statutes.[29]

There are a number of ways to avoid the confusions in *Eldridge*. Obviously, the Court could have retreated explicitly from the McKinney-Douglas College test for determining when an entity is private, and treated hospitals as public actors in everything they did. Or, avoiding a Charter-based decision, the Court might have interpreted the general medical care act directly to require the provision of sign language interpreters as medically necessary.

The most important alternative is suggested by language at the conclusion of Justice La Forest's state action analysis: "The Legislature, upon defining its objective as guaranteeing access to a range of medical services, cannot evade its obligations . . . to provide those services without discrimination by appointing hospitals to carry out that objective."[30] The Charter places the government under a *duty* of *nondiscrimination*, which means that, once it decides to enter a field by providing some social welfare services—perhaps with a proviso that it must provide a substantial amount of a genre of those services—it must provide *all* the services within that genre to the extent that failing to do so would amount to a prohibited form of discrimination. Conceptualizing the

---

[27] *Id.* at ¶ 49.

[28] *Id.* at ¶ 51.

[29] As Professor Hogg puts it, "[T]he hospitals did not need any power conferred by statute to provide a full range of medical services—they were doing so long before funding under the hospital insurance program started in 1958." 2 Peter W. Hogg, Constitutional Law of Canada § 34.2 (c) at 34–15 (looseleaf ed.).

[30] 1997 Can. Sup. Ct. LEXIS at ¶ 51. Later, in the course of his analysis of the substantive claim, Justice La Forest referred, not disapprovingly, to the possibility that the Charter placed affirmative obligations on legislatures. *Id.* at ¶ 78.

issue in *Eldridge* as implicating a duty to provide social welfare services would avoid the obfuscations occasioned by the state action doctrine. I emphasize once again the threefold equivalence here: identifying when state action is present is the same as specifying the social welfare rights guaranteed by the Charter, and both are the same as identifying the Charter's limits on background rights of property and contract.

Vriend is celebrated as a case about the rights of gays and lesbians.[31] It is also a state action case. In that aspect *Vriend* is a simple rerun of *Re: Blainey*, once we put aside the misleading assertion that *Re: Blainey* involved a discriminatory action that was permitted only because of statutory authorization. Vriend's employer, a private college, terminated his contract when it learned that he was gay. In doing so, the college was exercising its common-law right, which for present purposes I can describe as the right to hire and fire at will. Of course, statutes have limited quite substantially employers' rights under the common-law employment-at-will doctrine. But no applicable statute displaced the common-law right with respect to decisions to hire and fire based on sexual orientation. Vriend complained to the Alberta Human Rights Commission that he had been unlawfully discriminated against, but the commission, taking the apparently sensible view that, sexual orientation not being included in its mandate, it lacked jurisdiction to consider Vriend's complaint, refused to process the complaint. Vriend then sought a declaratory judgment that the exclusion of sexual orientation from the human rights statute violated his Charter rights.

Justice Peter Cory wrote an opinion explaining why there was state action. Undoubtedly, a statute is subject to Charter scrutiny. Further, it is straightforward to conclude that a legislature enacting remedial or protective legislation can violate the Charter's equality provisions by deliberately excluding a class of people from the legislation's coverage out of a desire to insulate actions that harm the unprotected class from the statute's protections.[32] Justice Cory, though, expressly disclaimed reliance on such an account of Alberta's exclusion of gays and lesbians from the scope of its human rights statute.[33] Rather, he argued that the statute's "underinclusiveness" was the problem. But, of course, to describe a statute as underinclusive is simply to assert that the statute does not modify background rights—such as the employment-at-will doctrine—as extensively as it constitutionally could.[34] As in *Eldridge*, the

[31] Vriend v. Alberta, [1998] 1 S.C.R. 493.

[32] That is one way of reading the U.S. Supreme Court's opaque opinion in Romer v. Evans, 517 U.S. 620 (1996).

[33] [1998] 1 S.C.R. at 533 (asserting that "it is not necessary to rely on" the position that "in this case . . . the deliberate decision to omit sexual orientation . . . is an 'act' of the Legislature to which the Charter should apply."

[34] I think it fair to say that the analysis contained in Justice Cory's opinion amounts to repeated restatements of the conclusion. Consider this, for example: "If an omission were not subject

opinion purported to reserve the question of "whether the Charter might impose positive obligations . . . such that a failure to legislate could be challenged under the Charter."[35] This is true, but only in the limited sense that neither *Eldridge* nor *Vriend* spelled out the legislature's positive obligations in detail. There is no doubt that both cases can only be understood as holding that the Charter imposes *some* positive obligations on legislatures. And, I think it worth emphasizing that the words Justice Cory used in connection with the issue of positive obligations is rather supportive of the claim that some positive duties exist.[36]

Eldridge and *Vriend* weaken *Dolphin Delivery* by identifying some circumstances under which the Charter requires legislatures to alter background rights. *Dolphin Delivery* retains some residual effect on judicial rhetoric if not on holdings, however. Justice Cory wrote that he could not accept the argument that "the effect of applying the Charter to the [human rights act] would be to regulate private activity."[37] But that is surely what happens as a result of *Vriend*: the Charter, taken in connection with underinclusive legislation, alters the *private* law of contract through new rules not themselves adopted by the legislature. More generally, we can describe the state of affairs in two ways. One description is that the Charter requires the legislature to enact rules regulating private activity. Under this description, the legislated rules, not the Charter, regulate private activity. But because the legislature acts under a Charter-imposed obligation, the alternative description—that the Charter sometimes (that is, when the Charter requires the legislature to act) regulates private activity—is more perspicuous.

THE STATE ACTION DOCTRINE AS A RESIDUAL CATEGORY

The analysis of omissions and failures to act brings out an important feature of the modern state action problem. In many ways the state action problem is a

---

to the Charter, underinclusive legislation which was worded in such a way a to simply omit one class rather than to explicitly exclude it would be immune from Charter challenge. If this position was accepted, the form, rather than the substance, of the legislation would determine whether it was open to challenge." *Id.* at 533. I take this to reject, reasonably enough, the argument that a statute enumerating protected classes and then stating explicitly, "By the way, you should notice that this list excludes gays and lesbians," would be subject to Charter review, but one that omitted the statement would not. Clearly, both statutes should be treated the same, but—*Re: Blainey* aside—this does not explain why the similar treatment should be to give both forms of exclusion Charter scrutiny or to refrain from giving such scrutiny to either.

[35] *Id.* at 534.

[36] Again, the contrast with the United States is striking. The U.S. Supreme Court forcefully rejected the argument that the U.S. Constitution imposes positive duties in DeShaney v. Winnebago County Dept. of Social Services, 489 U.S. 189 (1989).

[37] [1998] 1 S.C.R. at 534.

residual one, dealing with those aspects of the private economy left untouched by the relatively thick regime of statutory regulation applicable to most private actors.[38] So, for example, in such democracies most employers typically cannot discriminate on the basis of race or national origin, not because the doctrine of horizontal effect is vigorous, but because there are statutes prohibiting them from doing so. The state action doctrine has some bearing only with respect to employers who fall outside the scope of the statutory schemes, for example, in the United States because they have too few employees to come within those schemes.

One might think that the state action issue would disappear were the government to withdraw entirely from regulating some field. Then, after all, the arguments based on inequality in connection with regulation would, of course, disappear. So, for example, Christopher Manfredi suggests that Alberta might have "avoided the *Vriend* decision" by repealing the province's entire human rights statute, thereby "withdrawing from the human rights field altogether."[39] In modern circumstances, though, complete withdrawal from a field is essentially impossible as a political matter. Nor does complete withdrawal resolve the analytical problem, because all one must do is redefine the "field"—in *Vriend*, from "human rights regulation" to "employment regulation." The state action issue will then arise because of some failure to regulate in the newly identified field.

The residual nature of the state action doctrine has important consequences. Obviously, it reduces—or transforms—the concerns critics might have about an expansive doctrine. Often the critical concern about the doctrine is that it infuses a large domain of private life with constitutional norms, in a way that is inconsistent with the very idea that the domain is private. The thick statutory regulation of private life, often in the service of, if not necessarily compelled by, constitutional norms,[40] means that private life is already not *that* private. Once again, we see that the doctrine's effect lies in licensing *courts* to impose constitutional norms on private actors in the residual area. The proper concern with the doctrine, in this component, is therefore not about its effects of the domain of private life, which in a world thick with statutory regulation are inevitably small, but about the relationship

---

[38] It is important to note that *aspects* of what a private actor does can be left unregulated even while other activities by the same actor are regulated. For U.S. examples, see Moose Lodge No. 107 v. Irvis, 407 U.S. 163 (1972) (refusing to impose antidiscrimination requirements on an organization whose sale of alcoholic beverages was highly regulated); Rendell-Baker v. Kohn, 457 U.S. 830 (1982) (refusing to require that a school whose provision of educational services was highly regulated comport with constitutional norms in connection with discharging teachers).

[39] Christopher P. Manfredi, "The Life of a Metaphor: Dialogue in the Supreme Court, 1998–2003," (2004) 23 S.C.L.R. (2d) 105, 129.

[40] *See* Constitution of South Africa, Art. 9(4): "National legislation must be enacted to prevent or prohibit unfair discrimination."

between courts and legislatures. The doctrine comes into play only when the legislature has made a decision to refrain from extending statutory regulation, and the courts' application of the doctrine can therefore be described as overriding the policy-based decision the legislature made in defining the scope of statutory regulation. Notice, though, that at this point the concern about the doctrine is simply an instance of more general concerns about judicial review, understood as the power of courts to displace legislative policy judgments.

Another consequence of the residual nature of the state action doctrine is that the possibility of justifying the discrimination becomes larger, when, as is generally the case, substantive constitutional norms allow discrimination if there are strong enough reasons supporting it.[41] Consider a nation whose statutory ban on employment discrimination applies only to those who employ more than fifteen employees.[42] An employer with ten employees concedes that she discriminates in hiring on the basis of race or national origin, and then seeks to justify her decisions. This employer can invoke a number of justifications that would not be available to someone who employed a larger number of workers. If, as again is likely for small businesses, the employer actually works in close proximity to the employers, she might claim that imposing a norm of nondiscrimination on her would violate her right of privacy, forcing her to spend time and share space with people against whom she harbors ill feeling.[43] The constitutional nondiscrimination norm, that is, bumps up against another constitutional norm—but only in the context of small enterprises, which is, as I have argued, exactly the context where the state action doctrine has its effect.

Other examples could be developed, involving justifications predicated on religious belief or what in the United States is called the constitutional right of expressive association. The general form of the example is clear enough. Courts vigorously applying this component of the doctrine will have to accommodate competing *constitutional* values. Legislative schemes of statutory regulation accommodate constitutional norms and policy concerns too, and leave some range of discretion for private actors to decide as they will. This component of the doctrine also leaves some range of discretion for private actors, through the necessary accommodation of competing constitutional values. Yet, these accommodations are not fully responsive to one of the concerns about an expansive state-action doctrine: the private actors may prevail, but they do so only because their actions are defensible in the public terms of

---

[41] U.S. constitutional doctrine captures the idea with the concept of *strict scrutiny*, with its requirement that justifiable discriminations serve only the most important governmental interests ("compelling interests"), and do so in a way that has the smallest reach beyond those interests ("narrow tailoring").

[42] The figure is taken from some elements in U.S. antidiscrimination law.

[43] The example obviously can be adapted to deal with discrimination in housing as well.

an accommodation of competing interests, not because their actions are simply not subject to a requirement of public justification.[44]

The "Mature" Doctrine in Canada

By 2001, the Court diplomatically described its retreat from *Dolphin Delivery*, saying that its doctrine had "matured."[45] The case in which it made that observation extended the idea that sometimes the legislature has a duty to act. *Dunmore v. Ontario (Attorney General)* involved the province's regulation of labor relations. Absent a labor relations statute, employers have the right under background law to deal with workers on whatever terms they wish, including the right to refuse to bargain with workers collectively. Labor relations statutes typically change that background law and require employers to bargain collectively. Collective bargaining statutes emerged from labor conflict in industry, and historically many labor relations statutes applied only to industrial workers and did not extend to agricultural laborers. So, farm employers retained their unmodified common-law right to negotiate with their workers on whatever terms the employers chose. Ontario's labor relations statute was one of the usual ones, covering industrial but not agricultural workers. In 1994, the province's legislature enacted a statute requiring farm employers to bargain collectively with their agricultural laborers. In 1995, after a change in party control, the legislature repealed the 1994 statute. Agricultural workers then sought judicial relief, claiming that their inability to bargain collectively—or, more precisely, the absence of a legislative requirement that employers bargain with them collectively—violated their right under the Charter to freedom of association.[46]

The Supreme Court agreed. Justice Michel Bastarache's opinion *began* by finding that, in light of history, the government had a responsibility in the area of labor relations "to extend protective legislation to unprotected groups."[47]

[44] Perhaps the accommodation will define the boundaries of a large enough private domain, within which no public justification is required, to satisfy much of this concern. It remains possible, though, that the accommodation will be close to a case-specific balancing of interests; if so, the concern about preserving some private domain would be substantial. (I am grateful to Frank Michelman for directing my attention to this aspect of the problem.) *See also* Taylor, *supra* note 4, at 638–39 (observing that the state action doctrine identifies an area of private choice as to which the government is indifferent about the decisions private actors make).

[45] Dunmore v. Ontario (Attorney General), [2001] 3 S.C.R. 1016, ¶ 26.

[46] The precise formulation is important because it helps us understand why Justice Bastarache's statement that excluding agricultural workers from the general scheme of the labor laws excluded them "from the only available channel for associational activity." *Id.* at ¶ 44. That is clearly not true; agricultural workers can bargain collectively with any employer who wants to do so, that is, who exercises the common-law background right in a particular way. And the workers can increase the number of employers who wish to do so by exercising whatever economic power the workers have.

[47] *Id.* at ¶ 20.

Underinclusive legislation "may, in unique contexts, substantially impact the exercise of a constitutional freedom,"[48] and did so in this case. Only after reaching that conclusion did Justice Bastarache address the state action issue, saying that it was "not a quantum leap" from the mature state action doctrine "to suggest that a failure to include someone in a protective regime bay affirmatively permit restraints on the activity the regime is designed to protect . . . [by] orchestrat[ing], encourag[ing] or sustain[ing] the violation of fundamental freedoms."[49]

Dunmore's doctrinal innovation was this: *Eldridge* and *Vriend* involved claims that underinclusion violated the Charter's equality provisions. Finding a duty to act more expansively is a fairly natural response to claims of inequality. It is less natural as a response to a claim that substantive rights have been violated.[50] The Court was able to assimilate the claim in *Dunmore* to earlier ones essentially by finding a requirement of equal treatment implicit in the Charter's protection of the right of association.[51] I believe that this too is not a truly stable doctrinal resolution of the problems in the area.

Recognizing Social and Economic Rights in State Action Cases

The rule that emerges from *Dolphin Delivery*, its approval of the result in *Re: Blainey, Eldridge, Vriend,* and *Dunmore* is something like this: Sometimes the Charter imposes a duty on the legislature to modify background rules. That duty arises in settings where the legislature has *already* modified the background rules to some extent. The problem with this approach, apart from the obvious failure to identify precisely when the legislative duty arises, is that the legislature has *always* modified the background rules.

Professor Hogg observes about *Vriend*, "If Alberta had had no human rights statute at all, or perhaps one that dealt only with discrimination on the basis of age (for example), then the Charter challenge would have failed at the threshold, because there would be no statute or other governmental act to which the Charter could apply."[52] That seems plainly inaccurate in the case of

[48] *Id.* at ¶ 22.

[49] *Id.* at ¶ 26.

[50] Justice Christine L'Heureux-Dubé treated the exclusion of agricultural workers as an intentional one, in the sense that, given the background, it was intended to deny agricultural workers the rights to associate. *Id.* at ¶ 123. Presumably, the traditional exclusion would not be intentional in this sense; what matters, I would think, is the extension of collective bargaining rights followed by their withdrawal. I simply point out that such an analysis raises interesting questions about a legislature's ability to experiment with new forms of regulation and conclude that they have failed, and, even more obviously, about the role of a constitutional court in a world where party control over legislatures shifts regularly.

[51] *Cf.* Kenneth Karst, "Equality as a Central Principle in the First Amendment," 43 U. Chi. L. Rev. 20 (1975).

[52] 2 Hogg, *supra* note 29, at § 34.2 (b), 34-11.

a human rights act limited to age discrimination; nothing about the policy of the state action doctrine supports a distinction between a case where sexual orientation was omitted from an enumeration of five protected classes and one where it was omitted from an enumeration of two—or one. And even in the absence of a human rights act, there *is* a statute, indeed there are many statutes, to which the Charter could apply. Suppose, for example, a legislature enacts an antidiscrimination statute that covers all the protected classes one could imagine, prohibiting discrimination in housing and the provision of public accommodations, and then enacts an antidiscrimination statute prohibiting *employment* discrimination against only members of some of the protected classes. The exclusion of some protected classes from the employment discrimination statute is underinclusive in the appropriate sense.[53] And, more generally, there are always statutes that can be challenged as underinclusive—all the statutes modifying the employers' common-law background rights but not modifying the employment-at-will doctrine with respect to sexual orientation. All the analytic work is done by the words *relatively comprehensive* in Professor Hogg's formulation, "having enacted a relatively comprehensive statute providing redress for acts of discrimination, the Legislature subjected itself to the Charter,"[54] but there is no explanation of why a relatively comprehensive statute triggers the legislature's obligation while a less comprehensive one, or the absence of any such statute, does not.[55]

As I have already pointed out, a wide range of statutes that alter the common-law rights and duties of owners of private property characterize the modern welfare state. In *Dolphin Delivery* itself, for example, statutory labor law substantially changed the common-law right of contracting parties to decide for themselves whether and on what terms to engage in negotiations and come to terms. Employers may not insist on paying workers less than the statutory minimum wage, manufacturers may not insist on dealing with each worker individually, and so on. The Canadian Supreme Court's emerging understanding that the Charter sometimes requires legislatures to act—or, alternatively, that

---

[53] Macklem, *supra* note 14, at 221, hints at a distinction between comprehensiveness in *scope*—the protected classes—and comprehensiveness in *focus*—the subjects covered. He does not analyze such a distinction, but his criticisms of distinguishing between a statute that prohibits one ground of discrimination while omitting ten others and a statute that prohibits ten but omits one seem applicable to the distinction I have suggested between scope and focus.

[54] 2 Hogg, *supra* note 29, at § 34.2 (b), 34-11.

[55] Macklem, *supra* note 14, at 226, points out that this construal of the cases gives legislatures perverse incentives. They may be better off not attempting to do anything than in going only part of the way into a field. Suppose that there is some political pressure to adopt an antidiscrimination statute, but also substantial opposition to adopting one that goes "too far." Those who fear going too far might be willing to accept a limited statute, but they might prefer no statute at all to one that goes too far, and their opposition to an expansive statute might be weightier politically than support for a limited statute from proponents. Under these circumstances, politicians would be inclined to avoid adopting the limited statute for fear that they would be saddled with the expansive one.

the Charter authorizes the courts to displace the background rules more than the legislature had—immediately poses the question about *Dolphin Delivery*, Why did the Charter not require the legislature or the courts to alter the common-law rule barring people from inducing breaches of contracts through secondary boycotts? Only a full-fledged theory of social and economic rights can answer that question. *Dolphin Delivery* and its progeny distract the courts from addressing it.

Getting Out of the Hole by Changing the Common Law

By this point it should be obvious that nothing substantial remains of *Dolphin Delivery*. That is, we live in a world where legislatures have comprehensive power to regulate.[56] Couple that with two other propositions that emerge from the later cases: first, a legislature's failure to regulate can violate the Charter, and, second, to establish a Charter violation one need not show that the legislature's failure to regulate was deliberate or was intended to impose disadvantage on those who would have benefited from regulation. The first of these propositions implies that ordinary exercises of background rights of property and contract are subject to Charter scrutiny; such exercises are precisely what happens when someone acts in the context of a legislative failure to regulate. The second implies that the proper test for determining when background rights violate the Charter is outcome-oriented: do the background rights produce a normatively acceptable level and distribution of property and contract rights? And, finally, this last question is the same as this: to what extent does the Charter protect social and economic rights?

Why did the Canadian Supreme Court go wrong in *Dolphin Delivery*, in the face of the well-known and unhappy history of the state action problem in U.S. constitutional law? Here I return to the institutional and ideological accounts sketched earlier.

In *Dolphin Delivery*, the Court did address a constitutional question, albeit in what it acknowledged to be an unnecessary discussion in light of its resolution of the state action question. The union argued that an injunction against secondary picketing violated its right to freedom of expression. The Court used the standard two-step analysis in Canadian constitutional law by asking, first, whether the activity involved was protected by the Charter and, then, whether the restriction was a "reasonable limit [that is] demonstrably justified in a free and democratic society." The Court agreed that picketing did involve expression. In answering the second question, the Court concluded that limiting *secondary* picketing struck a reasonable balance between free expression

---

[56] Subject, of course, to prohibitions on regulation such as are embodied in the Charter and other national constitutions.

interests and Dolphin Delivery's "pressing and substantial" economic interests, because such a ban prevented the escalation of industrial conflict beyond the parties immediately affected.

Sixteen years later, the Court revisited the question of secondary picketing. The case arose when the union representing workers at a Pepsi-Cola bottling plant extended their pickets from the plant to retail stores and to the hotel where replacement workers were staying.[57] Pepsi got an injunction against the secondary picketing. The Canadian Supreme Court held that, under the common law, peaceful secondary picketing should generally not be treated as a tort. The Court's opinion argued that changing the common law in this way was appropriate, because the common law had to "reflect" the "fundamental Canadian value" of free expression as written into the Charter. Quoting an earlier decision, the opinion observed that "Charter values, framed in general terms, should be weighed against the principles which underlie the common law. The Charter values will then provide the guidelines for any modification to the common law which the court feels necessary." The opinion then engaged in an extensive examination of the interests to be balanced, beginning with a long and obviously sympathetic account of the free expression interests in picketing and following with a less sympathetic account of the need to protect innocent third parties from economic damage. The common law, the opinion concluded, should protect third parties from "undue" harm. The Court then turned to the possible doctrinal solutions to the question of determining what "undue" harm was, and found that the best answer was to allow secondary picketing unless it involved some independent tort or crime. In explaining why this common-law rule avoided undue harm to third parties, the Court's opinion returned to the Charter: more restrictive rules would "run[] counter to Charter methodology and values" and "contravene[] at least the spirit of the Charter by sacrificing an individual right to the perceived collective good rather than seeking to balance and reconcile them."[58]

Two things jump out from the *Pepsi-Cola* opinion. First, it is hard to imagine that an opinion *directly* applying the Charter to the problem would have read any differently. The Court's approach to the common-law question substantially narrows the distance between the position that the Charter does not apply to the courts in their law-interpreting and law-developing capacities, and the position that the Charter has direct horizontal effect. Like *Dolphin Delivery*, an opinion giving the Charter direct horizontal effect would have used the language of "reasonable limitations justified in a free and democratic society" to deal with the balance between free expression and burdens on third parties instead of saying that the common law required the courts to balance competing interests. Otherwise, it is hard to see how the opinions

---

[57] Pepsi-Cola Canada Beverages (West) Ltd. v. R.W.D.S.U., Local 558, [2002] 1 S.C.R. 156.
[58] *Id.*, ¶ 22 (quoting Hill v. Church of Scientology, [1995] 2 S.C.R. 1130, ¶ 97), ¶¶ 88, 91.

would have differed. Yet, having available to it the possibility of developing the common law in light of constitutional values, the Canadian Supreme Court had no need to take a position on the theoretical question—indeed, in this context the almost entirely theoretical question—of the Charter's direct horizontal effect.

Second, though, the Court indicated that there might be some limits on its ability to develop the common law. The Court identified two related propositions that preserved some distance between common-law development and Charter interpretation. It observed that the change in the court-made law was not particularly large or "far-reaching." Large changes, the Court's observation suggested, should be left to the legislature. In addition, the Court observed that the prior state of judge-made law was "unsettled and inconsistent" in the several provinces. The Court's observation suggests that "overturn[ing] a well-established" judge-made rule might be a task for legislatures rather than courts.[59]

According to these suggestions about the proper role of courts, courts can modify the rules they have made, but only when the changes are not too large and only when (if this is different) it is not at all clear what the existing rules actually are.[60] These suggestions would limit the influence of constitutional norms on the development of judge-made law, depending on what counts as a change that is too large for the courts to effectuate on their own, and on how much uncertainty there is about the content of existing law. I suggest that these criteria are not likely to limit the use of the processes of ordinary judicial lawmaking with respect to background rules in ways that approximate the direct horizontal application of constitutional norms: serious litigants will rarely pursue cases seeking large-scale modifications of existing law when existing law is absolutely clear.

A common type of case raising state action questions can illustrate this point. The pattern is this: People seek to hold a political demonstration at a privately owned shopping mall. The owner asserts that its property rights entitle it to bar the demonstrators from its property. The demonstrators claim (in this form of the argument) that the owner's property rights should be defined with constitutional norms in mind, and that, when those norms are taken into account, the owner's property rights should not contain an

---

[59] *Id.*, ¶ 22 (quoting Hill v. Church of Scientology, [1995] 2 S.C.R. 1130, ¶ 96), ¶ 15.

[60] For earlier suggestions along similar lines, see Southern Pacific v. Jensen, 244 U.S. 205, 221 (1917) (Holmes, J., dissenting) ("I recognize without hesitation that judges must and do legislature, but they do so only interstitially; they are confined from molar to molecular motions."); Li v. Yellow Cab Co., 13 Cal. 3d 804, 833 (1975) (Clark, J., dissenting) ("the Legislature is the branch best able to effect transition from contributory to comparative or some other doctrine of negligence"). In citing these cases, and invoking a distinction between large-scale transformations and small-scale developments, I take no position on what counts as the latter and what the former. My point is that our terminology would be clarified were we to replace terms like *direct application* and *indirect application* of constitutional norms with references to the scale of the change in background rules of law required by such norms.

absolute right to exclude demonstrators.[61] Put in the terms of the present discussion, the demonstrators are asking that the general law of property be modified to recognize a "free speech easement" over the shopping mall owner's property.[62] My sense is that constitutional courts typically reject the arguments made by the demonstrators,[63] but on the merits, and not because the demonstrators are asking for too large a change in clearly established rules of property law. The courts have recognized many novel easements over the years, and doing so for free speech would not, I think, in most instances be the kind of large change in established law that, according to the Canadian Supreme Court's suggestions, could be done only by the legislature.[64]

An Argentine case also shows how courts worried about making changes in background law that are, in their view, too "large" can revert to the constitution. In 1957 the Supreme Court of Argentina devised a remedy for unconstitutional actions in a lawsuit challenging the action of local police officials in closing down a newspaper.[65] A year later the Court took up a challenge by an employer to the occupation of its factory by union members—what in the United States was once known as a "sit-down" strike. The employer filed two lawsuits. One was a complaint under the background law, seeking police assistance in evicting the workers. The courts refused to issue the order because the union was engaged in a labor dispute and so was not attempting to "assume ownership of the property," as required by the relevant background law of property. The second was a "constitutional" claim for judicial protection against the union's deprivation of the employer's property. The Supreme Court of Argentina held that it *could* issue such an order. According to the court, the workers' "self-help" was illegal: they could not "invoke supra-legal rights," and they were illegally restricting the employer's "constitutional right to property and, above all, to work."

---

[61] *See* Lloyd Corp. v. Tanner, 407 U.S. 551 (1972) (finding no state action and therefore no constitutional violation in the shopping mall owner's exclusion of demonstrators); Appleby v. United Kingdom, No. 44306/98, Eur. Ct. H. R. (May 6, 2003) (finding no violation of the European Convention on Human Rights in defining a shopping mall owner's rights as including a right to exclude demonstrators).

[62] The term, as applied to *public* property such as streets and parks, was introduced in Harry Kalven, Jr., "The Concept of the Public Forum," 1965 Sup. Ct. Rev. 1, 13.

[63] *But see* PruneYard Shopping Center v. Robins, 23 Cal. 3d 899 (1979), aff'd 447 U.S. 74 (1980). The rejection occurs when the courts treat the property owner's rights as having some constitutional dimension, and find that the demonstrators have adequate alternative venues for their protest.

[64] This discussion leaves to one side the question of whether there is some sensible theory of the roles of courts and legislatures that would support the conclusion that only legislatures, and not courts, can make large changes in well-established judge-made law. The difficulty is that the law having been made by judges in the first place (at which point it almost certainly was a large change in well-established law), the reason for insisting that judges persist in their errors is unclear.

[65] I draw here on the presentation of the cases in Angel Oquendo, Latin American Law (2006).

The Court ended its analysis by explaining why "ordinary procedures"—that is, the procedures available under background law—were inadequate. Those procedures would have required the employer to bring each individual worker into court, where the worker would have a right to a lawyer and the right to introduce evidence. Using these procedures would postpone the time when the employer would be able to regain possession of the factory. Note that the *substantive* constitutional analysis is only slightly different from the substantive analysis of the background law. It would not have been difficult, I think, for the court to say that in the context of sit-down strikes, the background law did not require that the workers intend to deprive the employer of permanent ownership of the factory. The sticking point appears to be procedural rather than substantive. The question then is whether modifying the procedures in eviction cases, so that the employer could file a single case against all the strikers at once, would have been too great a change in the law.[66]

Again, the general point is a version of the argument in chapter 6 that distinguishing between legislatures and courts in their lawmaking and law-developing capacities is extremely difficult: judge-made law is rarely so settled and clear that a cogent case can be made for insisting that only the legislature can change it. The Canadian Supreme Court's suggested limitations on the influence of constitutional norms on judge-made law seem unlikely to do much to limit that influence. Here, too, the distance between the Canadian Supreme Court's approach and an expansive state action doctrine is likely to be rather small.

The Canadian Supreme Court was able to address the impact of constitutional norms on the background rules because it has the power to alter those background rules directly. In contrast, the U.S. Supreme Court must take the background rules as it finds them in state law. Unsurprisingly, the state action issue looms larger in the United States than in Canada, whose Supreme Court has straightforward legal techniques available to diminish the importance of the state action issue. Of course, those techniques can raise a question that should worry those concerned with an expansive state action doctrine: how large may a court's change in the background rules be before it becomes legislation rather than justified common-law development of the background rules? And, just as we appear to lack the conceptual resources to deal with the state action question directly, so we lack the resources to address this transformation of that question.[67]

---

[66] I do not know how Argentine lawyers would assess the magnitude of the changes in procedure the Court's analysis would have required. I use the case only to illustrate that magnitude is what matters.

[67] Notably, Richard Epstein's response to an earlier version of the arguments made here and in chapter 6 relies on classical legal theory, whose decay is precisely the reason why these questions have become extremely difficult. Richard Epstein, "Comparative Constitutionalism Meets the New Constitutional Order," 3 U. Chi. J. Int'l L. 455 (2002).

My account of the ideological explanation of this phenomenon is less complex and more speculative. It is this: In the early 1980s Canadians committed to a social democratic state, like such people in other Western industrial nations, found their commitments seriously challenged by a resurgent conservatism and, more important, neoliberalism. At that time, the prospect of expanding the social welfare commitments of social democratic states may have seemed to be receding. In 1986, the blunt answer to the direct question Does the Charter guarantee social and economic rights? would have been an equally direct no. Framing the question in the more traditional state action terms may have allowed judges ambivalent about the interaction between social democracy and neoliberalism, and uncertain in 1986 about the ultimate outcome of the conflict, to defer definitive resolution. Perhaps Canadian judges today are more confident about the persistence of social democratic traditions in Canada. The recent cases do not abandon the doctrinal state action framework created by *Dolphin Delivery*, but their focus on underinclusiveness, legislative duties, and the like brings the connection between the state action inquiry and the question of constitutional social and economic rights much closer to the surface of the analysis. Judges may be in the process of moving to confront the issue of social and economic rights more directly because social democratic norms have had a staying power that might not have been apparent in 1986.[68]

Social democratic commitments to social provision can be expressed as the courts develop the background law *or* as they enforce constitutional rights. But social democracies are always incomplete, in that social provision is not, and probably never can be, comprehensive.[69] Social democracies are also characterized by a public commitment to civil rights and civil liberties. One aspect of that commitment is a commitment to maintaining some private domain free from public regulation.

This combination poses another difficulty for social democracies with significant commitments to judicial review. The incomplete system of social provision induces constitutional courts to consider whether the actual level and distribution of material goods is consistent with the nation's constitutional commitment to social provision. The need to preserve a private domain leads constitutional courts to develop a state action doctrine. But preserving a private domain undermines efforts to sustain a constitutionally acceptable level and distribution of material goods. In traditional analyses that assume

---

[68] The U.S. comparison is again illuminating. Neoliberalism has strengthened in the United States over the past decades, and the national commitment to social welfare rights has weakened, though it has not disappeared. Under these conditions, the fact that the state action doctrine remains vibrant in the United States should not be surprising.

[69] For an illustration, see Gosselin v. Quebec, [2002] S.C.R. 429 (holding that the Charter's guarantees of a right to "life, liberty, and security of the person" did not provide "the basis for a positive state obligation to guarantee adequate living standards").

strong-form judicial review, a stable doctrine could take two forms. Developing a vigorous state action doctrine, the courts could constitutionalize background rights of property and contract, as the U.S. Supreme Court attempted during the *Lochner* era. Or, developing a vigorous doctrine dealing with social and economic rights, the courts could constitutionalize social provision. Both courses, however, raise important and difficult questions of judicial capacity and separation of powers. The only real conclusion I think can be drawn from the arguments developed here is that it would be better to deal with those questions directly rather than conceal them within the awkwardness of the state action doctrine. And, as I argue in chapter 8, weak-form review changes the picture by adding a third possibility: enforcement by means of a mechanism ensuring that judicial action *is* small-scale.

The normative payoff of the preceding analysis is limited but, I think, important. The state action doctrine obscures the question courts are actually confronting, which is the extent to which a nation's constitution guarantees social welfare rights. Once that question is brought to the fore, we can then ask, as I do in the next chapter, what role the courts might play in answering it.

THE EFFECTS OF THE GERMAN STRUCTURE OF JUDICIAL REVIEW

As I noted earlier, Germany's solution to the state action problem has been enormously influential. Indeed, the Canadian solution is essentially the same as the German one, although the Canadian Supreme Court has not referred to the German analysis in any detail, perhaps because of structural differences between the two nations' judicial systems.

The case for concluding that Germany was able to arrive at its solution because of its commitment to social welfare values is straightforward, yet making it brings out additional aspects of the state action issue in comparative constitutional law. In setting out the structure of government, Germany's Basic Law begins with a provision, described as providing the "basic principles of state order," saying that Germany shall be a *Rechtstaat* and a *Sozialstaat*.[70] The first term is usually translated as "state governed by the rule of law," and refers implicitly to the difference between the postwar German state and the Nazi regime it replaced. The second term is usually translated as "social welfare state."[71]

---

[70] Basic Law, art. 20 (1).

[71] The translation of Article 20 (1) distributed by the Press and Information Office of the Federal Government does not use the standard translations, probably for ease of reading. In that translation, Article 20 (1) is, "The Federal Republic of Germany shall be a democratic and social federal state." The Press Office's pamphlet, "Germany: Constitution and Legal System," says that Article 20 identifies "four fundamental principles": Germany is "a democracy, a state based on the rule of law, a social state, and a federal state."

The social welfare principle emerged in Germany in the late nineteenth century, when Prussian chancellor Otto von Bismarck responded to the rising political power of socialist parties by appropriating some of their programs, creating the first substantial program of social insurance to protect against economic losses caused by injury, sickness, and old age. In 1891 Pope Leo XIII issued an encyclical, "Rerum Novarum (On the Condition of Workers)," dealing with the "rights and duties of capital and labor," which committed the Roman Catholic Church to supporting even more extensive social welfare programs. That commitment was reaffirmed in 1931 by Pope Pius XI in the encyclical "Quadragesimo Anno (On Reconstruction of the Social Order)." The Irish Constitution of 1937, whose preamble was quoted in chapter 1, may be the first reflection in a constitutional document of the social teachings of the Catholic Church.

Constitutions drafted after World War II almost universally included social welfare provisions. Social democratic parties had substantial political power nearly everywhere, and had to be accommodated in the process of drafting the constitution, and Christian Democratic parties adopted the Catholic Church's social teachings as their own. All the important political actors, that is, were committed to restraints on unregulated market operations that threatened to deny human dignity to some.[72] In using the term *Sozialstaat*, the Basic Law, adopted in 1949, reflected these commitments. The state action problem arises when the distribution of wealth produces social outcomes that seem inconsistent with a nation's constitutional values. A social welfare state, though, is designed to address social outcomes that are thought to be normatively troubling. The deep commitments of a social welfare state, that is, are compatible with widespread interventions to address social outcomes produced by the distribution of wealth. It should not be surprising that the state action problem would seem less serious in a social welfare state.

The argument that the structure of constitutional review in Germany eases the state action problem is more complex than the argument regarding social welfare ideology. Germany has a specialized constitutional court, not a generalist one like those of the United States and Canada, and so has *only* the power to determine constitutional questions. For present purposes, the mechanism by which the Constitutional Court decides such questions is the "constitutional complaint."[73] A person who believes that the government has

---

[72] *See* Paul Misner, "Christian Democratic Social Policy: Precedents for Third-Way Thinking," in European Christian Democracy: Historical Legacies and Comparative Perspectives 68, 85–88 (2003) (describing the emergence of left-wing Christian Democratic groups after World War II and their emphasis on "social justice for a humane democratic regime").

[73] The Court also has the power to decide constitutional questions presented to it by state governments, the national government, or one-third of the members of the lower house in the legislature.

violated his or her constitutional rights can file a constitutional complaint. For example, suppose a veterinarian believes that the veterinary licensing board violated the Basic Law's guarantee of free expression by obtaining an injunction against him for unfair competition after the local newspaper ran a human (and animal) interest news story about the fact that he kept his office open around the clock to deal with emergencies.[74] The veterinarian must appeal within the "ordinary" courts, the ones that deal with unfair competition law. If they reject his constitutional claims, he can file a constitutional complaint with the Constitutional Court.

In this example, a public agency initiated the proceeding, and relied on licensing regulations as the basis for the unfair competition claims. State action here is obvious. Suppose, though, that a private party seeks an injunction for invasion of privacy, a claim founded on the background law of torts, not on any specific statutory regulation?[75]

That was the *Lüth* case. Erich Lüth was a prominent public figure in Hamburg. In addition to serving as the press minister of the Hamburg government in the 1950s, a position that gave him no formal authority to initiate prosecutions, he was head of the private Hamburg Press Club and was active in a group seeking to promote religious tolerance. In that latter capacity, he objected to Viet Harlan's return to the film business. Harlan had directed the notorious anti-Semitic film *Jüd Süss* in 1940, and Lüth urged the public to boycott Harlan's new film. Harlan went to court and got an injunction based on the background rule of law that one person cannot intentionally harm another "in a manner offensive to good morals." Lüth objected that the injunction was inconsistent with Germany's guarantee of free expression. He filed a constitutional complaint after the ordinary courts rejected that argument. The Constitutional Court found in Lüth's favor.

The Constitutional Court's decision in *Lüth* is usually described as the origin of the idea that constitutional norms should shape the way ordinary courts develop nonconstitutional law. The Constitutional Court began by asserting that the Basic Law regulated only "acts of public authority," thereby rejecting the position that the Basic Law had direct horizontal effect. Nor did the Basic Law directly control the content of "private law," that is, the background rules. But, according to the Constitutional Court, the Basic Law established an "objective order of values," which did affect private as well as public law. It followed that "[e]very provision of private law must be compatible with this system of values, and every such provision must be interpreted in its spirit."

[74] The example is based on the facts of Barthold v. Germany (8734/79), [1985] ECHR 3.

[75] The terminology here is made complex because German civil law—what I have called the background law (in part precisely for this reason)—rests entirely on a statutory code, the Civil Code. Neither German constitutional theorists nor anyone else, as far as I know, believes that the fact that the background law is ultimately statutory makes the state action problem a simple one in the way that the state action issue in the veterinarian's case is simple.

The ordinary courts had to bring the law they applied "into harmony with this system of values."[76]

The Constitutional Court recognized as well that it sat to *review* decisions by the ordinary courts, not to displace the role of those courts in developing the law. It would examine decisions of the ordinary courts to ensure that judges on those courts have "properly evaluated the scope and impact of the basic rights." But, the Court continued, its role was not to decide whether the ordinary courts had made some "legal error," but rather was to "make sure that the [ordinary courts have] correctly understood the constitutional principle."[77] One could read this as authorizing the Constitutional Court to displace the ordinary courts, by taking "correctly understood" to mean "determined correctly the implications of the Basic Law for private law." A better reading, though, is that the Constitutional Court was asserting the more modest power of ensuring that the ordinary courts attended to constitutional norms, took them seriously in developing the law under their control, and arrived at a solution that incorporated some reasonable understanding of constitutional norms into private law.[78]

Understood in that way, the Constitutional Court's power vis-à-vis the ordinary courts is quite similar to its power vis-à-vis the legislature. As the Court observed, "Newly enacted statutes must conform to the system of values of the basic rights," no more—or less—than does private law.[79] As with nearly

---

[76] *Lüth*, 7 BVerfGE 198 (1958), translated in Donald Kommers, The Constitutional Jurisprudence of the Federal Republic of Germany, at 363 (1997). For an interesting variant on the problem in *Lüth*, see the decision of the Constitutional Court of the Czech Republic, I. US 167/04 (May 12, 2004), reported in 11 E. Eur. Case Rptr. of Con. L. 139. There a lower court had refused to enforce a contract because one of its provisions was, in the court's view, ambiguous in designating the specific court that was to have the power to enforce the contract if a dispute arose. The Constitutional Court held that excessive formalism in contract interpretation violated the constitutional protection of "the autonomy of the will," that is, the protection of the parties' ability to determine the terms of their own agreement. For a similar holding, see the decision by the same court, I. US 185/04 (July 14, 2004), reported in Bulletin of Constitutional Case Law 2004/2, p. 254 (concluding that "by adopting [a particular] interpretation of ordinary law, [the ordinary courts] had failed to respect their obligation to protect the complainant's basic rights in the form of his legitimate expectation in obtaining the performance" of a contractual obligation contained in a contract modification that the ordinary courts interpreted to require a formal decision by the defendant's managing board).

[77] *Lüth*, in Kommers, *supra* note 76, at 364.

[78] A rough analogue in U.S. constitutional law arises in connection with the Constitution's prohibition on legislation that retroactively alters the "Obligation of Contracts." One needs to know what the initial contract was to know whether legislation changes the obligations it creates. Ordinarily, though, determining what a contract means is a question of state law. The U.S. Supreme Court has held that it can review a state court's determination of that question, giving "respectful consideration and great weight to the views of the state's highest court." Indiana *ex rel.* Anderson v. Brand, 303 U.S. 95, 100 (1938). For an overview of the areas in U.S. constitutional law where related issues arise, see Richard H. Fallon, Jr., et al., Hart and Wechsler's The Federal Courts and the Federal System 527–40 (5th ed., 2003).

[79] *Lüth*, in Kommers, *supra* note 76, at 363.

all the constitutional provisions I have discussed, that system of values is stated at a relatively abstract level, and there are many alternative, but reasonable, specifications, of what those values are in particular circumstances. A constitutional court reviewing legislation should ask whether the statute in question is consistent with a reasonable understanding of abstractly stated constitutional norms.[80] That is the posture the Constitutional Court said that it would take in reviewing the work of the ordinary courts.[81]

The institutional structure of the German court system brings out quite clearly the underlying conceptual structure of this aspect of the state action doctrine. The Constitutional Court cannot itself develop the background rules. It is confined to reviewing the decisions of the ordinary courts to see if the rules *they* have developed are consistent with constitutional norms. The distinction between "developing" and "reviewing" is crucial to understanding the conceptual structure of this component of the doctrine of indirect horizontal effect, and parallels the distinction between "large" and "small" changes in the common law that we saw in analyzing the Canadian *Pepsi-Cola* decision.

Another case from Germany, and a similar one from Great Britain, further illustrate how applying the constitution via indirect horizontal effect—the Lüth approach—is equivalent to developing background rules of law. In 1993, the German Constitutional Court directed the ordinary courts to reconsider a standard commercial case.[82] A bank agreed to lend a businessman over $50,000, but only if his daughter also signed the loan. A bank employee assured the young woman, who was unemployed and without substantial education, that signing the loan papers "won't make you enter into any important obligation." Several years later the father defaulted, and the bank sought repayment of the loan from the daughter, by then a single mother without any income. The ordinary courts enforced the contract, saying that anyone who cosigned a loan ought to know that doing so might lead to some real financial obligations. The daughter appealed to the Constitutional Court, arguing that the ordinary courts' interpretation of background contract law violated her constitutional right to dignity as it should be understood in light of the principle that Germany is a social welfare state. The Constitutional Court agreed, holding that the Basic Law required the ordinary courts to interpret

---

[80] *Cf.* Khumalo v. Holomisa, 2002 (3) SA 38 (T) (rejecting a common-law defamation claim after concluding that the common-law rules were an appropriate accommodation of interests in personal dignity and freedom of expression).

[81] For this reason, Taylor, *supra* note 4, at 627, is mistaken in asserting that the theory of direct horizontal effect "does not permit" the legislature "to alter and refine the common law as affected by the *Constitution*." The theory does so by the deference it requires the Supreme Court to pay to legislative choice.

[82] I draw my account of the case from Olha Cherednychenko, "The Constitutionalization of Contract Law: Something New under the Sun," Electronic J. Comp. L., vol. 8:1 (March 2004), http://www.ejcl.org/81/art81-3.html (visited Sept. 29, 2006).

background contract law as the daughter said, in cases where there was a "structural imbalance" in the bargaining power of the parties.

A parallel case arose in Great Britain in 1994. There a wife put up the family home as a guarantee for her husband's debts.[83] According to the House of Lords, the contract could not be enforced under principles of background law. The bank knew that the relationship between husband and wife was one in which the husband was likely to misrepresent the financial effects of using the house for these purposes, and knew that the transaction did not benefit the wife as an individual. Under the circumstances, the House of Lords said, the bank had a duty to inform the wife that she should get her own lawyer. Note that the German decision invokes constitutional law, the British one background law, but the two courts reach identical results. The House of Lords at the time (before the adoption of the Human Rights Act) lacked an enforceable constitution, but does not need one; the German Constitutional Court lacks the power to develop background rules of contract law, but does not need that power as long as it can use the Basic Law.

Can the Constitutional Court be as effective as the ordinary courts?[84] The ordinary courts are charged with developing the background rules. The question for the Constitutional Court is whether the ordinary courts' development of background law is consistent with constitutional norms. At least in theory, the Constitutional Court could end up determining quite precisely what those background rules are. It could do so by rejecting every background rule developed by the ordinary courts that was inconsistent with what the Constitutional Court believed to be the correct specification of constitutional norms. As a practical matter, though, that course is unavailable to the Constitutional Court, if only because it needs to maintain more or less harmonious relations with the ordinary courts. Those relations would be disrupted were it to become clear that the Constitutional Court was absorbing into itself the entire job of developing the background law.

Even putting practicality aside, though, the Constitutional Court is unlikely to engage in repeated efforts to pin down precisely the background law required by the constitution. The reason lies in the nature of constitutional norms, which are typically stated at a relatively abstract level. Constitutional review involves determining whether some particular enactment (or judicially developed legal rule) is consistent with some acceptable (or, as I would put it, reasonable) specification of the abstract norm's meaning in the enactment's context. The act of reviewing, that is, entails acknowledging that the body being reviewed (here, the ordinary courts) have some discretion in specifying the law they are charged with developing. The Constitutional Court

---

[83] Barclays' Bank PLC v. O'Brien, [1994] 1 AC 180.

[84] Cherednychenko, *supra* note 82, at § 5.3, suggests not, as I read the argument largely because the cases that come to the Constitutional Court are unlikely to give it a sufficiently comprehensive view of background law.

will therefore typically take the constitutional question before it to be, Is the background rule of law articulated by the ordinary courts consistent with a reasonable specification of constitutional norms?

Note here that this question is, or ought to be, the one a reviewing court should ask when it is considering the constitutionality of legislation. This component of the doctrine of indirect horizontal effect, that is, leads constitutional courts to act with respect to background rules just as they should act with respect to legislation. This component, that is, is simply ordinary constitutional law.

With this analysis in hand, we can return to *New York Times v. Sullivan*,[85] which held that Alabama's substantive rules in libel cases violated the First Amendment. On the analysis developed here, the fundamental question is the degree of deference the Supreme Court should give to state courts' construction of their common-law libel rules. Yet, the literature on the case rarely suggests that the Court should give the kind of deference to judicial common-law construction that is routine when the Court evaluates laws enacted by state legislatures. I suggest that this is a mistake. The issue in cases like *New York Times v. Sullivan* is, or at least includes, the degree of deference state courts should be accorded in developing the common law.

Conclusion

I have argued that the state action question is analytically identical to the question of identifying constitutionally protected social and economic rights. At least until quite recently, constitutional lawyers generally accepted a conventional wisdom about such rights: it was thought that courts cannot identify or enforce them. Doing so, it was thought, would require the courts to specify a comprehensive set of social and economic rights, enforce particular rights coercively at the instance of anyone who complained that he or she did not have the constitutionally required rights, and in the end prescribe a comprehensive budget for the nation so that constitutional rights would be respected.[86] As I noted in passing, this conventional wisdom ultimately rested on the view that judicial review could only take what I have called a strong form, that is, the form prevalent in the United States. In light of that conventional wisdom,

---

[85] 376 U.S. 254 (1964).

[86] *Cf.* 2 Hogg, *supra* note 29, at § 34.2 (i) at 34-27 (referring to "the limited range of relatively crude remedies that could be fashioned as Charter remedies by the courts"); Macklem, *supra* note 14, at 210 (arguing that courts enforcing social welfare rights would have to decide "whether health care should be public or private or something in between, . . . the level of funding health care should receive from the government, and . . . how that funding should be distributed. . . . It would be for the courts to set the direction for the economy, to establish the curriculum for the schools, to determine environmental policy—in short, to govern.").

judges may have thought that the state action question was exceedingly difficult, but that the question of constitutional social and economic rights was impossible. They might then have chosen to try to answer the hard question rather than address the impossible one.

As we saw in part 1, weaker forms of judicial review have been invented since the 1980s. Perhaps the Canadian Supreme Court's "mature" vision of the state action doctrine can be attributed in part to the fact that it has realized the difference between the strong-form review that makes judicial enforcement of social welfare rights nearly impossible in the United States, and the weak-form review enabled by the notwithstanding clause. The final chapter takes that suggestion seriously, examining in more detail the ways in which weak-form review might be a particularly appropriate mechanism for enforcing social welfare rights.

CHAPTER 8

Enforcing Social and Economic Rights

WRITING IN THE immediate aftermath of the adoption of new constitutions in central and eastern Europe, Cass Sunstein characterized the inclusion of social and economic rights in those constitutions as "a large mistake, possibly a disaster."[1] For Frank Cross, "reliance on positive constitutional rights is an ultimately misguided plan."[2] These statements are merely representative of the common wisdom among U.S. constitutional scholars, and are occasionally echoed elsewhere. South African Constitutional Court judge Albie Sachs describes the primary objection to including social and economic rights in constitutions as resting on questions about the capacity of courts to enforce such rights.[3]

Justice Sachs's observation is plainly accurate, as I will show. And yet, the concern about judicial capacity needs more elaboration than it usually gets, for two reasons. First, the discussion in the preceding chapters shows that the doctrines of state action and horizontal effect (whether direct or indirect) are also about the judicial enforcement of social and economic rights. Every constitutional court finds state action or gives some horizontal effect to constitutional provisions on *some* occasions where doing so calls into question the background rights of property, contract, or tort and thereby enforces some vision of social or economic rights. Yet, no one raises serious questions about the *capacity* of courts to develop and enforce a state action or horizontal effect doctrine. The first section of this chapter expands on this observation by discussing several areas of U.S. constitutional law in which the courts in effect displace the background rules in the service of constitutional values, again without controversy over their capacity to do so (however controversial particular decisions might be).

On analysis, the concern over judicial capacity turns out to be a concern about the ability of courts to coerce the political branches into making substantial changes in background rules, typically by large programs of social provision that require significant alterations in the distribution of wealth by means of taxes and transfer payments. That concern, though, rests on the

---

[1] Cass R. Sunstein, "Against Positive Rights," in Western Rights? Post-Communist Application (András Sajó ed., 1996). As we will see, Sunstein's views may have changed.

[2] Frank R. Cross, "The Error of Positive Rights," 48 UCLA L. Rev. 857 (2001).

[3] Albie Sachs, "The Judicial Enforcement of Socio-Economic Rights: The *Grootboom* Case" (unpublished manuscript in author's possession).

assumption that judicial enforcement of social and economic rights must take the form of coercive orders to the political branches. The second part of this chapter examines the conventional arguments against including social and economic rights in constitutions and demonstrates that those arguments do indeed make that assumption, usually without noticing.

The creation of weak-form judicial review places into question the assumption that judicial review must involve coercive orders. The third part of the chapter shows how courts in Ireland, South Africa, and the United States have begun to use various forms of weak-form review to enforce social and economic rights. These developments are relatively recent, and there remains some question about whether weak-form review can be a stable institution, that is, whether it can resist being transformed into either strong-form review or a rubber stamp for what the political branches decide on their own.

A final question is whether weak-form review can—or should—be confined to the enforcement of social and economic rights. Is it an institution well designed to enforce first-generation rights such as free expression and equality in political participation? I conclude this book with an argument that weak-form systems of judicial review—if they can be stably sustained—may indeed be the best institutional mechanism for enforcing *all* fundamental rights, first-, second-, and third-generation. The reason is that weak-form review acknowledges two basic features of modern constitutional order better than strong-form review does: the existence of reasonable disagreement over what an abstractly described constitutional right means in a particular context, and the imperfections of both unchecked political processes and unchecked judicial power in arriving at the best specifications of what constitutional provisions mean.[4]

Hints of Social and Economic Rights in U.S. Constitutional Law

Chapter 7 argued that nations with more expansive social welfare systems find the state action–horizontal effect problem easier to solve than nations with less expansive ones—which should be no surprise if, as I argued as well, that problem is equivalent to the question of whether social and economic rights should be enforced by the courts. As I argued, that doctrine always plays a residual role, dealing with areas left untouched by statutory regulation. The more extensive the statutory regulation, the less the state action–horizontal effect doctrine will matter to anyone except those directly affected by the legislature's failure to regulate some relatively small area. The United States has one of the thinnest systems of social provision among mature and economically prosperous democracies, which is why the state action problem is so difficult

---

[4] Weak-form review might be said to be a mechanism that brings the advantages of competition among institutions to the process of specifying constitutional meaning.

here. And yet, there are hints in standard constitutional doctrine outside the state action area that the U.S. Constitution does require the courts to displace the background rules in the service of constitutional values. After describing some of those hints, I take up their implications for the conventional criticism of judicial enforcement of social and economic rights.

Some elements of free speech law call into question the distribution of wealth resulting from background rules. These are the requirements that some public property be made available for political activity subject only to reasonable time, place, and manner regulations, and the problem of the heckler's veto. As noted in chapter 7, the heartland of the law on public protests gives demonstrators what could be called a First Amendment easement on public property.[5] The fact that the easement is on public property is misleading, though, because the easement affects private property as well. The Constitution requires the First Amendment easement because demonstrators believe that they lack adequate alternative resources—including money—to influence public policy in the direction they prefer. One must also consider the time (and work and income) lost by commuters delayed by a march along their usual travel route, or the business lost by stores on the line of march. Add these factors together and the conclusion is that the First Amendment requires an adjustment of the background rules: the demonstrators get more under this adjustment of rules and the store owners get less.

The heckler's veto cases have a similar structure. These cases arise when an extremely unpopular speaker is threatened with harm from the audience.[6] One could imagine a rule that left speakers vulnerable to whatever violence they could not prevent by hiring their own security forces. This rule would necessarily rely on the background rules of property law: speakers would devote some of their resources to protecting themselves and some to distributing their messages, and the police would intervene only to the extent that they would in nonspeech situations like bar fights. Standard First Amendment doctrine is different. The police have to devote a fair amount of resources to protecting the speaker—more than they would ordinarily devote to policing the area in which the speech is being held.[7] This, though, is simply a subsidy from the public generally to the speaker. Put another way, the First Amendment takes the property that taxpayers have under the background rules and gives it to the speaker threatened with harm.

---

[5] The First Amendment easement discussed in chapter 7 involved access to private property for free speech purposes.

[6] Geoffrey R. Stone et al., Constitutional Law 1108–17 (5th ed. 2005) (describing the "hostile audience" cases). For present purposes, it is irrelevant whether the speaker has hired a private arena in which to deliver the speech, or is using property made available because of a First Amendment easement.

[7] See Thomas I. Emerson, The System of Freedom of Expression 336–42 (1970) (discussing the problem of "hostile opposition").

Consider, finally, a third example from free speech law: suppose a group wishes to conduct a demonstration in a public park made available to them by the First Amendment easement. The city proposes to charge them the cost of cleaning up the park after the demonstration (beyond the cost of cleaning up the park after an ordinary day). The case law, though thin, tends to suggest that the city may not charge a group for these excess cleanup costs when the charges would be substantial relative to the group's resources (and that the city may charge the costs to a group that could afford them).[8] Again, the First Amendment requires a subsidy from taxpayers generally to demonstrators.

These elements of First Amendment law, then, are responsive to the distribution of wealth resulting from the background rules. I do not want to exaggerate the importance of these hints. They play a small, though important, role in standard accounts of First Amendment doctrine.[9] Perhaps, though, these and other hints of social and economic rights in standard constitutional doctrine would require only modest adjustments in the background rules. I am not certain that that is so. In the First Amendment cases, the problem the required-subsidy rules address arises *because* of the distribution of wealth: people who can afford to buy time on television to disseminate their messages do not need a First Amendment easement.[10]

Rattling around the arguments about constitutionally required subsidies are concerns about judicial capacity. The *means* of adjusting background rights are quite various. Recall the discussion in chapter 6 of homelessness: we could define the rules of property law (by refusing to require the police to eject the homeless person), or we could develop a tax-supported program of public housing, or a voucher program, or rely entirely on the tax system to eliminate disparities in access to housing, and so on almost endlessly. In the First Amendment context, the adjustments caused by creating a First Amendment easement seem "smaller" than those that some other means of addressing the underlying problem would be. We saw in chapter 7 how attractive—and yet misleading—are arguments that courts can make small but not large changes in the service of constitutional values.

Another take on the problem is this: To say that social and economic rights are constitutionalized is simply to say that courts will enforce them. But courts are quite ill-suited for making essentially strategic choices among means. We can refer to social and economic rights as constitutionalized if we are careful about what we mean: the Constitution imposes a moral or political obligation

---

[8] *See, e.g.*, Forsyth County v. Nationalist Movement, 505 U.S. 123, 133–37 (1992); Church of the Am. Knights of the Ku Klux Klan v. City of Gary, 334 F.3d. 676, 681 (7th Cir. 2003).

[9] For an argument that I take to suggest that the standard account should be revised so that these hints play a much larger role, see Rebecca Tushnet, "Copyright as a Model for Free Speech Law," 42 B.C. L. Rev. 1 (2000).

[10] And, indeed, the wealthy might not benefit from the First Amendment easement to the extent that they could be charged cost-justified fees for using the public area.

on legislatures to secure social and economic rights, but that obligation does not necessarily have to be judicially enforceable—or, at least, not judicially enforceable through strong-form judicial review.

THE CONVENTIONAL ARGUMENT AGAINST JUDICIAL ENFORCEMENT OF SOCIAL AND ECONOMIC RIGHTS

The assumption that courts exercise strong-form review pervades the literature critical of judicial enforcement of social and economic rights.[11] Frank Cross's discussion is exemplary.[12] He begins by *defining* "rights" as "constitutionally recognized, judicially enforced restraint[s] on popular government," justifying this definition on the ground that "most of the advocates of positive rights are contemplating something similar," and "[e]liminating judicial enforcement would considerably water down their proposals."[13] Cross sets up a dichotomy between judicial enforcement and no enforcement at all.

What *sort* of enforcement?[14] As the discussion proceeds, it becomes clear that Cross has strong-form enforcement in mind. Cross begins his discussion of "the politics of rights enforcement" by quoting an earlier statement of mine that opponents of social and economic rights regard them with horror because "their enforcement raises the spectre of 'the courts running everything—raising taxes and deciding how the money should be spent.'" But, Cross argues, courts are unlikely to enforce social and economic rights "aggressively." The reason is politics: the courts need the political branches to get anything done, and "[i]t is futile to rely on the judiciary to provide basic welfare for the disadvantaged, if the political branches are unwilling to do so." According to Cross, "Courts understand that requiring legislatures to provide minimal levels of subsistence for all Americans encroaches upon the jealously guarded 'power of the purse.'" He continues, "They could compel legislators to make

[11] I use arguments made in the legal literature as the vehicle for my analysis. There is a parallel literature in political philosophy, which, in my view, also makes the assumption of strong-form review. For example, Amartya Sen, "Elements of a Theory of Human Rights," 32 Phil. & Pub. Aff. 315, 346–47 (2004), describes what he calls an *institutionalization critique* of the idea of social and economic rights, and (at least implicitly) relates that critique to the view, expressed by Herbert Hart, that rights must be "made the subject of *coercive* legal rules." *Id.* at 326–27 (*quoting* H.L.A. Hart, "Are There Any Natural Rights?" 64 Phil. Rev. 175 (1955)). Sen argues that social and economic rights can be institutionalized by "social organizations," meaning the institutions of civil society. My discussion of weak-form review suggests that Sen may have overlooked some possibilities of institutionalization through courts. For a critical overview of the philosophical literature, see Cécile Fabre, Social Rights Under the Constitution: Government and the Decent Life (2000).

[12] Cross, *supra* note 2.

[13] *Id.* at 860–61.

[14] Cross's formulation *could* accommodate weak-form as well as strong-form enforcement, although the concern he expresses about watering down enforcement suggests that he does not regard weak-form review as an adequate enforcement mechanism.

politically difficult choices about raising taxes or cutting preferred programs, which could anger the legislators and cause them to deploy their power over the courts."[15] The analysis Cross offers indicates his commitment to the idea that judicial enforcement must take the form of strong-form review with coercive orders directing legislatures to appropriate money.

Cross addresses another aspect of the judicial capacity to enforce social and economic rights. The problem here, according to Cross, arises from the indeterminacy of guarantees such as the right to minimally decent housing. Such rights are, in his terms, "consequentialist, requiring the judiciary to create a program that achieves a given result."[16] (Note again the implicit reliance on the idea that judicial review takes a strong form, with courts "creating" social welfare programs.) Cross then examines "sincere" enforcement of social and economic rights, with this consequentialist aspect of such rights in mind.[17] Cross raises a series of questions about sincere enforcement when a litigant presents a claim that she has not received adequate government support:

> How would the Court decide if the individual were impoverished enough to qualify to invoke the right? Should it be an absolute or a relative standard? At what quantitative level should the standard be set? If the plaintiff qualifies under that standard, should the Court enter an order simply directing that this individual (and presumably all others similarly situated) be paid a certain amount of cash monthly or should in-kind services (such as food stamps or housing vouchers) be ordered? Should assistance be nationally uniform or geographically variable? Might the Court consider defenses to the government's constitutional obligations? What if the federal budget were strapped, and a court order would necessitate higher taxes or that money be taken from other programs, such as defense or environmental protection? Would alternative uses of the money be relevant? Could the Court consider the possibility that the plaintiff bore some responsibility for his impoverished status? What if he had gambled away a considerable sum of money? What if he had lost his job due to misfeasance?

As Cross notes, "All of these questions are potentially answerable, but," he writes, "they illustrate the complexity of enforcing a positive right."[18] Judges,

---

[15] *Id.* at 887 (quoting Mark Tushnet, Taking the Constitution Away from the Courts 169 (1999), 888, 890).

[16] *Id.* at 901.

[17] Cross also discusses what he calls a "realist" perspective on judicial enforcement, *id.* at 905–20, which, while interesting in itself, is peripheral to my concerns here. That perspective suggests that courts are more likely to enforce the social and economic rights of the already well-off than those of the poor, largely because the judges are members of the former group. This argument is made in nearly every constitutional system by those on the political left, who refer to the U.S. experience during the *Lochner* era. For an example, see Balakrishnan Rajagopal, "Judicial Governance and the Ideology of Human Rights: Reflections from a Social Movement Perspective," in Human Rights, Criminal Justice, and Constitutional Empowerment: Essays in Honor of Justice V. R. Krishna Iyer (C. Rajkumar & K. Chockalingam eds., 2004).

[18] Cross, *supra* note 2, at 904–05.

he continues, "are ill-suited for the evaluation and making of the trade-offs implied by many positive rights."[19] The fact that the courts have found a constitutional violation means that the legislature's own priorities placed attainment of the social welfare right below other social policies—national defense, building new roads, and the like. So, in enforcing social and economic rights, courts displace legislative judgments about how social policies should be ranked.

Justice Sachs presents, though he does not endorse, a shorter version of the conventional argument that the courts do not have the capacity to enforce social and economic rights. Echoing Cross's pragmatic concerns, Justice Sachs writes that judges "in general know very little about the practicalities of housing, land and other social realities."[20] Legislatures hold hearings and get information "from a variety of people with special expertise in particular areas." And, Justice Sachs points out, legislatures can engage in practical compromises in contrast to the "all-or-nothing" character of adjudication.

For present purposes, the important point here is the assumption that judicial review must take a strong form, with the judges themselves making the trade-offs, determining precisely what level of social support is constitutionally required, and on through the list of Cross's questions. I do not want to address the question of whether judges exercising strong-form review *could* answer the questions and make the trade-offs, but only to point out that Cross's skepticism about judicial enforcement of social and economic rights— typical of the critical literature on such rights—simply assumes that judicial enforcement must take a strong form.

A More Limited Version of the Conventional Argument

Cass Sunstein offers a more limited version of the argument that constitutions should not include social and economic rights. The argument is more limited in conceptual, geographical, and temporal scope. Conceptually, Sunstein recognizes that background rights of property, contract, and tort *are* social and economic rights.[21] Of course, courts *have to* enforce background rights, so it is a conceptual mistake to contend that courts lack the capacity to each and every social and economic right. The best response to this observation focuses on what we can call the *size* of the judicial role. Consider here the hints of judicial enforcement of social and economic rights we have already seen in U.S. constitutional law. The government must deploy some additional police officers to ensure that hecklers do not get a veto over what an unpopular speaker

[19] *Id.* at 905.

[20] Sachs, *supra* note 3.

[21] For an extensive discussion, see Stephen Holmes & Cass R. Sunstein, The Cost of Rights (1999).

can say. But the resources the courts compel the government to use to protect speakers from hecklers are small (relative to those involved in providing a guarantee of minimally decent housing). In addition, the judicial compulsion to spend money on police protection is implicit rather than explicit.

So, it is not that recognizing social and economic rights would have budgetary consequences, while recognizing other constitutional rights does not. Sunstein's conceptual analysis shows that the conventional claim must be that the size of the budgetary consequences matters. Protecting background private law rights and first- and second-generation constitutional rights is cheap, though not free. Protecting social and economic rights is expensive.

Sunstein restricts his argument against including social and economic rights in constitutions by geography and time. He is primarily concerned about recognizing such rights in nations making a transition from authoritarian, particularly communist, rule to market economies. Social and economic rights are in tension with the operation of a (relatively) unregulated free market, because markets produce the outcomes to which social and economic rights address themselves: some people who had decent work in an agricultural economy will drop into poverty as the economy responds to signals that manufacturing or tourism is better for the nation's economic position overall. Putting social and economic rights in the constitution of a nation undergoing a transition to a market society would interfere with that transition.

Supplementing this, Sunstein makes the "strong-form review" assumption. Describing a provision in the Hungarian Constitution dealing with compensation for work commensurate with the worker's effort and performance, Sunstein writes, "If the provision is to mean something, courts will have to oversee labor markets very closely, to make such that every bargain produces the right wage. We know that government is ill-equipped to undertake this task. Courts are in an even worse position to do so." Writing even more generally, Sunstein emphasizes that "[m]any positive rights are unenforceable by courts," which "cannot create government programs." Sunstein recognizes that constitutions are in part aspirational documents. But, he argues, the constitutions of new democracies should be primarily legal documents "in the sense that an individual citizen may count on the constitution to protect his or her rights, whatever a police officer, a legislature, or even a Prime Minister or President may say." Those who grow up in authoritarian regimes are likely to have "a cynicism about the efficacy of legal texts." Courts might refrain from enforcing social and economic rights because they acknowledge their own incapacity. That might have two adverse consequences: citizens might begin to regard the entire constitution as "a mere piece of paper," and they—and, worse, courts—might begin to regard all constitutional rights as equally unenforceable.[22]

[22] Sunstein, *supra* note 1, at 228, 229.

Sunstein's concern that placing social and economic rights in constitutions might interfere with the emergence of a stable market society seemed prescient when the Hungarian Constitutional Court invoked ideas associated with ideas of social and economic rights to invalidate portions of the government's program for placing the nation's system of pensions and social security on a more stable economic foundation.[23] The government was responding to demands from international lenders that it get the nation's budget under control. The government adopted an austerity program that included substantial changes in social provision. To summarize complex legislation: The austerity legislation affected two types of programs. The first were nominally social insurance schemes, like the U.S. Social Security system, in which people had previously made "payments" through their taxes that, they believed, were designated for repayment as pensions. The second were programs of entitlement, such as provisions for pregnancy and maternity benefits, and family allowances, that is, sums given to a family based on the number of children in the household. The austerity plan eliminated some entitlement programs entirely, and made all payments for the other programs subject to a means test, whereby only those determined to need the payments would receive them.

The Hungarian Constitutional Court invalidated the austerity program for several reasons. The primary one was that sudden changes in the system of social provision defeated legally protected expectations among Hungary's citizens. The government did have the power to change the social security system, but it had to do so with an adequate transition period that would allow people to adjust their expectations—and lifestyles—to take account of the system that would soon take effect. Changing the family allowances, though, required some transition period, because people had children and made long-term financial plans based on their expectation that they would have money from the family allowance system.[24] Short-term benefits, such as those for pregnancy and maternity, could be limited only under extremely stringent conditions, because the recipients would rarely have enough time to adjust their expectations and plans.

András Sajó, a leading scholar of Hungarian constitutional law, regarded the Constitutional Court's decision as a disaster, writing an article with the suggestive title, "How the Rule of Law Killed Hungarian Welfare Reform."[25] For Sajó, as for the international lenders, substantial restructuring of the

[23] The most important case is translated in László Sólyom & Georg Brunner, Constitutional Judiciary in a New Democracy: The Hungarian Constitutional Court 322–32 (2000). I rely heavily on the analysis in Kim Lane Scheppele, "A *Realpolitik* Defense of Social Rights," 82 Tex. L. Rev. 1921 (2004).

[24] The Court also held that restricting the pregnancy and maternity benefits was inconsistent with the constitutional protection given to fetuses, and indeed had been adopted in order to encourage women to carry their pregnancies to term.

[25] East European Constitutional Rev., vol. 5, no. 1 (Winter 1996), p. 31.

Hungarian economy was an essential predicate for future economic development, and getting control of the state budget, of which expenditures for social
provision were a large and controllable part, was an essential predicate for
that restructuring. So, it seemed to Sajó, the Constitutional Court's decision
was precisely the kind of interference with a transition to a market economy
that Sunstein feared would occur were social and economic rights enforced by
courts.[26]

Kim Lane Scheppele has argued that "the disaster that critics of the Court
predicted did not come to pass."[27] And, certainly, looking at the bottom line
within a decade of the Court's action, we see in Hungary a nation that has a
reasonably well-functioning market-centered democracy. Scheppele suggests
that the Constitutional Court's decision may actually have facilitated the
dual transition. For, she argues, Hungary was facing demands from international lenders that constrained political choice at least as much as constitutional provisions do. That is, the international lenders were depriving
Hungary's citizens of their ability to become effective in politics in just the
way that, Sunstein argued, judicial enforcement of social and economic rights
would. The Constitutional Court relied on notions of the rule of law to
counter that external pressure. And, as Scheppele argues, the international
lenders were placed at a strategic disadvantage by the Court's action, because
they were committed to the belief not only that austerity programs were
needed but that adherence to the rule of law was a prerequisite to a stable
market society. The Hungarian Constitutional Court in effect told the international lenders that they would have to adjust their commitment to austerity
in light of the lenders' own commitment to the ideal of the rule of law. Further, the Court's decisions sketched out what the accommodation would look
like. Hungary's constitution did not require the government to continue the
Communist-era programs of social provision for all eternity. All the government needed to do was come up with some reasonable program for shifting
from the existing system to a means-based one. And, Scheppele points out,
that is just what the government did.

Scheppele's analysis of the Hungarian case suggests some broader though
more speculative conclusions. Sunstein worried that recognizing social and
economic rights would impede the transition to a market society. Yet, though
all the nations in eastern and central Europe included social and economic
rights in their post-Communist constitutions, some—including, notably,
Hungary—appear to have made the transition to a market economy without
much difficulty. And, in light of the universal inclusion of social and economic rights in these constitutions, it cannot be that doing so accounts for

[26] Scheppele, *supra* note 23, at 1947–48, summarizes similar reactions from Hungarian scholars
and writers.
[27] *Id.* at 1948.

the failed or delayed transitions in nations such as Slovakia. It may be that including social and economic rights in these constitutions did not have the disastrous effects Sunstein feared because constitutional courts did little to enforce them. Then, though, Sunstein's concerns about the spillover effects—that citizens would come to regard all constitutional provisions as mere words on paper—of nonenforcement of social and economic rights were misplaced. For, once again, some of the nations of central and eastern Europe have developed reasonably well-functioning constitutional systems in which basic first-generation rights are generally recognized (at least to the degree they are recognized in western Europe and elsewhere).

Scheppele's analysis of the Hungarian austerity decision offers a pragmatic corrective to the pragmatic case against judicial enforcement of social and economic rights. For my purposes, the key aspect of that decision was that it prohibited an abrupt shift in the system of social provision while allowing a gradual one. As Scheppele puts it, "[W]e might expand the normal conception of the role of courts in a democratic society to include the role of 'policy partner' in ongoing bargaining about how a state should use its scarce resources."[28] The "normal conception" is that judicial review takes a strong form. The conception of judicial review, though, has already been expanded by the development of weak-form review. What happened in Hungary embodied some of the dialogic features of weak-form judicial review. I turn, then, to exploring the possibilities of weak-form review itself.

Forms of Weak-Form Review for Social and Economic Rights

As part 1 showed, weak-form review comes in several variants. Courts in Ireland, India, and South Africa have used weak-form review to enforce social and economic rights.[29] Their experience illuminates the possibilities of weak-form enforcement and suggests some of its limitations.

To begin, I distinguish among types of *substantive* rights—those that are merely declaratory, those that provide weak guarantees of social provision, and those that are interpreted to provide relatively strong guarantees. Afterward, I discuss the relationships among the types of rights, weak and strong, and strong and weak enforcement mechanisms. I argue that, though sometimes it is important to insist that the substance of a right cannot be disentangled from the remedies used to enforce it, sometimes it is equally important to stress that strong rights can be enforced *politically* as well as judicially, and in particular that weak judicial enforcement does not in itself undermine the

[28] *Id.* at 1935.

[29] For a related discussion, see Rosalind Dixon, "Creating Dialogue About Socio-Economic Rights: Strong v. Weak-Form Judicial Review Revisited," 5 Int'l J. Con. L. (2007).

claim that a right is a strong one, to be enforced through politics backed up and encouraged by the courts.

MERELY DECLARATORY RIGHTS

Perhaps most surprising are cases enforcing rights that seem to be merely declaratory or, in other terms, nonjusticiable. A constitution can enumerate social welfare rights but exempt them from judicial enforcement. The Irish Constitution contains a list of social welfare rights in a part headed "Directive Principles of Social Policy." The opening paragraph includes the following: "The principles of social policy set forth in this Article are intended for the general guidance of the [Parliament]. The application of those principles . . . shall not be cognisable by any Court under any of the provisions of this Constitution."[30]

Nonjusticiable rights need not be legally irrelevant. It seems clear, for example, that they can be used as the basis for defenses to ordinary tort and contract actions—for example, in identifying contract provisions that might be void as against public policy, to interpret ambiguous statutes, and even to support interpretations that, absent the Directive Principles or similar nonjusticiable rights, would not be the natural ones according to accepted standards of statutory interpretation. In addition, nonjusticiable rights can be invoked to explain why the courts refuse to recognize other rights, where the recognition of those other rights would impair the government's ability to implement—at its discretion—the nonjusticiable rights. A South African case makes the point. The South African government confronted a situation in which about three hundred poor people were displaced from their homes by flooding due to heavy rains.[31] The government responded by creating a temporary housing camp on the grounds of a large prison complex. Residents of a nearby town raised numerous challenges to the government's decision, which can be summarized as claims that the government's action constituted a regulatory taking of their property and was not in accordance with existing statutory restrictions on the government's power to use its property as it chose. The Constitutional Court of South Africa rejected the challenges, which were not frivolous.[32] Its decision can be understood as influenced by

---

[30] Art. 45, § 1, Constitution of Ireland, 1937. Similarly, the Indian Constitution makes the social welfare rights listed in its "Directive Principles of State Policy" judicially unenforceable. India Const. pt. IV, art. 37.

[31] Minister of Pub. Works v. Kyalami Ridge Envtl. Ass'n, 2001 (7) BCLR 652, P 2 (CC) (S. Afr.).

[32] Id. ¶ 51 (rejecting the claim that the government acted beyond its powers in establishing the transit camp and violated the constitutionally mandated separation of powers); id. ¶¶ 75–90 (rejecting the claim that the government's actions violated several statutes, ordinances, and the

the idea that social and economic rights deserve some recognition, if only indirectly.[33]

Courts can make social welfare rights nonjusticiable as well. Again, Ireland provides an example. The Irish Constitution contains a complex provision dealing with the right to education.[34] This provision concludes with the following social welfare right:

> In exceptional cases, where the parents for physical or moral reasons fail in their duty towards their children, the State as guardian of the common good, by appropriate means shall endeavour to supply the place of the parents, but always with due regard for the natural and imprescriptable rights of the child.[35]

Notably, this provision falls within the sections of the Constitution that are judicially enforceable.

In the 1990s Irish courts confronted a series of cases involving children with mental retardation, psychological disturbances, or other conditions that led them to be placed in state control.[36] The children and their parents claimed that the government was failing to provide adequate education.[37] Confronted with what they regarded as particularly strong cases of inattention to the circumstances of particular children, some lower courts first suspended the

---

town planning scheme); *id.* ¶¶ 109–10 (rejecting the claim that the government did not take the procedurally fair action required by the Constitution). The challengers claimed that the government was required to comply with environmental laws even when it was acting in its capacity as landowner, and that an array of statutes indicated that the government could create the housing camp only if it pursued a more formal process for doing so. *Id.* ¶¶ 10–11, 33, 65–89. The Constitutional Court rejected the latter challenge as having been raised too late in the expedited proceedings and rejected the former one on the merits. *Id.* ¶¶ 51, 75–90.

[33] In addition, nonjusticiable rights might be invoked as reasons for upholding national legislation against federalism-based challenges that the legislation lies outside the powers granted the national government by the constitution.

[34] Art. 42, Constitution of Ireland, 1937.

[35] Art. 42, § 5, Constitution of Ireland, 1937.

[36] *E.g., F.N. v. Minister of Educ.,* [1995] 1 I.R. 409, 412 (Ir. H. Ct.) (involving a child with "a hyperkinetic conduct disorder" who, the court concluded, "required a period of time in a secure unit which would contain him safely while confronting his behaviour"); *D.G. v. E. Health B.,* [1997] 3 I.R. 511, 517 (Ir. S.C.) (involving a child who "exhibited behaviour that was dangerous to himself and potentially to others," and who required "suitable residential care facilities"); *D.B. v. Minister for Justice,* [1999] 1 I.L.R.M. 93, 94–95 (Ir. H. Ct.) (involving a child who the court noted was "one of an increasing number of young people coming before this Court who, for their own welfare, require to be cared for . . . in a secure environment from which they cannot readily escape").

[37] *E.g., F.N.,* [1995] 1 I.R. at 412 (noting that F.N., through his solicitor, complained that the government had failed to provide him with "secure accommodation" or "religious and moral, intellectual, physical and social education"); *see also D.G.,* [1997] 3 I.R. at 518 (explaining that on five occasions D.G.'s solicitor had "written to the solicitor to the first respondent requesting that proper accommodation be made available" for D.G.); *D.B.,* [1999] 1 I.L.R.M. at 95 (noting that D.B.'s solicitor complained to the court that "there has been, and continues to be, a chronic shortage of places available in secure high support units" for young persons in need of such care).

litigation pending the promised adoption of new education initiatives,[38] and then, when those initiatives failed to materialize, entered comprehensive injunctions directing the government to develop adequate education programs for these children, essentially ordering them to do what they had promised.[39]

The Supreme Court of Ireland eventually rejected the argument that the government's failures violated the children's constitutional right to education.[40] In a judgment, joined by a majority of the Court's justices, that sounded all the themes of the conventional arguments against the enforcement of social and economic rights, Chief Justice Ronan Keane found the injunctions impermissible because they violated the principle of separation of powers. He agreed that the courts could issue declarations that Parliament and the executive had failed to comply with their constitutional duties. That, however, was as far as the courts could go. They should expect the officials to comply with the duties once the court clarified those duties. According to the chief justice, the injunctions impermissibly involved the courts "in effectively determining the policy which the Executive [is] to follow in dealing with a particular social problem." Paraphrasing an earlier opinion, the chief justice observed that "it is not the function of the courts to make an assessment of the validity of the many competing claims on national resources." That is not "administering justice in the normal sense," but rather is "an adjudication on the fairness or otherwise of the manner in which other organs of State had administered public resources."[41] The injunctions gave the courts a policymaking role that the Constitution lodged only in the Parliament and the executive.

The idea of nonjusticiability is that some constitutional provisions are not subject to judicial enforcement because, as the U.S. Supreme Court has put it, they are committed by the Constitution to another branch.[42] To say that separation-of-powers principles bar courts from enforcing a particular right—here, a social welfare right of a particular, and in some ways rather narrow, type—is simply to say that the right is nonjusticiable.

Yet, the Irish Court did indicate a willingness to *declare* that government social welfare policies violated constitutional guarantees. Declaratory rights are marginally different from nonjusticiable rights, in ways that are contingent on the place courts have in a nation's political culture. A standard concern about nonjusticiable rights—and, almost by definition, about merely declaratory rights (by which I mean rights that the courts are willing to declare violated by government policy without issuing enforceable orders)—is that they are not

---

[38] See, e.g., F.N., [1995] 1 I.R. at 416–17 (declaring that the court would not "make any immediate declaration or order" in the case, but would instead adjourn the case for the time being).

[39] See, e.g., D.B., [1999] 1 I.L.R.M. at 105 (ordering an injunction to "ensure that the [Minister for Health] who has already decided on the policy lives up to his word and carries it into effect").

[40] D. v. Minister for Educ., [2001] 4 I.R. 259 (Ir. S.C.).

[41] Id. at 287, 288.

[42] Baker v. Carr, 369 U.S. 186, 217 (1962).

rights at all. As the conventional arguments have it, a purported right without an accompanying judicially enforceable obligation is, almost literally, toothless.

Why would a legislator take seriously a constitution's identification of non-justiciable rights? As I argued in part 2, legislators might do so because they take the constitution seriously. That is, they might feel a moral obligation, enforced through politics, to do what the constitution says. Additionally, independent of—or perhaps causally related to—legislators' desires to comply with the constitution, civil society can read the constitution, conclude that it is being violated, and place pressure on legislators to enact policies that comply with the constitution. Gary Jacobsohn quotes a speaker in the debates on the adoption of the Directive Principles in Ireland who makes the following point: "They will be there as a constant headline, something by which the people as a whole can judge of their progress in a certain direction; something by which the representatives of the people can be judged as well as the people judge themselves as a whole."[43] That response might be adequate in nations with entrenched democratic cultures—where civil society stands ready to inflict political damage to legislators who depart from the constitution's requirements—and advanced welfare states.[44]

Nonjusticiable rights are enforced by civil society through political mobilizations and the like. Are merely declaratory rights meaningfully different? To some degree perhaps, because civil society can rely not merely on the constitution (and on what civil society organizations say the constitution implies about existing government policies), but on a judicial declaration of a constitutional violation. In the Irish cases, a judicial declaration of unconstitutionality might supplement the moral-political compulsion exerted by the constitution itself if the public gives some distinctive weight to statements—not judgments—made by courts.[45] Perhaps civil society institutions could make more headway with such a declaration in hand than they could otherwise with only the constitution's language to rely upon. But perhaps not; it will depend on the weight civil society itself gives to judicial declarations, and that weight will pretty clearly vary from one nation to another.[46]

[43] Gary Jacobsohn, "The Permeability of Constitutional Borders," 82 Tex. L. Rev. 1763, 1770 (2004) (quoting 67 Dail Deb. col. 69 (May 11, 1937), available at http://www.oireachtas-debates. gov.ie/D/0067/D.0067.193705110029.html) (visited Sept. 29, 2006).

[44] Ireland today might satisfy those requirements, although Ireland did not when the Directive Principles were inserted into the Constitution, and India today does not satisfy those requirements either.

[45] Consider in this connection a report by an ombuds office stating that the government's policy is unconstitutional. Polities that establish such offices might give their reports the kind of weight other polities give declarations by courts.

[46] Civil society might overestimate the effect a declaration will have on government officials, and might as a result mobilize less effectively after a declaration than it would with only the constitution's language to rely on. Finally, it deserves noting that the argument for declaratory rights gives a large place to the political effects of judicial declarations.

Weak Substantive Rights

Constitutions can recognize judicially enforceable social and economic rights, but give legislatures an extremely broad range of discretion about providing those rights (or, equivalently, direct that courts defer substantially to legislative judgments). That, formally, is the position taken in U.S. constitutional law. In *San Antonio Independent School District v. Rodriguez*, for example, the Supreme Court addressed a claim that Texas's system for financing public education violated the Fourteenth Amendment's equal protection clause.[47] The Court held that the Constitution required only that the legislature's choices satisfy a standard of minimum rationality.[48]

Unlike nonjusticiable rights, weak substantive rights are not immune from judicial enforcement. The celebrated case of *Government of the Republic of South Africa v. Grootboom* provides a good example of a weak judicially

---

[47] 411 U.S. 1 (1973).

[48] *Id.* at 55. *Rodriguez* and most other U.S. cases raising basic questions about the constitutional protection of social and economic rights have taken the form of equal protection challenges. *Rodriguez* did reject the claim that education was a "fundamental right," on the (circular) ground that fundamental rights for equal protection purposes were those that were implicitly or explicitly protected by the Constitution. *Rodriguez*, 411 U.S. at 33. It is at least theoretically possible to argue that social and economic rights are protected by the due process clause, the privileges or immunities clause, or other discrete constitutional provisions (that is, provisions interpreted as dealing with specific social welfare rights). On the privileges or immunities clause possibility, *see, e.g.*, Saenz v. Roe, 526 U.S. 489, 501–4 (1999) (discussing how the privileges or immunities clause protects the right of citizen travelers who become permanent residents of a state to be treated like other citizens of that state and, in particular, to receive the same amount of welfare benefits as citizens of that state). For a prescient argument that social welfare rights should be rooted in provisions other than the equal protection clause, see Frank I. Michelman, "Foreword: On Protecting the Poor Through the Fourteenth Amendment," 83 Harv. L. Rev. 7, 13 (1969) (noting that social and economic rights do not fit well within the scope of the equal protection clause because it is difficult to construe such rights as "inequalities," since the government's failure to provide adequate funds to those in need is a deprivation rather than discrimination). In addition, during the *Lochner* era, the Court enforced economic rights through the due process clause. That experience made the *Lochner* era a "counter-canon" in constitutional law, suggesting that it is quite unlikely that the Court would somehow manage to protect social welfare rights through the due process clause. *See* Richard A. Primus, "Canon, Anti-Canon, and Judicial Dissent," 48 Duke L. J. 243, 244 n. 10 (1998) (discussing the concept of the "anti-canon," which mirrors the constitutional canon by containing "highly important but normatively undesirable texts"). Welfare rights litigants believed that they could move toward the provision of a full set of social welfare rights by ratcheting up the procedural protections in place before existing rights could be terminated. That strategy rested on the hope, eventually proven empty, that the nonpoor would prefer to provide more generous benefits over eliminating benefits to the obviously needy. For a description of the strategy, see Frances Fox Piven & Richard A. Cloward, Poor People's Movements: Why They Succeed, How They Fail 264–357 (1977) (discussing the strong impact that the riots of the 1960s had on the development of new service programs and how the welfare rights activists should use a similar strategy when demanding payments and procedural protections for qualified recipients).

enforceable social welfare right.[49] I begin by noting that in both *Grootboom* and the subsequent *Treatment Action Campaign* (*TAC*) case, discussed in more detail later, the Constitutional Court rejected one version of strong substantive rights. In that version, the Constitution requires the provision to all of some minimum amount of health care or shelter, referred to doctrinally as a "minimum core" requirement. In *TAC*, the Court wrote, "[I]n dealing with such matters the courts are not institutionally equipped to make the wide-ranging factual and political enquiries necessary for determining what minimum core standards should be, nor for deciding how public revenues should most effectively be spent," and continued, "Courts are ill-suited to adjudicate upon issues where Court orders could have multiple social and economic consequences for the community."[50] This is the language of nonjusticiability. Yet, the Court went on in both cases to enforce the relevant social welfare right.

Grootboom involved the plight of a group of desperately poor people in South Africa. Originally they lived in terrible housing conditions in one of South Africa's shantytowns. Subsequently, they moved on to unoccupied, privately owned land that was included in an existing plan for the construction of low-cost housing. Although they were on the list for low-cost housing, many had no real prospect of obtaining it in the short run. The landowner obtained an order evicting them from the land, and the shacks they had built were demolished. The evictees eked out an existence by occupying a public football stadium, which lacked even the minimal, though still inadequate, facilities their shacks had provided.

The evictees sued, claiming that the government's housing policies, taken as a whole, failed to provide them with their constitutionally guaranteed right of access to adequate housing. They relied on the Constitution's guarantee of social welfare rights, which is itself qualified in the following way: "The state must take reasonable legislative and other measures, within its available resources, to achieve the progressive realisation of" the enumerated social welfare rights.[51] While expressly finding that the Constitution's socioeconomic rights were justiciable, the Constitutional Court noted that the trial court had rejected the evictees' argument that the constitution gave them a right to "a minimum core entitlement to shelter," but entered an order declaring that "the Constitution requires the state to devise and implement within its available resources a comprehensive and coordinated programme progressively to realise the right of access to adequate housing." The justifications for the order were that the Constitution required the government to take "reasonable" steps toward the realization of its social welfare rights, and that the

---

[49] 2000 (11) BCLR 1169 (CC) (S. Afr.)

[50] Minister of Health v. Treatment Action Campaign, 2002 (5) SALR 721, 722 (CC)(S. Afr.).

[51] S. Afr. Const. ch. 2, § 27(2).

exclusion of the "people in desperate need" from plans to provide housing to the poor were unreasonable because a "programme that excludes a significant segment of society cannot be said to be reasonable."[52]

The Court's order has several notable features. First, although in form the order simply declared that the Constitution imposed a duty on the government, the rights recognized were not merely declaratory. The order was made in a context where the government did have a program for building low-cost housing, which implies that the existing plan had to be adjusted to ensure that it contained an element that would provide housing opportunities for the "people in desperate need."[53] Despite the Court's rejection of the "minimum core" requirement, the Constitution's social welfare rights provisions have some judicially enforceable content.[54]

Requiring the government to include a provision for "people in desperate need" in its plans does shift the government's priorities to some extent. Yet, the Court's order was quite limited in its effects. In particular, under the Court's order the individual plaintiffs need not receive any relief at all.[55] The government's program would have been acceptable had it promised to provide some housing for people in desperate need "within a reasonably short time." Existing plans did not hold out that prospect. But, according to the Court, it would have been enough to have a program that had some "end in sight."[56]

Treating the rights as weak ones is consistent with the Constitution's language, and particularly its requirement of reasonableness. Constitutional provisions allowing governments to adopt reasonable programs to achieve social welfare rights, a willingness to find some programs unreasonable, and a remedial system that does not guarantee that any particular plaintiff will receive individualized relief: these are the characteristics of weak substantive social welfare rights.

---

[52] *Grootboom*, at ¶¶ 20, 14, 99, 43, 64.

[53] *Id.* at ¶ 69.

[54] *Id.* at ¶¶ 47, 64. The Court did not explicitly reject the "minimum core" requirement entirely, leaving the door open for defining such a requirement in the future by asserting that it was unable to formulate the requirement in *Grootboom* because it lacked relevant information. *Id.* at ¶33. The remainder of the opinion did, however, focus on whether the government's efforts to provide the housing rights contained in § 26 of the South African Constitution were reasonable in light of all the constrain's on affording those rights. In doing so, the Court suggested that its analysis would not focus on a "minimum core" requirement.

[55] *Id.* at §¶¶ 95–96. A newspaper report four years after the Court's decision indicated that members of the plaintiff class were living in conditions not materially different from the ones that had precipitated the litigation. *See* Bonny Schoonakker, "Treated with Contempt," Sunday Times (S. Afr.), Mar. 21, 2004, *available at* http://www.suntimes.co.za/2004/03/21/insight/in01.asp (visited Sept. 29, 2006) (describing the conditions and noting that Mrs. Grootboom had "apparently disappeared").

[56] *Grootboom*, ¶ 65 (noting that under the existing program, "people in desperate need are left without any form of assistance with no end in sight").

Strong Substantive Rights

Social welfare rights can be strong ones, in the sense that courts will enforce them fully, without giving substantial deference to legislative judgments, whenever they conclude that the legislature has failed to provide what the constitution requires.

The *TAC* case is a good illustration of a strong social welfare right.[57] Nevirapine is a drug that substantially inhibits the transmission of HIV/AIDS from infected pregnant women and nursing mothers to their children, reducing the risk of transmission from about 25 percent to about 12 percent. Nevirapine's manufacturer was willing to supply as much of the drug as was needed at no cost. The government of South Africa made nevirapine available at a limited number of "experimental" sites. The government took the position that distribution of nevirapine should be limited in that way because there was inadequate information on the long-term effects of nevirapine and, more plausibly, because the effective administration of the drug required its recipients to undergo some counseling from trained medical personnel. Although such personnel were widely available at public hospitals, the government's view was that requiring them to give the appropriate counseling would burden them with additional work and divert them from other, more pressing tasks.

An HIV/AIDS activist group challenged the government's policy, arguing that it violated the constitutional guarantee that "everyone has the right to have access to health care services."[58] The trial court ordered the government to make nevirapine available to everyone who would benefit from its use, and to develop "an effective comprehensive national programme to prevent or reduce the mother-to-child transmission of HIV, including the provision of voluntary counselling and testing, and where appropriate, Nevirapine or other appropriate medicine, and formula milk for feeding."[59]

The Constitutional Court modified the lower court's injunction, but in doing so recognized that the right to health was, in some respects, a strong substantive one. The Constitutional Court examined the government's justifications for refusing to make nevirapine available outside the experimental sites. In response to the government's claim that administering the drug outside the context of a comprehensive counseling program would be ineffective, the Court observed that the drug alone would have some beneficial effects for some women and their children even in the absence of counseling and other forms of support. The government expressed concern as well that widespread administration of the drug might lead to the development of a drug-resistant virus, to which the Court responded that the risk of such a development was

---

[57] Minister of Health v. Treatment Action Campaign, 2002 (5) SALR 721 (CC) (S. Afr.).

[58] S. Afr. Const. ch. 2, § 27(1)(a).

[59] *Treatment Action Campaign*, at 730.

"well worth running" in light of the life-threatening nature of HIV/AIDS. The Court said that the government's asserted concern about the long-term effects of administering the drug was "no more than a hypothetical issue," relying on the recommendation to use the drug made by the World Health Organization.[60] According to the Court, the government had good reason to monitor what happened after nevirapine was administered, so as to determine its long-term effects and to determine how effective it was when administered without counseling. But, the Court concluded, "this is not a reason for not allowing the administration" of the drug outside the experimental sites "when there is the capacity to administer it and its use is medically indicated." The Court concluded that the government's policy of limiting the drug to the experimental sites "fails to address the needs of mothers and their newborn children who do not have access to these sites." It therefore directed that the government "[r]emove the restrictions" on the distribution of the drug, "[p]ermit and facilitate" the drug's use when appropriate, according to a doctor's medical judgment, and "make provision if necessary for counsellors."[61]

The Constitutional Court's examination of the government's justifications for restricting the drug's availability was quite searching, and nothing in the relevant sections of the opinions indicates that the Court was giving any real deference to the government's judgments.[62] Further, the Court expressed the view that the courts had the power to enter mandatory injunctions directing the government to develop policies that would lead to the "progressive realization" of social welfare rights, although it concluded that no detailed injunction was necessary in the nevirapine case in light of changes in government policy.[63]

---

[60] *Id.* at 744, 745, 746. Lawrence K. Altman, "Infant Drugs for H.I.V. Put Mothers at Risk," New York Times, Feb. 10, 2004, at A22, reports on a study showing that the administration of nevirapine to mothers as a means of preventing transmission of HIV to their babies increases the risk that the mothers will develop resistance to drugs used to treat their own HIV infection.

[61] *Treatment Action Campaign*, at 747, 765.

[62] One reason for the Court's willingness to be relatively aggressive may have been the fact that, as the Court noted, the government's policy had changed as the litigation proceeded. The government abandoned what the Court called its "rigid" policy, *id.* at 760–62, and began to make nevirapine more widely available, although still not at all public hospitals, and it appropriated substantial new funds for the treatment of HIV/AIDS. The question then is *why* the government changed its position. It may have done so because of widespread criticism, including, of course, the lower court decision, which the Constitutional Court had refused to suspend during the appeal. In addition, perhaps the government changed its position because it expected the Constitutional Court to agree with the lower court that its prior position was unreasonable and because the government may have hoped that the Constitutional Court would weaken the remedy once it was faced with the more reasonable position the government was taking. My own view is that the widespread judgment among South Africa's political elites that President Thabo Mbeki's position on the cause of AIDS—he was reported to believe that the human immunodeficiency virus did not cause AIDS—was scientifically unsupportable played a more important role in the controversy's outcome than any technical legal factors.

[63] *Treatment Action Campaign*, at 757–60.

Unlike the Irish Court, the South African Constitutional Court found no separation-of-powers barrier to the use of such injunctions to enforce constitutional social welfare rights.[64]

TAC illustrates another point about strong substantive rights: the concern that strong enforcement of such rights might have troubling budgetary consequences can be reduced when, as in TAC itself (because nevirapine's manufacturer would provide the drug without cost to the government), the fiscal impact of compliance is small. That, in turn, can occur either when the number of beneficiaries of the strong right is quite small, or when the benefit provided to a larger class is itself inexpensive. Critics of strong enforcement of strong rights worry about the doctrinal implications of such enforcement in cases with small fiscal effects; they are concerned that the next case to arise might have much larger effects and yet be indistinguishable in principle from the first, "cheap" case. Yet, one might respond that the size of the fiscal impact is itself a principle relevant to the choice of enforcement mechanisms. If so, courts could invoke that principle to enforce some rights strongly, others weakly.

WEAK AND STRONG FORMS OF JUDICIAL ENFORCEMENT OF SOCIAL WELFARE RIGHTS

For many years, U.S. constitutionalists thought that judicial review necessarily took the strong form of completely displacing a legislative judgment with a judicial one. Finding a statute unconstitutional, a court would enjoin prosecutions or vacate convictions. The standard catchphrase was that constitutional rights were "personal and present,"[65] meaning that each person whose constitutional rights were violated was entitled to a remedy that immediately eliminated the constitutional violation.[66]

As the South African cases indicate, for practical reasons, the remedies for violations of social and economic rights cannot be "personal and present." It will necessarily take time to locate a housing unit for a person denied a constitutional right to shelter, and much more time to construct a housing unit. But the problem of deferred remedies is not unique to social and economic rights, and the U.S. experience with deferred remedies suggests an alternative to strong remedies.

[64] The Court referred to decisions by the highest constitutional courts in the United States, India, Germany, Canada, and the United Kingdom to support its conclusion that "courts in other countries" accept the possibility of entering mandatory injunctions. Id.

[65] See, e.g., Sweatt v. Painter, 339 U.S. 629, 634 (1950) ("It is fundamental that these cases concern rights that are personal and present.").

[66] Or, in the case of a completed violation, each person is entitled to a remedy that fully compensates for the damages caused by the unconstitutional action.

After holding that segregated elementary and secondary schools were unconstitutional, the U.S. Supreme Court ordered that desegregation occur
"with all deliberate speed."[67] That remedial approach did not make conceptual sense given the nature of the constitutional violation—the violation of
assigning students to schools on the basis of race could have been remedied
immediately by an injunction directing that school boards refrain from using
race as a criterion for such assignments—but the Court adopted the "all deliberate speech" remedy because it hoped that a gradualist approach would elicit
less resistance than an immediate remedy. That pragmatic judgment proved
mistaken, but the Court's approach does provide a model for a weak form of
remedy for the violation of constitutional rights.

Weak remedies may come in a number of forms. There is the pure declaration discussed earlier. Notably, the declaratory *remedy* for violations of social
and economic rights reproduces one version of weak-form *substantive* review
such as that created by the British Human Rights Act. Another weak remedy
is, in essence, a requirement that government officials develop plans that hold
out some promise of eliminating the constitutional violation within a reasonably short but unspecified time period. Once the plan is developed, the courts
step back, allowing the officials to implement the plan.[68] Although examples
of the effective deployment of weak remedies are relatively few in number, another characteristic might be judicial encouragement of negotiations among
affected parties over the contours of a more detailed plan, which the courts
might ratify rather than develop independently. Similarly, because no one ex-
pects immediate results, the courts would provide only light oversight of the
plan's implementation. Courts and implementing officials would interact,
though. Plaintiffs may periodically complain to the courts that the plan is not
being implemented vigorously or according to its terms. The implementing
officials may respond to such complaints or may come to the courts themselves to ask for a modification of the plan in light of the experience they have
had in attempting to implement it. Sometimes the courts will agree with the
plaintiffs and ratchet up the requirements, setting more precise timetables or
identifying specific benchmarks the officials must reach. Sometimes the courts
will agree with the officials and loosen the requirements to accord with the
realities as they have developed.

---

[67] Brown v. Board of Education, 349 U.S. 294, 301 (1955).

[68] The best theorization of weak remedies of this sort is the work of Charles Sabel and his collaborators. *See, e.g.,* Michael C. Dorf & Charles F. Sabel, "A Constitution of Democratic Experimentalism," 98 Colum. L. Rev. 267, 452–69 (describing how U.S. courts have shaped remedies
allowing for government experimentation while setting baselines for the protection of fundamental constitutional rights); Charles F. Sabel & William H. Simon, "Destabilization Rights: How
Public Law Litigation Succeeds," 117 Harv. L. Rev. 1015, 1062–73 (2004) (discussing experimentalist remedies in recent cases and arguing that experimentation can solve problems associated with stronger forms of remedy).

Once again I emphasize the parallelism between this remedial form and some versions of weak-form substantive review. Sunstein calls the remedial form "administrative review," Charles Sabel and his collaborators call it "experimentalist" review. In part 1 we saw dialogic versions of weak-form substantive review. Consider the enforcement of social and economic rights in a system with a notwithstanding clause, for example. The constitutional court might find that the legislature failed to provide the promised level of social protection. Suppose it entered a coercive injunctive order of the sort common in strong-form systems. The legislature could respond by complying with the order, or by modifying the underlying substantive guarantee by specifying that the legislative program—or, more interestingly, one changed a bit to respond to the court's concerns, but not so extensively as to comply with the coercive order—should take effect notwithstanding the constitutional guarantee. Worked out suitably, this process—that is, the exercise of weak-form substantive review of social and economic rights—could closely approximate the experimentalist remedial form.

The alternative to weak remedies is strong ones. Strong remedies are mandatory injunctions that spell out in detail what government officials are to do by identifying goals, the achievement of which can be measured easily, for example, through obvious numerical measures.[69] Such injunctions also set specific deadlines for the accomplishment of those goals. The interaction between the courts and government officials is close, not loose. Instead of relying on plaintiffs to complain, for example, the injunctions may impose reporting requirements, directing that the officials tell the courts periodically how the process of implementing the plan has gone. Typically, the courts will resist easy modification of their orders when officials say that practical difficulties have stood in the way of full implementation.

Finally, one important theorization of weak remedies suggests that weak remedies must, in the first instance, become converted into strong ones before they can be reconstituted as better weak remedies.[70] The idea is that planning remedies will work only after people become convinced that strong remedies have not addressed what remains a pressing social problem. The dynamic, then, is this: weak remedy found to be ineffective; replaced by strong remedy found also to be ineffective; replaced finally by a different form of weak remedy, which promises to be effective.

[69] In what follows I describe a *model* of strong remedies, developed from the materials provided by U.S. case law. I do not contend that *current* U.S. law fits the model well. For example, the U.S. Supreme Court has told lower courts to accede to officials' requests to modify strong remedies more readily than they would in the model I describe. *See* Rufo v. Inmates of Suffolk County Jail, 502 U.S. 367, 390–93 (1992) (adopting a standard under which the party seeking the modification bears the burden of establishing that a significant change in the facts or law warrants revision of the decree and that the proposed modification is appropriately tailored to fit the change in facts or law).

[70] *See* Sabel & Simon, *supra* note 68, at 1065–67 (describing the removal of "political blockage" as an important precondition to the development of weak remedies).

We have, then, a pair of remedial forms, each with its characteristic advantages and disadvantages. Weak remedies might turn out to be ineffective, but—perhaps for that very reason—they are unlikely to generate strong political opposition. Strong remedies might work in the short run, but—again perhaps for that very reason—they may become intensely controversial.[71]

Weak remedies might go well with weak substantive social and economic rights, a possibility I mention only to put aside. The more interesting questions, I think, involve strong substantive rights. In the terms I have developed here, the conventional wisdom about judicially enforceable social and economic rights rests on the assumption that remedies for rights violations must be strong ones. The possibility of using weak remedies for strong substantive rights seems worth exploring.

Can Strong and Weak Rights Really Be Distinguished?

My description of weak and strong substantive rights regularly slides between identifying a standard of review, which goes to the strength of the right, and mentioning what courts do when they find violations of the weak or strong rights, which goes to the remedies available for violations. A critic of this presentation might say that the distinction between weak and strong substantive rights is simply one about the timing of the remedy, with strong rights receiving immediate judicial remedies, weak ones receiving deferred judicial remedies, and nonjusticiable rights not being rights at all. The critic might add that the constitutional provisions I have described use terms such as "within available resources" and "progressive realization" as part of the definition of the right, seemingly folding the remedy into the rights definition itself. Further, the critic might note that what makes a right strong is the fact that legislatures have a quite narrow range of choices available to them with respect to the right, and that in such circumstances, all enforcement must be strong in the sense that it forces policy outcomes into the narrow range the constitution permits. And, finally, the critic might suggest that, in a world of reasonable disagreement about what a constitution's provisions mean, *no* rights can be strong in the appropriate sense.

All these points have some force. Yet, using the term *rights* to describe even nonjusticiable rights brings out that we have a number of institutional

---

[71] On the effectiveness of strong remedies, see Malcolm M. Feeley & Edward L. Rubin, Judicial Policy Making in the Modern State: How the Courts Reformed America's Prisons 366–75 (1998) (describing the major effects the federal judiciary produced in prison reform cases, including the extension of well-recognized constitutional rights to prisoners and the abolition of the South's "plantation model" of prisons). On the ensuing political controversies, see, for example, Ross Sandler & David Schoenbrod, Democracy by Decree: What Happens When Courts Run Government 139–61 (2003).

mechanisms by which rights can be enforced, including enforcement by a mobilized civil society. A nation's constitutional culture, perhaps reinforced by court decisions, can give particular rights a "feeling" of strength or weakness. Rights that feel strong might generate distinctive political claims. That, at least, is the case for strong rights enforced by weak courts.

Weak Remedies for Strong Rights?

We are familiar with the use of strong remedies—damage awards and mandatory injunctions, for example—for violations of first-generation civil and political rights.[72] Indeed, the emergence of weak-form judicial review in systems previously committed to parliamentary supremacy suggests that a fixed point in modern constitutionalism is that first-generation rights *must* be enforced in the courts. Another fixed point, as we have seen, is that modern constitutions must *contain* guarantees of social and economic rights. My previous discussion stopped with constitutions adopted in the immediate aftermath of World War II. The wave of constitutions adopted after 1989 and the return of constitutionalism to Latin America around the same time added another concern. After 1989, confidence that freedom and democracy would produce social democratic policies was tempered by concern that they would lead instead to a market society that was too free and unrestrained. Constitutional social and economic rights would obstruct that development.

Yet the accommodation of a market society to constitutionalized social and economic rights could not go too far without alienating other important political actors. For example, in South Africa the inclusion of social welfare rights itself had to accommodate the interests of the (white) capitalist class, which everyone knew was going to play an important role in the post-apartheid regime.[73] In addition, the post-1989 constitutions were created in a world with relatively fluid capital, whose reigning ideology was the so-called Washington consensus.[74] That consensus placed substantial constraints on the ability of

[72] Remedying violations of equality rights sometimes requires more complex steps. The Canadian jurisprudence on "reading in" legislation to remedy constitutional violations by including within a statute's scope a group whose exclusion violates the Constitution's equality provisions or "reading down" to exclude other groups from the statute's coverage is the best developed among the jurisdictions with which I am familiar. For a brief discussion, see Peter W. Hogg, 2 Constitutional Law of Canada 37.1(f)–(g) (looseleaf ed., 1997).

[73] For a clear demonstration of the effects of this constraint on the development of the South African Constitution, see Heinz Klug, Constituting Democracy: Law, Globalism, and South Africa's Political Reconstruction 118–38 (2000).

[74] One often-cited source describes the Washington consensus's "core tenets" as "deregulation, privatization, 'openness' (to foreign investment, to imports), unrestricted movement of capital, and lower taxes." William Finnegan, "The Economics of Empire—Notes on the Washington Consensus," Harper's, May 2003, at 41–42.

national governments to implement social democratic policies, and more important in the present context, on the ability of the drafters of national constitutions to include robust social welfare rights in their constitutions.[75]

In these circumstances, a strategy of writing strong social welfare rights into the constitution but enforcing them only through weak remedies seems particularly attractive.[76] This is especially so because, at least as the Washington consensus evolved, its supporters came to believe that social provision of basic education and public health made worthwhile contributions to development by subsidizing the development of human capital. Can this strategy work?

Professor Sunstein's argument about the need of nations without strong constitutionalist traditions to develop one might weigh against this position. One of the most effective ways of developing a constitutional tradition, he argues, is for a nation's political elite to demonstrate to the public that the new constitution's words actually mean something—that the words have some effects on their lives. Coupling strong rights with weak remedies, particularly when those remedies are rarely deployed because of resource constraints on plaintiffs, may be a formula for producing cynicism about the constitution.

The possibility of coupling weak rights with strong remedies seems unattainable as well. The risk of cynicism recurs. Citizens would observe constitutional language seeming to guarantee some social and economic rights and the lack of any real enforcement thereof, not because no one is available to enforce the rights—in a system with strong remedies, the courts themselves do so—but because the rights are not strong.[77]

Professor Cross raises another concern. He argues that even weak remedies for social and economic rights are unlikely to succeed.[78] His reason is that enforcing rights, even in a weak-form system, requires resources that the beneficiaries of social and economic rights typically lack. He relies on the important work of Charles Epp describing the "support structure" needed to produce a true rights revolution.[79] A constitution's social welfare provisions might not be enforced at all, even through weak remedies, because no one is available to help the courts run the remedial process.

---

[75] See Ran Hirschl, Toward Juristocracy: The Origins and Consequences of the New Constitutionalism 46–47 (2004) (describing how "international political economy factors" advocated by actors such as international banks and corporations may push "domestic economic elites to advocate constitutionalization" as a method of protecting transnational capital).

[76] I use the language of strategy here, although I do not believe that the process whereby constitutional courts came up with weak remedies for strong substantive rights was always consciously strategic, although on occasion it might have been.

[77] Perhaps the Irish approach might be adapted so that, instead of making it clear that the social and economic rights are nonjusticiable principles of social policy, the constitution makes it clear that it will be rare for the legislature to violate such rights.

[78] Cross, *supra* note 2, at 880–85 (discussing "the economics of rights enforcement").

[79] Charles R. Epp, The Rights Revolution: Lawyers, Activists, and Supreme Courts in Comparative Perspective (1998).

Professor Cross's concerns about the "support structure" for social and economic rights can be alleviated a bit. As he notes, the support structure need not be provided by the beneficiary groups themselves.[80] Civil society can sometimes supply the support structure. For example, the South African nevirapine case was litigated in the name of the Treatment Action Campaign, described by some as South Africa's most well-organized civil society group.[81] In addition, remedies can be structured to reduce the resources the beneficiary groups must deploy. *Grootboom* required the representatives of the homeless to come back to court to complain if the government's plan was, in their judgment, inadequate. The court might instead have required the government to report in six months, and at intervals thereafter, on its plans and their progress. True, the homeless would have to come to court to point out whatever deficiencies there might be in the government's plans and progress, but the burden on them is smaller than it was in the remedy the court developed.[82]

These observations about civil society may be insufficient to allay all reasonable concerns. Civil society institutions need to gain domestic legitimacy. To some extent they can do so from their activities themselves, as they claim to be working to enforce the nation's constitution. Yet, sometimes these institutions have stronger nondomestic than domestic support, which might undermine their effectiveness.[83] Civil society's institutions might be thin, leading to essentially random interventions by the courts (which might, however, be a signal to other institutions about the possibility for new mobilizations). The thicker the world of nongovernmental organizations (NGOs), the more systematically issues will be presented to the courts, but the more likely as well will be decisions that have, at least cumulatively, a significant fiscal impact. And, finally, the distribution of NGOs in society might be skewed in just the

---

[80] Cross, *supra* note 2, at 882 (observing that "[r]epresentatives of the impoverished sometimes prevail in court," because they have counsel provided "either pro bono or through the support of an interest group").

[81] Sachs, *supra* note 3, quotes the group's lawyer as making that claim.

[82] Justice Sachs defends the court's refusal in *TAC* to require the government to report on two grounds, that the government had "responded correctly in the past in terms of complying with orders that came from the Court," and that the dialogue between the court and the government had to be "civil in tone and reasonable in substance." Sachs, *supra* note 3. *But see* Lynn Berat, "The Constitutional Court of South Africa and Jurisdictional Questions: In the Interest of Justice?" 3 Int'l J. Con. L. 39, 70 (2005) (noting that at the time *TAC* was decided, "two years after *Grootboom*, the government had done virtually nothing to improve the lot of Grootboom and people like her"). The focus on Grootboom individually, and on the class she represented in the litigation itself, is mistaken, for reasons discussed in the text. Reliance on government's good faith might be misplaced had the government not been engaging in any sort of planning to provide housing for the desperately needy.

[83] For a discussion, see Rita Jalali, "Foreign Aid and Civil Society:How External Aid Is Detrimental to Southern NGOs and Social Movements," Democracy & Society, vol. 2, no. 2, p. 6 (Spring 2005), available at http://www.georgetown.edu/centers/cdats/DemocracyAndSocietyS05.pdf (visited Sept. 29, 2006).

way that other social institutions are, thereby leading to the reproduction in NGO activities of the limitations of more obviously political organizations.

There are clear obstacles to the effective enforcement of social and economic rights, even through weak remedies. And there is another difficulty. I argued in part 1 that weak-form systems of judicial review might not be stable, using the Canadian example to suggest that weak-form systems might transform themselves into strong-form ones. Similarly, weak remedies might become strong ones.

Consider the South African cases that refer to the constitutional requirement that the government seek the progressive realization of social and economic rights. Assume that the South African courts enforce those rights with weak remedies. Occasionally, litigants will raise the question of whether the rights are indeed being progressively realized. Or, more precisely, litigants will claim that the weak remedies are not producing an acceptable rate of realization. Moreover, litigants will be able to point to a systemic reason for the (low) rate they, and the courts, observe: Weak remedies give government officials weak incentives to do much to realize the social and economic rights. Short-term concerns may overwhelm the long-term ones embodied in the weak remedies; even weak remedies displace other policy choices officials might prefer to make, if only by forcing them to devote time to issues they think have low priority; officials may repeatedly believe that they will be able to persuade the courts, in the occasional interactions contemplated by weak remedies, that the courts should reformulate their understanding of what the social and economic rights provisions require—and, even if those hopes are repeatedly defeated, the officials will know that they have already delayed the realization of the rights somewhat.

If courts have some unstated sense of what an appropriate rate of realization would be, they may come to find that weak remedies are too weak. And I believe that judges may well come to have such a sense. What they seek is the realization of the social and economic rights—that is, their coming into being as a real-world phenomenon. What are judges likely to do if they observe nothing happening as a result of their weak remedial orders? One possibility is that they will begin to strengthen the orders, moving in the direction of converting strong rights protected by weak remedies into strong rights protected by strong remedies. The same course of action may be likely as well if judges observe almost nothing happening—that is, if the rate of realization seems to them too slow.[84]

The best case study supporting the claim that this response may occur is the U.S. experience in school desegregation cases. That experience might be taken

[84] The slide into strong remedies may occur even if the starting point is merely a declaratory right. Courts may expect civil society mobilizations to induce politicians to do something to ensure the provision of such a right and, observing politicians doing nothing, may begin to impose weak, then stronger, remedies.

to indicate that weak remedies are no remedies at all. The U.S. Supreme Court did indeed step back from supervising the desegregation process,[85] and the lower courts gave school authorities a great deal of latitude. The result, especially in the Deep South, was that nothing much happened in the way of desegregation for a decade.[86] The Court's response was to convert the weak remedies into strong ones, authorizing the lower courts to mandate detailed desegregation plans and closely supervise their implementation. The Supreme Court's impatience with the failure to accomplish much desegregation—its concern that the rate of realization of the right to nonsegregated schooling was too low—propelled the change.[87]

The unfolding story of school adequacy litigation in North Carolina is also instructive.[88] In 1997 the North Carolina Supreme Court held that the state had a constitutional duty to provide children "the opportunity to attain a sound basic education."[89] After an extensive hearing, the trial court then entered an order directing the state "to conduct self-examinations of the present allocation of resources and to produce a rational[], comprehensive plan which strategically focuses available resources and funds towards meeting the needs of all children . . . to obtain a sound basic education."[90] It left the details to the state education authorities, but it indicated that the remedy should ensure that each classroom have a competent and well-trained teacher, each school a competent and well-trained principal, and that each school be provided with the resources needed to provide all children the opportunity to obtain a basic education. The court ordered the state to report on its progress every three months.

The North Carolina Supreme Court affirmed this planning order. It praised the trial court for exercising "admirable restraint" by leaving so much to the defendants to work out, although it added the qualification "initially at least." At the same time, the court reversed another component of the trial court's order, this one requiring the state to expand existing prekindergarten

[85] See Brown v. Bd. of Educ., 349 U.S. 294, 300 (1955) (giving lower courts the authority to enforce desegregation and allowing them to give segregated schools the "additional time necessary to carry out [the Supreme Court's] ruling"); Shuttlesworth v. Birmingham Bd. of Educ., 358 U.S. 101, 101 (1958) (affirming without opinion a district court decision upholding the facial validity of a pupil placement law).

[86] See Lino A. Graglia, Disaster By Decree: The Supreme Court Decisions on Race and the Schools 38–45 (1976) (describing circuit court decisions that essentially allowed school segregation to continue).

[87] See, e.g., Green v. County Sch. Bd., 391 U.S. 430, 439 (1968) (requiring the school board to "come forward with a plan that promises realistically to work, and promises to work now"), 438 (citing the school board's "deliberate perpetuation of [an] unconstitutional dual system" as a reason for imposing a stricter desegregation imperative).

[88] The most recent decision, at the time this is written, is Hoke County v. State, 358 N.C. 605 (2004).

[89] Leandro v. State, 346 N.C. 336 (1997).

[90] Hoke County, 358 N.C. at 635.

programs so that all "at risk" children could enroll. Such a "specific" remedy was "inappropriate at this juncture."[91] So far, then, the opinion resembles *Grootboom*: a planning remedy and a refusal to enforce a specific substantive standard. Yet, I wonder why the trial court issued the prekindergarten order, and I note the Supreme Court's repeated hints that it might later ratchet up the requirements—presumably, moving from a planning order to one requiring that specific actions be taken.

The lessons to be drawn from these experiences are complex and to some extent contradictory. They suggest that there might well be a dynamic, born of frustration, leading the courts to convert weak remedies into strong ones. Perhaps, though, that frustration might itself take a long time to realize. In contexts other than segregation, the courts might not become impatient as quickly—within seventeen years—as the U.S. Supreme Court did. They might, for example, conclude that rights dealing with education, housing, and jobs might take at least a generation to realize. James Liebman and Charles Sabel suggest another constraint on this dynamic. Consider the South African Constitutional Court's reasons for rejecting a "minimum core" interpretation of social and economic rights: Judges cannot, the Court said, come up with adequate definitions of what that core might be. Liebman and Sabel suggest that the courts can overcome this difficulty by transforming the "minimum core" requirement from an absolute to a comparative one. In the education context, for example, do not try to define what a good basic education is; rather, look at schools that are uncontroversially providing such an education, and direct "the laggards to adopt strategies with effects equivalent to those pursued by the leading schools and districts."[92] Courts might eventually become frustrated if the laggards continue to lag, but perhaps they will be more patient than they would be had they themselves developed the standards the schools were to achieve.[93]

The courts might respond to a rate of realization that seems too low in another way. They might reconceptualize the constitution's social and economic rights. Instead of treating such rights as strong ones protected by weak remedies, courts may treat them as weak rights or even nonjusticiable ones. The (psychological) mechanism here is that judges will infer from the failure of weak remedies to accomplish much change in the actual provision of social and economic rights that the task is beyond judicial capacity—that, despite the promise of weak remedies, constitutions ought not recognize strong judicially enforceable social and economic rights.

The idea that this second response might occur comes not primarily from judicial behavior, but from the ingenious—some would say cynical—suggestion

[91] *Id.* at 638, 643.

[92] James S. Liebman & Charles F. Sabel, "The Federal No Child Left Behind Act and the Post-Desegregation Civil Rights Agenda," 81 N.C. L. Rev. 1703, 1720 (2003).

[93] I note that in some contexts, this comparative strategy might not be easily pursued. I wonder, for example, whether it could be used in the setting of the Grootboom case.

by former senator George Aiken that the best way to extricate the United States from the war in Vietnam was for the president to declare victory and bring the troops home.[94] There are some judicial analogues, though. Some state courts that ordered revisions in their states' systems of financing public education encountered such strong resistance that they basically withdrew from the field, saving face by declaring that what the state legislature had done actually did satisfy the constitutional requirements the courts were enforcing.[95] I should note, though, that there is an alternative reading of the evidence from these cases. Charles Sabel and James Liebman suggest that courts succeed when they utilize creative weak remedies and fail when they use the politically more problematic strong remedies.[96]

In some aspects, transforming strong rights into weak ones might converge with the first response, transforming weak remedies into strong ones. Consider here yet another perspective on the U.S. desegregation. The experience with strong remedies in desegregation cases was not an entirely happy one in the United States. Those remedies accomplished a fair amount in the short run, and particularly in areas with school districts that encompassed urban and suburban areas. They also engendered a great deal of resistance, which in the end produced a political reaction that, working through the process by which federal judges are appointed, eventually led the courts to withdraw from the desegregation process. The arguments for the conventional wisdom about the incompatibility between strong social welfare rights and strong remedies are tied directly to judicial capacity, but it would not be difficult to incorporate the likelihood of this sort of political response into those arguments. The idea is that judges should interpret resistance to the implementation of strong substantive rights as civil society's mobilization in support of a conception of rights different from the one the judges have offered. Further, judges should also come to see that mobilization is itself a way of enforcing what civil society understands social and economic rights to be.

We might then have in hand the following argument: courts should not enforce strong social and economic rights with weak remedies because those remedies may well become strong ones, which in turn will lead courts to transform the strong rights into weak ones. In this way, the Irish model of declaratory

[94] For the aphorism and its origin, see Pamela S. Karlan, "Exit Strategies in Constitutional Law: Lessons for Getting the Least Dangerous Branch Out of the Political Thicket," 82 B.U. L. Rev. 667, 667 n. 2 (2002).

[95] The most comprehensive study is Douglas S. Reed, On Equal Terms: The Constitutional Politics of Equal Opportunity 22–34 (2001). Reed describes a number of states in which judicial action did push legislatures in the direction of equalizing resources, although in my view he somewhat overestimates the degree of movement and the contribution the courts made to that movement.

[96] Charles F. Sabel & James S. Liebman, "A Public Laboratory Dewey Barely Imagined: The Emerging Model of School Governance and Legal Reform," 28 N.Y.U. Rev. L. & Soc. Change 183 (2003).

but otherwise nonjusticiable rights—analogous to the British Human Rights Act approach—may turn out to be the best, because it at least allows for the permanent articulation of the view that social and economic rights should be strong.

Social Welfare Rights from the Right and the Left

Canada's Supreme Court issued a decision in 2005 that illustrates many of this book's themes: the possibility of enforcing constitutional social welfare rights, the possibility that doing so will serve conservative rather than progressive goals, the importance of attention to innovative forms of remedy.

The *Chaoulli* case involved a challenge to a central provision in Quebec's system for providing health care.[97] All public health care systems that seek to serve a high proportion of the population face several problems. One is cream skimming—the concentration in the public system of people whose health care costs are extremely high. Another is sustaining political support by ensuring that nearly everyone, including the well-to-do who have disproportionate influence in politics, has a stake in guaranteeing that the system operate reasonably well. The basic strategy for doing so is well-known: the system's designers must discourage the migration of low-cost and high-income people from the public system into some alternative.[98] The techniques of discouragement vary. Quebec chose to prohibit people from purchasing insurance to cover the cost of medical services provided outside the public health care system.[99]

Public health care systems have another characteristic—rationing. Rationing takes the form of waiting periods before a person can obtain a desired, or needed, medical service. Those challenging Quebec's health care system contended that the length of the waiting periods deprived them of a constitutionally protected interest in personal security.[100] The Canadian Supreme

---

[97] Chaoulli v. Quebec (Attorney General), [2005] 1 S.C.R. 791.

[98] Everyone knows as well that complete prohibition is impossible. At the limit, a high-income person can go to some other jurisdiction to obtain the medical services he or she desires.

[99] Note that the law did not prohibit the provision of services outside the public system. At least in theory, a doctor could sustain a practice by providing services to patients—ordinarily, of course, quite high-income ones—who could pay in cash, that is, without reimbursement from some insurance policy.

[100] Technically, the challenges rested on Section 1 of the Quebec Charter of Human Rights, which provides, "Every human being has a right to life, and to personal security, inviolability and freedom," and on Section 7 of the Canadian Charter, which provides, "Everyone has the right to life, liberty and security of the person and the right not to be deprived thereof except in accordance with the principles of fundamental justice." Except where the precise language of these provisions matters, I will not distinguish between them, and will refer to a general right to personal security.

Court agreed.[101] Then, following its well-established jurisprudence, the Court asked whether the government had demonstrated that the impairment of the constitutional right was adequately justified. Four justices agreed that the government had failed to do so. The core of the argument was this: the government attempted to justify the impairment occasioned by waiting periods by pointing to the need to discourage migration out of the public health care system, but, the justices said, a complete ban on private medical insurance was an arbitrary method of doing so. The justices canvassed practices in other public health care systems, and observed that many other techniques for discouraging migration existed. Indeed, they found that Quebec's approach was unique, and—or so it seems from reading the opinions—uniquely restrictive of a personal liberty to enter into contracts. Finally, one would have thought that there would be some examination of whether adopting an alternative method of discouraging migration would reduce waiting periods in Quebec. There was none, because, again under well-established jurisprudence, the government had the burden of showing that its approach did not *increase* waiting times compared to other methods, and the government had made no attempt to do so.

Initially—and, as I will argue, even after a more elaborate analysis—the Court's opinions evoke the discredited period in U.S. constitutional history known as the *Lochner* era, during which the U.S. Supreme Court invalidated social welfare legislation on the ground that some social welfare statutes violated a constitutionally protected liberty of contract.[102] The surveys of policy approaches taken in other public health care systems to the problem of migration certainly lent the opinions an air of pure policy disagreement: it is relatively easy to read the opinions as finding the government's policy unconstitutionally arbitrary because, after all, there were, in the justices' view, alternative policies that could have done at least as good a job. Further, the opinions had a tone, confirmed by the Court's unconsidered choice of remedy, that the underlying constitutional problem combined the progressive concern for ensuring adequate health care for all with a conservative concern for preserving the liberty of every person to enter into insurance contracts that were intrinsically perfectly ordinary.

Yet, the case is something more than a reactionary reversion to a jurisprudence that the United States abandoned during the New Deal. How might a progressive defender of constitutional social welfare rights see the problem? Most obviously, as one in which the real constitutional claim was a social

---

[101] The Court was shorthanded when it delivered the judgment, with two justices having been appointed but not sitting on the case. Four justices found that the Quebec statute violated the Quebec Charter, three of whom found as well that it violated the Canadian Charter. Three justices dissented.

[102] The extent to which there *was* a "*Lochner* era" has become contested recently, but for my purposes, there is no need to engage or even describe that controversy.

welfare one, that the waiting periods in Quebec deprived people of their constitutional right to decent health care, where decency includes some concern for the timely delivery of needed services. The issue in the *Chaoulli* case would be one of *remedy*, not of substantive violation, once a litigant established that the waiting periods were long enough to cross some threshold of "indecency."

Seen in that way, much of the Supreme Court's opinion can be defended,—although on new grounds—and crucial parts remain questionable. First, with long waiting periods established, it might make sense to ask the government to explain, if it could, why the waiting periods resulted from something other than the ban on private insurance. Second, if the government failed in that task, it might make sense to look around for other approaches to discouraging migration that held out the possibility of reducing waiting periods. Third, the Court could then draw on the remedial innovations I have already discussed. Most modestly, the Court could require the government to investigate alternative approaches and report to the Court within a year on which alternative it proposed to adopt. Somewhat less modestly, the Court could receive such a report and itself impose the alternative as a remedy. Or—and this is the most interesting possibility—the Court could choose a provisional remedy at the time of the initial decision that the substantive constitutional right to health care was violated. It might tell the government to implement a specific policy alternative, but only provisionally, giving the government an opportunity to substitute some other alternative of its own choosing. Which is, in some sense, what the Court actually did.

The problem in the *Chaoulli* case was rather modest, though revealing. The Court followed the course of imposing a remedy, the elimination of the ban on private insurance. The resonances of *Lochner* arise because that choice seems to rest on an unstated assumption that the default remedy is always reversion to the institutions of the private market economy. Still, even here there might be something to be said on behalf of the Canadian Supreme Court. That Court's choice of remedy is always only provisional given the existence of the override mechanism discussed in part 1.[103] By invoking the notwithstanding clause (and its Quebec equivalent), the government of Quebec could restore the prohibition on private insurance or choose some approach to discouraging migration other than a flat prohibition on private insurance.[104]

---

[103] The Quebec Charter of Human Rights contains a provision allowing its legislature to derogate from the Charter's protection by explicit legislation. Quebec Charter of Human Rights, ch. 5, § 52 ("No provision of any Act, even subsequent to the Charter, may derogate from section 1 to 38, except so far as provided by those sections, unless such Act expressly states that it applies despite the Charter.").

[104] Apparently the Quebec government chose not to use the override or derogation mechanism, which, as discussed in part 1, can be a defensible ordinary political calculation or a less defensible delegation of final authority to the Supreme Court.

The *Chaoulli* case thus demonstrates both the utility and the perils of judicial enforcement of social welfare rights.[105]

Weak Remedies for *First*-Generation Rights?

The double transformation I have sketched returns us to some basic questions about weak-form judicial review, bringing back into focus the proposition that disagreements between courts and legislatures about constitutional meaning typically involve reasonable differences about what the constitution's general or abstract terms mean. That proposition, in turn, bears on another objection that has been raised to providing weak remedies for violations of strong social and economic rights. As I have observed, there is general agreement that *first*-generation rights are strong ones. Professor Sunstein has suggested that providing weak remedies for social and economic rights might lead to providing equally weak remedies for traditional civil liberties and civil rights.[106] Similarly, Professor Richard Epstein worries about the use of experimentalist techniques of review for first-generation rights.[107] And, notably, two proponents of experimentalist modes of judicial review note the possibility of using those

---

[105] *See also* Sandra Fredman, "Human Rights Transformed: Positive Duties and Positive Rights," [2006] Pub. L. 498, 514 (citations omitted):

[The Indian Supreme Court] has fashioned its own remedial orders to provide ongoing management. For example, in the "Right to Food" case, it has issued a continuing mandamus to require states to fully implement specific schemes including mid-day meals at school. Secondly, affirmation of wide duties is often used to counter maladministration rather than to initiate new projects. Thus the right to livelihood of pavement dwellers gave rise only to a duty to complete a project for which funds had already been allocated. In the right to food case, a primary problem was maladministration: the Court found that about half of the food subsidy was being spent on holding excess stocks; reducing stocks would free up large resources to distribute food and provide hot mid-day meals for school children.

[106] *See* Sunstein, *supra* note 1, at 229 ("One of the enduring legacies of communism is a cynicism about the efficacy of legal texts. . . . If positive rights are not enforceable, the constitution itself may seem like a mere piece of paper.").

[107] Richard A. Epstein, "Classical Liberalism Meets the New Constitutional Order: A Comment on Mark Tushnet," 3 Chi. J. Int'l L. 445, 464 (2002):

[T]his exercise in democratic experimentalism may have bad spillover effects if it leads courts to rethink the strength of negative liberties guaranteed in the American and other constitutions. Take the simplest question of whether ordinary citizens have the right to criticize the incumbent government, which goes to the core of American First Amendment liberties. I regard this guarantee as essential to the well-being of any political state. But this guarantee is reduced to rubble if the court merely instructs the legislature (or dictator) to recognize the role of critics in a democratic society before locking up all political dissidents.

modes in connection with free speech rights, but provide worked-out examples of using them only in *other* areas.[108]

As a matter of legal analysis, there is no reason why an approach adopted for one category of cases (social and economic rights), for reasons specific to that category (such as concerns about fiscal impact), will leak over into another category (traditional civil liberties and civil rights), where those reasons are irrelevant. Nor is there an obvious mechanism that would induce judges to make that sort of analytic error. Still, I too share the intuition that leakage is a more than trivial possibility. It is less clear to me, though, that it is a possibility worth worrying too much about.

Earlier in this chapter I argued that one could find "hints" connecting First Amendment law to social and economic rights. These hints show that, at least with respect to some doctrines, we cannot sharply distinguish between first- and second-generation rights. One response to that observation might be that these doctrines are not at the heart of free speech law. Perhaps the conclusion we should draw is that free speech doctrine developed out of these hints ought to treat them as weak substantive rights subject to strong remedies. So, for example, the courts should apply a deferential standard when asked whether the police did "enough" to protect a speaker from a hostile audience before they arrested the speaker for provoking a riot.

Yet, there are some additional hints in U.S. law, this time of the use of weak-form review in connection with core First Amendment rights.[109] The Supreme Court has acknowledged the importance of giving Congress room to experiment in cases involving regulations of cable television that would plainly be unconstitutional bans on ideas of which Congress disapproved were the regulations to be applied to longer-established media.[110] Its decision striking down some regulations of the distribution of indecent material over the World Wide Web merely approved a trial court's decision that, given the record before it, the government had not shown that technology was inadequate to limit minors' access to such material without limiting the access of adults as well.[111] In the latter case, Justice Breyer's dissenting opinion referred to an earlier opinion that had praised "constructive discourse between our courts and our legislatures" that "is an integral and admirable part of the constitutional design."[112]

---

[108] Dorf & Sabel, *supra* note 68, at 456–57 (noting the relevance of their analysis to First Amendment doctrine), 459–64 (working out the analysis in conjunction with criminal procedure rights).

[109] I do not consider here the use of weak-form review in free speech cases in Canada or elsewhere, because the nervousness I am addressing arises precisely from the fact that weak-form review is unfamiliar in the United States.

[110] *See, e.g.,* Turner Broadcasting v. FCC, 520 U.S. 180 (1997) (upholding a regulation that required cable systems to transmit programs originating on local broadcast stations).

[111] Ashcroft v ACLU, 542 U.S. 656 (2004).

[112] *Id.* at 689, quoting Blakely v. Washington, 542 U.S. 296, 326 (2004) (Kennedy, J., dissenting). Justice Kennedy was the author of the Court's opinion from which Justice Breyer was dissenting.

Justice Breyer referred to the fact that the statute the Court was evaluating resulted from deliberations in Congress responding to a prior decision invalidating Congress's first stab at the problem. Even though Justice Breyer was writing in dissent, his observations indicate that the idea that experimentalism and dialogue might matter in constitutional adjudication of first-generation rights has reached the U.S. Supreme Court.

The Court itself endorsed experimentalism with respect to political speech, the core of the First Amendment, when it upheld the McCain-Feingold campaign finance reform law. The doctrine the Court articulated is far too complex to outline here. What matters is something Justices Stevens and O'Connor wrote at the end of their opinion for the five justices who joined their opinion upholding the statute: "We are under no illusion that [the McCain-Feingold law] will be the last congressional statement on the matter. Money, like water, will always find an outlet. What problems will arise, and how Congress will respond, are concerns for another day."[113] As—they need not have added—is the question of how *the Court* will respond. That is, the opinion came close to explicitly endorsing the idea that the *substantive* law of the First Amendment would be shaped by interactions among the public acting as campaign donors, Congress acting as regulator, and the Supreme Court acting as the (provisionally) final determiner of the Constitution's meaning. But that idea simply *is* the one that underlies weak-form judicial review.[114]

One point about these examples deserves emphasis: in the main, they involve relatively new *social* phenomena—cable television and the Web obviously so, the new technologies of campaigning only slightly less. Experimentalist modes of review might be particularly appropriate in such cases. In contrast, perhaps we have enough experience with such core problems of free expression as efforts by government to punish those who simply disagree with its policies to conclude that experimentalism—or weak-form review—has given us all the benefits it can. Chapter 2 argued that weak-form review differs from strong-form review only in that the dialogic interaction between courts and legislatures occurs over a shorter period in weak-form systems than in strong-form ones, illustrating that proposition with the example of free speech law and speech critical of the government. The example also shows how experimentalist or weak-form review can generate rules that can be enforced in a strong form.

My suggestion, that is, is that weak-form review can be replaced by strong-form review when enough experience has accumulated to give us—judges, legislators, and the people alike—confidence that giving the judges the final

---

[113] McConnell v. Federal Election Comm'n, 540 U.S. 93, 224 (2003).

[114] For a related example of dialogic review, dealing with the problem of articulating constitutional doctrine in a domain where the factual predicates for applying doctrine change rapidly, see Stuart M. Benjamin, "Stepping Into the Same River Twice: Rapidly Changing Facts and the Appellate Process," 78 Tex. L. Rev. 269 (1999).

word will not interfere with our ability to govern ourselves in any significant way. The reason, of course, is that when the experiments have run their course, few legislatures will adopt regulations that courts will *need* to invalidate because everyone will have learned from the experiments.

And this, finally, returns us to the most basic point about constitutionalism and judicial review. As I argued in part 1, weak-form judicial review respects the right, grounded in democratic theory, for majorities to prevail when, acting through their representatives, they enact statutes that are consistent with reasonable interpretations of the constitution even if those interpretations differ from those the courts offer. The dual transformation of weak-form remedies for violations of social and economic rights occurs because legislatures and the courts disagree over the constitution's meaning. It thereby illustrates why weak-form judicial review is *generally* attractive, notwithstanding its own imperfections. Nervousness about extending weak-form review to first-generation rights is misplaced.

Table of Cases

Index